The Earliest View of New Testament Tongues

The Earliest View of New Testament Tongues

Understood as Non-Supernatural, Learned Earthly Languages

MAURICE E. VELLACOTT

RESOURCE *Publications* · Eugene, Oregon

THE EARLIEST VIEW OF NEW TESTAMENT TONGUES
Understood as Non-Supernatural, Learned Earthly Languages

Copyright © 2024 Maurice E. Vellacott. All rights reserved. Except for brief quotations in critical publications or reviews, no part of this book may be reproduced in any manner without prior written permission from the publisher. Write: Permissions, Wipf and Stock Publishers, 199 W. 8th Ave., Suite 3, Eugene, OR 97401.

Resource Publications
An Imprint of Wipf and Stock Publishers
199 W. 8th Ave., Suite 3
Eugene, OR 97401

www.wipfandstock.com

PAPERBACK ISBN: 979-8-3852-2842-3
HARDCOVER ISBN: 979-8-3852-2843-0
EBOOK ISBN: 979-8-3852-2844-7

11/01/24

Unless otherwise indicated, English language quotations from the Bible, in this book, will be taken from the (NASB®) New American Standard Bible®, Copyright © 1960, 1971, 1977 by The Lockman Foundation. Used by permission. All rights reserved. lockman.org

Contents

Preface | ix

Acknowledgments | xi

1. Introduction | 1
    1.1 Subject background | 1
    1.2 Personal background | 2
    1.3 State of research | 2
        1.3.1 Insufficient scope of research | 5
    1.4 Problem statement | 10
    1.5 Aim and objectives | 11
        1.5.1 Aim | 11
        1.5.2 Objectives | 12
    1.6 Central theoretical argument | 12

2. Linguistic Analysis of γλῶσσα/γλῶσσαι (glṓssa/glṓssai) | 13
    2.1 Hebrew | 14
    2.2 Greek | 19
    2.3 Conclusions | 21

3. Cultural Analysis | 22
    3.1 Roman Perspective—the "Way" as a sect of Judaism | 22
    3.2 Jewish influence bearing on the Corinthian assembly | 25
        3.2.1 Paul's Hebraistic upbringing and training | 32
            3.2.1.1 Many quotations from the Older Testament | 46

CONTENTS

    3.2.2 Aquila and Priscilla—Jewish co-workers from Rome | 49

    3.2.3 Apollos—an Alexandrian Jew | 51

    3.2.4 Silas, Timothy—circumcised Jews, troubleshooters, Paul's protégés | 52

    3.2.5 Peter—of the Jerusalem mother assembly | 56

    3.2.6 Judaizing Christians referred to in 2 Corinthians | 62

  3.3 Synagogue influence on Corinthian Assembly | 65

    3.3.1 Origin of Corinthian Congregation | 77

        3.3.1.1 Synagogue ruler Crispus and his entire household | 80

        3.3.1.2 "A worshipper of God" Titius Justus | 81

    3.3.2 Composition of Corinthian Congregation | 84

  3.4 Aramaic influence on Corinthian Assembly | 88

  3.5 Greek influence on Corinthian Assembly | 89

  3.6 Roman influence on Corinthian Assembly | 94

  3.7 Delphine Oracle influence on Corinthian Assembly | 98

  3.8 Low literacy influence on Corinthian Assembly | 99

  3.9 Conclusions | 105

4. Historical Analysis of "Language/Languages" | 108

  4.1 Post-Apostolic time until 1516 AD | 108

    4.1.1 Post-Apostolic time until 500 AD | 112

        Clement of Rome, Irenaeus, Montanism, Tertullian, Novatian, Origen, Epiphanius, Pachomius, Hilary of Poitiers, Filastrii/ Filastrius, Ambrosiaster, Gregory of Nazianzus, Ambrose, Chrysostom, Severian of Gabala, Jerome, Augustine of Hippo, Cyril of Alexandria, Pope Leo I the Great, Theodoret of Cyrrhus

    4.1.2 500 AD until 1000 AD | 130

    4.1.3 1000 AD until 1516 AD | 131

        Michael Psellos, Hildegard of Bingen, Thomas Aquinas

  4.2 Reformation period (1517–1648 AD) | 138

    Francis Xavier, Martin Luther, John Calvin

CONTENTS

4.3 Post-Reformation (1649–1905 AD) | 140

Quakers, Shakers and Ranters, French Huguenot Protestants, Catholic Jansenists, Moravians, Edward Irving, Mormons (LDS)

4.4 Modern period—Azusa until Third Wave (1906–1980 AD) | 151

4.5 Present time (1980off AD) | 156

4.6 Conclusions | 159

5. Contextual and Exegetical Analysis of γλῶσσαι (*glōssai*) | 162

5.1 Contextual/Exegetical Analysis of Acts 2 event (Jerusalem Jewish recipients) | 165

5.2 Contextual/Exegetical Analysis of Acts 10 event (Caesarea Gentile recipients) | 192

5.3 Contextual/Exegetical Analysis of Acts 19 event (Ephesus Diaspora recipients) | 195

5.4 Contextual and Exegetical Analysis of 1 Corinthians 14 | 203

5.4.1 Contextual Analysis of 1 Corinthians 14 | 230

5.4.2 Exegetical Analysis of 1 Corinthians 14 | 234

5.5 Conclusions | 303

6. Translation Analysis of Any Shift in Meaning | 305

6.1 Wyclif Bible translation of "languages/tongues" (1380 AD) | 305

6.2 Tyndale Bible translation of "languages/tongues" (1535 AD) | 306

6.3 Cranmer Bible translation of "languages/tongues" (1540 AD) | 306

6.4 Geneva Bible translation of "languages/tongues" (1562 AD) | 307

6.5 Rheims Bible translation of "languages/tongues" (1582 AD) | 308

6.6 Bishop's Bible translation of "languages/tongues" (1568/1602 AD) | 308

6.7 Authorised (KJV) Bible translation of "languages/tongues" (1611/1873 AD) | 309

6.8 Luther's translation of "languages/tongues" (1483–1546 AD) | 312

CONTENTS

6.9 Calvin's translation of "languages/tongues" (1509–1564 AD) | 313

7.0 Conclusions | 316

7. Summary, Findings, Conclusions | 318

8. Contribution and Recommendations | 325

Bibliography | 331

Preface

AS A STUDENT OF church history, Dr. Vellacott was aware that in the last 145 years, the 1 Corinthians 14 phrase "speaking in tongues" and the underlying Greek terms γλῶσσα *(glóssa* singular) or γλῶσσαι *(glóssai* plural) have been a subject of considerable debate. Some would understand those Greek terms to mean "language" or "languages" in the sense of *miraculously endowed, earthly languages*. Others hold that these terms mean ecstatic or non-ecstatic languages in the *non-normative, non-earthly sense*, as particularly promoted by those of Pentecostal and Charismatic persuasion. The intriguing question for Dr. Vellacott was: which is the more appropriate intent of the Greek text in 1 Corinthians 14 or is there a viable third explanation of *normally acquired languages*? What can we glean from the Hebrew Older Testament and the Greek Old and New Testaments on the matter? Are there parallel synagogue customs that would shed some light on the subject? Is there relevant New Testament era culture that would aid in understanding of the pertinent terms? What were the uses and abuses of γλῶσσα/γλῶσσαι *(glóssa/glóssai)* in the New Testament era and post-Apostolic history? What do exegetes of the pivotal 1 Corinthians 14 passage have to say? As a result, is there a present-day practice of "tongues" which finds support from this passage?

After five years of diligent research, Dr. Vellacott concluded that there is considerable merit to the interpretation of early church father, the Jewish Bishop Epiphanius, who wrote that the γλῶσσαι/*glóssai* conflict in the first-century AD assembly of believers at Corinth involved different dialects of Greek (Attic-Ionic, Aeolic and Doric Greek) with inconsiderate congregants using the Hebrew language and the aforementioned Greek dialects in their assemblies without translation. This interpretation would mean that 1 Corinthians chapter 14 is not referring to a non-earthly (ecstatic or non-ecstatic) phenomena nor being miraculously and instantaneously given a previously unlearned, earthly, foreign language. The Older Testament Scripture, which was originally in Hebrew, the inconsiderate use of minority Greek dialects, teaching the Law—these components seem to have created a significant issue around the lack of translation and a resulting teaching problem within the multilingual Corinthian assembly.

With *diglossia* existing among first-century Judeans, Dr. Vellacott concurs that it was a key factor in understanding what was meant by "other tongues" in Acts 2:4. "Among first-century Judeans, the religious language, *leshon ha-kodesh* ["holy language"], Hebrew, was the language that both Palestinian and Diaspora Judeans expected to hear in the Temple liturgy, during the feast of Pentecost" (Zerhusen, 1995:126). "Instead of *leshon ha-kodesh*, the disciples of Jesus, inspired by the Holy Spirit, began speaking in 'other tongues' (i.e., languages other than Hebrew). The speakers spoke Aramaic and Greek, languages they knew, languages that were simultaneously the native languages of the crowd assembled in Acts 2" (Zerhusen, 1995:126).

By the different sections and chapters in this book, this Epiphanius interpretation is shown to be linguistically sound, culturally relevant, historically viable, contextually consistent, compatible with the intent of the earliest English translations, and therefore exegetically preferable.

Acknowledgments

ALTHOUGH ONE PERSON'S NAME appears as the author on the title page, others have contributed to this work lasting over several years.

I first express my gratitude to my gracious Redeemer and Lord, who gave me this important project to keep me occupied before, and in the aftermath of, tragically losing our first-born, 42-year-old, married son, Chad Maury Vellacott, to the dread mental health illness of schizophrenia. I long for the day when I will hold him in my arms again at that glad reunion in the Lord's presence. This project has engaged my mind and been a God-given, positive relief amid this long, dark night of my soul.

I also pay tribute to my dad and mom, Ed and Mary Vellacott, who were great encouragers of me and my five siblings. I am grateful for dad and mom having come to know Jesus, the Messiah, as their Savior and Lord and helping me know that sin separated me from my Creator, but because of Jesus' death and resurrection I could be reconciled to God. As humble folk, they modelled what it was like to be spiritually "born again," which spurred me on to walk that same path of service to God and others. I also look forward to reuniting with them in heaven or on earth in the days ahead. I am eternally grateful to my dad for having pointed me to Nipawin Bible College.

I am indebted to Nipawin Bible College faculty, staff and students there in the 1970s, who challenged my thinking and provided the seedbed for everything I did thereafter, as a Pastor, college teacher, Canadian federal Member of Parliament, and whatever else God has in store for me in my remaining days on this earth. Briercrest College, Canadian Theological Seminary, Trinity International University (T.E.D.S.), Dallas Theological Seminary, and Jerusalem University College have also played important roles in shaping me.

ACKNOWLEDGMENTS

I thank my dear wife, Mary, whom I met at Nipawin Bible College, who has supported me, challenged me, and shown a keen interest in these studies. I have much appreciated those engaging discussions with her on this research of mine and her sharing with me all that she is learning through her weekly Bible Study Fellowship International program. In addition to being a diligent student of the Bible, Mary has also been a much appreciated, meticulous proofreader of this manuscript.

I would be remiss if I did not express my heart-felt appreciation to my promoter and North-West University professor, Dr. Philip Du Toit, who patiently and professionally guided me through the PhD thesis on which this book is based. He was firm in direction and a good resource person in view of his considerable knowledge in the New Testament and expertise in the Greek.

I am also grateful to my Wipf and Stock book editor, Dr. Robin Parry, from Worcester in the UK, who has been accommodating and had good advice along the way in preparation of this manuscript for typesetting and publication. Wipf and Stock Managing Editor Matt Wimer, Assistant Managing Editor Emily Callihan, Editorial Administrative Assistant George Callihan, and typesetter Ian Creeger have all been helpful and encouraging at different points in the process. In the final phase, Dr. Savanah N. Landerholm used her expertise in copyediting, typesetting, and design to prepare a final product that is attractive and more readable.

I dedicate this work to my family, and in particular to my living children, Lisa (spouse Paul), Josh, and Jay, and daughter-in-law, Melissa, as well as my grandchildren, with the prayer that they too will be diligent students of the Word to the honor and glory of the coming King of Kings and Lord of Lords.

1

Introduction

1.1 SUBJECT BACKGROUND

In the last 145 years, the 1 Corinthians 14 phrase "speaking in tongues" and the underlying Greek terms γλῶσσα/*glōssa* (singular) or γλῶσσαι/*glōssai* (plural) have been a subject of considerable debate. Some would understand those Greek terms to mean "language" or "languages" in the sense of miraculously bestowed, earthly languages. Others hold that these terms mean ecstatic or non-ecstatic languages in the non-normative, non-earthly and esoteric sense, as particularly promoted by those of Pentecostal and Charismatic persuasion. The intriguing question for this book: which is the more appropriate intent of the Greek in 1 Corinthians 14 or is there a viable third explanation of normally acquired languages? What can we glean from the Hebrew Older Testament and the Greek Old and New Testaments on the matter? Are there parallel synagogue customs that would shed some light on the subject? Is there relevant New Testament era culture that would aid in understanding of the pertinent terms? What were the uses and abuses of γλῶσσα/γλῶσσαι (*glōssa/glōssai*) in the New Testament era and post-apostolic history? What do exegetes of the pivotal 1 Corinthians 14 passage have to say? As a result, is there a present-day practice of "tongues" which finds support from this passage?

1.2 PERSONAL BACKGROUND

Over the years, although wary, I have not been closed to the supposed "gift of tongues" as understood by my Pentecostal and Charismatic friends. I have in fact prayed that, if there is such a gift for today, and if the Holy Spirit, the Sovereign Bestower of gifts, has such a gift for me, whatever it be, then I'm willing to receive it. In that regard, I would at this point not be labelled a "continuationist" or "cessationist" but term myself a "skepticist." I have a high view of Scripture and don't want my position on the issue to be determined by my subjective experiences and feelings. Rather, my spiritual experiences should be subjected to the Word of God and appropriate conservative methodologies to discern the meaning of the text, so I and others will not be led astray.

I've witnessed the scenario on videos where a "tongues seeker" is told to repeat the sounds the leader makes. If she does, she's told she's speaking in "tongues"! Was this the procedure in the Corinthian assembly of Christ followers in the first century? What are we to make of this present-day form of "tongues-speaking"? How do we account for the modern manifestations of what is claimed to be biblical "tongues-speaking" in view of 1 Corinthians 14 in particular?

1.3 STATE OF RESEARCH

In this sphere of study, a significant portion of the contemporary academic literature reflects the view of the last 145 years that γλῶσσα/glōssa (singular) or γλῶσσαι/glōssai (plural) means an ecstatic, non-earthly language, as held by those of Pentecostal and Charismatic persuasion. Of those consulted firsthand, this assumption of it not being an earthly language is held by scholarly commentators on 1 Corinthians such as Anthony Thiselton (2000), Gordon Fee (2014, 1990, 1987), Roy Ciampa and Brian Rosner (2010), Craig Blomberg (1994), Leon Morris (1958), C.K. Barrett (1968, 2004), Archibald Robertson and Alfred Plummer (1911), Craig Keener (2005), Ben Witherington (1995), Hans Conzelman (1975), Raymond Collins (1999), Charles Talbert (2002), Pheme Perkins (2012), David Garland (2003), Paul Gardner (2018), Mark Taylor (2014), Jerome Murphy-O'Connor (2009), and D. A. Carson (1987).

Collins (1999:456) urges that 1 Corinthians "12–14 is different from the disciples' experience at Pentecost (Acts 2:5–13)."

INTRODUCTION

Joseph Fitzmyer (2008:513–514) acknowledges that: "The neg. of *eusemon logon*, 'intelligible, recognizable speech,' could be illustrated by someone speaking a foreign language that is not understood by those present, but more likely it refers to an inarticulate succession of words that give the impression of language but are unintelligible to the hearers."

In taking a contrary view, Thomas Schreiner (2018:Kindle Location 5400) writes that "human languages are likely in view. First, as noted earlier, the word *glōssai* refers to human languages, not ecstatic utterances."

Verbrugge and Harris (2008:Kindle Location 5075) hold the view that γλῶσσα/*glōssa* (singular) or γλῶσσαι/*glōssai* (plural) may mean ecstatic "tongues" in the esoteric sense of a non-earthly language, as held by those of Pentecostal and Charismatic persuasion, but it could mean supernaturally bestowed, known earthly languages as on the Day of Pentecost (Verbrugge & Harris, 2008:Kindle Location 5064). The mishmash view of Verbrugge and Harris (2008:Kindle Locations 5062–5063) is reflected in their allowing that it may also be represented in "people who have a tremendous gift of picking up a foreign language easily and quickly."

In an assessment of *Prophecy and Inspired Speech in Early Christianity and Its Hellenistic Environment* (Forbes, 1995), Thiselton concedes:

> Certainly the main thrust of Christopher Forbes' warnings against assuming that tongues denotes *ecstatic speech* on the basis of overly selective and unrepresentative examples of "inspired speech" in Graeco-Roman texts should be heeded and accepted. The instances of irrational frenzy described by Euripides concerning the Dionysiac cult in *The Bacchae* and similar phenomena concerning the frenzied antics of the Sibyl in Virgil's *Aeneid*, often familiar from classes in school should not be taken as models for an understanding of 1 Corinthians 12–14 . . . Forbes suspects the approach of history-of-religion writers since Reitzenstein of special pleading, and his wide review of primary sources in Graeco-Roman literature entirely vindicates his scepticism (2000:971).

Irenaeus (130–202 AD) tells about "many brethren in the church who possess prophetic gifts, and who through the Spirit speak all kinds of languages" (1885:*Against Heresies*, Book V, Chapter 6, section 1).

The Earliest View of New Testament Tongues

The writings of the church fathers, initially scanned, reflect an understanding of the γλῶσσαι/glóssai at Pentecost as either spoken or heard foreign languages (Roberts et al, 1885; Lake, 1912). Church leaders through the centuries have been of the view that the Acts chapter 2 phenomenon was foreign human languages for the predominate purpose of evangelization (cf. Thiselton, 2000:973–974). Robert Gundry (1966:299–307) propounds this perspective in an article entitled "'Ecstatic Utterance' (N.E.B.)?" Gundry also expounds this particular point of view in his work on 1 Corinthians in the Commentary on the New Testament (2010).

These church fathers, in the context of Acts 2 and 1 Corinthians 12–14, were not aware of an alternate interpretation of γλῶσσαι/glóssai as ecstasy (nor *glossolalia* which is not a word in the Greek New Testament). Tertullian (155–220 AD), who became a Montanist in his later days (Tertullian, 1972), needs be examined more closely in this book's chapter 4 Historical Analysis.

Thiselton (2000:973–974) summarizes:

> It is usually claimed that the most widespread pre-modern view held among the Fathers, medieval writers, and Reformers perceives tongues as *the miraculous power to speak unlearned foreign languages.* Among the Fathers, it is generally claimed that Origen, Chrysostom, Theodore, Cyril, and Theodoret held this view; among medieval writers and Reformers, Thomas Aquinas, Photius, Estius, and Calvin; among modem writers especially J. G. Davies, Robert Gundry, and Christopher Forbes.

The Princeton theologian Charles Hodge (1797–1878) also forcefully argued that γλῶσσαι/glóssai was unlearned foreign languages (1860:247–252) but interestingly seems to concede that a speaker's own native, non-Greek language might rise to the fore in some situations (1860:252). Hodge (1860:251) also says in respect to the attainment of these foreign languages: "It is said God is not wont by miracles to remove difficulties out of the way of his people, which they can surmount by labor."

In a scholarly article entitled "The Gift of Tongues: Comparing the church fathers with Contemporary Pentecostalism" (2006:61–78), Nathan Busenitz asserts that:

> The patristic evidence supports a rational foreign language as the proper and normal manifestation of tongues. Conversely, unintelligible babblings and irrational gibberish are never associated with the gift (p. 63–64).

Nevertheless, the heart of the problem is implicit in our review of patristic, medieval, and Reformation interpretations. Edwards (1886:319) declares:

> But it is evident that the Corinthians did not use their gift of tongues to evangelize the heathen world. They spoke with tongues in their Church assemblies, and not once does the Apostle urge them to apply the power to the purpose for which it would be so eminently serviceable.

1.3.1 Insufficient scope of research

The current problem is whether the "tongues" of 1 Corinthian 14 is a non-earthly expression or speaking in a hitherto unlearned, earthly language. Poythress (1977:132–135) hypothesizes degrees of known earthly languages and degrees of an unknown or non-earthly language. Poythress' dicing into five parameters of classification still boils down to degrees of the two commonly-held categories: a non-earthly (ecstatic or non-ecstatic) expression or speaking in a hitherto unlearned, earthly language. So, the common two-fold categorization still holds, and Epiphanius of Salamis offers a third proposal.

Now I turn to a deficiency in the literature. This proposed study will help to remedy a deficiency and provide a valued contribution to the scholarly literature.

The pertinent Epiphanius text is potentially insightful for explaining the γλῶσσαι/glōssai problem at Corinth. The text is customarily credited to Epiphanius (310–403 AD; according to Bartolocci born 288 AD), the Romaniote Jewish Bishop (consecrated approximately 365 AD) of Salamis, an ancient Greek city-state on the east coast of Cyprus. (Salamis and Paphos on Cyprus are places where Paul spent time on his first missionary journey.) It is valuable to note that Epiphanius was born of Jewish parents in Judea and spent much of his life there (Thomassen & van Oort, 2009:xiii–xiv, xix, et al.), which would tend to his having a more Hebraistic and less Gentile mindset. That he knew Hebrew seems likely based on his periodic Hebrew quotations. This Jewish Hebrew background is unique among the post-Apostolic Fathers (Greek and Latin) where we get the first mentions of γλῶσσαι/*glōssai*.

Epiphanius' Book 1, which contains the central text under consideration herein, was greatly indebted to the prolific writer, Hippolytus of Rome (c. 170–c. 235 AD), and Irenaeus (c. 130–c. 202 AD), both of whom had Justin Martyr (c. 100–c. 165 AD) for a predecessor (Thomassen & van Oort, 2009:xx, xxiii). Photios I of Constantinople describes Hippolytus in his *Bibliotheca* (cod. 121) as a disciple of Irenaeus (Thomassen & van Oort, 2009:xxvi), who in turn was said to be a disciple of Polycarp (c. 69–c. 155 AD) and Polycarp was a disciple of the Apostle John (Irenaeus, *Adversus Haereses* III.3; Tertullian, *De praescriptione haereticorum* 32.2). Thus, with this chain of connections, Epiphanius' information on the first-century Corinthian congregation may have been a linear transmission from an apostolic source. Epiphanius has little or no independent information about what he writes on in his *Panarion* (Thomassen & van Oort, 2009:xxiii). Epiphanius cites Clement of Rome (c. 35 AD–99 AD) and Clement of Alexandria (c. 150–c. 215 AD) and Eusebius (c. 260/265–30 May 339 AD), among other church leaders (Thomassen & van Oort, 2009:xxiii–xxv). Epiphanius is quite dependent on his predecessor sources (Thomassen & van Oort, 2009:xxiii–xxvi) but draws from personal experience (Thomassen & van Oort, 2009:xxv) and prefers quoting from Holy Scripture (Thomassen & van Oort, 2009:xxvii).

Manfred Bietak (2003:4; cf. Murray, 1987:93–115; Burkert, 1995:139–148) in writing about the historical reliability of oral traditions, states that they can be sustained for up to six generations or approximately 200 years. If an oral description about the cause of the divisive Corinthian γλῶσσαι/*glōssai* problem began to circulate in the second century, Epiphanius having picked up on this strain of thinking is within the previously referred to limits of historical reliability, meaning that his very intriguing account likely contains an accurate recital of core history. It is certainly much, much closer in time than the speculations of academics two thousand years later.

Orality expert Pender-Cudlip (1972:12; also Dorson, 1973:9) argues that normally "oral tradents" are just as concerned "to receive and render a precise, accurate and authentic account of the past" as would a modern historian. Miller (1980:51, 52) portays these oral transmitters as "professional historians in the sense that they are conscious of history and evidence" and further, that "oral historians are . . . no less conscious of the past than are historians in literate cultures." (The Jesus Legend: A Case for the Historical Reliability of the Synoptic Jesus Tradition by Eddy and Boyd includes some relevant chapters for recommended reading on ancient literacy and oral tradition, published by Baker in 2007).

In respect to orality, one must also keep well in mind that "written records may serve as a fountainhead for oral tradition" (Vansina, 1985:31). After all, written sources and literacy were valued in a greater degree by the Judaeo-Christian community (Gerhardsson, 1990:538; Meier, 1991:vol. 1, 275). "In societies where writings have been in use for a long time it is very hard to find source material that is completely uninfluenced by writing" (Gerhardsson, 1986:31).

The pertinent Epiphanius passage is the most straighforward and potentially most insightful by a church father on the Pauline address to the divisive Corinthian γλῶσσαι/*glōssai* problem (Thomassen & van Oort, 2009:349–351). The pertinent Epiphanius passage is cited from the Second Edition 2009 translation by Frank Williams of the *The Panarion of Epiphanius of Salamis*. Book I (Sects 1–46), which is a revised and expanded version (Thomassen & van Oort, 2009). Numerous editions and works were consulted in determining and laying out the best Greek text of Epiphanius' Panarion, Book I, Section III, Heresy 42 beginning at Scholion 13 and 21 (Thomassen & van Oort, 2009:xxxv–xxxix). Among the several recent works of significance, Philip Amidon's *The Panarion of St. Epiphanius of Salamis, Selected Passages* (1990) was consulted (Thomassen & van Oort, 2009:xi). In determining and laying out the best Greek text of Epiphanius' Panarion, of extreme importance, careful account was taken of Collatz's (et al.) 2006 titled *Register zu den Bänden I–III, Ancoratus, Panarion 1–80, De Fide* (Thomassen & van Oort, 2009:xi–xii). This was a revision of Karl Holl's 1910 *Die handschriftliche Überlieferung des Epiphanius (Ancoratus und Panarion). Texte und Untersuchungen* 36.2 (Leipzig : J. C. Hinrichs), which was an extensive textual criticism of the Epiphanius writings.

"Holl's is a carefully edited critical text . . . . there can be little doubt that Holl has given us a fair approximation of what Epiphanius wrote" (Thomassen & van Oort, 2009:xii). Thus, Frank William's translation used in this book is a rendering of Karl Holl's critical text of his second volume, republished in 1980 by Jürgen Dummer (Thomassen & van Oort, 2009:xii).

The Earliest View of New Testament Tongues

The thesis statement attributed to Epiphanius appears to evince an atavistic and early patristic viewpoint. Later copyists or translators would not likely have added Epiphanius' postulation of an explicit Jewish link as a cause of the γλῶσσαι/glōssai controversy in the first-century Corinthian church. "Attic [Greek] was already the dominant language during and after Epiphanius time; literary conflicts between its Doric and Aeolic counterparts had long been settled. Hebrew had no place in any Christian liturgy at the time of Epiphanius or later. These would not be issues that later copyists or editors would see important to insert as an emendation" (Sullivan, 2013). In view of diligent scholarly work, it is judicious to understand that this text, to immediately follow, was part of the original Epiphanius manuscript.

The relevant words of the text are in Epiphanius' Panarion, Book I, Section III, Heresy 42 beginning at Scholion 13 and 21 (Thomassen & van Oort, 2009:349–351):

> (a) Elenchus 13 and 21. Thus the languages too are by the gift of the Spirit. But what sort of languages does the apostle mean? He says, "languages in the church," to show those who preened themselves on the sounds of Hebrew, which are well and wisely diversified in every expression, in various complex ways—on the pretentious kind of Greek, moreover, the speaking of Attic, Aeolic and Doric—that God does not permit just one language in church, as some of the people supposed who had stirred up the alarms and factions among the Corinthians, to whom the Epistle was being sent.
>
> (b) And yet Paul agreed that both using the Hebrew expressions and teaching the Law is a gift of the Spirit. Moreover, to condemn the other, pretentious forms of Greek, he said he spoke with "tongues" rather (than those) because he was an Hebrew of Hebrews and had been brought up at the feet of Gamaliel; and he sets great store by the scriptures of these Hebrews, and makes it clear that they are gifts of the Spirit. Thus, in writing to Timothy about the same scriptures, he said, "For from thy youth thou hast learned the sacred scriptures."
>
> (c) And further, he said the same sort of thing to the people who had been trained by the Greek poets and orators, and added in the same way, "I speak with tongues more than ye all," to show that he was more fully versed in the Greek education as well. . . .

(f) And yet you see how the holy apostle explains of languages, "Yet in church I had rather utter five words with my understanding," that is, "in translation." As a prophet benefits his hearers with prophecy in the Holy Spirit by bringing things to light which have already been furnished to his understanding, I too, says Paul, want to speak so that the church may hear and be edified—not edify myself with the boast of Greek and Hebrew which I know, instead of edifying the church with the language which it understands.

What did Epiphanius mean by this? The Epiphanius text, in the passages quoted above, refers to the use of Attic (included Ionic), Aeolic and Doric Greek. These classic Greek dialects were in contrast to the lower-style, levelled, common *koine* Greek, also known as Hellenistic/Alexandrian, broadly spoken in the New Testament era. Use of the classic dialects often indicated an attempt at a more complex, lofty literary style.

In the second paragraph quoted above, Epiphanius speaks of "pretentious forms of Greek" and, in the third paragraph quoted above, he speaks of "the people who have been trained by the Greek poets and orators." Epiphanius implies that the γλῶσσαι/*glōssai* conflict in Corinth was a problem of pompous people using the inscripturated Hebrew and the aforementioned Greek dialects in elevated manner to pridefully posture as superior to others in the assembly. This interpretation would mean that 1 Corinthians chapter 14 is not referring to a non-earthly (ecstatic or non-ecstatic) phenomena nor being instantaneously given a previously unlearned, earthly, foreign language. The Older Testament Scripture, which was originally in Hebrew, the pompous use of classic Greek dialects, teaching the Law—these components seem to have created a significant issue around the lack of verbal interpretation/translation and a resulting teaching problem within the Corinthian assembly because of the snobbery and inflated egos of some.

Following are a couple of journal articles that give support to the Epiphanius thesis as they lean in a different direction than the two typical explanations of the "tongues" conundrum. In a scholarly piece in the July issue of the Concordia Journal, Edward Engelbrecht (1996:1) writes:

> Since 'to speak in a tongue' occurs a number of times in the Old Testament, the Dead Sea Scrolls, and Rabbinic literature, it is necessary to consider these writings to determine the origin

and meaning of Paul's expression. This article proposes that 'to speak in a tongue' was a common Semitic idiom adapted by Paul. It was suggested to him by the prophecy of Isaiah 28:11, which he used to address the difficulties at Corinth. The expression's application in Semitic literature is not to ecstatic speech but to speaking in a foreign language.

Bob Zerhusen in "The Problem Tongues in 1 Cor: A Reexamination" (1997:151), in making his case on the matter, concludes with:

> If the reader has read the earlier article ["An Overlooked Judean Diglossia in Acts," Biblical Theology Bulletin, Vol. 25] on the violation of the Judean diglossia in Acts 2 and now has read about the language problem of 1 Corinthians 14, he will note that four assumptions have been challenged: (1) that the language-speaker spoke a language he had never learned before, (2) that the language-speaker did not know or understand the language that he was speaking, (3) that the language speaking was miraculous, and (4) that this miraculous ability in languages was one of the manifestations of the Spirit (1 Corinthians 12:7).
>
> The cultural, historical, linguistic, and exegetical evidence presented in these two articles demonstrates these assumptions to be false. In both Acts 2 and 1 Corinthians 14 the language-speakers knew and understood exactly what they were saying because they were speaking the languages with which they were most familiar (i.e., their native or first languages).

1.4 PROBLEM STATEMENT

The Epiphanius contention is that the γλῶσσαι/glóssai conflict in Corinth was a problem of pompous people using Older Testament Hebrew and classic Greek dialects in elevated manner to pridefully posture as superior to others in the assembly. This pomposity around the role of the inscripturated Hebrew and classic Greek dialects in the Corinthian assembly has never been adequately explored in the published academic literature. The two major interpretations in the published academic literature until now, as outlined above, are that 1 Corinthians chapter 14 refers to a non-earthly (ecstatic or non-ecstatic) phenomena or an opposing view that Corinthian congregants were instantaneously being given a previously unlearned, earthly, foreign language. As aforementioned, these other two interpretations do not explain some of the key exegetical issues.

Because Epiphanius' interpretation offers a serious potential solution, there needs to be a thorough examination of this Jewish Christian Bishop Epiphanius' contention that it was rather a matter of the Hebrew Older Testament Scripture, the pompous use of classic Greek dialects, and teaching the Law in the broad sense. Rather than a non-earthly utterance or supernaturally bestowed earthly languages, there appears to have been a significant issue around the lack of verbal interpretation/translation and a resulting edification void and teaching deficiency within the Corinthian assembly because of the snobbery and inflated egos of some. That the Epiphanius explanation has not been fully explored, is a major problem that will be addressed by this study.

1.5 AIM AND OBJECTIVES

1.5.1 Aim

My aim is to rigorously test this unique Epiphanius proposition that the γλώσσαις-speaking in 1 Corinthians 14, with the terms γλῶσσα/glōssa (singular) or γλῶσσαι/glōssai (plural), was a controversy around the use of the Hebrew Older Testament Scripture and classic Greek dialects in the assembly and the need to interpret into a common Greek language so others could be edified.

In a cosmopolitan city like Corinth, with people from all over the Roman Empire, if there were multilingual individuals (polyglots), this would probably have affected the dynamics of the Corinthian congregation. The Epiphanius text may be pointing to various immigrants in Corinth articulating their regional classic Greek dialect in the worship service and Paul's admonition for those lesser known, stilted dialects to be interpreted into the more commonly used dialect of the congregants so that all the assembled believers could be edified.

The "tongues" issue being an on-going, significant church problem justifies this particular angle of inquiry.

1.5.2 Objectives

The following objectives flow from this aim:

a. To test the Epiphanius thesis against a linguistic analysis of the relevant words in the Hebrew and Greek texts of the Bible to see whether his contention is viable.

b. To probe the legitimacy of the Epiphanius thesis by doing a cultural analysis of the pertinent Roman government perspective of "the Way," the Jewish influence bearing on the Corinthian assembly, the derivative synagogue influence on the Corinthian assembly, the Aramaic, Greek and Roman life and influence on the Corinthian assembly, the Delphine Oracle influence on the Corinthian assembly, and the low literacy influence on the functioning of the Corinthian assembly.

c. To do a historical analysis to assess whether the Epiphanius thesis is explicitly or indirectly contradicted, and if so when, why and by whom.

d. To do a contextual and exegetical analysis of corollary Acts passages, 1 Corinthians 12–13 and the central 1 Corinthians chapter 14 to determine if there is anything inherent in the textual data that would refute the Epiphanius thesis.

e. To determine whether the Epiphanius thesis is undermined or contradicted in the earliest English translations.

1.6 CENTRAL THEORETICAL ARGUMENT

The central theoretical argument of this book is that the best way to understand the 1 Corinthians 14 phrase "speaking in tongues" and the underlying Greek terms γλῶσσα/*glŏssa* (singular) or γλῶσσαι/*glŏssai* (plural) may be in view of the contribution of early church Jewish Bishop Epiphanius, namely, that it centred around an interpretive or didactic problem within the Corinthian assembly, being a matter of the Hebrew Older Testament Scripture, differing classic Greek dialects, and the need to teach the Hebrew Older Testament Scriptures in understandable language.

2

Linguistic Analysis of γλῶσσα/γλῶσσαι (glōssa/glōssai)

THE RELEVANT GREEK TERMS for this study are γλῶσσα/*glōssa* (singular form) and γλῶσσαι/*glōssai* (plural form).

The singular γλῶσσα (*glōssa*) is used in the Gospels and Acts (Mark 7:33 and 7:35; Luke 1:64 and 16:24; Acts 2:26) where the reference is to the bodily organ of speech.

The plural γλώσσαις (*glōssais*) appears in Mark 16:17 but there it is part of the longer disputed ending of Mark 16:9–20. These twelve verses don't appear in the two earliest and most trustworthy manuscripts of the New Testament nor numerous other collaborative manuscripts (Metzger, 1975: 122–123). In fact, in other manuscripts, ancient copyists mark this passage with asterisks or obeli to indicate a spurious addition (Metzger, 1975:123). After laying out about three pages of cogent documentation on the earliest Greek, versional, and patristic evidence, Metzger (1975:126) succinctly concludes, "Thus on the basis of good external evidence and strong internal considerations, it appears that the earliest ascertainable form of the Gospel of Mark ended with 16:8." This suffices to determine that this is not a legitimate New Testament text which needs to be dealt with in this book nor does one need to get into the interesting conjectures of why Mark appears to have ended his Gospel so abruptly (Metzger, 1975:126).

The plural γλῶσσαι (*glōssai*) is used in Acts 2:3; Acts 2:4; Acts 2:11; Acts 10:46; Acts 19:6. In Acts 2:3, the term is used figuratively to refer to the shape of what seemed to be flames of fire resting on the gathered disciples on the day of Pentecost. The context surrounding Acts 2:4 and 11, seems to be clear that the reference is to known languages of this world, as in the intervening verses 6 and 8, the assembled crowd, who understand what was being said, refer to it as their very own native "dialects." Because Acts 10:46 and Acts 19:6 are in dispute, these verses will be dealt with in chapter 5 in the contextual and exegetical analysis.

In the New Testament, these terms γλῶσσα (*glóssa* singular form) and γλῶσσαι (*glóssai* plural form) are the subject of debate only in the earlier chronologic books of Acts and 1 Corinthians. In New Testament writings outside of these two books, the meaning of γλῶσσα/γλῶσσαι (*glóssa/glóssai*) is not disputed and is understood to mean either languages of this world or the bodily organ of speech.

Elsewhere in the Pauline corpus, the terms γλῶσσα/γλῶσσαι (*glóssa/glóssai*) are used thrice more, in Romans 14:11 (singular form) and Romans 3:13 (plural form) and in Philippians 2:11 (singular form), all indisputably referring to the tongue as the organ of speech. In the Bible, γλῶσσαι (*glóssai*—languages/tongues) is listed in 1 Corinthians 12:10 and 28. No one such list of roles and functions is comprehensive. These lists seem to be suggestive and not exhaustive.

There is only one use of γλῶσσα (*glóssa*) in the New Testament writings of Peter (1 Pet 3:10) referring to the organ of speech, five uses of the singular γλῶσσα (*glóssa*) by James (Jas 1:26; 3:5–8) clearly denoting the organ of speech and no use at all by Jude.

John uses the term γλῶσσα or γλῶσσαι (*glóssa/glóssai*) seven times in the book of Revelation (5:9, 7:9, 10:11, 11:9, 13:7, 14:6, and 17:15) where the references are indisputably to languages of this world, and once in Revelation 16:10 and 1 John 3:18 where the reference is to the bodily organ of speech.

The controversial matter of γλῶσσα/γλῶσσαι (*glóssa/glóssai*) in the Christ assembly at Corinth seems not to have been an issue in any of the other New Testament congregations and the subject receives no mention.

2.1 HEBREW

Because the disputed use of the terms γλῶσσα/γλῶσσαι (*glóssa/glóssai*) comes early in the New Testament chronology and the meaning in later passages, as cited above, is used in respect to the organ of speech or human language, one needs to turn to the Hebrew Older Testament Scriptures for more background in respect to the Acts and 1 Corinthians meanings in the earlier New Testament chronology. The Septuagint Greek translation of the Hebrew Older Testament and the Masoretic Hebrew text of the Older Testament will be used.

In the Greek-English Lexicon of the Septuagint (Lust, 2003:305–306), we have,

> Glossa, γλῶσσα,-ης+ N1F 5-6-27-83-48=169 LSJ LSJ Suppl = Liddell-Scott-Jones. Supplement (→ LIDDELL) Gn 10,5.20.31; 11,7; Ex 11,7 tongue, language Gn 10,5 γλῶσσα χρυσῆ golden ingot, bar of gold Jos 7,21; φαῦλοι γλώσσῃ they who speak evil Sir 20,17; ὁ δυνατὸς ἐν γλώσσῃ an eloquent man Sir 21,7; γλῶσσα τρίτη slander (lit. a third tongue) Sir 28,15 → TWNT.

Even the seeming strange translation, at first glance, of γλώσσαν (*glōssan*), deriving from the Hebrew noun לשון (*lashon*) in Joshua 7:21, has the meaning of *tongue* (and in this case also translated *bar/wedge*) of χρυσήν (*chrysēn*—gold). Here γλώσσαν (*glōssan*) is understood to mean a *tongue* referring to the general shape of the gold ingot. So, in this instance, *tongue* is used in a figurative sense. All the Genesis passages referred to above (Gen 10:5, 20, 31; 11:7) are naturally understood to mean real earthly languages.

The Hatch and Redpath Concordance to the Septuagint (1983: 271–272) has a comprehensive listing of γλῶσσα/γλῶττα (*glōssa/glōtta*) occurring in the Greek Older Testament. In the preponderance of the references of the Hatch and Redpath Concordance to the Septuagint (1983:271–272), indeed, in over a hundred cases γλῶσσα (*glōssa*) or γλῶττα (*glōtta*) derive from the Hebrew noun לשון (*lashon*) and is straightforwardly translated *tongue*, the organ of speech, or in a few cases refers to *language* in the earthly and ordinary sense of that word.

In the few remaining Older Testament cases, in the Hatch and Redpath Concordance to the Septuagint (1983:271–272), where γλῶσσα (*glōssa*) or γλῶττα (*glōtta*) derive from other Hebrew nouns, the meaning is patently *language* or *tongue* in the earthly and ordinary sense of those words (all the citations in Daniel; Gen 11:7; Ps 81:5; Prov 17:4; Zeph 3:9; Isa 19:18).

The Maccabees citations, in the Hatch and Redpath Concordance to the Septuagint (1983:272), refer to the bodily organ, the *tongue*, often in brutal reference to it being cut out. In III Maccabees 2:17, γλώσσης (*glōssēs*) is best translated "speech." The one outlier in the books of the Maccabees is in II Maccabees 3:26 where the description is to a flogging.

In the entirety of the Septuagint with the only pertinent terms of γλῶσσα (*glōssa*) or γλῶττα (*glōtta*) and the underlying Hebrew derivative words, there is no intimation of ecstatic language nor angelic/heavenly language for public or private use.

Carson (1987: 100) writes, "The range of the 'prophet' word group was certainly broad enough to encompass tongues-speaking," but he cites no sources or adduces no proof. Carson may have in mind certain references in the Hebrew Bible to *prophesying* (1 Sam 10:15–13, 19:18–24; 2 Sam 6:13–17) but these contexts do not include the Hebrew words for *language(s)* or *tongue(s)*. Moreover, the Greek Septuagint translation, of these Older Testament passages, doesn't use the terms γλῶσσα (*glōssa*) or γλῶσσαι (*glōssai*) or their cognates. Thus, from a strict scholarly point of view it would appear to be too conjectural to link these to γλῶσσα (*glōssa*) or γλῶσσαι (*glōssai*) of the New Testament.

On the other hand, of necessity, one must delve into the expression "speaks in a tongue(s)/language(s)" (λαλῶν γλώσσῃ/*lalṓn glṓssē*), which, with slight variation, occurs ten times in 1 Corinthians 14 (2, 4, 5a, 5b, 6, 13, 18, 23, 27, 39). Engelbrecht (1996:295) proposes that 'to speak in a tongue' was a common semitic idiom adapted by Paul . . . . suggested to him by the prophecy of Isaiah 28:11, which he used to address the difficulties at Corinth."

In critiquing Nils Engelsen's (1970) doctoral thesis and an article by Roy Harrisville, Engelbrecht (1996:295) emphatically states that, "The difficulty with this thesis is that there are no specific sources which use the expression [γλώσσα λαλεῖν/*glōssa lalein*] to describe unintelligible, ecstatic speech prior to Paul, making the conclusions of Engelsen and Harrisville rather tenuous." On the contrary, Engelbrecht (1996:295) asserts that, "The expression's application in Semitic literature is not to ecstatic speech but to speaking a foreign language."

Ironically, Harrisville, in the Septuagint, finds that γλώσσα/*glōssa* is used with λαλεῖν/*lalein* a number of times (Job 33:2; Ps 37:30, 39:3, 109:2; Isa 19:18, 28:11) but sweeps these examples aside as not precedential to Paul's use in 1 Corinthians 14, because they don't fit Harrisville's assumption that Paul must have meant "ecstatic speech" (Engelbrecht, 1996:296–297). Engelsen rather than examining the uses of γλώσσα/*glōssa* with λαλεῖν/*lalein*, sought out examples of ecstatic speech in

LINGUISTIC ANALYSIS

pre-Christian Greek literature (Engelbrecht, 1996:296). Because Engelsen also operated under the assumption that Paul must have meant "ecstatic speech" when writing in 1 Corinthians 14, he concluded that any expression referring to inarticulate speech is essentially unknown in pre-Christian Greek (Engelsen, 1996:296–297). Because of this *a priori* assumption, Engelsen and Harrisville fail to objectively consider how their own specific Older Testament Greek Septuagint examples relate to Paul's use in 1 Corinthians 14. If they would have just dispassionately looked at those verses (Job 33:2; Ps 37:30, 39:3, 109:2; Isa 19:18, 28:11) found in the Septuagint, where γλῶσσα/*glōssa* is used with λαλεῖν/*lalein*, they would have concluded that these terms, used in close conjunction, meant "speaking with a tongue" or "a tongue speaking" or "speaking a foreign (earthly) language" all without any mystical meaning. After all, context is the main determining factor in ascertaining meaning. Instead, without any empirical evidence, Engelsen and Harrisville conclude that Paul must have meant ecstatic speech based on something prior to him, although they can't list a single text of support (Engelbrecht, 1996:298).

In addition, examples in the Older Testament in the Hebrew language of the phrase "to speak in a tongue," in their respective contexts, uniformly mean "to speak a foreign language(s)." The Hebrew verb דָּבַר (*dabar*—to speak) and the Hebrew noun לָשׁוֹן (*lashon*—language/tongue) are the operative words.

The Apostle Paul uses the Isaiah 28:11 passage as a proof text to show that foreign languages are meant as a sign of God's rebuke to the unbelieving. God will use the conquering Assyrians—"with ones of foreign lip and tongue strange" he will speak to the resistant and rebellious Israelites (Isa 28:11).

In Esther 1:22, the King's decree uses the same Hebrew verb דָּבַר (*dabar*—to speak) and noun לָשׁוֹן (*lashon*—language/tongue) as in Isaiah 28, with its meaning being synonymous (i.e., "to speak a foreign language).

Nehemiah 13:24 uses the same Hebrew verb דָּבַר (*dabar*—to speak) and the same Hebrew noun לָשׁוֹן (*lashon*—language/tongue) and the meaning once again is "to speak a foreign language."

Lastly, in Jeremiah 5:15 which uses the same Hebrew verb דָּבַר (*dabar*—to speak) and the same Hebrew noun לָשׁוֹן (*lashon*—language/tongue), the Lord warns that he will bring a nation that speaks a foreign language to severely rebuke his people.

In the above Isaiah and Jeremiah examples, the theme is that the speaking of a foreign language will be a sign of God's judgement upon an unbelieving people (cf. Deut 28:49). "It is this tradition of foreign language as a sign of God's punishment that lies behind Paul's quotation and application of Isaiah 28:11" (Engelbrecht, 1996:299).

In light of the foregoing, complete coverage of Older Testament passages where "speak" and "tongue" are used together, "to speak in a tongue" appears to be a semitic idiom, which, thereafter, Paul drew on in 1 Corinthians 14. Engelbrecht (1996:302) argues, "It should also be noted that 'to speak in a tongue' is never used in the sense of 'ecstatic utterance' and . . . consistently refers to the speaking of a foreign language or the holy language, Hebrew." The last phrase by Engelbrecht (1996:297) about "the holy language, Hebrew" is very interesting because he bases this intimation on the Mishnah (second century AD). He does acknowledge that this source is later than the Apostle Paul's time but notes that it may reflect early tradition (Engelbrecht, 1996:297).

The pseudepigraphic *Testament of Job* (Charlesworth, 1983) must be referred to, as chapters 49 to 52 are oft referred to in support of the origin of the modern-day phenomena of "tongues." In these chapters, it is said that Job's daughters speak and sing in the "languages" of the angels. The phrase "to speak in a tongue" is never actually used. Rather, the Greek term used is διαλέκτω (*dialektō*) which is the same term used in Acts 2:6, 8, on the Day of Pentecost.

The notable church historian Eusebius (265–339 AD) preserves the argument of an anti-Montanist (HE 5.17.1–4) who demanded to know where in biblical history any precedent appeared for ecstatic prophecy (Charlesworth, 1983:834). R.P. Spittler believes that, subsequently, the original Jewish work was amended by the Montanists in the second century AD as an apologetic for ecstatic speech, adding the references to angelic languages (Charlesworth,1983:834). There are weighty reasons internal to the document that demonstrate there was likely the significant addition of chapters 46–53 to the original *Testament of Job* composition (Charlesworth, 1983:834), specifically: "Job's first-person address ends at chapter 45" (Charlesworth, 1983:834); "Testament of Job 46–53 supplements 1–45 in reporting Job's recovery" (Charlesworth, 1983:834); "Apocalyptic language more conspicuously appears in chapters 46–53, which contain no extended poetic piece to match those found in chapters 1–45" (Charlesworth, 1983:834); "In the single reference to the devil found in 46–53, he is called 'the enemy'

(TJob 47:10), while the terms 'Satan,' the 'devil,' and the 'evil one' appear in 1–45" (Charlesworth, 1983:834). The work remained in Montanist hands as a propaganda text for quite some time (Charlesworth, 1983:834).

2.2 GREEK

As noted at the outset of the Hebrew section above, the relevant Greek terms for this study are γλῶσσα (*glóssa* singular form) and γλῶσσαι (*glóssai* plural form). In the New Testament, these terms are the subject of debate only in the earliest chronology, namely Acts and 1 Corinthians.

We begin this section, exclusively focusing on a Greek analysis, by turning to the present standard Greek Lexicon. The Greek terms at the heart of the 1 Corinthians chapter 14 discussion "γλώσσῃ" (singular) or "γλώσσαις" (plural), in Bauer, Danker, Arndt and Gingrich (2021, hereafter referred to as BDAG) are defined as meaning the literal organ of speech or figuratively as the shape of the tongue (BDAG, s.v. γλῶσσα, §1), language/languages (BDAG, s.v. γλῶσσα, §2) or "an utterance outside the normal patterns of intelligible speech and therefore requiring special interpretation, ecstatic language, ecstatic speech" (BDAG, s.v. γλῶσσα, §3) with this latter option listing 1 Corinthians 14:1–27, 39; 12:10, 28, 30; 13:1 (BDAG, s.v. γλῶσσα, §3). To include these very verses which have been the subject of vigorous dispute, seems to beg the question. BDAG then continues "There is no doubt about the thing referred to, namely the strange speech of persons in religious ecstasy. The phenomenon, as found in Hellenistic religion . . . " (BDAG, s.v. γλῶσσα, §3). Christopher Forbes (1995), after extensive review of the cited Hellenistic sources, as delineated below, dismantled this supposedly pre-Christian parallel for early Christian *glossolalia* (non-earthly languages).

Forbes (1995:152) pinpoints the problem of the suggested Hellenistic parallels brought forward by modern authors. ". . . these references come from the mid-second century or later." He argues, "In the light of the problems to do with changing views of paranormal phenomena in Hellenistic culture between the first century and the end of the second, mentioned in the introduction, the lateness of the evidence cited above must raise very real doubts" (Forbes, 1995:152).

Forbes (1995:160) also refutes the suggestion that Montanist ecstatic prophecy reflects the similar postulated Hellenistic background. Forbes (1995:160) writes, "Indeed, the evidence of Eusebius who knows of collections of Montanist oracles, and actually cites the contents of some of them, makes it luminously clear that these oracles were delivered in plain Greek." Maximilla's and Montanus' preserved oracles were quite intelligible (Forbes, 1995:160). The Montanist prophetic utterances resembled Delphic enthusiasm in that the speech was intelligible (Forbes, 1995:162). "There is no evidence that glossalalia was practised among the Montanists, or that they understood their prophecy to include angelic languages" (Forbes, 1995:184).

In summarizing his search for ecstatic and unintelligible speech in the Hellenistic world prior to the Christian era, Forbes (1995:168) reiterates that the oracle of Apollo at Delphi "was neither 'ecstatic' nor unintelligible" but was commonly cryptic and obscure in archaic and poetic form. The enthusiastic worship of Dionysus and Cybele included ritual and invocation which was intelligible (Forbes, 1995:168).

Forbes also did a survey of proposed parallels within intertestamental Judaism (Jubilees 25:14, Testament of Judah 25:2–3, 1 Enoch 40, 71:11, 4 Maccabees 10:21, and Martyrdom of Isaiah 5:14 and various references from Philo). None of those passages suggested either an unintelligible form of ecstatic speech or the human use of heavenly languages (Forbes, 1995:182).

Forbes (1995:316) concludes that the Apostle Paul's use of γλώσσαίς λαλείν (*glōssais lalein*) has no precedents or parallels, as technical terminology, in Greek literature.

Thumb (*Gr. Dial.* p. 22), cited in Moulton and Milligan (1930:128), "points out that grammarians used γλῶσσα not only for 'language' but also for 'local peculiarities of speech': thus . . . 'sub-dialects.'" The alternate definition from the papyri and other non-literary sources refers to the organ of speech (Moulton and Milligan, 1930:128). There is no mention of "ecstatic speech" or anything alluding to such nor anything to do with extraterrestrial speech. There was no separate listing of the plural γλῶσσαι/*glōssai*.

The Classic Greek Dictionary defines γλῶσσα/*glōssa* as the organ of speech, physically or metaphorically, and alternately in reference to using "a language" or "dialect" (Berry, 1956:143). There is no mention of "ecstatic speech" or anything alluding to such nor anything to do with extraterrestrial speech. There was no separate listing of the plural γλῶσσαι/*glōssai*.

Liddell and Scott (1968:353), under γλῶσσα/*glōssa*, lists three primary meanings, namely, the organ of speech, a language or dialect, and anything shaped like a tongue. There is no mention of "ecstatic speech" or anything alluding to such nor anything to do with extraterrestrial speech, and similarly in an earlier abridgement (Liddell and Scott, 1892:143). There was no separate listing of the plural γλῶσσαι/*glōssai*.

Lampe's *Patristic Greek Lexicon* (1961:316), under γλῶσσα/*glōssa*, showed up definitions of: (1) tongue, as an instrument of speech, (2) language(s), (3) metaphorically with an example of γλῶσσα being used as metonymy for "psalterion/harp of the Lord," (4) thong, (5) ingot, of gold. There is no mention of "ecstatic speech" or anything alluding to such nor anything to do with extraterrestrial speech. There was no separate listing of the plural γλῶσσαι/*glōssai*.

2.3 CONCLUSIONS

To test the thesis that γλώσσα/*glōssa* (singular) or γλώσσαι/*glōssai* (plural) means "language" or "languages" in the Epiphanius sense of those words, the preceding linguistic analysis used all tthe essential tools. In thus testing the Epiphanius thesis against a linguistic analysis of the relevant words in the Hebrew and Greek texts of the Bible, there is nothing that appears to undercut the viability of the Epiphanius assertion that γλώσσα (singular) or γλώσσαι (plural) means "language" or "languages" in the ordinary sense of those words.

On the contrary, from the foregoing, linguistic analysis, in which γλῶσσα/γλῶσσαι was examined in its various contexts, it appears, thus far, that there is no defensible definition of ecstatic or non-ecstatic angelic/heavenly language for public or private use out of the Greek terms γλῶσσα/*glōssa* (singular) or γλῶσσαι/*glōssai* (plural).

3

Cultural Analysis

PROBING THE LEGITIMACY OF the Epiphanius thesis by a cultural analysis will in this chapter involve an examination of the pertinent Roman government perspective of "the Way," the Jewish influence bearing on the Corinthian assembly, the Apostle Paul's Hebraistic background and that of his co-workers, the derivative synagogue influence on the Corinthian assembly, Aramaic, Greek and Roman influence on the Corinthian assembly, the Delphine Oracle influence on the Corinthian assembly, and the low literacy influence on the functioning of the Corinthian assembly.

3.1 ROMAN PERSPECTIVE—THE "WAY" AS A SECT OF JUDAISM

"The Way" is mentioned a number of times in the book of Acts (9:2; 19:9, 23; 22:4; 24:14, 22) as a designation for the early followers of Christ. Possibly, the early followers of Christ self-designated as followers of "the Way" because of Jesus' statement in John 14:6 that he is "the way, and the truth, and the life."

Saul of Tarsus went to Damascus to take prisoner men and women "belonging to the Way" (Acts 9:2; 22:4). After Saul was converted, he became a missionary and went by the name of Paul. In Ephesus, Paul met some in the synagogue who "were becoming hardened and disobedient, speaking evil of the Way" (Acts 19:9).

CULTURAL ANALYSIS

During his trial before Felix, Paul said, "I admit to you, that according to the Way which they call a sect, I do serve the God of our fathers" (Acts 24:14). In view of Paul's statement, it appears that "the Way" was considered to be a sect of Judaism rather than a separate religion. In Acts 24:22, we are also told that Felix had an exact knowledge about "the Way." Felix's Judaean Governor successor, Festus, made a similar assessment about "the Way" being a sect of Judaism when he said that "they [the accusing Jews] simply had some points of disagreement with him [Paul] about their own religion and about a certain dead man, Jesus, whom Paul asserted to be alive" (Acts 25:19).

The Roman authorities were aware of "the Way" as another Jewish sect (Acts 24:14) who read the same Scriptures (the Older Testament), worshipped the same God, practiced similar customs, celebrated the same festivals, and likewise saw themselves as distinct from the beliefs and practices of the society around them. At this early stage, the great difference between "the Way," as they were oft referred to, and the rest of Judaism was the belief by the former that Jesus of Nazareth was the Davidic Messiah. In the early going, the majority of Jesus followers were Jewish, with a rapidly growing number of Gentiles, many of whom had already been either proselytes (converts who had been fully integrated into the Jewish synagogue community) or the "God-fearers" (Gentiles adhering to some Jewish beliefs without the full conversion rites).

Schiffman (2015:52), in reviewing what has been learned from the Dead Sea Scrolls, notes the importance of the insights "the scrolls tell us about the ferment and debate that took place within the Jewish community in the second and first centuries B.C.E. and the early first century C.E." Schiffman (2015:53) emphasizes that, "The scrolls have been part of a wider, post-Holocaust phenomenon of understanding earliest Christianity as a Jewish sect."

Specifically in the Corinthian first-century context, the Jews must have complained that these Christians were not a sect of the Jewish religion (Judaism), whereupon proconsul Gallio, in judgement (Acts 18:14–15), said in effect "Settle your own internal religious squabbles."

Acts 16:20, 21 also shows that Paul and his companions were perceived as proclaiming Jewish customs. The net effect is that because the Jewish synagogues were sanctioned by Roman law, Christianity could take advantage of this protection as long as it sheltered itself under the auspices of the Jewish religion (Bruce, 1977:254).

The Earliest View of New Testament Tongues

As Bruce Winter (1999:223) writes in respect to Acts 18:14, 15, "... they secured the very ruling that no Jew wanted to hear. Christianity was a sect within Judaism and therefore a *religio licita*, part of the *mos maiorum*. This was how Christianity was judged in the eyes of a Roman governor with expertise as a jurist." Winter (1999:223) goes on to write, "What Gallio ruled . . . had implications for this early Messianic movement. Whether Jewish Christians or Gentile Christians, Roman citizens, or provincials, they were all seen as 'a party' operating under the Jewish umbrella." Gallio saw the Corinthian dispute, between the Jews and Paul, as "questions about words and names and your own law" (Acts 18:15). Gallio saw the disputants as having the same sacral writings, worshiping the same God, observing the same customs, and distinct from the society around them.

Winter (1999:224) understands that the consequence of Gallio's decision was to exempt from emperor worship, not only the Jews, but now the Christians also. Winter (1999:224), in referencing the first twelve pages of A.N. Sherwin White's, *Roman Society and Roman Law in the New Testament,* states, "This judgement was valid for the province of Achaea by reason of his *imperium*, but although it was not legally binding beyond it, an opinion of a leading jurist could not be lightly disregarded."

Ford (1966a:406) writes, regarding the Jewish community in Corinth, that "to its Roman governors the Christians differed not at all from it; indeed, it is unlikely that there was an actual separation between Church and synagogue at this time." In view of this fact on the ground, Ford (1966a:406) suggests that it is easier to understand Paul's reference to the courts (1 Cor 6:1–8) and the collection (1 Cor 16:1–4).

Even in his latter ministry, when the Apostle Paul was accused by the Jews of being "a ringleader of the sect of the Nazarenes" (Acts 24:5), the use of the term "sect" demonstrates that these clashes were viewed as internal Jewish conflicts by proponents of Second Temple Judaism (Acts 24:5, 14; 28:22). The Sadducees were referred to as a "sect" (Acts 5:17) and the Pharisees were also referred to as a "sect" (Acts 15:5; 26:5).

As above, at this early stage, the great difference between the "Way" and other Jews was the belief of the former that Jesus of Nazareth was the Davidic Messiah (Acts 18:4, 5).

"Jesus' followers constituted a radical Jewish sect that neither Roman nor Greek could distinguish from the rest of Jewry at first sight" (Oliver, 2021:23).

The demarcation between "Christians" and "Jews" is described in scholarly literature as "the parting of the ways" (Dunn, 2006). As Dunn's book shows, this didn't happen in a historical moment, but was a gradual process, and was not complete for centuries (Dunn, 2006). As Meyers (2013:133) concludes: "The older view that the split occurred early in the Roman period after the two Jewish revolts against Rome (66–70 C.E. and 132–135 C.E.) can no longer be maintained. The separation came much later."

3.2 JEWISH INFLUENCE BEARING ON THE CORINTHIAN ASSEMBLY

Over a century ago, Harnack (1908:9) gauged that about 7 percent of the approximate sixty million population of the Roman Empire was Jewish. His rough appraisal was that there were about one million Jews in Syria, another one million in Egypt, one and a half million in Asia Minor, Greece, Cyrene, Italy, Gaul and Spain, and 700,000 in Israel (Harnack, 1908:6–8). With Judaism embracing about 4 to 4.5 million (7 percent) of the total population of the Roman Empire in those days "one begins to realize its great influence and social importance" (Harnack, 1908:9).

Josephus has preserved a series of first-century AD, Roman, governmental edicts affirming the rights and privileges of various Jewish communities in Asia Minor in the face of local opposition and hostility (Levine, 2005:113). The various edicts presume the Jews were well organized, with their own communal framework, and practicing their own social and religious customs (Levine, 2005:113–114).

These decrees seem to derive from the basic recognition extended by Julius Caesar to the Jews in the Roman Empire, in appreciation of the support he received from Antipater, Hyrcanus II, and the Jews in his struggle against Pompey (Josephus, 1963:115).

Josephus (1963:129) states his general view on the Roman governmental perspective on the Jewish religion practiced throughout the Roman Empire. "Jewish citizens of ours have come to me and pointed out that from the earliest times they have had an association of their own in accordance with their native laws and a place of their own, in which they decide their affairs and controversies with one another." The verdict of Gallio recorded in Acts 18:14–15 in the Corinthian context seems to bear this out. Even Paul's 39 lashes on each of five occasions indicates that he customarily submitted to the authority granted to Jewish synagogues (2 Cor 11:24; cf. Deut 25:1–3), at least for awhile.

Various modern authors make the same point. In writing of the treatment of Jews of the dispersion even after AD 70, Bruce (1977:29) avows, "In fact, a succession of edicts issued by the highest authorities had secured to Jews throughout the Roman Empire quite exceptional privileges, and these were not rescinded."

Levine (2005:130–131) summarizes these general rights of the Jews in the pre-70 Diaspora as: the right to maintain their own courts, the right to attend to their own food requirements, the right to avoid worshipping the civic deities or appearing in court on Sabbaths and festivals, the right to be exempt from serving in the army, the right to send monies to Jerusalem, and the more general right to conduct a wide range of communal affairs. Sanders (1999:2) also compiled a similar list. Despite these protections, Flusser (1989:75) states the caveat that, "The Jews of the Diaspora felt that they were in constant danger of anti-semitism and were faithful to Palestine."

The Jews of the Diaspora had to be constantly vigilant that these granted privileges were not in any way undermined. Because they were not on their home soil, there was a sense of insecurity and suspicion about anything under the umbrella of Judaism that might erode their social stability (Flusser, 1989:75).

Runesson (2008) documents the attraction, in varying degrees, of many pagans to Judaism. "In fact, the status enjoyed by many Diaspora communities may have been due, at least in part, to the presence and support of a large number of pagan sympathizers" (Levine, 2005:118).

In addition to its Davidic kingly associations, Jerusalem also set the standard for faithfulness to Jewish traditions in the Apostle Paul's day (Malina and Pilch, 2006:371–374).

In view of the wealth of new epigraphic material such as the manuscripts from Qumran and documents from the Judaean desert, linguists, archaeologists and most biblical scholars began to change their views and now readily accept that Hebrew, as well as Aramaic, was spoken and written in the time of Jesus (Baltes, 2014:60).

The findings from the Dead Sea Scrolls reverberated throughout the academic world. In view of the impact of the Dead Sea Scrolls, the reputable Oxford Dictionary of the Christian Church, in relation to the Hebrew language, had to revise its statement. In its first edition, in regard to the Hebrew language, it stated that, "It ceased to be a spoken language about the fourth century B.C." (The Oxford Dictionary of the Christian Church, 1958:614), but had to revise that statement in the third edition to read: "Hebrew continued to be used as a spoken and written language after the classical period, and is found in texts from Qumran and in the Mishnah..." (The Oxford Dictionary of the Christian Church, 1997:741–742).

As former Professor of Hebrew University, David Flusser (1989:11–12) writes:

> The spoken languages among the Jews of that period [at the time of Jesus] were Hebrew, Aramaic, and to an extent Greek. Until recently, it was believed by numerous scholars that the language spoken by Jesus' disciples was Aramaic. It is possible that Jesus did, from time to time, make use of the Aramaic language. But during that period Hebrew was both the daily language and the language of study... Today, after the discovery of the Hebrew Ben Sira (Ecclesiasticus), of the Dead Sea Scrolls, and of the Bar Kochba Letters, and in light of more profound studies of the language of the Jewish Sages, it is accepted that most people were fluent in Hebrew. The Pentateuch was translated into Aramaic for the benefit of the lower strata of the population... There is thus no ground for assuming that Jesus did not speak Hebrew; and when we are told (Acts 21:40) that Paul spoke Hebrew, we should take this piece of information at face value. This question of the spoken language is especially important for understanding the doctrines of Jesus. There are sayings of Jesus which can be rendered both in Hebrew and Aramaic; but there are some which can only be rendered into Hebrew, and none of them can be rendered only in Aramaic. Their language was early Rabbinic Hebrew with strong undercurrents of Biblical Hebrew.

Lexicographer Moses Segal (1927:1) categorized the Hebrew language into four periods: (1) Biblical Hebrew (BH), from the earliest times to the end of the Biblical period, about 200 BC; (2) Misnaic Hebrew (MH), from about 400–300 BC to about 400 AD; (3) Medieval Hebrew, from the redaction of the Babylonian Talmud, about 500 AD, to 1700 AD; and (4) Modern Hebrew, from the beginning of the eighteenth century AD to the present. Segal (1927:1) views the first period overlapping the second period, as Biblical Hebrew continued to be used as literary idiom long after the rise of Misnaic Hebrew.

The Earliest View of New Testament Tongues

Segal (1927:2) regards Misnaic Hebrew to be the vernacular and colloquial language spoken in Judaea during the first century. "In earlier Misnaic literature no distinction is drawn between Biblical Hebrew and Misnaic Hebrew. The two idioms are known as לְשׁוֹן הַקֹּדֶשׁ (*Leshon Hakodesh*), the Holy Tongue, as contrasted with other languages ... " (Segal, 1927:2). Segal (1927:17) acknowledges that "With regard to the language of Jesus, it is admitted that in the Roman period, and perhaps earlier, Aram[aic]was the vernacular of the native Galilean Jews. But even in Galilee, M[isnaic] H[ebrew] was understood and spoken, at least by the educated classes."

On the basis of research on Matthew's Gospel, Josephus and other contemporaneous literature, Grintz (1960:32–47) writes: "We conclude that in the last days of the Second Temple, Hebrew was a living language."

The homeland of the Jews, with its interrelationship of Greek, Hebrew and Aramaic, had a reputation as being the region where plurilingualism was the most common (Christidis, 2007:639). As summarized by Spolsky (1997:138), by the beginning of the Common Era two thousand years ago, a pattern of triglossia had emerged, with Hebrew, Judeo-Aramaic, and Greek all playing meaningful roles. Baltes (2014:62) admits the same. Ong (2016:182) contends that the first-century Jewish homeland was multiglossic with adding Latin, the Roman administrative language (Ong, 2016:166).

This model of language organization became the norm for the Jewish people during most of their dispersion, with separate defined functions for the different languages: Hebrew was used for religious and literacy purposes; a Jewish language [dialect] was used for most other community and home functions, and one or more "co-territorial vernaculars" was used for communication with non-Jews (Spolsky, 1997:138).

In view of ten years of discovery in the wilderness of Judaea, Milik (1959:130) categorically avowed that the findings "... prove beyond reasonable doubt that Mishnaic [Hebrew] was the normal language of the Judaean population in the Roman period." Even if this be judged an overstatement, there appears to be a broad consensus in the current scholarship that, at a minimum, Hebrew was used for religious purposes.

As Joosten (2010:335), based on the recent research and discovery of new manuscripts, remarks that, in Jewish Israel, through the first century, "Hebrew remained the language of the Bible .... the Hebrew Scriptures were widely read and studied in the original text."

"Hebrew was used, much more than Aramaic as far as we can judge, in liturgy and religious teaching" (Joosten, 2010:335). This contention would be bolstered by John 19:20 which tells of the inscription above Jesus on the cross, "written in Hebrew, Latin, *and* in Greek." Hughes (1974:134) asserts, "Linguistic research is making it increasingly difficult to maintain that by terms like *Hebraisti* (John 19:20; Acts 21:40; 22:2; 26:24) and *Hebraikos* (Luke 23:28) the Aramaic language is unquestionably intended." The actual reality is that Aramaic was called "Syriac" [an Aramaic dialect] as "Syria" was the Greek name for "Aram" (Hughes, 1974:138–139). Grintz (1960:33–34) also maintains that Hebrew is meant in these various New Testament passages, not Aramaic (Luke 23:28; John 19:20; Acts 21:40; 22:2; 26:24). The Roman authorities would have meant for all the passers-by to understand the inscription on Jesus' cross, so it is telling that Hebrew and not Aramaic was written on that placard (John 19:20).

The presumption of the death of Hebrew as a spoken language after the Babylonian exile is no longer a viable theory in view of the evidence establishing that Hebrew was a living language in the first century AD (Baltes, 2014:62).

The picture that emerged from the epigraphic and literary evidence during the Second Temple period is that Hebrew had the status of a national language being used in literature, religion and to express national identity (Baltes, 2014:37). For the Jews, "Hebrew would still have remained as the Jewish religious, linguistic symbol and identity marker in the first century CE" (Ong, 2016:183). The use of Hebrew was needed "in the reading of the Scripture in the synagogues" and for "the recitation of the Torah, as well as in other ceremonial rituals that would have required the language" (Ong, 2016:182).

Rajak (2009:8) comments that those who have written about the Greek Bible tended to overlook the Jewish side of the equation altogether. She writes of the rather static and old ideas about the "dispersion" and the diminished role of the Hebrew language, when in fact, based on extensive research, there has been a dramatic reassessment on the Jewish Diaspora in particular (Rajak, 2009:8).

As Joosten (2017:44–49, 62) writes, ". . . in the late Persian and Hellenistic periods, 'classical' Hebrew was not a dead language to be deciphered respectfully, but a living language to be exploited as much as possible. Whether in the diaspora or in their occupied homeland, the Jews considered Scripture their real home country, and its language their native idiom." In this regard, Wright (2008:271) makes some interesting comments on the Septuagint, after it became established as an independent text whose reading and use was divorced from its Hebrew source text. Wright (2008:271) remarks that thereafter the concept of the divine inspiration of Scripture became very relevant and debate ensued over the relative authority of the Hebrew and Greek texts.

Translation, from the second century BC onward, was a distinctive and valuable part of literary activity for the Jewish Diaspora, as indicated in the preface of the Greek Ben Sira (Rajak, 2009:114). Ben Sira's grandson explained how and why he worked diligently to produce a Greek version of his wise grandfather's book of instruction (Rajak, 2009:14). Rajak (2009:14) asserts that, "This interest also demonstrates that esteem for Hebrew as holy tongue and national language persisted and it presupposes a functioning bilingualism at least within a scholarly element of the diaspora population." Joosten (2017:46) also maintains that Hebrew may reasonably be considered a holy tongue, in that "originally an ordinary human language, over time it became a sacred idiom, fit for religious purposes and ever so slightly unfit for everything else." During the first century, Hebrew was "known as לְשׁוֹן הַקֹּדֶשׁ (Leshon Hakodesh), the Holy Tongue, as contrasted with other languages" (Segal, 1927: 2). Even years later, the Church Father, Cyril of Alexandria (c. 370-c. 444 AD), was still gripped by the mystique of the Hebrew language and maybe the more so because he had never learned it. In *Contra Julianum*, Cyril referred to Hebrew as the sacred language and lamented that he had to resort to the Greek language (Migne, 1863:Vol. 76, Lib. VII, Section 234, Col. 857–858).

Coming into the first century AD, there were numerous revisions of the Greek Septuagint in an effort to bring it into greater congruence with the Hebrew text of the Bible (Wright, 2008:271). Brock (1992:321) imputes these "corrections," at the turn of the common era, to the growing certitude that the Hebrew language should be thought of as the singular medium of authority and revelation. He writes, "Such an attitude to the unique role of Hebrew as the language of divine revelation effectively ruled out the possibility that a biblical translation could legitimately enjoy any authority at all independently of the Hebrew original" (Brock, 1992:321). On the other hand, the Jewish Philo, who was from Egypt and thoroughly Hellenized, took the position on the

Greek Septuagint translation, that it enjoyed equal status, as "sister," with the original Hebrew (Brock, 1992:328).

"It was against this general background of varying, and increasingly polarized, attitudes to biblical translation, that Christianity emerged" (Brock,1992:327–328).

Cohen (1998:3) observes that "the Diaspora communities formed the Jewish network which early Christians as Jews were able to use for their own purposes."

In addition to the potential significant influence of the Hebrew language on the Corinthian Christ assembly, the Corinthian believers, via the Apostle Paul's teaching, seemed to be influenced by Jewish apocalyptic thought. Paul wrote that "the time has been shortened" (1 Cor 7:29–31; cf. 1 Cor 15:51–57) and exhorted the Corinthian believers to eagerly anticipate the imminent end of the age and the coming of Christ (*parousia*/παρουσία).

Gregory Dix (1953:3), in his extensive evaluation of the question of the Hellenization of the gospel, concludes that the core of the gospel message is comprised of "a Jewish Monotheism and a Jewish Messianism and a Jewish Eschatology; which is expressed in a particular pattern of worship and morality."

This assessment runs contrary to a particular bias in the early twentieth century, which claimed that many early Christian beliefs and practices were adapted from Hellenistic pagan cults. By now, scholarship has mostly discarded this theory. The more recent body of information shows that early Christianity arose from the Jewish world of thought. Nash (1984:270) grappled with the assertions of the History of Religions School, and responded unambiguously to their claims: "Was early Christianity a syncretistic faith? Did it borrow any of its essential beliefs and practices either from Hellenistic philosophy or religion or from Gnosticism? The evidence requires that this question be answered in the negative."

This appraisal of Nash is corroborated by the research of other historians and scholars like Wright (1992) and Flusser (1989) who attest that first-century Judaism provides the unique framework and influences to comprehend the development of early Christianity.

"The very mode of first-century Messianic faith was intrinsically Jewish. Gentiles participating in apostolic communities were, by default, already deep into Jewish practice" (Michael & Lancaster, 2009:61).

3.2.1 Paul's Hebraistic upbringing and training

Since F.C. Baur's major work, *Paulus, der Apostel Jesu Christi, sein Leben und Wirken, seine Briefe und seine Lehre* (1845; *Paul the Apostle of Jesus Christ: His Life and Works, His Letters and His Teaching*, English Translation 1875), New Testament scholars have debated the seeming discrepancies between Paul's self-portraiture in his own letters and the Lukan depiction of him in the book of Acts.

Legitimate discussion as that is, if Luke, however, is deliberately skewing his portrayal of Paul and falsifying information to do so, that would be inconsistent with Scripture's inerrancy, but also inconsistent with Luke's writing his Gospel and Acts so that Theophilus "might know the exact truth about the things [he had] been taught" (Luke 1:4). Luke would not be providing certitude to Theophilus if he was intentionally distorting the facts for whatever ulterior motive.

Respected classicist and historian, Paul Barnett (2012) who, in brief, harmonizes some of the seeming differences, says, "Although the various criticisms of Acts appear to damage the credibility of that text for commentary on Paul, those criticisms diminish when carefully evaluated." The relative adroitness with which former Anglican Bishop and New Testament scholar Barnett ameliorates some of the vaunted contradictions leads one to believe that studious examination of other purported contradictions can result in their being harmonized.

Without ignoring the apparent differences, emphasizing dissimilarities between Luke's depiction of Paul and Paul's self-portraiture in his own letters is like drawing attention to the variance between the biography and the autobiography of the same person. Not unlike the synergy of the Synoptic Gospels, we have two valid and captivating pictures of Paul. One could say that Acts is an external picture, as taken by a professional photographer, and Paul's own writings present an internal picture of the man—an X-ray or ultrasound, so to speak. Each vantage point gives us a fuller picture of the Saul, who in due course became known as the Apostle Paul.

With that said, Saul was of the tribe of Benjamin, and as a Hebrew of Hebrews was circumcised on the eighth day (Phil 3:5), and spent his younger years growing up in Tarsus. Marulli (2011/2012:87) states that Paul is probably claiming a Benjamite pedigree to enable him "to compete in authority with the Judaizers." Marulli (2011/2012:88) says that Paul brings up the fact that he has been circumcised to communicate that "he does not come from a family who detached itself from the language and the tradition of his ancestors and of his land." By such a statement, Paul avers that "he is neither a Gentile, nor a Proselyte, nor a Jew that has been Hellenized to the point of losing contact with his mother country and sacred language" (Marulli, 2011/2012:88).

For all of Paul's exemplary Jewish pedigree, he counted it as "loss" compared to the surpassing value of knowing Christ Jesus (Phil 3:8–9).

Saul's father must have been a Roman citizen because Paul (pre-conversion known as Saul) says that he himself "was actually born a *citizen*" (Acts 22:28). In Acts 22:3, Paul recounts "I am a Jew, born in Tarsus of Cilicia, but brought up in this city [Jerusalem], educated under Gamaliel, strictly according to the law of our fathers. . ." Gamaliel, a most illustrious Pharisee of his day, was renowned as "a teacher of the Law and respected by all the people" (Acts 5:34). Gamaliel is also portrayed as a persuasive influencer of his religious colleagues in the Sanhedrin (Acts 5:40).

So, because Saul's parents were of the sect of the Pharisees (Acts 23:6), probably just after puberty at about age 12 or 13, Saul went to Jerusalem to live with relatives and receive this additional biblical training under the Pharisee Gamaliel. Under Gamaliel, Paul would have developed an expert knowledge of the Hebrew Scriptures. Even the Roman Governor Festus acknowledged Paul's "great learning" (Acts 26:24).

Gamaliel followed the more lenient or liberal philosophy of Hillel his grandfather, juxtaposed against the pharisaical school of Shammai. In some ways this was very providential because it prepared Paul (pre-conversion known as Saul) to eventually be more broad-minded in his encounters with the Gentile world. As noted, under Gamaliel's tutelage, Paul acquired an expert knowledge of the Hebrew Scriptures, and in the providence of God, it may be that this educational pedigree gave him access to teach in the synagogues of the Jewish Diaspora on his missionary travels (Acts 17:2).

Saul apparently was an ambitious student and Pharisee, as he reports that he was "advancing in Judaism beyond many of [his] contemporaries . . . being more extremely zealous for my ancestral traditions" (Gal 1:14). It seems that Saul was well connected with the Jewish leadership of his day, as indicated by his relationship of obtaining religious favors from the High Priest and Sanhedrin (Acts 9:1–2).

The Earliest View of New Testament Tongues

Saul was no doubt fluent in Hebrew, being he was educated as a Pharisee in Jerusalem under the esteemed Rabbi Gamaliel (Acts 21:40 and 22:2). The fact that, on the Damascus Road, as Paul recites his conversion to King Agrippa in Acts 26:14, the ascended Lord Jesus addressed Saul in Hebrew is a fair inference that this was his mother tongue (Bruce, 1977:43). Hughes (1974:134) and Grintz (1960:33–34) assert that, by terms like *Hebraisti* (John 19:20; Acts 21:40; 22:2; 26:24) and *Hebraikos* (Luke 23:28), the Hebrew language is meant in these various New Testament passages.

After citing the Apostle Paul's use of Aramaic and Hebrew expressions and "Greek words with Hebrew meanings," Joosten (2010:344) acknowledges that "Paul probably knew both Aramaic and Hebrew, and may have used traditional material formulated in these languages." Although Paul appears to predominantly quote from the Greek Septuagint translation when referring to Older Testament passages, he sometimes clearly makes use of the Hebrew text (Job 41:3 in Rom 11:35; Job 5:12f in 1 Cor 3:19; Exod 16:18 in 2 Cor 8:15; Num 16:5 in 2 Tim 2:19), so from even these few passages, it would seem that Paul had a facility in the Hebrew language.

Nevertheless, because his hometown of Tarsus was a major city in eastern Cilicia, part of the Roman province of Syria, by the time Paul was a child, he would have learned Aramaic. Because, for a time, Paul resided in Damascus (Acts 9:20–23) and Antioch (Acts 11:25–30; 13:1–3), two of Syria's most important cities, he would likely have picked up the Syriac dialect also.

Paul would have also been fluent in Greek as attested by his birthplace of Tarsus, his missionary focus west of Israel and his frequent use of the Greek Septuagint translation of the Hebrew Scriptures, a discussion to which we turn in the next section of this book. Over the course of his lifetime, Paul would have become familiar with various Greek dialects.

As Latin was the administrative language of the Roman Empire (Kent, 1966:18; Engels, 1990:67–74) and having to interface with the Roman authorities from time to time, Paul likely had an acquaintance with that language also. From another perspective, Ong (2016:186) states that Jews, like Paul, who likely studied such subjects as philosophy, law, grammar, rhetoric, would have perhaps been exposed "to Latin in some cases, as these subjects were taught in that language."

Paul tells us that after his Damascus Road experience, regaining his sight by the hands of Ananias, being baptized, and preaching Jesus in Damascus synagogues (Acts 9:1–22), he then went to Arabia (Gal 1:17–19). Paul did not revisit Jerusalem until three years later to become acquainted with Peter and during that time he met James the Lord's brother (Gal 1:18,19). Paul emphasized that the gospel he preached was not received from man nor was it taught to him, but he "*received* it through a revelation of Jesus Christ" (Gal 1:12).

In Philippians 3:6, Paul admitted that before his momentous shift to trust in the resurrected Christ, he was blameless as to the righteousness which is in the law. In accord with the Judaism of his day, Paul had believed in the possibility of salvation through works of the law, but after trusting in the resurrected Christ Jesus, Paul recognized that only through the enabling power of the Spirit of Christ could the righteous stipulations of the law be wholly met in redeemed sinners like himself (Rom 8).

It is likely that Paul would have been influenced by the hermeneutical principles passed on from his teacher Gamaliel. For example, Paul uses the interpretive principle of arguing "from the lesser to the greater" in 1 Corinthians 9:9–12, which begins as follows: "You shall not muzzle the ox while he is threshing." Subsequent to this quote of Deuteronomy 25:4, the Apostle Paul applies this Hebrew Scripture, stressing that, if God cares about the humane treatment of oxen, he is all the more attentive that his devoted human laborers receive the sustenance they are worthy of. Paul used this interpretive principle of arguing "from the lesser to the greater" in a number of other places in the New Testament as well (Rom 5:8–9, 10, 15, 17; 11:12, 24; 1 Cor 12:22; 2 Cor 3:7–9, 11; Phil 2:12; Phlm 1:16; Heb 2:2–3; 9:13–14; 10:28–29; 12:9, 25).

Tomson (1990:69), in an extensive study of the Pauline epistles, summarizes: "First Corinthians is not only remarkable among Paul's letters for its 'legal' and 'Jewish' character, but it appears very much to reflect Paul's own thinking and was recognized as such in the early church." Tomson (1990:82) refers to basic categories of tradition and in respect to the category of Scripture remarks:

> Second Temple Jews accepted [OT] Scripture both as the basis of practical life and thought; so did Paul. Scriptural verses are generally introduced with quotation formulae such as: ' . . . as it is written', as is common in Hebrew, Aramaic and

Greek Jewish works. Often short explanatory phrases are inserted or, as in 1 Cor 10:1–4, a paraphrase is given.

As a source of authority, from the Older Testament Scripture, under the formula "it is written" or citing "the Law" for general support or paraphrases of it, Tomson (1990:82) cites numerous examples of it from 1 Corinthians, cross-referencing the relevant Older Testament passage.

In a lengthy journal article, Drimbe (2019:81–82) concludes: "Paul approaches the OT using contemporary Jewish exegetical techniques and devices; the same as used by the rabbis, Philo or Qumran, for instance." Sometimes Paul even cites the same Older Testament passages as they quote (Watson, 2004:167–513). "Yet, the interpretive results are *fundamentally* different" (Watson, 2004:219–220). The Older Testament texts that Paul refers to are applied to Christ and the community of Christ believers (Drimbe, 2019:82). Paul explains the meaning of Older Testament words or passages to meet the demands of new situations. Because of Paul's different interpretive convictions, he arrives at distinctive, interpretive results (Drimbe, 2019:82; Dunn, 1985:423; Bernadette, 1990:72–73).

In 1 Corinthians 14:21, Paul quotes Isaiah 28:11f as a citation from "the law"—the inclusion of the prophetic book of Isaiah in the "law" category is a descriptor which widens considerably the conventional Hebrew definition of what "the law" is. However, this would have been quite appropriate for a student of the more accommodating Gamaliel school (cf. Acts 5:34ff episode).

The book of Acts, which recounts Paul's evangelistic activity and the social disturbances that often followed, illustrates the general truth that non-Jews made no distinction between Christ-following Jews and other Jews. As a case in point, in the Roman colony of Philippi, Paul reportedly caused problems by casting out a demonic spirit from a slave-girl who "was bringing her masters much profit by fortunetelling" (Acts 16:16). Paul's casting out the evil spirit angered the slave-girl's masters because "their hope of profit was gone" (Acts 16:19). In retaliation, they seized Paul and Silas and dragged them before the local chief magistrates, identifying both men as Jews and accusing them of disrupting the peace of Philippi by promoting customs that were unlawful for Romans "to accept or observe" (Acts 16: 21). That Paul and Silas were identified as Jews is notable. How was this known—by their dress, by their manners, by their speech, or by the public declarations of the demon-possessed slave-girl who incessantly hounded them? In any event, the local inhabitants recognized them as Jews and did not differentiate them from other Jews. Paul and Silas were accused of illicitly propagating Jewish customs and values among Romans.

In Acts 19:23–40, the local Jewish community of Ephesus was called upon to give account for Paul's opposition to the prevalent occultic activity in the city. The temple for the goddess Artemis (Diana for the Romans) was located in Ephesus, to which devotees from all over Asia came. A trade union of workers, whose income depended on the cult of Artemis, was upset with Paul's message and mission because he had turned people away from their craft. Paul's traveling companions, Gaius and Aristarchus, were dragged into the city theatre where they faced an angry mob. Jewish inhabitants of the city were in attendance, and they put forward a Jewish man by the name of Alexander. According to Acts 19:33–34, when Alexander motioned with his hand to make a defense to the assembly, the crowd became even louder because they "recognized that he [Alexander] was a Jew," and shouted in unison "Great is Artemis of the Ephesians!" (Acts 19:34). Keener (2014: 2921) says in respect to this incident that "Leaders in the Jewish community would be anxious to preserve their community's favorable status and reputation." Oliver (2021:18–19) suggests that maybe Alexander, on behalf of the local Jewish community, wanted to clarify that they had already disowned Paul and his associates (Acts 19: 9). Similarly, as in Philippi, the non-Jewish population of Ephesus made no distinction between Christ-following Jews and other Jews (Oliver, 2021:19).

There is sometimes bandied about the idea that at a singular point in time the Apostle Paul made a general announcement that henceforth he would abandon any attempts at evangelizing the Jews and singularly focus on evangelization of the Gentiles. Paul never made such a grand announcement. Runesson (2008:123) draws our attention to the fact that Paul's abrupt departure from the synagogue in any given locale to minister among the Gentiles does not mean that his mission to the Jews had finished. For example, in Corinth after his pronouncement to the Christ-rejecting Jews that he would now go to the Gentiles, Crispus, the leader of the synagogue, among others, became a believer. Again, in the next town, Paul first turned to the Jews in the city's synagogue. So, Paul's censure of the Jews of a local synagogue in Acts 18:6 refers only to Corinth, not to a general policy (Runesson, 2008:123; Acts 13:46,

Acts 18:6, Acts 28:28). Paul never categorically rejected his own people and in fact was dogmatic that "God has not rejected His people [Israel/the Jews]" (Rom 11:1). Paul asserts that he is a physical descendant of Abraham "according to the flesh" (Rom 4:1).

It is agreed that Paul came to a place in some cities, where the local synagogal Jewish community, in the main, became hostile to his Christocentric gospel message, whereupon he pivoted and began to focus on an outreach to the Gentiles, and likely to the Gentile "God-fearers" (φοβούμενοι τὸν Θεόν, *phoboumenoi ton Theon*) or "God-worshippers" (θεοσεβεῖς/*Theosebeis*), from the synagogue at that (Acts 18:4, 7). It was theologically and strategically driven—first to the Jews, then to the Gentiles. Right to the end of the New Testament account of his life and ministry, Paul went to the Jews first. Even when he was taken as a captive to Rome, from his rented quarters under guard, he reached out to the Jewish leadership there (Acts 28:17) "trying to persuade them concerning Jesus, from both the Law of Moses and from the Prophets" (Acts 28:23).

Korner (2015:78) suggests that:

> "... irrespective of whether Paul's communities were perceived as "satellites" of Judean *ekklēsiai* or as diasporic Jewish associations, his designation of them as *ekklēsiai* would have served to minimize Jewish perceptions of his communities as being "other" relative to "Judaisms" within the matrix of pluriform Second Temple Judaism (and vice versa). The widespread use of *ekklēsia* terminology within the Greco-Roman and Jewish worlds granted Paul's trans-local associations an increased missional relevance within the Diaspora and in particular would have served, not least at the institutional level, to locate them socially with Jews, Jewishness, and "Judaism."

As Campbell (2016:309) asserts, it is erroneous to separate the Apostle Paul from his Judaic roots and to abandon his "previous" Jewish identity, when Paul was Jewish ethnically, linguistically, culturally, and religiously. In Romans 4:1, Paul points out that he is a descendant of Abraham "according to the flesh." Thus, Barclay (1958:11) describes the Apostle Paul as "proudly, stubbornly, unalterably a Jew" and asserts that "if ever there was a Jew who was steeped in Judaism, that Jew was Paul" (Barclay, 1958:15).

For a time, at least, subsequent to his Damascus Road experience, Paul still submitted to Jewish synagogue discipline, as evidenced in his testimony that on five occasions, he "received from the Jews thirty-nine lashes" (2 Cor 11:24). Paul could have claimed exemption from this synagogal jurisdiction and punishment on the basis of his Roman citizenship but that would have denied his Jewishness and prevented him from having access to the synagogues as was his normal practice upon entrance to a new mission field (Bruce, 1977:127–128).

Significantly, in adherence to his Jewish background, Paul claims this Roman and Jewish jurisdictional principle for the Christ assemblies in 1 Corinthians 6:1–8. There Paul urges his Corinthian congregants to do exactly what Gallio in Acts 18 commanded, to follow the regular Jewish custom and try non-capital cases. In 1 Corinthians 6, Paul alleges that the Corinthian believers are disregarding the Jewish jurisdictional precedent of dealing with non-capital cases (Ford, 1966a:406).

In 1 Corinthians 6:2, Paul refers to a Jewish concept, which would not be familiar to pagan Gentiles, specifically, that "the saints of the Highest One" will judge the world when they take possession of the kingdom (Dan 7:22; cf. Wis 3:8). In 2 Corinthians 13:1, Paul warns the Corinthian congregation that, if necessary, when he comes, internal "trials" would be held on undealt-with moral matters, using Jewish rules of evidence (i.e., "the testimony of two or three witnesses" Deut 19:15).

When looking at 1 Corinthians 15, regarding Paul's doctrine of the resurrection, Daube (1956:303, 332) asserts that the chapter deals with ideas and questions that were long being raised in Jewish circles.

Gabriele Boccaccini (2016:3) warns, that "making a distinction within Paul between his 'Jewish' and 'non-Jewish' (or 'Christian') ideas does not make sense. Paul was blatantly 'Jewish' in his traditional thought processes and remained such even in his 'originality.'" Boccaccini (2016:3) directs attention to the diversity within Second Temple Judaism, and that there never was a monolithic form of Judaism or Christianity. Paul did not rebel against his Jewish heritage (Boccaccini, 2016:14). Paul's gospel message was in accord with that of the early Christ-movement (Boccaccini, 2016:14). Instead, the Apostle should be understood as a zealous missionary who had dramatically encountered the risen Lord and been commissioned by the resurrected Messiah. Therefore, the Apostle Paul did not need to deny his Jewish identity.

As Bruce (1977:126) emphasizes, "The direction of his [Paul's] faith and life was by now too firmly fixed—first by his Jewish upbringing and then by his submission to Jesus as Lord—for Hellenism to exercise a decisive influence on his mind." Bruce (1977:126) further writes of the Apostle Paul:

> ... while he preached the gospel to the Hellenes, it was no hellenized gospel that he preached. His proclamation of deliverance and life through Christ crucified brought his gospel into basic conflict with accepted standards of Hellenistic value and gave it the quality of "folly" which it had in the eyes of those of his hearers who made their assessments by what Paul called "the wisdom of the world" (1 Corinthians 1:20ff).

In Acts 23:6, many years post-conversion, Paul says, "I am (present tense) a Pharisee." One might attempt to rebut this by saying that it was only a tactical maneuver when Paul's strategy was to split the Pharisees from the Sadducees on the doctrine of resurrection, in his appearance before the Sanhedrin Council (for a lucid argument on this and the larger Torah observant issue, see Du Toit, 2016:1–9).

Pharisees believed in a resurrection, whereas Sadducees did not. Indeed, it probably was a tactical maneuver! However, based on the "present tense" (Acts 23:6), it would be presumptuous to say that Paul was being deceptive or had dementia and really meant that he had been a Pharisee in the past and now totally disavowed it. Maybe in the world of that day, there was a loose categorization that Paul could still legitimately claim, in view of his earlier Pharisaic formation and being in general agreement with the core Pharisaic doctrinal beliefs over against the views of the Sadducees. The Pharisees and Sadducees were both powerful, religious-political "power groups" (Black, 1962:777). The Apostle Paul identified with the Pharisees.

The Pharisaic reformation movement was sparked by their acceptance of the Hebrew prophetic writings and the wisdom literature, in addition to the five books of Moses known as the Torah (Black, 1962:777). The Pharisees allowed their interpretation of the Torah "to be influenced by this wider scriptural authority to an extent which the Sadducees, with their narrower views of scripture, were prevented from doing" (Black, 1962:777). It was among the Pharisees "that the Jewish messianic hope was nourished on the ancient prophetic scriptures, as well as on the Torah" (Black, 1962:777). The five core tenets of the Pharisees (Black, 1962:777–779) which Paul would have had general agreement with were: God's sovereignty, the resurrection, angelology, eschatology, and the eventual world-wide rule of Messiah.

However one dices it, Paul still felt some affinity to that "Pharisee" label and his rhetoric in that situation was probably also governed by his overriding dictum of becoming "all things to all men" that he might "by all means save some" (1 Cor 9:22).

Nevertheless, it is crucial to note that post-conversion, Paul is clear that faithful adherence to the Law and its prescriptions will not earn salvation. "Being 'under the Law' [ὑπὸ νόμον, *hypo nomon*] (1 Corinthians 9:20; Gal 3:23; Gal 4:4–5, 21; 5:18; Rom 6:14–15) refers to a condition that makes Jewish identity markers (strict keeping of laws and prescriptions) as necessary to soteriological purposes. To Paul, this is not sufficient for the Jews, nor required anymore for Gentiles (Gal 5:18)" (Marulli, 2011–2012:89). In light of the cross, the Apostle Paul opposed "from within" the diseased Judaistic legalism of his day (Smith, 2013:12). As Sandmel (1978:305) aptly put it: "Christianity perpetuated some central aspects of Judaism unchanged; it altered some of what it inherited; it rejected a large portion of its legacy; it created its own materials and embellished these creations."

Toward the end of the New Testament accounting of his life, Paul in an audience with the leading men of the Jews in Rome said, "Brethren, though I had done nothing against our people, or the customs of our fathers . . . " (Acts 28:17). Paul didn't consider himself as committing any "offense either against the Law of the Jews or against the temple" (Acts 25:8) or against the customs of their fathers (Acts 28:17). The "customs of our fathers" would likely have, at least, included temple and synagogal involvement as Paul's travel and ministry allowed.

Retaining the seventh day of each week for participating in scriptural study and delivering a sermon does not appear to have been a problematic issue for Paul. Actually, it served Paul's purposes, and often the seventh-day sabbath, in a synagogue, was an evangelistic outreach day for him (Acts 13:14, 42, 44; 16:13; 17:2; 18:4, 11; cf. Rom 14:5–6). In addition, the Saturday Sabbath was likely kept by the Jewish and Gentile believers for quite some time, as "it is difficult to imagine that a new day of worship was introduced prior to the Roman destruction of the city [Jerusalem] in 70 AD" (Geraty, 2013:257).

As to how the Apostle Paul related to the Jewish festivals, it appears that Paul delayed in Philippi out of respect for the Passover Feast as reported in Acts 20:6 ("And we sailed away from Philippi after the days of Unleavened Bread, and came to them at Troas within five days; and there we stayed seven days;" cf. Lev 23:4–8). In Acts 20:16, author

Luke notes that Paul was in a hurry to get back to Jerusalem in time for the Feast of Pentecost (cf. Lev 23:15–22).

Paul is possibly referencing the Feast of Firstfruits in 1 Corinthians 15:20–23 (cf. Lev 23:9–14). In respect to Paul's travel itinerary, Luke casually references the Day of Atonement ("the fast") in Acts 27:9 (only one fast was prescribed by the law and that on the Day of Atonement in Leviticus 16:29–34). These above passages are more inferential about Paul and his team's observance of the Jewish festivals but are not the nature of explicit commands. One could argue that the keeping of the Jewish festivals was assumed so there is no need for Paul to reiterate a command about it. In most of these examples above, the obvious intention of Luke in the passing mention of a particular festival is to denote an approximate timeline on the Jewish calendar in the chronologue of Paul's missionary journeys.

The passages of Acts 16:15, 34 and Acts 18:7 are probably an indication that Paul was not strictly adhering to the Levitical food laws or the prohibition on eating with non-Jews. At some point, Paul had challenged Peter "to his face" on this issue of Peter avoiding table fellowship with Gentile believers (Gal 2:11ff).

Based on the foregoing allusions, to claim that Paul was fully Law observant is probably going too far. The most that could be argued from these references is that Paul and the Corinthian congregation remained under the cover of Judaism as far as the authorities were concerned, at this transitional period of the first century, while denying the basic tenet of circumcision.

Although Paul, possibly, personally, practiced certain of the foregoing Jewish "customs," the unbearable yoke of the law (Acts 15:10) and circumcision for Gentile converts (cf. Gal 2:3–5) were watershed matters he vociferously opposed and upon which he would not vacillate (Acts 15; Gal *et al.*). Paul viewed himself as having "died to the Law" (Gal 2:19) and not "under the law" (Rom 3:19; 6:14–15; Gal 3:23 and 4:4–5). Paul was clear that having the Law, including circumcision, would not secure or preserve right standing before God (Rom 2:23–29).

Ciampa and Rosner (2006:205–218) have put forth the "Judaism" approach, suggesting that the argumentation in the Apostle Paul's Corinthian correspondence flows from standard Jewish ethical concerns. They assert specifically that, "A biblical/Jewish approach provides a better basis for appreciating the structure and coherence of Paul's response to Corinthian problems" (Ciampa and Rosner, 2006:218). Ciampa and Rosner (2006:205–218) view the Apostle Paul's rhetoric as being influenced by his Jewish roots and cultural context. Paul would dip into his Jewish and rabbinic training and dish out wise counsel to address the problematic issues. This would particularly come in handy when Paul perpetually faced off against Jewish opponents whereupon he would turn their pseudo-spiritual issue on its head and use Jewish scriptural insights to counter and defeat his foes.

Brian Tucker (2011:75) sees Paul's rhetoric in the Corinthian epistles as offering Older Testament guidance for Jewish life within the new Christ assembly there. Indeed, the Apostle Paul's counsel on a variety of topics to the Corinthians, seems to provide a soft silhouette of the rights of pre-70 Diaspora Jews delineated by Levine (2005:130–131): maintaining their own courts, attending to their own food requirements, avoiding worship of the civic deities, sending monies to Jerusalem, and other communal affairs. The Apostle Paul has rabbinic-like counsel on all these issues in his letters to the Corinthian congregants who believed in Jesus as the Messiah.

Paul's Jewish indictment on the illicit relationship of a stepson and his stepmother found in 1 Corinthians 5:1–13 is taken from the incest prohibitions of the Older Testament (Lev 18:7; 20:11; Deut 13:5; 17:7, 12; 21:21; 22:21; 22:30). Assuming Hebrew Scripture awareness on the part of his readers, he pejoratively states that they have *porneia* (πορνεία) in their midst that "does not exist even among the Gentiles" (1 Cor 5:1) which can spread through their whole assembly like leaven (1 Cor 5:6), as Paul infers Hebrew Older Testament Scripture passages of Christ our Passover Sacrifice (1 Cor 5:7). In his strong rebuke, Paul assumes an understanding of basic Jewish Passover customs (1 Cor 5:8).

In 1 Corinthians 9:9, on the issue of remuneration, Paul draws on an interpretation of Deuteronomy 25:4. Paul's mention of the Temple in 1 Corinthian 9:13 and the support owed to its functionaries undergirds his argument for the support an apostle should be able to expect from a community he serves. Paul would not likely have used this argument had he been writing to those converted directly out of paganism, but he is writing to Jews, proselytes and "God-fearers" and he expects them to find the argument tenable (Ford, 1966a:409; Daube, 1956:396).

Borgen (1996:31) asserts that, "Paul sided with the predominant Jewish traditions, in saying an emphatic 'no' to idolatry, 1 Cor 10:7 and

The Earliest View of New Testament Tongues

14–22." Borgen (1996:35), further writes that, "Paul draws on Jewish ideas about the importance of the attitude, intention and criteria held by a person when one is judging whether food is sacrificial or not." Borgen (1996:37) agrees that 1 Corinthians 10:25 and 27 are related "to rabbinic ideas and practice."

In that 1 Corinthians chapter 10:1-4 passage, Paul repeats the theme of food and idolatry using the familiar Exodus story inferring that his readers had enough of an acquaintance with the Jewish Scriptures and would be able to grasp his symbolism and would appreciate and defer to the edicts of the Hebrew Scriptures.

Ford (1966a:407) makes the point that "the collection which St. Paul appears to emphasize so much in his correspondence (1 Cor 16:1-4 and 2 Cor 8 and 9) can perhaps be best seen against a Jewish background." The references to this collection in the epistles to the Romans (16:26) and the Galatians (2:10) "are directed to communities in which there would be many Jews" (Ford, 1966a:407).

In 1 Corinthians 16:2, in describing the method of storing up contributions, the Apostle Paul uses a Hebraistic phrase κατὰ μίαν σαββάτου (kata mian sabbatou), literally "every one (first) of the 7 days (week)" (Robertson & Plummer, 1914:384). In the Hebraistic phrase κατὰ μίαν σαββάτου (kata mian sabbatou), Paul instructs that the collection should be set aside on the first of the week, which means on Sunday (cf. Mark 16:2; Luke 24:1; John 20:1, 19; Acts 20:7). As Ford (1966a:407) points out, "a collection could not be made on the Sabbath in a Jewish community." The specifics of this directive seem to emphasize that there was a very significant Jewish composition to the Corinthian *ekklesia* of believers and that Paul obviously had first-hand knowledge of this significant Jewish composition, being he planted this congregation.

In the epistles to the Corinthians, only "a few biblical texts are quoted in full and others remain covert" (Ford, 1966a:411). The Older Testament passages referred to in the Corinthian epistles are not clearly from the Masoretic Text or the LXX [Septuagint] in the form we have it now (Ford, 1966a:411), because they are not word-for-word quotations but are indirect citations. Nevertheless, De Waard (1965:83) asserts that overall "51 of the 93 Old Testament quotations in the Pauline epistles completely agree with the LXX." This last statement has to be qualified because the number of Older Testament attributions in the Newer Testament depends on whether just obvious citations have been included and whether all strong allusions or verbal parallels have been excluded.

To wrap up this section, it is instructive to return to the beginning of the Corinthian congregation as reported in Acts18:7, where it's indicated that when Paul departed from the Corinthian synagogue, he "went to the house of a certain man named Titius Justus, a worshipper of God, whose house was next to the synagogue." Koet (1996:409) asserts, "The fact that Luke shows that Paul remains spatially as near to the synagogue as possible is more or less a metaphor for his being as closely connected to the synagogue as can be and that thus Luke makes a point about Paul's desire for a continuing relationship with the Jews."

The Acts 18:7 Greek term συνομοροῦσα (*synomorousa* from *synomoreó*) which bespeaks very near proximity to the synagogue is a word only found here in the New Testament and is variously translated as "to border on, be next door" (BDAG, s.v συνομορέω), "having joint boundaries, to border on, be contiguous to" (Thayer, συνομορέω, 606), "adjoining" (INT), "joined hard" (KJV). The colour of these meanings is that the synagogue and house of Titius Justus may have shared a common wall. In any event, instead of running away, by remaining in proximity, the calculation seems to suggest that Paul and the Corinthian congregation, literally and figuratively, stayed close to their Jewish roots, but it would always be walking a tight rope.

Paul was adhering to the Jerusalem Council decision in opposition to certain Christ-believing Pharisees who insisted on circumcision and keeping Torah for Gentile believers (Acts 15:5). Paul was adamant not to compromise the gospel of grace. As Paul says, in 1 Corinthians 7:19, "Circumcision is nothing and uncircumcision is nothing, but *what matters is* the keeping of the commandments of God." By his own admission, Paul was clearly teaching Gentiles not to undergo "circumcision" because it was code for Jewish identity (Gal 5:3–4). Paul doesn't want to encourage converts to become Jewish nor does he want the Gentile believers to be lawless.

Once Paul and his converts were rebuffed by a local synagogue, the believing Jews and Gentile "God-fearers" and subsequent converts needed written instruction from Paul infused with Older Testament principles to address the problematic situations they were encountering in this new life in Christ.

The Earliest View of New Testament Tongues

3.2.1.1 Many quotations from the Older Testament

The Apostle Paul uses the Older Testament in the Corinthian context for a variety of quite necessary reasons. Paul cites the customary Jewish dyad, the vertical act of idolatry in tandem with the horizontal act of sexual immorality. These two always occur in the many Pauline vice lists. Paul warns the Corinthian believers of idolatry (1 Cor 10:7ff; cf. Ex 32:4, 6, 19 and Num 16; 17; 21:5f; 25:1ff) and the harmful consequences of illicit sexual behaviour (1 Cor 6:9–11, 16; cf. Gen 2:24; Isa 57:7–8, Hos 4:12–14, Gal 5:19–21, Eph 5:5, Col 3:5, Rev 2:14, 20, 21:25). Paul assumes that these Corinthian Messianic believers know these Older Testament stories, so he pointedly refers to the tragic example and moves on.

Paul uses Older Testament verses to rebuke their exaltation of human wisdom over God's wisdom (1 Cor 1:19, 31; 2:9, 16; 3:19–20; cf. Isa 29:13–14; 22:13; Jer. 9:24; Prov 16:1, 9, 33; 19:21).

To bolster his doctrinal teaching on the resurrection (1 Cor 15), Pauls draws on the Older Testament writings (Gen 1:11; 2:7; 5:3; Isa 25:8; Dan 12:3; Hos 13:14).

Centrally, the Apostle Paul utilizes the Older Testament to show that Christ fulfilled certain Hebrew Scriptures (1 Cor 15:27, 55; cf. Ps 18:6; Hos 13:14).

Suffice to say, as exhibited with these above examples, Paul has a powerful arsenal of Older Testament verses at his command and doesn't hesitate to wield this array as the spiritual situation demands. The Apostle Paul basically takes Old Testament principles and tweaks them for application to the various situations that the infant mixed Jewish-Gentile congregation faced.

Now to move through 1 Corinthians chapters 1 to 3 as an example of commentary on Older Testament passages. 1 Corinthians appears to be based on the motif of wisdom in the prophets (Isa 29:14 cf. 1 Cor 1:18; Isa 33:18 cf. 1 Cor 1:20; Jer 9:24 cf. 1 Cor 1:30–31; Isa 64:3 & Isa 65:17 cf. 1 Cor 2:9; Isa 40:13 cf. 1 Cor 2:16; Isa 61:3 cf. 1 Cor 3:9; Isa 5:21, Job 5:13, and Psalm 94:11 cf. 1 Cor 3:18–20). As these verse connections make clear, the early chapters of Paul's first letter to the Corinthians assume reader familiarity with the Older Testament Scriptures. These references "would suggest that the recipients were familiar with the OT, in which case it is hardly likely that they were recently converted pagans" (Ford, 1966a:412).

> Indeed, so strong are some of the allusions that St. Paul seems deliberately to be stressing that the Old Testament has indeed been fulfilled in the New, and at several points the Corinthian correspondence bears affinity to the Epistle to the Hebrews in this respect (Ford, 1966a:412).

Paul presupposes that the Corinthian believers know about the Passover (1 Cor 5:6–8), the Shema (1 Cor 8:4–6; cf. Deut 6:4), Pentecost (1 Cor 16:8) and other Deuteronomic ordinances and customs from the Torah (1 Cor 5:13; 9:9–13; 2 Cor 13:1). The recipients of Paul's letter are obviously aware of the Hebrew creation story, as Paul presumes it in his teaching on male/female one-flesh union (1 Cor 6:16), male/female roles (1Cor 11:2–16), and the sure hope of the resurrection for the believer (1 Cor 15:20–23, 43–49). In 1 Corinthians 10:1–11 (cf. 2 Cor 3:16–18), Paul assumes knowledge about the place of Moses in Israelite tradition and familiarity with accounts of the exodus from Egypt and the subsequent Israelite wilderness wanderings.

Silva (1993:631) lists 107 explicit citations of the Older Testament in Paul's writings. Many of these passages are introduced by stock phrases like "as it is written," "for the scripture says," "for [prophet] says," or "according to the law" (See chart by Silva, 1993:631). Silva's list doesn't contain allusions, which would make the list very long. The influence of the Older Testament obviously predominates in Paul's thinking and communication. In the acknowledged Pauline writings, the greatest number of Older Testament citations are in Romans followed by the Corinthian epistles.

Although Paul appears to frequently quote from the Greek Septuagint translation, in whatever form he possessed it, when referring to the Older Testament passages, he sometimes clearly makes use of the Hebrew text (Job 41:3 in Rom 11:35; Job 5:12f in 1 Cor 3:19; Ex 16:18 in 2 Cor 8:15; Nu 16:5 in 2 Tim 2:19). In some instances, even Paul's quotations from the Greek Septuagint seem to more closely parallel the Hebrew Masoretic text, perhaps because he's familiar with a proto-Masoretic Hebrew text or he is attempting to conform the Greek translation to an existing Hebrew text (Fotopoulos, 2010:423). Silva (1993: 632) asserts that "there is good reason to think that he [Paul] was familiar with the original Hebrew and that the latter, in at least some cases, determined how he used the OT [Old Testament]."

The earliest extant Greek translation of the Older Testament Scripture is reputed to have been instigated at Alexandria in the third century BC. This version is commonly known as the Septuagint, although in view of its supposed origin, it could more correctly be designated as the Alexandrian version. Paget (2014:105) writes:

> What do scholars generally agree upon in the study of this subject? First, that when we talk about the origins of the Septuagint, we are referring to the origins of the translation of the Pentateuch alone. The reasons for the translation of that set of books were probably different from that of other books. Second, most scholars are clear that this translation took place sometime in the third century BCE. Third, the translation was probably the product of Egyptian Jewry, and, more specifically, Alexandrian Jewry.

So, strictly speaking the first translation of Hebrew Scripture to Greek, refers to the Torah (Pentateuch) alone, which translation took place sometime in the third century BC (Paget, 2014:105–106). The rest of the Older Testament was not translated into the Greek at that time, but there is a general agreement that the Greek translations of most of the remaining Older Testament books are from the second century BC (Beckwith, 2008:382, 383).

The variable styles of the individual Septuagint translators are demonstrated by the uneven character of the eventual completed Greek translation of the Older Testament. By comparison, some books show that the particular translator was more paraphrastic, such as in Job, Proverbs, and Isaiah, while others generally display a more word-for-word in-order translation. The Torah (Pentateuch) seems to be the most carefully translated, while the rest of the Older Testament books (Tanakh) vary considerably in quality.

Pietersma has argued that the Septuagint's textual-linguistic nature, one in which many aspects of the Greek text are unintelligible without resort to the Hebrew original, indicates that the linguistic relationship of the Greek to the Hebrew was originally one of subservience and dependence (Wright, 2008:299). Pietersma (2002:350) argues that the Septuagint Greek frequently "cannot stand on its own feet." Wright (2008:299) suggests that the Greek Septuagint translation was intended from the outset to be used alongside the Hebrew source text. Such a relationship, Pietersma (2002:350) characterizes by the term "interlinear."

Pietersma (2002:360) proposes that the most appropriate place for a translation with the Septuagint's textual-linguistic makeup would be in the school, where the subservient and dependent Greek translation would assist students as an aid to the Hebrew text. In other words, the Septuagint translation was meant as an auxiliary teaching tool to lead to the underlying original Hebrew. Brock's (1972:11–36) analysis of the Septuagint has also convinced him that the textual-linguistic nature of the translation indicates that it tries to bring the reader to the original, not the original to the reader.

> The Septuagint's textual-linguistic makeup points to its intended original function, one in which the Greek was dependent on rather than a replacement for the Hebrew. One might also conclude that such a relationship between the Greek and the Hebrew meant that *the Greek translation was most likely not at first considered authoritative scripture* [italicized emphasis mine] but instead it provided a means of gaining access to the Hebrew scriptures (Wright, 2008:308–309).

The bottom line is that Paul's quotations of and allusions to the Older Testament show how deeply he was steeped in the Older Testament Scriptures. It demonstrates the Hebraistic mind-set that Paul brought to bear in founding and instructing this first-century Corinthian congregation.

3.2.2 Aquila and Priscilla—Jewish co-workers from Rome

Aquila (Ἀκύλας, *Akylas*) and Priscilla (Πρίσκιλλα, *Priskilla or Priscila*) were a first-century, Christ-believing, Jewish, married, missionary couple described in the New Testament. The Apostle Paul described them as his "fellow workers in Christ Jesus" (Rom 16:3). In the New Testament, this Jewish couple, Priscilla and Aquila, strengthened the early Messianic congregations in Corinth, Ephesus, and Rome. Paul was very grateful for these fellow workers in Christ who "risked their own necks" for him (Rom 16:3–4).

Aquila and Priscilla are named as a couple six times in four different books of the New Testament. It was first at Corinth that the Apostle Paul "found a certain Jew named Aquila, a native of Pontus, having recently come from Italy with his wife, Priscilla, because Claudius had commanded all the Jews to leave Rome . . . and because he was of the same trade, he stayed with them and they were working; for by trade they were tent-makers" (Acts 18:2–3). In this passage, the Jewish pedigree of Aquila is noted and then underscored by the fact that they were expelled from Rome along with Jewish compatriots. In the absence of a reference in this passage to Priscilla being a Jewish woman, it is likely that Priscilla was a Jewish proselyte. As a presumed devout Jewish man, Aquila would have only married a genetic Jewish woman or a proselyte. All proselytes would also have been caught up in the expulsion decree. Paul would have lived and laboured and ministered with this fine Jewish Christ-believing couple in Corinth during the time of his sojourn there, which was about 18 months.

Priscilla and Aquila had a timely influence on Apollos, the Alexandrian Jew, when after picking up on certain deficiencies ("being acquainted only with the baptism of John" Acts 18:25) in his preaching in the Ephesus synagogue, Priscilla and Aquila discreetly "took him [Apollos] aside and explained to him the way of God more accurately" (Acts 18:26). Apollos became a powerful apologist among the Jews for this new Messianic faith (Acts 18:28). It is of significance that Priscilla and Aquila's first encounter with Apollos was in a Jewish synagogue (Acts 18:26). In other words, they were all in attendance at the local Ephesian synagogue. Admittedly Apollos was there for evangelistic purposes, but in view of the Jewish background of each of these three persons, it should not be seen as out of the ordinary for all three of them to be in such a setting.

At the point of writing 1 Corinthians 16:19, Paul had returned to Ephesus, and concludes the Corinthian epistle: "The churches of Asia greet you. Aquila and Prisca greet you heartily in the Lord, with the church that is in their house [in Ephesus]." Several Western texts (D F G goth Pelagius) add "with whom also I am lodging" (Metzger, 1975:570). Because this Jewish couple, Aquila and Priscilla, now in Paul's company in Ephesus, had been involved in the founding of the Corinthian fellowship, they would have known many there at Corinth, and therefore the enthusiastic greeting from them that Paul conveys.

By the time of Paul's writing to the Romans, Priscilla and Aquila must have been back in Rome, among the Jewish and Gentile Christ-believers there. Paul writes to "Greet Prisca and Aquila, my fellow workers in Christ Jesus" (Rom 16:3). It would seem that at this point, the expulsion decree of Claudius Caesar in respect to Jews was no longer in effect or was not being enforced anymore.

Toward the end of his life, from a Roman prison, Paul again sends warm greeting to his devoted friends: "Greet Prisca and Aquila, and the household of Onesiphorus" (2 Tim 4:19).

From the New Testament, we know that these Jewish compatriots, Aquila and Priscilla, were of great help to the Apostle Paul in establishing congregations in Corinth, Ephesus and Rome.

3.2.3 Apollos—an Alexandrian Jew

Apollos (Ἀπολλώς) was a first-century Alexandrian Jewish believer in Jesus as Messiah and he was a co-worker of the Apostle Paul. Apollos served in the early development of the churches of Ephesus and Corinth.

In Acts 18:24–26, we read this account:

> Now a certain Jew named Apollos, an Alexandrian by birth, an eloquent man, came to Ephesus; and he was mighty in the Scriptures [Older Testament]. This man had been instructed in the way of the Lord; and being fervent in spirit, he was speaking and teaching accurately the things concerning Jesus, being acquainted only with the baptism of John; and he began to speak out boldly in the synagogue. But when Priscilla and Aquila heard him, they took him aside and explained to him the way of God more accurately.

Apollos did not resist the wise counsel of these fellow Jewish believers. He must have been teachable because right thereafter, the Ephesian brethren encouraged him on to Achaia and wrote a letter of recommendation for him (Acts 18:27, 28). When Apollos arrived there in Achaia "he helped greatly those who had believed through grace, for he powerfully refuted the Jews in public, demonstrating by the Scriptures that Jesus was the Christ" (Acts 18:27–28, 19:1).

In 1 Corinthians 3:6, Paul acknowledges the indispensable role of Apollos at Corinth, the capital of the province of Achaia, by writing: "I planted, Apollos watered, but God was causing the growth." That Apollos watered what Paul sowed meant there was no undermining of Paul's message. Their roles were symbiotic.

The Apostle Paul says that both he and fellow Jewish believer Apollos were tasked with building up the body of Christ. Specifically, Paul says "Let a man regard us in this manner, as servants of Christ, and stewards of the mysteries of God" (1 Cor 4:1).

That Apollos was a devout Jew born in Alexandria has led to speculation that he would have adopted the allegorical style of Philo.

Murphy-O'Connor (1996:275) remarked: "It is difficult to imagine that an Alexandrian Jew . . . could have escaped the influence of Philo, the great intellectual leader . . . particularly since the latter seems to have been especially concerned with education and preaching."

Further testament to the Apostle Paul's positive, collegial relationship with fellow Jew, Apollos, is Paul's urging Apollos to go back to Corinth (1 Cor 16:12a). It didn't suit Apollos at that time, although Apollos was open to going to Corinth later when he had opportunity (1 Cor 16:12b).

The last time this Jewish comrade, Apollos, is mentioned is in Titus 3:13, when Titus is urged to "diligently help Zenas the lawyer and Apollos on their way so that nothing is lacking for them."

3.2.4 Silas, Timothy—circumcised Jews, troubleshooters, Paul's protégés

Silas or Silvanus (Σίλας/Σιλουανός) was a Jewish believer in Christ who was also a Roman citizen (Acts 16:37). *Silas* is a Greek name and possibly a contraction of *Silouanos*, which is a transliteration of the Latin *Silvanus*. Therefore, he is probably also the "Silvanus" in Paul's Epistles (2 Cor 1:19; 1 Thess 1:1; 2 Thess 1:1) and the "faithful brother" in 1 Peter 5:12. Bigg (1902:84) writes, "There can be little doubt that the Silas of Acts is the Silvanus of the Pauline and Petrine Epistles . . . "

When we first meet Silas in Scripture, he is an elder and prophet in the Jerusalem church (Acts 15:22, 32). In addition to being a leading man of the Jerusalem church (Acts 15:22, 23), Silas would thereafter accompany Paul on most of his second missionary journey (Acts 15–18).

In that first appearance of Silas at the Acts 15 Jerusalem Council, the apostles acknowledged that God was drawing the Gentiles to hear the gospel and believe and receive the Holy Spirit without the need to follow all the ritual laws of the Jews (Acts 15:7–11). After "much debate" (Acts 15:7), the verdict was reached that Gentile converts need not be circumcised and only minimal conditions for fellowship would be imposed (Acts 15:20). The apostles and elders at the Jerusalem Council decided to send Judas and Silas with Paul and Barnabas to report back to the brethren in Antioch, Syria and Cilicia (Acts 15: 22ff).

Because they were trusted Jewish brothers, Judas and Silas were given the very important task of carrying the letter from the Jerusalem

Council to Antioch. The letter is a summary of the decision of the Jerusalem apostles and elders (Acts 15:23–29). The letter points out that Judas and Silas "will also report the same things by word *of mouth*" (verse 27). Silas and Judas were also prophets and so could encourage and strengthen the brethren (Acts 15:32). Judas and Silas were entrusted with the crucial task of explaining the specifics and reasons for this paradigm-shifting decision. This decision was a momentous one and this first appearance of Silas in the New Testament record makes it clear that the early church Jewish leadership trusted Silas with a crucial responsibility. "He must, therefore, have been heartily in accord with the substance of the Decree" (Bigg, 1902:84).

Barnabas accompanied Paul on his first missionary journey, which had taken place prior to the Jerusalem Council. Before Paul's second journey, they had a "sharp disagreement" (Acts 15:39), about whether they should again take with them the younger John Mark who had deserted them on the first missionary journey. So, Paul and Jewish co-laborer Barnabas parted, with Barnabas sailing to Cyprus with Mark, and Paul chose a new Jewish companion, Silas, to accompany him.

Luke's twelve references to Silas correspond to Paul's second missionary journey. Silas accompanied Paul through most of his second missionary journey, during which Silas endured a beating and imprisonment in Philippi (Acts 16:22–24), the amazing conversion of the Philippian jailer and his household (Acts 16:25–33), and an escape to Berea (Acts 17:10–12).

Silas, independent of Paul, ministered to the Macedonian churches, because subsequently in the Acts record, these two Jewish brethren, "Silas and Timothy came down from Macedonia," and rejoined Paul in Corinth to assist him there in the evangelism campaign in the synagogue that founded the Christ-believers' fellowship there (Acts 18:5).

Silas was a reputable Jewish leader and a faithful brother, so the aid that he and Timothy provided to Paul when they got to Corinth enabled the Apostle to devote full time to his apologetic ministry among the Jews and Gentiles at the local synagogue (Acts 18:5). According to 2 Corinthians 1:19, a Silvanus and Timothy joined Paul in that initial preaching in Corinth. The writer Luke does not refer to a Silvanus in any of Paul's journeys recorded in the book of Acts. As above, Luke chronicles Silas and Timothy rejoining Paul in Corinth in Acts 18:5, so "Silas" and "Silvanus" are likely one and the same person. Bigg

(1902:84) writes, "There can be little doubt that the Silas of Acts is the Silvanus of the Pauline and Petrine Epistles..."

The name "Silvanus" is usually conjoined with "Timothy" (2 Cor 1:19; 1 Thess 1:1; 2 Thess 1:1), as in the authorial greeting in both letters to the believers in Thessalonica, the very city from which Paul and Silas made their escape from a Jewish-led mob (Acts 17:5–10). The salutation in both Thessalonian epistles is word-for-word the same in acknowledging the co-authors: "Paul and Silvanus and Timothy, to the church of the Thessalonians" (1 Thess 1:1; 2 Thess 1:1). Milligan (1908:xxxv) asserts that both these epistles were written from Corinth, where Silas and Timothy rejoined Paul. Milligan (1908:xxxix) also states that the Second Epistle to the Thessalonians "shows that in the main, the historical conditions of the Thessalonian Church were very little altered, and that consequently the Second Epistle must have been written not many months after the First. We therefore date it also from Corinth within the period already specified 50–51 A.D."

The final mention of Silvanus (a.k.a. Silas) is in 1 Peter 5:12, where it reads: "Through Silvanus, our faithful brother (for so I regard *him*), I have written to you..." It is quite possible that this phrase is to be understood to mean that Silvanus was "the bearer as well as the draughtsman of the Epistle" (Bigg, 1902: 5). Selwyn (1947:241) also maintains that Silvanus was actually involved in both the *composition* and *transmission* of the epistle. This suggests that the role of Silvanus was more than simply recording dictated words. The Greek phraseology translated "our faithful brother" of 1 Peter 5:12 suggests the Apostle Peter's implicit trust in Silvanus. Selwyn (1947:242) writes that, "In all the other passages in the N.T. where πιστός is used of a particular individual... it means 'to be relied on for a particular mission or purpose.'" In respect to the wording of 1 Peter 5:12, Selwyn (1947:242) offers a possible inference from Peter, regarding Silvanus, "whom I reckon I can rely upon implicitly to interpret my message and meaning faithfully."

Because Silvanus (Silas) was a "faithful brother" (1 Pet 5:12), was one of the "leading men among the brethren" (Acts 15:22), experienced a peaceful outcome when commissioned to relay the decision of the Jerusalem Council (Acts 15:33), and was an invaluable colleague on the Apostle Paul's second missionary journey (Acts 15–18), it is quite possible that he helped in formulating the language of the First and Second Epistles of Peter. At a minimum, some polishing of Peter's Greek may have been necessary.

In the context where the Apostle Paul was still "reasoning" and "trying to persuade Jews and Greeks [God-fearers]" in the Corinthian (Hebrew?) synagogue, in addition to Silas, a Jerusalem Jew (Acts 15:22, 27, 32), there also came down from Macedonia (Acts 18:5) to assist Paul, a circumcised Greek Jew named Timothy (Acts 16:1ff), to whom we now turn our attention.

Timothy was a Greek Jew who was circumcised by Paul (Acts 16:3). His name Τιμόθεος (*Timótheos*), means "to honor God" or "be honored by God" (https://en.wikipedia.org/wiki/Saint_Timothy in the Greek; cf. BDAG, s.v. τιμή, §2).

When Paul and Barnabas visited Lystra on the first missionary journey, Paul healed a man "lame from his mother's womb" (Acts 14:8–10), subsequent to which a number of Lystran residents received the message of Paul and Barnabas and became disciples (Acts 14:21–22). When Paul returned that way sometime later, on his second missionary journey with Silas, Timothy already "was well spoken of by the brethren who were in Lystra and Iconium" (Acts16:2). After having just mentioned Lystra in Acts 16:1a, author Luke writes that "a certain disciple was there, named Timothy" ("there"—εκε). So it seems that Timothy was from that Lycaonian city of Lystra in Asia Minor. Timothy was born of a Greek Gentile father and a devout Jewish mother, Eunice, who had become a believer (Acts 16:1).

Timothy's mother Eunice and his grandmother Lois had taught him the Hebrew Scriptures since he was a young boy (2 Timothy 3:15) and laid the groundwork that enabled Timothy to have a "sincere faith" of his own (2 Tim 1:5).

The Apostle Paul recruited Timothy fairly early in his second missionary journey and thereafter Timothy became Paul's constant companion and his missionary partner, alongside Silas at this point in time (Acts 16:3).

Because Timothy's father was a Greek Gentile, Timothy had not been circumcised, so before they set out, Paul "took him [Timothy] and circumcised him because of the Jews who were in those parts" (Acts 16:3). This action did not undermine the verdict of the Jerusalem Council, that Gentile believers did not have to be circumcised (Acts 15). It seemed to be more a matter of expediency to ensure Timothy's acceptance in the synagogues and among the Jews whom they would be evangelizing. Larsson (1985:431) remarks that it was "to remove an obstacle to his missionary work."

Timothy, along with Silas came down from Macedonia and greatly assisted Paul in establishing the Corinthian fellowship of believers (Acts 18:5).

There is an intimation in Scripture that Timothy was apprehensive about a subsequent Corinthian assignment, as Paul writes to the Corinthian believers: "Now if Timothy comes, see that he is with you without cause to be afraid [ἀφόβως/ *aphobōs*], for he is doing the Lord's work ... Let no one therefore despise him ... " (1 Cor 16:10–11).

In Ephesus, it appears that Paul assigned Timothy to confront some false doctrine (1 Tim 1:3ff). Paul knew he could rely on Timothy. When Paul had challenging and conflictual situations to deal with in Thessalonica (1 Thess 3:2), Corinth (1 Cor 4:17), Philippi (Phil 2:19), or Ephesus (1 Tim 1:3ff), he sent Timothy. Paul wrote about Timothy to the Philippians, "I have no one *else* of kindred spirit who will genuinely be concerned for your welfare (Phil 2:20).

Timothy is listed as the co-author of 2 Corinthians, Philippians, Colossians, 1 Thessalonians, 2 Thessalonians, and Philemon. It's while he's in prison that Paul writes four epistles, three of which mention Timothy being present with him (Phil 1:1, 2:19, Col 1:1, Phlm 1:1). Timothy is also the recipient of two epistles in his name from his mentor, the Apostle Paul.

The writer of Hebrews announces that Timothy has been "released" so we know that Timothy was imprisoned at least once during his life time (Heb 13:23).

When Paul was languishing in prison and awaiting execution, he called his faithful friend and "beloved son" (2 Tim 1:2) Timothy, for a final farewell (2 Tim 1:4 and 2 Tim 4:21). This Jewish believer, Timothy, obviously had a very close relationship with Paul, as his protégé, trouble-shooter and his "true child in *the* faith" (1 Tim 1:2).

3.2.5 Peter—of the Jerusalem mother assembly

"Hellenistic Jewry accepted with joy the achievements of Palestinian Jewry. It is well known that Palestinian Sages, like Rabbi Akiva and his pupil Rabbi Meir, visited the countries where they [Diasporan Jews] were settled ... " (Flusser, 1989:78). Flusser (1989:75) states "The Jews of the Diaspora ... were faithful to Palestine."

CULTURAL ANALYSIS

There was likely a similar, natural orientation to Jerusalem, as well, by Messianic Jews and Messianic "God-fearers," at the Diaspora assemblies of Jesus' believers. Malina and Pilch (2006:371–374) assert that Jerusalem did indeed set the standard for adherence to Jewish traditions in the Apostle Paul's day among Christ believers. This attitude appears to have been picked up by a segment of the Christ assembly in Corinth as reflected in 1 Corinthians 1:12. Some were indicating that they followed Cephas (Peter), the Apostle from Jerusalem. Barentsen (2011:5), in a paper exploring social identity theory in the Corinthian context notes that, in the six years since its founding, the different teachers under whom the Corinthian believers grouped themselves were all Jewish, "which reflects their respect for the Jewish origins of the gospel."

"The Jewish *ekklēsia* in Jerusalem, which boasted the Jewish likes of Peter, John, and James, retained a certain prestige among Christ-followers despite the initial success of the gospel among gentiles" (Oliver, 2021:24).

Robertson and Plummer (1914:12) represent the "classical" approach to the factions in 1 Corinthians with the Paul group reflecting Paul's own preaching and teaching, the Apollos group standing for "hellenistic intellectualism," the Cephas group advocating for "the Gospel of the circumcision," and the "Christ" group, perhaps being "zealots for the law, hostile to the Apostleship of St. Paul."

Barrett (1968:44) avows that "the Cephas-group represented Jewish Christianity" and would be the ones pressuring "for the observance of food laws and the judicial rights of the community, and in a questioning of Paul's apostolic status."

In his first canonical epistle to the Corinthians (1 Corinthians 15:11), Paul diplomatically emphasizes that it does not matter whether it was "I or they [the other Apostles]" who preached and "so you believed," reiterating the issue of different leaders at the beginning of this epistle (cf. 1 Cor 1:12). By the time of his second epistle to the Corinthians, Paul's tone was not so conciliatory.

In his first and second letters to the Corinthian believers, Paul devotes a great deal of space in defence of his apostolic authority, from which we can deduce that his opponents were directly attacking or a least undermining his apostolic authenticity. It's probable that Paul's opponents did not recognize him as a bona fide Apostle, because unlike Peter and the rest of the Apostles, Paul had not known Jesus on a personal basis during Jesus' earthly ministry. Also, Jesus had given to Peter the primacy among the Apostles (Matt 16:18–20).

In 1 Corinthians 15:6–9, in a creedal-type statement, Paul acknowledges that Cephas (Aramaic for "Peter") and the twelve apostles preceded him, and "last of all, as it were to one untimely born, He appeared to me [Paul] also . . . the least of the apostles" (1Cor 15:8–9). In 1 Corinthians 15:10, Paul makes the surprising claim that he "labored even more than all of them [Apostles]." That would be quite the "boast" if Paul had not immediately qualified it by attributing his extensive and exhaustive labour to "the grace of God with me" (1 Cor 15:10; cf. 2 Cor 3:5; 1 Cor 3:6). Paul felt the need to assert his apostleship at other points in these letters to the Corinthian Christ-believers, defensively comparing himself to the other apostles, particularly naming Cephas (1 Cor 9:1–5; cf. 2 Cor 12:11–12). Suffice to say, Paul was more than a little sensitive on this apostleship issue contra Cephas and the original 12 disciples.

Because Paul mentions Peter/Cephas several times in 1 Corinthians (1:12; 3:22; 9:5; 15:5), there is the legitimate question of whether Peter came to Corinth during the "unknown" period of his life in the middle of the first century. From about 50 AD onwards, Peter seems to have begun a more widespread mission, probably focusing on Jewish communities in different Diaspora cities (Edmundson, 1913:80, 84; Manson, 1962:38–40). Ferguson (2013:38) acknowledges that "It is impossible to trace Peter's journeys after his departure from Jerusalem, but his presence in Antioch is attested by Paul, a ministry in parts of Asia Minor is implied by 1 Peter, and the presence of a 'Peter party' in Corinth suggests his activity there at some point." Barrett (1982:32) suggests that "it seems far more probable that he [Peter] had himself been in Corinth than that members of the church there had simply heard of him as a notable Palestinian Christian." Barrett (1982:37) adds, "The evidence of 1 Corinthians shows the certain influence, and probable presence, of Peter in Corinth. He was an embarrassment to Paul, and his characteristically Jewish-Christian opinions take some hard knocks."

In regard to Peter's presence in Corinth and his faction in 1 Corinthians 1:12, Barrett's insight (1982:29) is pertinent, when he notes: "The fact that Paul immediately (1 Cor 1:13) goes on to speak of baptism suggests that converts tended to align themselves with the evangelist under whom they had been won to the faith." This may be a reasonable argument for Peter's presence and evangelistic effort in Corinth sometime after Paul founded the ἐκκλησία there (1 Cor 3:10). Manson (1962:190-224) builds a convincing case for Peter having been in Corinth. Witetschek (2018:66-82) concludes similarly. Hengel (2010:92) argues that Peter journeyed through the west of the Empire in a continuing, counteractive campaign against Paul, following the pattern of their confrontation in Antioch.

Paul indicates in 1 Corinthians 9:5 that Cephas (Peter) had the "right to take along a believing wife" on his mission journeys and out of that Barrett (1982:29, 32) implies that Peter had visited Corinth with his wife, both of whom enjoyed the Corinthian congregation's hospitality. These trips, for Peter (and his wife), would have been to people of Jewish background (to the "circumcised" per the agreement in Galatians 2:7-10). However, that agreement is "easier said than done." Ironically, that agreement of Paul going to the Gentiles and Cephas to the Jews, was "bound to cause difficulty because there were few places that were purely Jewish or Gentile in population" (Barrett, 1982:19-20). The agreement was additionally compounded by Paul's propensity to start each new mission in any given city by arguing the case for Jesus as Messiah in the local Jewish synagogue. Barrett (1982:20) remarks that "there is no reason to be surprised that trouble of precisely this kind arose in Corinth."

Ellis' (1975:264-298) excellent and indispensible summary of "Paul and His Opponents" surveys the research on this topic from the time of Reformer John Calvin to F.C. Baur right up until 1975. Ellis (1975:264-298) concludes that Paul's primary opponents were the "ritually strict *Hebraioi*" out of the Jerusalem church whose features and beliefs were exhibited in different ways, counteracting Paul's mission or attempting to influence the congregations Paul founded.

In the middle of the nineteenth century, Ferdinand Baur proposed that the major cause of the conflict in Corinth was two major groups, and "the basic cause of the conflict and division at Corinth, then, was the tension and disagreement between Jewish Christians, linked with Peter, and Pauline Christians, who followed Paul's critical stance toward the law" (Adams, 2004:14).

Baur's viewpoint has established a lasting influence even until today. There were quite a number of scholars in the twentieth century who predicated a distinct contrast between Peter and Paul (Grosheide, 1953:15). More recent advocates of Baur's position are Barrett

(1971:233–254), Thrall (1980:42–57), Martin (1987:279–289), Goulder (1995, 2001), and Sweet (1991:372–382), to name a few.

Although the dialectal premise of Baur's Hegelian philosophy of history (1831) has fallen out of favour, nevertheless, with the backdrop of Paul being undermined in most congregations he founded by a persistent Judaistic band, it is quite conceivable that in the Corinthian Christ assembly there was residual conflict between Gentile and Judaic-disposed factions (i.e., Paulinists versus Petrinists). Barrett (1982:21–22) remarks that "if there is a connection between the troubles of 2 Cor. 10–13 and those of 1 Corinthians, it is to be found, not, as is often supposed, in the Christ-group, but in the group of Cephas." The context of each Pauline letter and particular verses and cross-references of Scripture tend to support the assumption of a rift between Peter and Paul.

Brown and Meier (1983:2–8) categorized "Jewish-Gentile Christianity" into four groups which formed in the pre-70 AD era. Group One consisted "of Jewish Christians and their Gentile converts, who insisted on *full observance of the Mosaic Law, including circumcision*" (Brown & Meier, 1983:2). Brown and Meier (1983:3–4) placed Peter into Group Two "consisting of Jewish Christians and their Gentile converts, who did *not* insist on circumcision but did require converted Gentiles to keep *some Jewish observances*." The proponents of this approach would have been particularly associated with the Jerusalem apostles, in accord with the mandate of Matthew 28:16–20, which speaks of a church founded on Peter, and gives the Jewish Apostles a mission to all nations (Brown & Meier, 1983:4).

Brown and Meier (1983:4–6) placed Paul into Group Three "consisting of Jewish Christians and their Gentile converts, who did *not* insist on circumcision and did *not* require observance of the Jewish ("kosher") food laws." This Pauline type of Jewish/Gentile Christianity was more liberal than that of James and of Peter regarding certain obligations of the Law (Brown & Meier, 1983:5). Paul's admonitions in the latter half of many of his letters show that he expected all believers to live by the Decalogue and by the high morality of Judaism (Brown & Meier, 1983:5). Brown and Meier (1983:5), based on Acts 20:6 and 16, suggest that Paul kept the Jewish feasts, such as Unleavened Bread and Weeks (Pentecost) and that Paul worshipped in the Jerusalem Temple.

Brown and Meier's (1983:6) Group Four consists "of Jewish Christians and their Gentile converts, who did not insist on circumcision or

CULTURAL ANALYSIS

observance of the Jewish food laws and who *saw no abiding significance in Jewish cult and feasts*." These Hellenistic Jews had broken with Judaism in a radical way (Brown & Meier, 1983:6-8).

So, by Brown and Meier's (1983:2-8) analysis, Paul (Group Three) would have taken a more liberal approach than Peter (Group Two), but more conservative than Group Four which Paul was accused of being a part of by his opponents (cf. Acts 21:20-21).

Peter's personal actions alone had a huge effect on other believers, Jews and Gentiles (Gal 2:12-13). Barrett (1982:37) deduces of Peter that,

> . . . he was easily frightened, and therefore easily influenced and used. More subtle and less scrupulous ecclesiastical politicians found him useful as a figure-head. Hence Paul's embarrassment. He could not simply repudiate Peter; yet Peter, in the hands of those who made use of him, was on the way to ruining Paul's work at Corinth.

If Peter's name is in the mix in Corinth, it's within the realm of reason to believe that, at minimum, the name and clout of the Apostle to the Jews would be appealed to in order to promote a Jewishness that differed with Paul and by contrast to question Paul's apostolic authenticity. If you have partisans lining up behind Paul or Peter, it's not going to be over areas where they were in lock step, but rather on areas where there were differences.

Paul's juxtaposing his name with Peter's in these occurrences in 1 Corinthians (1:12; 3:22; 9:5) suggests definite tension with Peter, the Apostle to the Jews (i.e., "circumcision"), or those enamoured with Peter's special mandate and his primacy among the apostles (cf. Matt 16:18-20).

As a minimum, it may be that Cephas (Peter) himself had no explicit part in the divisive faction which carried his name in Corinth. Barentsen (2011:14), in reply to the question of whether the Apostle Paul was successful in his plan to initiate a new social identity and cohesion among the Corinthian believers, posits that those plans were almost overturned "by Jewish-Christian teachers who arrived in Corinth soon after the delivery of 1 Corinthians, before Paul could arrive personally." Second Corinthians 11:13 (cf. 1 Cor 11:22) speaks of Judaizing false apostles who had been in Corinth. These false apostles may have traded on Peter's name, formally or informally. Paul also alludes to letters of recommendation brought to the Corinthian congregation by others (2 Cor 3:1).

3.2.6 Judaizing Christians referred to in 2 Corinthians

From the Acts record and the Pauline epistles, the controversy that was supposed to have been settled at the Jerusalem Council (Acts 15) seemed to dog Paul and his mission, wherever he went and all of his days. Paul tussled with what appears to have been an influential group of Jewish believers who still wanted to define their identity in relation to the Law, at least in part, which Paul opposed entirely. His Judaizing opponents just didn't give up as recorded in Paul's epistle to the Galatians. However, different than in Galatians, here in the Corinthian epistles there are no explicit references, at this stage, that Judaizers are presently pressuring the Corinthian Christ-believers about circumcision, kosher diets, or Sabbath observance (Oropeza, 2009:8).

They may have received some of their tacit encouragement from Cephas (Peter), as Barrett (1982:21) bluntly posits: "There were Judaizers who did not call for circumcision, and one of them had most probably been in Corinth already before 1 Corinthians was written—Cephas. Without demanding circumcision he had attempted to impose a Judaic pattern of thought and religious life" on the Corinthian assembly of believers. Barrett (1982:21) draws attention to the fact that Paul uses the expression "to Judaize" of Peter in Galatians 2:14, where he accuses him of compelling the Gentiles to ἰουδαΐζειν (*ioudaizein*).

MacGregor (2018:22–28) contends that there was a Judaizing faction in the first-century Corinthian congregation, which faction promoted the oral Torah, an example being 1 Corinthians 14:34-38, with a quotation attributed to them (1 Cor 14:34–35), followed by the Pauline refutation (1 Cor 14:36–38).

Oropeza (2009:7–8) asserts that this "second canonical letter of Paul to the Corinthians was written about a year after the first, and ... the opponents of Paul are the same throughout. These adversaries are not belligerent members of the congregation but Jewish-Christian missionaries (2 Cor. 11:13, 22– 23)." Bruce (1977:278) writes, "These intruders were not judaizers in the narrower sense ... "

> They [the judaizers] conceived it as their mission to impose the authority of the mother church over the Christian world. It

was nothing to them that this contravened the agreement over which the Jerusalem leaders had shaken hands with Paul and Barnabas some years previously . . . . For a time they clearly made some headway at Corinth. Ten or eleven years later their policy must have collapsed in any case; the dispersal of the Jerusalem church at the time of the Jewish revolt against Rome which broke out in A.D. 66 put an end to such authority as that church had enjoyed throughout the Gentile mission-field (Bruce, 1977:278).

By way of his counter claims, in 2 Corinthians 11:22, Paul infers that his opponents are Judaizers. Paul writes, "Are they Hebrews? So am I. Are they Israelites? So am I. Are they descendants of Abraham? So am I" (2 Cor 11:22). In 2 Corinthians 11:23ff, the Apostle Paul denounces his Judaizer opponents with biting sarcasm, as he reluctantly boasts of his indefatigable labour and zeal for the spiritual welfare of the Corinthian believers and converts in all the churches he had helped establish.

Paul likely stresses the Spirit's glory exceeding that of Moses and the old covenant (2 Cor 3:1–4:6) to counter accusations against the credibility of his ministry and because his opponents appear to be using their heritage as Moses' successors to gain authority among the Corinthians (Oropeza, 2009:8). From what we can deduce of Paul's own words, at this time, the strategy of his opponents is to discredit Paul's apostolic authority (Oropeza, 2009:8). Paul writes, "For I consider myself not in the least inferior to the most eminent apostles" (2 Cor 11:5).

It seems implied in 2 Corinthians 11:5ff that these "super-apostles" (ὑπερλίαν ἀποστόλων, *hyperlian apostolōn*) were accepting remuneration from the Corinthians, but Paul did not. This approach seems to have backfired on Paul. Because Paul received no material support from the Corinthian believers, it was deemed that his message was without charge, and therefore perceived by at least some of the Corinthians to be a less valuable message than that of the "super-apostles."

It was probably only in the general deterioration of the Corinthian situation, after the writing of 1 Corinthians, that Paul realized how detrimental was the impact, on the Corinthian congregation, of outside Jewish emissaries who professed to be believers (Barrett, 1982:37). For Paul, it was then no more diplomatic allusions and no longer possible to repeat the words of 1 Corinthians 15:11 that it was inconsequential who preached the message, because, never mind that they flagrantly contravened the agreement of Galatians 2:7–9, these "super-apostles" preached "another Jesus" and "a different spirit" and "a different gospel"—in other words it was not the gospel he had proclaimed (2 Cor 11:4, 5).

Paul again refers to these "super-apostles" in 2 Corinthians 12:11, reiterating that "in no respect was I inferior to the most eminent apostles (ὑπερλίαν ἀποστόλων, *hyperlian apostolōn*)." In 2 Corinthians 11:13 "the gloves are off" and Paul bluntly calls these interlopers "false apostles, deceitful workers, disguising themselves as apostles of Christ." These Hebraic (cf. 2 Cor 11:22), pretentious "super-apostles" designed to "enslave" them, "devour" them (i.e., "to take their money" as in Mark 12:40) and subject them to physical abuse (2 Cor 11:20).

Paul expresses great dismay that the Corinthian Christ-believers would let these Judaizers enslave them (2 Cor 11:20a). So, although "Paul versus Judaizers" may not explain all the conflicts in the Corinthian Christ assembly, it surely was an element—a strong undercurrent—that periodically erupted to the surface. In 2 Corinthians 10:7, Paul reminds those pretentious Hebraic leaders and their followers, who regard themselves to be in the "superior" Christ party, that he, Paul, too, is Christ's and can claim higher authority from the Lord but doesn't wish to terrify them (2 Cor 10:8–9).

Mason (2009:324–325) posits that in writing to Corinth, Paul cites the εὐαγγέλιον/*euangelion* (gospel/good news) as the basis of the bond with his readers because he had established them in the εὐαγγέλιον/*euangelion* (gospel/good news), and he urges them to preserve their allegiance (1 Cor 4:15; 9:18; 2 Cor 4:3; 9:13). After his departure, Paul's teaching is contested by those advocating a Judaizing Christianity which proves very attractive to his Corinthian converts. Paul strongly condemns these intruders and their beliefs (Mason, 2009:324–325).

Mason (2009:325) asserts that the Apostle Paul claims to have birthed the Corinthian believers through the εὐαγγέλιον/*euangelion* (gospel/good news), and now in the face of a Judaizing challenge Paul sardonically accuses them in the following manner:

> If one comes and preaches another Jesus, whom we have not preached, or you receive a different spirit which you have not [formerly] received, or a different (ἕτερον) *euangelion*, which you have not [formerly] accepted, you bear *this* beautifully (2 Cor 11:4).

In this passage, Paul is unwilling to link a regressive Judaizing Christianity with the good news (εὐαγγέλιον/*euangelion*) he proclaimed (Mason 2009:325). In this conflictual situation with "Judaizers" who wanted to impose Levitical laws on all Christians, Paul strenuously qualifies his proclamation of the good news (Mason 2009:325).

Though the Apostle Paul faces many other problems in other Christ assemblies he planted, he does not link those problems to a "different εὐαγγέλιον" (*euangelion*/gospel) as he does in 1 and 2 Corinthians (Mason 2009:325).

3.3 SYNAGOGUE INFLUENCE ON CORINTHIAN ASSEMBLY

> It appears quite certain that the Jewish population of the Diaspora, estimates of which ranged between two and five million, outnumbered that of Judaea well before 70 AD. It is reasonable to assume that almost any Jewish community would have had its own "place" (*topos* per Josephus), i.e., a synagogue. Thus, the number of such institutions throughout the Empire undoubtedly reached into the many hundreds, if not thousands (Levine, 2005:82).

The New Testament alone records the names of 23 specific cities which had synagogues, sometimes more than one. There were synagogues (συναγωγή/*synagōgē*) in Antioch of Pisidia (Acts 13:14), Antioch of Syria (Acts 6:5), Athens (Acts 17:17), Berea (Acts 17:10), Cana (John 2:1), Capernaum (John 6:59), Corinth (Acts 18:7, 8), Cyrene (Mark 15:21), Damascus (Acts 9:2), Ephesus (Acts 16:13; 18:19ff), Iconium (Acts 14:1), Jericho (Luke19:1), Jerusalem (Acts 24:12), Laodicea (Col 4:16), Miletus Acts 20:17), Magdala (Mark 5:21), Nazareth (Luke 4:16), Pergamum (Rev 2:12), Philadelphia (Rev 3:7), Salamis (Acts13:5), Smyrna (Revelation 2:8), Thessalonica (Acts 17:1), Thyatira (Acts 16:14; Rev 2:18), and a place of prayer (προσευχή/*proseuchē*) in Philippi (Acts 16:13). The New Testament makes 15 general references to synagogues in Galilee and 13 general references to synagogues in Judea.

It is very interesting to note that Bruce (1977:42), citing Powell, brings attention to the apparent fact that, based on inscriptions, Rome and Corinth contained a "synagogue of (the) Hebrews" in contrast to a synagogue used by Greek-speaking Jews. Bruce (1977:42) explains that in the dispersion throughout the Greco-Roman world, the Hellenists would be the majority of the Jews residing in the respective Diaspora cities, "while the Hebrews would be recent immigrants from Palestine or members of families which made a special point of preserving their Palestinian ways." Bruce (1977:42) continues, "Paul's contemporary, Philo of Alexandria, himself a Hellenistic Jew, employs the word 'Hebrews' to denote those who speak Hebrew."

Powell (1903:60–61), under number 40, provides a hand-drawn picture and a description of a particular block demarcating [Συνα]γωγὴ Ἑβρ[αίων] (transliterated [Syna]gogue of Hebr[ews]), from a multi-year archaeological dig at Corinth, which Powell says probably formed the lintel over the top of the synagogue doorway (Powell, 1903:61). Deissmann (1927:16) enthused, "It is therefore a possibility, seriously to be reckoned with, that we have here the inscription to the door of the Corinthian synagogue mentioned in Acts xviii. 4, in which St. Paul first preached!"

Assuming his restoration is correct, Powell (1903:61), accompanies the picture and description, with a very detailed explanation of this stone's significance, as follows:

> We know that there was a Jewish synagogue at Corinth, where St. Paul preached during his sojourn there (cf. N.T. *Acts*, xviii. 4). If our restoration be correct, this stone was part of that synagogue. The poor cutting displayed in the letters and the use of a second-hand block may point to the poverty of this foreign cult at Corinth. If we may judge from the place where the stone was found (and the size of the block favors the supposition that it had not been moved far), we can place the Jewish synagogue in the region east of the road to Lechaeum, and but a short distance north of the great fountain of Pirene. This district was a residence quarter, as many house walls (cf. *Am. J. Arch.* Vol. I, 1897, p.p. 465–467) and the remains of a Roman house with a central court, a few metres north of Pirene, bear witness; we know that the synagogue was in a residence quarter, for when Paul went out from it, after forsaking the Jews who had opposed him, he entered the dwelling of a certain Justus, "whose house joined hard to the synagogue " (cf. N T. *Acts*, xviii. 7). It is not likely that the synagogue was on the west side of the road, for this side was flanked by a colonnade and a series of shops or small buildings close under the hill where stood the old temple of Apollo. The building was probably not more than a hundred metres from the Propylaea which

marked the entrance to the market-place (cf. Paus. II, 3, 2), and in the market-place was probably situated the "judgement seat," to which Paul was brought by the Jews to be tried before the Roman proconsul, Gallio (cf. N.T. *Acts,* xviii. 12).

Thus, at the outset of this section, we confirm that the literary and the archaeological/epigraphical spheres corroborate that there was at least one synagogue in first-century Corinth. Furthermore, the archaeological/epigraphical evidence cited immediately above seems to point to a Hebraic background, rather than Hellenized background for this particular Corinthian synagogue.

This apparent Hebraic synagogue in Corinth may also explain why Paul describes himself as "a Hebrew of Hebrews" (Phil 3:5), which in Paul's writings, as certainly in Luke's, "is probably a more specialized term than 'Israelite' or 'Jew'" (Bruce, 1977:42). In 2 Corinthians 11:22, Paul provides a similar emphatic response to those who were trying to undermine him. These false apostles (2 Cor 11:13ff) were probably Judaizers, in view of how Paul customized his sortie against them. That context (2 Cor 11:22), where Paul emphasizes that he is a "Hebrew" suggests a more restricted sense for the term than the expressions "Israelites" or "descendants of Abraham" which follow in the same verse (Bruce, 1977:42). "In Acts 6:1 'Hebrews' is used in contradistinction to 'Hellenists', although both Hebrews and Hellenists were Jews . . . . The distinction was probably linguistic and cultural: the Hebrews, in that case, attended synagogues where the service was conducted in Hebrew . . . (Bruce, 1977:42).

Ford (1966a:404) suggests, "Perhaps one should not think of a homogeneous group but of Jewish communities having their own synagogues, St. Paul leaving one, for example, the 'conservative,' or pure Jewish, and attaching himself to another, the Greek or the proselyte." Ford (1966a:404–405) adds:

> We have such a situation in Rome and Jerusalem. The synagogues in Rome were named after their patrons. This may provide a clue to the divisions in Corinth; the four parties may be four synagogue communities who adopt the name of their Christian patrons, or they may be divided according to nationalities or language.

"The Diaspora synagogue fulfilled much the same function as a communal and religious center within each Jewish community, and

Roman authorities clearly articulated the rights and privileges of this institution and the community in general in a number of contemporary decrees and edicts" (Levine, 2005:81; see also previous section 3.2 "Jewish influence bearing on the Corinthian assembly" in this chapter 3).

A general edict of Augustus to the Jews of Asia Minor from 12 BC is of special note: "And if anyone is caught stealing sacred books or sacred monies from a Sabbath-house [σαββατεῖον] or a banquet hall [ἀνδρών], he shall be regarded as sacrilegious, and his property shall be confiscated to the public treasury of the Romans" (Levine, 2005:115).

In comparing the functions of the Second Temple and synagogues in the same period, Levine (2005:79) writes "... one focused on sacrifice, the other on Torah reading and prayer; one demanded silence in the cultic ritual, the other public recitations; one required a priestly leadership, the other did not (in other words, a sacral hierarchical framework par excellence in contradistinction to a communal one)." Thus, in Israel and in the Diaspora, the synagogue appeared to be a supplement to the Temple worship, rather than in competition with it. Particularly in the Diaspora, and the parts of Israel more distant from Jerusalem, a centre for Jewish community and spiritual life was needed that would complement and supplement the functions of the Temple.

Thus it was that the synagogue had communal and religious functions. We'll deal with the communal functions first. In terms of communal functions, the synagogue served as a place for administering justice and discipline. We see in the intertestamental book Susannah (Sus chapter 2) in the Septuagint version, adjudicating cases was one of the basic privileges of Diaspora communities. The New Testament reinforces this aspect. Each of the Synoptic Gospels reiterates this point: "Beware of men; for they will deliver you up to the courts, and scourge you in their synagogues..." (Matt. 10:17–18; Mark 13:9; Luke 21:12; cf. Luke 12:11). In Matthew 23:34, Jesus is recorded as having said: "Therefore, behold, I am sending you prophets and wise men and scribes; some of them you will kill and crucify, and some of them you will scourge in your synagogues, and persecute from city to city." Paul's speaking on the steps of the barracks in Jerusalem (Acts 22:19) once again recalls this judicial function. He retells his personal experience in the following words: "And I said: 'Lord, they themselves understand that in one synagogue after another I used to imprison and beat those who believed in Thee'" (Acts 22:19). In 2 Corinthians 11:24, Paul speaks of being lashed by the Jews thirty-nine times on five different occasions.

In view of no clear outward differentiation between a synagogue and a Christ assembly *(ekklésia/ἐκκλησία)*, in the middle of the first century AD, in Corinth, Ford (1966a:406) writes that it is easier to understand the Apostle Paul's reference to the courts (1 Cor 6:1–8).

Although without the harsh physical aspect of discipline, Paul carried over the synagogue concept of judging internal civic affairs to the Corinthian assembly of Christ believers, when he chides them (1 Cor 6:2ff) for not handling communal matters of discipline within their own ranks. After all, Paul says that the saints will judge the world and [fallen] angels (cf. 2 Pet2:4, 9 and Jude 6). This Jewish concept, likely unfamiliar to Gentiles outside the synagogue, is also in Daniel 7:22 and in the Septuagint apocryphal Book of Wisdom (Wisdom of Solomon), dated mid-first century BC, which reads, "They [the righteous] shall judge the nations, and have dominion over the people" (Wis 3:8).

Another communal aspect was the sacred meals which are documented in a number of first-century Jewish contexts (Pharisaic *ḥavurot*, Essenes or Qumran sectarians, and the Therapeutae), primarily in connection with religious associations (Levine, 2005:115, 141). However, it would appear that such communal meals were not foreign to the wider Jewish community, as reflected in the decree regarding Delian Jews (Levine, 2005:115, 142). At times, these communal meals were intimately connected to cultic acts, as was the Passover sacrifice in the Jerusalem Temple (Levine, 2005:142). Such meals became a central feature in the nascent Christian church as well (Levine, 2005:142). Communal meals, centred around Christ's substitutionary death, became a distinctive trait in the inceptive Christ assembly at Corinth (1 Cor 11:17–34).

A third communal aspect of pre-70 AD Diaspora synagogues, is noted by Levine (2005:115), who writes of the official sanction, of Emperor Augustus, in 12 BC for the Jews in Asia Minor to collect monies:

> Finally, the reference to a synagogue as a repository for sacred books and sacred monies is invaluable. These monies were probably donated for local use as well as for the Jerusalem Temple, a practice that, as we have seen, was widespread among first-century Diaspora communities.

From the accounts in Acts, we learn of a fourth communal aspect, that of the ancient custom of reading the Hebrew Scriptures in the synagogue on the Sabbath, which custom supposedly originated from

Moses himself (Acts 15:21). In the pre-70 Diaspora, Levine (2005:131) asserts that the reading of the Hebrew Scriptures involved congregational participation. The gathering on the Sabbath in the synagogue was the place for the community to congregate, fellowship and learn from their Hebrew Scriptures. We learn that it is the synagogue Sabbath gathering that provides the setting for Paul's meeting the local Jewish community (e.g., Acts 13:42; 16:13; 17:2; 18:4).

As to those in the synagogue in Berea, the author of Acts notes that some Jews were gathering daily to eagerly examine the Hebrew Scriptures, especially to evaluate Paul's message. The author Luke describes an incipient Messianic community whose devotion and commitment led to daily study of the Hebrew Scriptures. These Berean Jews were described as "more noble-minded" than those of the nearby Thessalonian synagogue (Acts 17:11).

In summarizing his research on the reading of the Hebrew Scriptures in the synagogue before 70 AD, Perrot (1988:149) states "The custom of reading the Law of Moses was well established in the first century AD, both in Israel and the Diaspora" (cf. Acts 15:21; 2 Cor 3:14–15).

Acts 13:15 offers us a glimpse of the Sabbath-morning liturgy in the synagogue at Antioch of Pisidia. Four elements are featured on this occasion: a portion from the Torah is read; then a passage from the Prophets is read; the synagogue officials invite Paul to speak; and Paul addresses the congregation (This sequence parallels Luke's description of the synagogue service at Nazareth in Luke 4:14–30). What's remarkable is the receptivity of the Antioch synagogue community to the participation of an outsider. We have no information in the text to tell us whether Paul's arrival at the Antioch synagogue was foreknown. As a non-local rabbi, maybe because he was from Jerusalem, he was asked to address the congregation. Although we don't know if this practice was customary, it may have been a common courtesy, as we notice that something similar happened at Ephesus. We read in Acts 18:24–26 of an Alexandrian Jew named Apollos who came to the local synagogue there and spoke fervently and accurately about Jesus.

By the first century AD, readings from the Prophets in the synagogue service also seemed to be normative from indications in the New Testament noted above (Acts 13:15). Jesus was asked to read from Isaiah 61 when attending a synagogue in Nazareth (Luke 4:17–19) and Paul delivered "a word of exhortation" at the synagogue in Antioch in

Pisidia following readings from the Torah (the five books of Moses—the Pentateuch) and the Prophets (Acts 13:14–15). The regularity of the prophetic readings in the context of the first-century Sabbath service is referred to in Acts 13:27: "For those who live in Jerusalem and their rulers, recognizing neither him nor the utterances of the prophets which are read every Sabbath, fulfilled these [words] by condemning *Him*."

In the case of Luke 4:16–20, it was the Prophetic reading—and not the Torah passage, strictly speaking—that determined the nature of the sermon subsequently delivered (Luke 4:21–27). From this account and the instance concerning Paul (Acts 13:15), it appears typical for the sermon to follow the Prophetic reading and be related to it. A sermon based on the Prophetic passage "... would seem to have been the norm with oppositional, messianically oriented groups, such as early Christians and members of the Qumran sect. The books of the Prophets lent themselves to revolutionary messages, be they of a political, social, or religious nature" (Levine, 2005:158). In his section on "Sabbath Day Readings" before 70 AD, Perrot (1988:157) writes:

> The prophetic text complements that of the Tora to clarify its meaning. Hence a section from the Pentateuch cannot be accompanied by any random prophetic text. A verbal and thematic link between them was needed, so that the passage from the prophet 'resembled' the passage from the Tora .... It was precisely this similarity which was to give some of its later dynamism to the homily. But this 'magnetizing of texts' existed already before the fall of the temple.

Luke 4:16–30 provides a precise example of the connection of the homily to the prophetic passage when Jesus followed up the reading of Isaiah 61:1f, about the liberation brought by the sabbatical year, by pronouncing that he was the fulfilment of that prophecy in those very days. In this Luke passage, it is quite fascinating that Jesus stopped reading in the middle of Isaiah 61:2, since at his first coming he proclaimed only the "favorable year of the Lord" (Luke 4:19), whereas the "day of vengeance of our God" (Isa 61:2b) is retained for his second coming. Long-suffering forbearance and the cross was his essential mission at his first coming; judgement of the conquering King is inextricably linked to his coming again (Isa 61:2bff).

Although it is challenging to figure out the form(s) of homiletics at this stage, Perrot (1988:158), suggests that "... the opening of the reading of the day could be used as starting-point, to be followed by an exposition where texts from the whole of Scripture were formed into a long chain." In the previous paragraph of his writing on this matter, Perrot (1988:158) had given the example of Paul's using the launch pad of the Hebrew Scriptures, on three Sabbaths in the synagogue, to make an evidential, logical case for Jesus being the crucified, resurrected Messiah (Acts 17:2–3). Paul seemed pretty adept at stringing together relevant Hebrew Scriptures to persuasively make his case on whatever the issue he was dealing with, in spoken or written form.

It has also been suggested that the prophetic reading, along with its related homily, may have concluded the synagogue service (Levine, 2005:154). The New Testament literary evidence seems incontrovertible that the sermon (i.e., the expounding on an idea from the scriptural reading) was a usual part of the Sabbath synagogue service. Jesus preached in the synagogue in Nazareth (Luke 4:20–21) and Paul preached a sermon in the synagogue in Antioch in Pisidia (Acts 13:15) and many elsewhere also (Acts 17:2a "according to Paul's custom;" Acts 13:5, 16ff; 14:1; 17:10, 17; 18:4, 19; 19:8).

As a consequence of Jews from Israel immigrating westward, liturgical developments progressed at different rates in the Diaspora synagogues, although "by the first century torah reading liturgies were firmly established everywhere" (Runesson, 2001:470, 480).

McNamara (1983:210) writes: "Moses, that is the Pentateuch, was not merely read; his message was preached, proclaimed. James put the origins of this custom back into very ancient times ... They had to hear the law and hear it explained." Levine (2005:155) writes that, from all sources, it is very clear that the reading from the Hebrew Scriptures in the early synagogue was more than reciting the text, but whether in Judaea or the Diaspora, the readings from the Torah and the Prophets functioned as a springboard for further instruction and edification.

Levine (2005:159) indicates there is a consensus that the custom of translating Scriptures into the vernacular at the synagogue service already existed in the Second Temple period. Levine (2005:159) suggests that in the Roman Diaspora ". . . the Septuagint translation (or variations thereof) may have been used after the Hebrew reading ..." "Passages in Philo, Josephus, and the NT (Luke 4:16–21; Acts 15:21; 17:1) refer to the regular reading of Scripture in synagogues in the original languages [Hebrew and some Aramaic] as well as in translation" (Tov, 2008:174).

CULTURAL ANALYSIS

Although conceding that in the pre-70 AD period, the Greek Septuagint may have been more at play in the Alexandrian context of Egypt, Perrot (1988:155) counters: "Still one may suppose that in the 'synagogues of the Hebrews' which are mentioned several times in connection with the Diaspora at Rome and Corinth, reading was also in Hebrew."

Tov (2008:184) corroborates this assessment when he writes:

> ... there is no direct archeological data for the use of specific copies of *Greek* Scripture in synagogues in Israel or in the diaspora. It is likely that the Greek translation of the Torah was used in Egypt in the third and second centuries BCE, but this assumption cannot be proven.

That the Hebrew Scripture scrolls were stored in the synagogue is inferred by Luke 4:16–21, where we have the account of Jesus entering the synagogue in Nazareth. A scroll of Isaiah was handed to Jesus, he unrolled it, read the text, rolled the scroll back up and handed it to the attendant. Because the Scripture scrolls were very expensive, they were normally owned by the community rather than by individuals (Runesson, 2014:272). The implication for Acts 17:10–11 is that this passage should probably also be read with an understanding that the first-century "noble-minded" Bereans, of necessity, congregated at their Diasporan synagogue daily to examine the Scripture scrolls there in the repository in order to check out the Apostle Paul's claims that Jesus was the Messiah.

In responding to the question about the details and nature of the readings in the synagogue on the Sabbath before 70 AD, Perrot (1988:154–155) responds that "All synagogues must surely have possessed the whole Tora in its five volumes and some other Bible scrolls, like Isaiah and the Twelve Prophets, and no doubt the Psalms. These were the books most in use." Perrot (1988:155) conjectures that the Palestinian synagogues being small and numerous, probably could not afford all the scrolls because of their considerable expense.

Taking up a second religious aspect of the synagogue, during the Second Temple period, some Diaspora synagogues were denoted as προσευχή (*proseuchē*), literally, "house of prayer." "On the basis of the name alone, it is rightfully assumed that prayer was a significant element of Jewish worship in such places" (Levine, 2005:164). In Philippi (Acts 16:13), we have the only occurrence in New Testament literature of a Diasporan assembly being denoted as a place of prayer (προσευχή/ *proseuchē*).

In first-century synagogues, in the Diaspora, the aspect of prayer seems to have had a far lesser role, comparative to the centrality of the Torah-reading. The Torah reading may indeed have been the primary focus of Jewish worship in the Diaspora, in part, because it "was undoubtedly the most dramatic and participatory component of Jewish worship and thus the one most likely to be described" (Levine, 2005:165). Additionally, it may be that corporate prayer hardly receives a mention in the first century and Diasporic literature regarding synagogue ritual because of the singular importance of the Torah reading and that being the focal point "around which most of the other liturgical elements revolved, i.e., . . . sermon, and *haftarah* [reading from the Prophets]" (Levine, 2005:165). Matthew 6:5 alludes to prayer in the synagogue: "And when you pray, you are not to be as the hypocrites; for they love to stand and pray in the synagogues and on the street corners, in order to be seen by men." Prayer is assumed in a corporate setting in the Corinthian assembly of those who believed in Jesus (1 Cor 11:4, 5, 13 and 14:14, 15).

Sanders (1999:7) proffers, "In 1 Corinthians 14, Paul refers also to hymns . . . This inclines me to add singing to the list of possible synagogal activities." Bradshaw (2008:21), in sorting out first-century Judaism from possible later Talmudic practice, writes:

> What was certainly happening in the first century, however, was that new psalms and hymns were being composed for use in worship, to which the large collection of *hodayoth* from the community at Qumran bears witness [Vermes, 150–201]. Philo speaks of chants, hymns, and songs being employed in Jewish worship [Philo, *In Flaccum*, 121–122], and when describing the customs of the Therapeutae says that in their solitude "they do not only contemplate but also compose songs and hymns to God in all sorts of metres and melodies" [Philo, *De Vita Contemplativa*, 29].

Bradshaw (2008:22) concludes his chapter on Jewish precedents for early church worship by affirming that this element, among others, formed the backdrop for early Christian converts and their manner of worship services in the various Pauline-founded congregations (cf. 1 Cor 14:26; Eph 5:19; Col3:16).

Luke 13:10ff infers one other possible feature of synagogues in the first century. In that account, the synagogue official is not indignant that Jesus had healed in the synagogue, but that Jesus had done it on the Sabbath. In rebuking Jesus for having so done, the synagogue official invited the assembled audience to come back to the synagogue for their healings on the other six days of the week—just not on the Sabbath (Luke 13:14). In the pre-70 AD Diaspora Christian context, "gifts of healing" are referred to in 1 Corinthians 12:9, 28, 30, and of note is the only "manifestation of the Spirit" referred to as a gift(s). The subject of healing is only introduced in one other New Testament epistle—namely the book of James. Ford (1966a:405) comments that "both [1 Cor. and James] may have Jewish backgrounds."

Sanders (1999:7; 1992:202) remarks on Paul's directive in 1 Corinthians 14:26: "His assumption of active participation by many probably reflects synagogue practice as he knew it." "This democratic attitude to permit the participation of laymen in the service . . . " (Idelsohn, 1932:16) eventually made its way into the Second Temple period synagogues with lay people called forward to read Scripture or speak a word of encouragement and ultimately segued into the Pauline Christ assemblies and the Corinthian congregation in particular (cf. 1 Cor 14:26).

Because of the broad range of primary material at our disposal (archaeological, epigraphical, and literary), several aspects common to the pre-70 Diaspora synagogues or προσευχή (*proseuchē*) become quite obvious (Levine, 2005:127).

In summarizing the above section, regarding the synagogue's communal functions in the Diaspora, pre-70, it served as a place for dispensing discipline. Another communal aspect was the sacred meals which are documented in a number of first-century Jewish contexts (Pharisaic *ḥavurot*, Essenes [Qumran], Therapeutae). Thirdly, monies were collected for local needs or sending on to the Temple in Jerusalem. These three communal aspects are reflected in Paul's letters to the Corinthian assembly of Christ believers (cf. 1 Cor 5 and 6:1–8; 11:20–34; 16:2–3).

Regarding the synagogue's religious functions in the Diaspora, pre-70 AD, it seems evident that those basic functions were Torah reading, reading from the Prophets, study and instruction, sermons, some measure of prayer, singing of songs/hymns, and possibly healing. It appears that these forms of religious expression, in a similar context of encouraging lay participation, were all replicated to one degree or another in the Corinthian assembly (cf. 1 Cor 11:4, 5, 13; 12:28, 30; 14:14, 15; 1 Tim 2:8, 11, 12 and 1 Tim 4:11, 13, 16).

The Lord's Supper is based on the Jewish Passover traditions and believer's baptism is obviously similar to Jewish practice as well (Lamm, 1991). Without doubt, the Apostles and early believers in Jesus as Messiah took their cue for their initiation rite from the similar Jewish practice.

The presence of "prominent women," in Paul's audience at Berea was also noted (Acts 17:12). Luke in writing Acts, makes a habit of singling out Gentiles, both men and women, as also having frequented Diaspora synagogues (Acts 13:43; 14:1–2; 17:4, 12; 18:4).

The only synagogue official named in these pre-70 AD Acts Diaspora accounts is the ἀρχισυνάγωγος/*archisynagōgos* (cf. Mark 5:22, 35, 36, 38; Luke 8:49; 13:10–17; Acts 18:8, 17). In Acts 13:15, these officials (ἀρχισυνάγωγοι/*archisynagōgoi*) invite Paul to speak to the synagogue meeting in Antioch of Pisidia following the reading of the Torah and Prophets. It's apparent that the position of ἀρχισυνάγωγος/*archisynagōgos* involved responsibility and authority. In the second case of this type of official in Acts, Luke notes that Crispus, the ἀρχισυνάγωγος/*archisynagōgos* of the Corinthian synagogue, became a believer (Acts 18:8), and, characteristically in the culture of the day, his whole household followed suit. In the literary and epigraphical material, the ἀρχισυνάγωγος/*archisynagōgos* (synagogue ruler), in addition to being the one in charge of worship was also a financial patron of the synagogue (Levine, 2005:416).

The Christian term of *diakonos* (deacon) "had a precedent in the officers of the synagogue who had charge of the collection and distribution of alms" (Schaff, 1910a: 499). The Christian concept of *presbuteros* (elder) derives from the Hebrew Older Testament context and synagogue (Schaff, 1910a: 491–492; cf. Luke 7:3–5).

With the uniqueness of the Torah-reading ceremony and its related components in the synagogue worship context, especially when compared to other religious institutions in the first-century Greco-Roman world (Levine, 2005:165), it would be difficult to imagine these distinctive elements just dropping out of sight in the meetings of first-century Christian assemblies in the Diasporan world, particularly, as we shall shortly see, when the synagogue provided the initial converts in Paul's mission-plants in Corinth and elsewhere.

Runesson (2014:291) deduces: "While Jesus never established an association [synagogue], it is sociologically highly likely that his followers soon began forming such institutions, and that they patterned those settings on already existing Jewish association synagogues." Runesson (2014:292) further appraises, "As Christ-belief spread in the Diaspora, such an institutional [synagogue] pattern would have been familiar also to non-Jews as they gathered in private homes and, later, in separate buildings."

Leithart (2002:122) writes,

> It is certainly true that the actions of the church's worship ... are very much like the actions performed by worshipers in the synagogue. So far as it is possible to determine, synagogue worship in the first century seems to have consisted of reading Scripture, teaching, prayer, fellowship meals, and Psalms, an ensemble of liturgical actions that closely matches Luke's descriptions of the meetings of the early Christians. It is also evident from Acts that Paul drew many of his early converts from the synagogue, and it is plausible to assume that they continued to worship in much the same way that they had before their incorporation into the church.

1 Corinthians 14:40 implies there was a "fixed order" (BDAG, s.v. κατὰ τάξιν, §1) of their congregational services in first-century Corinth. Being that the initial leaders and congregants of this fledgling assembly came out of the synagogue, it would be safe to conclude that, the outline of whatever that "fixed order" was, likely derived from their immediately prior, synagogue customs.

3.3.1 Origin of Corinthian Congregation

From Acts 18:4, it appears that the recipients of the Apostle Paul's message in the Corinthian synagogue are stated to be "Jews and "Greeks" as he "reasoned" and "persuaded." Thus, Paul's initial converts in Corinth were Jewish (Acts 18:8) plus a Gentile named Titius Justus (Acts 18:7), who was said to be "a worshiper of God" (σεβομένου/*sebomenou*"). This is one of the Greek terms for the category called "God-fearers" (Feldman, 1986:58). These are Gentiles who "attached themselves in varying degrees to the Jewish worship and way of life," but in the case of the males did not take the final step of circumcision necessary to become a proselyte to Judaism (Bruce, 1977:128). The other requirements of undergoing a ceremonial bath/baptism, offering a sacrifice, and undertaking to keep the law of Moses were the only ones that applied for women, thereby making less of a barrier for Gentile women to become proselytes (Bruce, 1977:129). Luke frequently refers to such people (Acts 13:43, 50; 16:14; 17:17; 18:7).

In the Book of Acts we find the Greek terms φοβούμενοι/*phoboumenoi* ("those fearing") and σεβομένοι τὸν θεόν/*sebomenoi ton theon* ("those reverencing God") and elsewhere in classical Greek literature we find the term θεοσεβαις/*theosebeis* ("God worshippers"), which for convenience, we refer collectively to these Greek terms as "God-fearers" (Feldman, 1986:58).

Feldman (1986:58–63) examined the evidence independent of the book of Acts, to see whether it demonstrated the existence of a substantial group of "sympathizers" or semi-Jews. Contrary to MacLennan and Kraabel (1986:46–53), Feldman (1986:58) contended that the evidence indicated the existence of such "sympathizers" in rather large numbers. Feldman (1986:59) wrote: "Whether such people are called 'God-fearers' or 'sympathizers' or 'semi-Jews' is relatively unimportant. The fact is they existed . . . . The evidence is circumstantial, literary and epigraphic."

So as Bruce (1977:128) proposed above, these "God-fearers" were Gentiles who "attached themselves in varying degrees to the Jewish worship and way of life without as yet becoming full proselytes."

The term "proselytes" (προσήλυτον/*proselyton*) seems customarily to have referred to converts who were fully integrated into the Jewish synagogue community. In Acts 13:42–43, in Psidian Antioch, we have an interesting juxtaposition, which may be a caveat to the norm.

> And as Paul and Barnabas were going out, the people kept begging that these things might be spoken to them the next Sabbath. Now when *the meeting of* the synagogue had broken up, many of the Jews and of the God-fearing proselytes followed Paul and Barnabas, who speaking to them, were urging them to continue in the grace of God.

The expression "God-fearing proselytes" (σεβόμενοι προσηλύτων/ *sebomenoi proseluton*) here is a unique combination where προσηλύτων (*proseluton*/proselytes) is possibly being used in an ambivalent sense, indicating that in this part of the world these Gentile proselytes were still categorized as "God-fearers" and were not technically regarded as being in full communion with pure-bred ethnic Jews. This surprising distinction seems borne out in the verses to follow where author Luke has it that only the Jews contradict Paul's message and "blaspheme." The "God-fearing proselytes" are not thus incriminated, whereas when Paul for the first time announces that he will henceforth turn to the "Gentiles," the Gentiles upon hearing the inclusivistic Isaiah 49:6 quote, begin "rejoicing and glorifying the word of the Lord; and as many as had been appointed to eternal life believed" (Acts 13:48). Attentive to how Luke carefully parses his words and what he says and doesn't say, a fair-minded deduction would be that the receptive "Gentiles" here were probably the "God-fearing proselytes" of the synagogue setting in the earlier verse 43 of this same chapter 13. It is hardly likely that hitherto completely uninformed Gentiles would respond so enthusiastically and sincerely. After all, it was Paul's apt quotation of the Lord's injunctive about Gentile inclusion in the offer of salvation (Isa 49:6) that so powerfully resonated with these seeming biblically literate hearers.

We cannot escape the historical fact that the Corinthian congregation of believers in Christ originated from the synagogue in Corinth. As recounted in Acts 18:4–8, the nucleus was comprised of Jews and Greeks (i.e., Gentile "God-fearers") who believed Paul's message, in the synagogue, that Jesus was the Christ (Messiah). Additionally, this community of Christ believers at Corinth was supported and nurtured, from its earliest days, by several Jewish believers, in addition to Paul (Aquila, Priscilla, Silas, Timothy, Apollos, Crispus, Gaius/Titius Justus, and possibly Sosthenes and Peter).

Furthermore, when writing from Corinth to the Roman believers, Paul passes greetings (Rom 16:21) from fellow believers Lucius, Jason and Sosipater, likely of the local Corinthian congregation, at least for a time, and refers to them as his "kinsmen" (συγγενεῖς/*syngeneis*). For συγγενεῖς/*syngeneis*, see especially Romans 9:3 where Paul uses the same Greek term and adds "according to the flesh" and glosses "my brethren," which within that context, Paul is clearly referring to his Jewish brethren. BDAG defines the word συγγενεῖς as "belonging to the same extended family or clan, related, akin to" (s.v. συγγενεῖς, §1) or "belonging to the same people group, compatriot, ext. of 1" (s.v. συγγενεῖς, §2). With either BDAG shade of definition, Paul, in Corinth, is passing along greetings of "fellow Jews" from whence he writes.

Lastly, in 1 Corinthians 7:18–19, Paul goes into a brief exhortation about neither circumcision nor uncircumcision being anything of consequence. This brief doctrinal counsel signifies a continuing Jewish presence in Corinth or it would be without point.

This Jewish DNA, as delineated in the foregoing and subsequent, would understandably and inevitably have a bearing on the congregational life in Corinth in the years ahead.

3.3.1.1 Synagogue ruler Crispus and his entire household

The Acts 18:8 record simply states that after the initial evangelism of Paul within the Corinthian synagogue, that "Crispus, the leader of the synagogue, believed in the Lord with all his household, and many of the Corinthians when they heard were believing and being baptized." The term "household" would have inferred spouse, children and spouses of adult children, and servants. The number may have been sizeable, unlike modern nuclear families of a mom, dad, and a minor-age son and daughter. Luke, being one to not waste words, apparently wants us to understand that the sway and standing of Crispus was considerable, because Crispus believing in the Lord influenced many others to believe also. We know, according to 1 Corinthians 1:14, that Crispus was baptized by Paul.

From the literary and epigraphical material, as an ἀρχισυνάγωγος/ *archisynagōgos* (synagogue ruler), in addition to being the person in charge of synagogue worship, Crispus would have been a person of financial means and a financial patron of the synagogue (Levine, 2005:416).

It would seem that, in some manner, Crispus relinquished his ἀρχισυνάγωγος/*archisynagōgos* (synagogue ruler) position, as by the time of the Gallio incident (Acts 18:12–17), the Corinthian Jewish synagogue had selected Sosthenes as his successor (Acts 18:17).

In concluding this section, it is of interest to note that possibly the successor of Crispus also became a Christ believer and joined the Pauline-founded congregation in Corinth. Acts 18:17 refers to a Sosthenes who was "the leader of the synagogue" in Corinth at the time of the hearing before proconsul Gallio. If this is the same Sosthenes mentioned in 1 Corinthians 1:1 as the co-author of 1 Corinthians, perhaps he subsequently became a believer in Jesus as the Messiah also. "This connection has a long connection in church tradition and has much to commend it, although it cannot be conclusively demonstrated"

(Richards, 2004:113). Thiselton (2000:70) asserts that Paul's inclusion of Sosthenes as his 1 Corinthians co-author was meant to be a "poignant reminder of the power of the gospel." I would add that it might also serve as an interesting parallel to the conversion testimony of the Apostle Paul. As a synagogue leader, Sosthenes too was a man of advanced standing in Judaism. As evidenced by Sosthenes pressing charges against the Christ-follower Paul before the Achaian proconsul Gallio (Acts 18:17ff), Sosthenes too was zealous to protect Judaism from those making claims that the crucified Jesus was the Messiah. If this Corinthian epistle co-author (1 Cor 1:1) be the same former Corinthian synagogue leader, Sosthenes too had a dramatic change of mind, and in a remarkable about-face, was now preaching the very Christ he had previously maligned and persecuted.

Richards (2004:114) suggests that Paul had Sosthenes join him because Sosthenes intimately knew the Corinthian congregation and culture. Sosthenes was an "insider," whereas Paul as an "outsider" was not aware of the intricacies and nuances of Corinthian culture (Richards, 2004:114). If Paul's co-author for 1 Corinthians be Sosthenes, a former local synagogue leader, with standing in the community, not being Paul's younger protégé, he was less likely to be cowed by Paul and more likely to interject in Paul's writing as required (Richards, 2004:114).

3.3.1.2 "A worshipper of God" Titius Justus

Philip Schaff opines that the Jewish religion "attracted proselytes who longed for a purer and more spiritual worship" (Schaff, 1910a: 459–460), which contention would be supported by the account of the devout Gentile Centurion Cornelius (Acts 10).

Flusser (1989:73) succinctly sums up the mood of the first century AD:

> In those days a sense of the emptiness of polytheistic beliefs and of the moral corruption of mankind was widespread throughout the world, and there was a growing sympathy for the Jews and for their attitude to religion. Many people joined Judaism as full proselytes, and others, who were called "God-fearing," did not take upon themselves the full yoke of the Commandments, but undertook to keep some of the obligations of Judaism. Such men were the first to join Christianity as a result of the preaching of Paul and his sect.

The Earliest View of New Testament Tongues

Acts 18:7 describes Titius Justus as "a worshipper of God" (σεβομένον τὸν Θεόν/*sebomenon ton theon*). Titius Justus had a house adjacent to the synagogue in Corinth which he put at Paul's disposal when Paul had to depart the synagogue (Acts 18:7). In regard to Titius Justus, Bruce (1977:251–252) posits:

> If, as is probable, he is identical with the Corinthian Christian described by Paul as "Gaius, who is host to me and to the whole church" (Romans 16:23), then his full name, Gaius Titius Justus, marks him out as a Roman citizen. Paul singles out Crispus and Gaius, together with one Stephanas and his family, "the firstfruits of Achaia" [Corinth was the capital of this Roman province], as the only ones of his Corinthian converts whom he baptized personally [1 Cor 1:14–16; cf. 1 Cor 16:15].

This baptism reference in 1 Corinthians 1:14–16 would probably coincide with the Acts 18:7 mention of one of Paul's first Corinthian converts, a man Titius Justus by name. Goodspeed (1950: 382), after referring to unique, Roman, naming traditions, remarks that it is "altogether likely" that Gaius (1 Cor 1:14; cf. 1 Cor 16:15) is one and the same as Titius Justus (Acts 18:7), his full name being Gaius Titius Justus (in the Latin sequence *praenomen*, then *nomen*, then *cognomen*). "Gaius is a *praenomen*, as in Gaius Julius Caesar; . . . so that Caesar, while he was often called Julius Caesar, might be informally referred to by his friends as Gaius, a man named Gaius Titius Justus, in a historical narrative such as the Acts, could naturally be called Titius Justus, and yet in a familiar letter like Romans 16, be spoken of by his *praenomen* as Gaius" (Goodspeed, 1950:382).

Runesson (2008:121) gives us some further clues about Gaius Titius Justus, when he writes:

> In Luke, God-fearers are separate from the proselytes. They visit the synagogues on the Sabbath, take part in Jewish prayers, practise some of the laws of the Torah, and make charitable gifts to the Jews. . . . Luke has his own interests in these God-fearers as the first Gentiles who hear Paul's message about God's salvation together with Jews. When he refers to "Jews and Greeks" in the synagogue, the latter is probably an allusion to God-fearers (18:4).

In this case, it's probably safe to say that Gaius Titius Justus had been part of the Corinthian Hebrew synagogue, for him to have so quickly found out about Paul's expulsion from there and quickly offering to host Paul and ultimately the newly forming congregation of Christ believers. This Titius may in fact have witnessed the scene where Paul "shook off his garments," turned his back on the recalcitrant Jews and dramatically departed the Corinthian synagogue (Acts 18:6–7).

It is interesting that even after Paul's dramatic pronouncement, and move over to the house of Gaius Titius Justus, there was no violent opposition from the ethnic Jews for about eighteen months (1Cor 18:11), despite Paul's new accommodation being right next to the synagogue. The Jews and these Gentiles were living side by side in civil coexistence. When the animosity flared into the open again and the Jews brought Paul before Gallio's judgement seat, the allegations against Paul are not to do with fraternizing with pagans, but rather "questions about words and names" and Jewish law (Acts 18:15)—internal sectarian matters. One wonders if there were accumulating losses from their Hebrew synagogue to the new adjacent congregation that was being hosted by Gaius Titius Justus, which caused the Jews to attempt legal action against Paul before the Achaian proconsul Gallio.

It is instructive to note, that what triggered Paul's departure from the Corinthian synagogue, was when the Jews "resisted and blasphemed" (Acts 18:5–8). Acts 18:4 refers to Paul "reasoning" and "trying to persuade Jews and Greeks [Gentile God-fearers]" in the Corinthian synagogue. For the pronoun "they" in the first clause of Acts 18:6, the obvious antecedent noun is "Jews" in the last part of the preceding verse 5. This is to say that the author Luke does not include the "Greeks" (Gentile God-fearers") in the resistance and blasphemy. It was the Jews who "resisted and blasphemed." So, when Luke has Paul saying in dramatic fashion (Acts 18:6) that from now on he will "go to the Gentiles," it's not clear, if it's meant that the Apostle Paul will go to the Gentile "Godfearers" or to completely pagan Gentiles in Corinth. Based on this missionary enterprise being headquartered right next door to the Corinthian synagogue, in the house of a "God-fearer" named Gaius Titius Justus (Acts 18:7; cf. Rom 16:23), it would be more prudent to err on the side of the first option, that thereafter the target audience was Gentile "God-fearers"—those who attended the synagogue and were quite familiar with the Hebrew Scriptures taught therein. In any event, because of the Lord's words to Paul in a night vision, the Apostle had the assurance of the Lord's presence, that he would not be harmed and that many people would accept his message (Acts 18:10) and so he settled in at the home of Gaius Titius Justus for 18 months "teaching the word of God among them" (Acts 18:11).

3.3.2 Composition of Corinthian Congregation

As recounted in Acts 18:4–8, the nucleus was comprised of Jews and "Greeks" (i.e., Gentile God-fearers), from the local synagogue, who believed Paul's message that Jesus was the Messiah ("Christ" translated from the Greek).

Acts 15:21 is an acknowledgement that even Gentile "worshippers of God" and "God-fearers" who became new Christ believers would be accustomed to the normal synagogue content and ordering of the weekly Sabbath service.

External evidence that the Apostle Paul's readers in Corinth had been very significantly impacted by Jewish background, worship and teaching is found in the First Epistle of Clement (of Rome) to the Corinthians. This Clement (c. 35–c. 99 AD) was bishop of Rome in the late first century AD (Chapman, 1908:13). He is listed by Irenaeus and Tertullian as the bishop of Rome, holding office from 90 AD to his death in 99 AD (Chapman, 1908:16). He is considered to be the first Apostolic Father of the Church (Chapman, 1908:12–13). Lightfoot, Funk, Nestle and others suggest that Clement was of Jewish origin, which may explain his continual use of the Older Testament throughout his Epistle to the Corinthians (Chapman, 1908:14).

Clement's epistle to the Corinthians is replete with references to Older Testament verses and principles. There are about 105 references to the Older Testament in the entire body of Clement's First Epistle to the Corinthians (Lake, 1912; ANF, Vol. 1, *First Epistle to the Corinthians, Clement of Rome*).

Ford (1966a:416) asks some very discerning questions:

> Why should St. Clement have assumed (1) so much acquaintance with the OT, and (2) that the arguments from the OT would carry conviction, if his readers were former pagans? Could the Corinthian Church have appeared so Jewish to St. Clement and yet so Gentile to St. Paul? They both wrote in the same century, and one would not expect a sudden influx of Jewish influence between the Pauline correspondence and the Clementine. It is easier to presume a predominantly Jewish background from the beginning.

CULTURAL ANALYSIS

Obviously, the Jewish heritage was an important factor in the Corinthian assembly at the time of the Apostle Paul's writing and supports the Epiphanius thesis. By the time of Paul's authoring 1 Corinthians, there may have been a sizeable percentage of Gentiles in the Corinthian Christ-believer community, as Paul refers to their Gentile past (ὅτε ἔθνη ἦτε/*hote ethnē ēte* in 1 Cor 12:2), although this may simply refer to the more remote past of the "God-fearers" who were converted out of the Corinthian synagogue context. This is the only instance of 53 occurrences where the New American Standard Version translates ἔθνη/*ethnē* as "pagans" which translation may be heavily influenced by the immediate context of the phrase "dumb idols" in the same verse (1 Cor 12:2). In all other occurrences of the term ἔθνη/*ethnē* in the New Testament, the NASV translates it "Gentiles" or "nations."

At the time of Paul's writing 1 Corinthians, there must have still been a consequential proportion of the congregation comprised of Jewish or "God-fearer" backgrounds because of Paul's address to topics that would greatly concern them, such as the consumption of "meat sacrificed to idols" (1 Cor 8–10). There must have still been a significant enough percentage of Jews and Gentile proselytes for Paul to urge Corinthian congregants not to undo their circumcision (1 Cor 7:17–18), known as epispasm. Also as mentioned earlier, the Corinthian congregants seemed to have had a good grasp of the Hebrew Scriptures from the outset of its founding, which concurs with their origination from the adjacent Jewish synagogue. Based on Paul's Hebrew Scripture illustrations, examples, allusions and the way he frames issues in the Corinthian letters, a consequential, continuing Jewish presence cannot be denied.

Though Latin was the official language in Corinth (Kent, 1966:18; Engels, 1990:67–74), the urban masses were of a diverse ethnicity such as Greeks, Jews, Egyptians, Syrians, Anatolians, and Phoenicians (Engels, 1990: 70–71). Archaeologically salvaged sherds of pottery or small pieces of stone that have writing scratched onto them and lead curse tablets from the first century AD in Corinth are almost entirely in Greek (Winter, 2001:14), so that would have been the trade language, used as a medium of basic communication by people in Corinth whose native tongues may have been different (Kent, 1966:18; Engels, 1990:67–74). So even if their mother tongue was not intelligible to another person they needed to converse with, some dialect of Greek, probably Doric, served as that bridge language. Nevertheless, from what social level did the Corinthian believers come from?

Some hypothesize that anywhere from 68–99 percent of the Roman Empire's population was poor, with defining poverty as: "the poor are those living at or near subsistence level, whose prime concern it is to obtain the minimum food, shelter, and clothing necessary to sustain life, whose lives are dominated by the struggle for physical survival" (Garnsey and Woolf, 1989:153). There were famines in mid-first-century Greece and the Greek East, with possibly one at Corinth in the early fifties AD (Winter, 2001:216–25). The economy of Corinth was dependent on trade, and the urban city and its immediate surrounding area could not supply sufficient food for the population of Corinth (Williams, 1993:31–33, 38).

Current scholarship has correctly drawn attention to this poverty in the environs of Corinth. However, taking our cue from the qualified language of 1 Corinthians 1:26, that even though, in their midst, "there were not many wise according to the flesh, not many mighty, not many noble," the implication is that there were some Corinthian believers in those categories (Theissen, 1982:72). These representatives of the upper class were a dominant minority in the congregation (Theissen, 1982:73).

Because of the resulting social divisions among the Christ believers in Corinth and the seeming, inordinate influence of a small elite group within the church, who were prejudiced against their social inferiors, a number of scholars see class discrimination at the root of most of the problems addressed in this epistle (Theissen, 1982; Chow, 1992; Clarke, 1993; Martin, 1995; Meeks, 1983). Meggitt (1998) counters this prevailing perspective. Yet Paul's remarks, about the composition of the Corinthian assembly (1 Cor 1:26-29), do support the dominant view that within the Corinthian ἐκκλησία (ekklēsia) there were some members of status, and some of the individuals whom Paul names appear to be in a higher tier of Corinthian society. For example, in writing from Corinth to the Roman believers, the Apostle Paul refers to Gaius (1:14), who must have been a man of substantial means in order to "host" Paul and "the whole [Corinthian] church" in his house (cf. Rom 16:23; this "Gaius" would likely be the same "Titius Justus" referred to in Acts 18:7. Whether this was a "hosting" of the "whole church" every week or a less frequent assembling together of all the home groups to this one location, we know not.) Nevertheless, Gaius must have had a large house or villa because the Corinthian congregation was large, as implied in Acts 18:10 ("many people" λαός πολὺς/*laos polys*).

If Crispus and, subsequently, Sosthenes were ἀρχισυνάγωγοι/ *archisynagōgoi* (rulers) of the synagogue, as previously discussed in this section (cf. Acts 18), they must have been from wealthy families (as previously noted the title ἀρχισυνάγωγος/*archisynagōgos* normally infers financial patronage of the synagogue). Additionally, the Erastus who sends greetings from Corinth to the Roman believers (Rom 16:23) is designated as "city treasurer" (Kent, 1966:100; Meeks, 1983:58–59). It is pretty uncommon for Paul to mention the roles and vocations of fellow believers, but it does give us a glimpse into the social stratification of the Corinthian congregation, with a few such elevated individuals having a significant leadership impact in respect to the body of believers across the city of Corinth.

Corinthian believers having cases against one another in the secular courts (1 Cor 6:1–8) may have been the wealthy patrons of the respective house gatherings competing with one another for greater overall prestige. Those with "knowledge" who were insensitive to the qualms of their "weaker brethren" in respect to food sacrificed to idols (1 Cor 8–10) could have been individuals of higher status not wanting to break off contact with their secular social peers by a strict separatist position. The discriminatory conduct against poorer members by the well-to-do surrounding the communal meal as part of the Corinthian Lord's Supper memorialization (1 Cor 11:17–34) was a prominent display of the social inequality among Corinthian believers. Because of the disparity of wealth and status within the Corinthian groups of believers, there was serious potential for inflated egos, snobbery, pomposity, and prideful posturing as Epiphanius indicated.

In concluding this section on the composition of the Corinthian congregation, it is worth reiterating that in Paul's day the congregations of believers had to meet in private homes. The residential sectors of Corinth have for the most part not been excavated, but archaeologists have carefully studied a suburban first-century villa in nearby Anaploga (Furnish, 1988:27). Only 30 or 40 people could have assembled in that spacious house, so the Corinthian congregation was probably comprised of subgroups which only amalgamated periodically (Furnish, 1988:27). Murphy-O'Connor (2002:153–161) suggests that this may have contributed to the factions which became more pronounced when the whole Corinthian body of believers had to crowd into one house for the Lord's Supper.

3.4 ARAMAIC INFLUENCE ON CORINTHIAN ASSEMBLY

Before the Common Era, Aramaic (and its Syriac dialect) became a major language to the East of what's today termed Israel, while Greek was in a similar position West of Israel (Egypt, Asia Minor, Greece, Italy, etc.). (Mendels, 2011:49, 50). It's not outside the realm of possibility that Jews and others from the East would have carried Aramaic with them if they migrated to the West where Greek held sway. However, aside from this conjecture, there is no research material that points to any role of consequence for Aramaic in Corinth in the first century AD. Therefore, it would seem, for the purposes of this study, that compared to Greek and Roman influence, the Aramaic would have been a much lesser influence on the Corinthian assembly of Christ believers.

If Aramaic had influence in the Corinthian congregation of believers, it would have been in the aggregate, indirectly, and in combination with other Mediterranean linguistic minorities. Since the time of Corinth's re-establishment with a few hundred people sent from Italy by Julius Caesar in about 43 BC, it became a leading city, by the time the Corinthian believers' congregation began, and became Greece's largest city by the end of the first century AD (Pawlak, 2013:158). The significant population growth came because of "migration from close and far corners of the Mediterranean world" (Pawlak, 2013:158). These people from all over the Mediterranean world made it a buoyant and ethnically diverse city. Pawlak (2013:160) therefore counsels: "Multi-ethnicity leads to cultural diversity, so caution should be called for whenever we try to classify Corinth using the terms 'Roman' or 'Greek.'" So, although Roman and Greek cultures dominated, the intermingling of various other language groups was probably part of the amalgam that created the Corinthian γλῶσσαι (languages/tongues) challenge that required rules to be laid down for its resolution to the benefit of the growing and diverse congregation.

Mendels (2011:49–54, 68) aptly develops the contradistinction of Hebrew and Aramaic in the East and Greek and Latin dominance in the West and the reason why Paul went West. However, there's a reverse irony in the infrequency of Hebrew use in the Western Diaspora (that is west of modern-day Israel), of which Corinth was a part. The use of the Hebrew original and related Aramaic expositions and early versions of the Peshitta were routinely read in the East (Mendels, 2011:50). The commonness of Hebrew in the synagogues of the East (east of modern-day Israel) meant that the use of Hebrew was no big deal, whereas in the Western Diaspora, with Greek and Latin dominating, and the use of Hebrew being not so readily understood and a more rare commodity, an individual with some facility in that "holy tongue" of Hebrew (Rajak, 2009:14; Joosten, 2017:46) would more easily stand out and would impress others not conversant in the perceived sacred and original language of the Older Testament.

3.5 GREEK INFLUENCE ON CORINTHIAN ASSEMBLY

The ancient tradition, from approximately 700 BC to the first century AD was to classify the many Greek dialects into three basic groups, namely Attic-Ionic, Aeloic and Doric (Karali, 2007: 392). Some scholars incline to add a fourth group, lesser known, referring to it as Arcado-Cypriot (Karali, 2007:393). These four groups, with their multiple variants, is what is meant by the classical Greek languages. Suffice to say there was no uniformity and indeed a competitiveness among the different dialects until the Hellenistic/Alexandrian *koine* began to have an impact and slowly began to erode the predecessor dialects in any given locale. Even as late as the first century AD and beyond, there was a jockeying for pre-eminence among the various dialects still surviving (Bubenik, 2007:482).

It is an established fact in the history of the Greek dialects that during Hellenistic times, under the Achaean and Aetolian Leagues, an Achaean Doric *koine* appeared, which formed the basis of all Doric dialects, which retarded the spread of the Attic-based Hellenistic/Alexandrian *koine* Greek into Western Greece of which Corinth was a part (Buck, 1900:193).

Dosuna (2007:444) writes of the Doric/Dorian Greek (Δωρισμός/ *Dōrismós*), also known as West Greek, which was a group of ancient Greek dialects spoken in a vast area, that included northern Greece, most of the Peloponnese (Achaea, Elis, Messenia, Laconia, Argolid, Aegina, Corinth, and Megara), the southern Aegean, as well as the colonies of some of the aforementioned regions, in Cyrene, Magna Graecia, the Black Sea, the Ionian Sea and the Adriatic Sea. It was also spoken in the Greek sanctuaries of Dodona (Epirus), Delphi (Phocis), and Olympia (Elis), as well as at the four Panhellenic festivals; the Isthmian (Corinth), Nemean (Nemea), Pythian (Delphi), and Olympic Games (Olympia) (Dosuna, 2007:444).

Of those numerous Doric Greek dialects functioning at the time of the first century AD, the Corinthian dialect was one of the several variants (Dosuna, 2007:444). The Corinthian dialect was obviously spoken on the Isthmus of Corinth plus the colonies of Corinth in western Greece like Leucas, Ambracia and others, and at the trade route settlements such as Apollonia in southern Illyria all the way to Italy from the Gulf of Corinth (Dosuna, 2007:445). The significant place accorded to the Doric Greek dialect in Corinth is seen in the account of first-century orator, Favorinus, who had fallen out of favour with the Corinthian authorities and had his statue displaced. In what has become known as the *Corinthian Oration* (Oration 37), Favorinus spoke with high praise for the Doric language to impress the locals so they'd lobby the authorities to reinstall his statue in a conspicuous location in Corinth (Dio Chrysostom, 1946:25).

The misunderstandings that can develop in new cultural settings with a dialect difference would possibly be paralleled by the account of Paul and Barnabas in Acts 14:8ff where at Lystra there was serious miscommunication with the locals who spoke the Lycaonian/Lycian language. "The Lycian [Lycaonian] alphabet is of Greek origin with slight modifications and with certain letters assigned to a different use" (Adiego, 2007:765). It would seem that "the Lycaonian language," (possibly influenced by the Greek masculine name Lycaon) of the towns of Lystra and Derbe, was possibly a Greek dialect in view of the populace thinking Barnabas and Paul were the Greek gods Zeus and Hermes come down from the heavens. Even if not a Greek dialect, the Greek language and Lycaonian/Lycian language are related, both being Indo-European (Brixhe, 2007:926). The priest of the Greek god Zeus, whose temple was near at hand, wanted to put garlands on Paul and Barnabas and sacrifice oxen to them. Once they understand what was going on, with great difficulty, Paul and Barnabas managed to restrain the crowds from so doing.

Based on research, Bubenik (2007:482) attests that, "The 'strict' Doric dialects of Laconian, Messenian, Cretan, and Cyrenaean proved to be the most stubborn in ceding their place to Helenistic *koine*." We don't find any purely Hellenistic *koine* inscriptions in Cyrenaica until the second century AD (Bubenik, 2007:482–483). It could be argued that the regional power Cyrenaica may be an outlier because it is a federation of Greek colonies in North Africa centered on the city of Cyrene and known as an important cultural and intellectual center of the Hellenistic world. However, the Greek island of Rhodes is clear evidentiary testimony to the survival of the "middle" Doric dialects, with more than half of the public inscriptions discovered there being in a "middle" Doric dialect, during the entire Hellenistic period, from the third century BC to the third century AD (Bubenik, 2007:483). On this Greek island, "middle" Doric dialects, peculiar to a particular locality or district, persisted right through until the third century AD (Bubenik, 2007:483).

The Hellenistic *koine* gradually supplanted the Doric vernaculars but for awhile a number of regional *koinai* developed (Dosuna, 2007:446). Dosuna's research (2007:446) indicates that,

> Laconian was the dialect [in the Spartan state] that offered the greatest resistance. There is both epigraphic and literary evidence that attests to the persistence of the vernacular in the fifth century A.D. These testimonies are corroborated by the survival of modern Tsakonian.

So, it varied in the Aegean Sea area. In Crete, once the Hellenistic *koine* gained momentum in the first century AD, there are almost no dialectal inscriptions anywhere on the island (Bubenik, 2007:482)

Bubenik (2007:485), cross-referencing Hodot (1976), reports that: "The Aeolic speaking communities proved to be quite stubborn in clinging to their old dialects. In Lesbos the dialect continued to be used in inscriptions until the first century AD."

From the fifth century BC onwards, Attic Greek became the dialect of all educated Greek rhetoricians (Panayotou, 2007:409).

As Hellenic culture began expanding under Philip of Macedon in the middle of the fourth century BC, the Attic dialect started spreading geographically, eventually developing into a Hellenistic *koine*, challenging the other Greek dialects for prominence (Woodard, 2004, 614). This Hellenistic period of Greek continued until the fourth century AD (Woodard, 2004, 614). There is an excellent visual representation of these competing Greek dialects of that era, on a map prior to the page 650 section, "Greek dialects," in The Cambridge Encyclopedia of the World's Ancient Languages (edited by Roger Woodard, 2004, Cambridge University Press). Depicting this dialectal contention, the same map can be found prior to the page 50 section, "Greek dialects," of The Ancient Languages of Europe (edited by Roger Woodard, 2008, Cambridge University Press).

Similar understanding of this diversity of Greek dialects at that time can also be seen on a colored re-drawn map (https://commons.wikimedia.org/wiki/File:AncientGreekDialects_(Woodard)_en.svg). On that insightful map, note that Corinth, of Doric Greek dialect, is in very close proximity to several other Greek dialects, namely, Attic, Ionic, Aeolic, Arcado-Cypriot, Achaean and Northwest Greek. Keep in mind that there were also subdialects of the various major dialects.

The gradual divergence of the *koine* Greek from the Greek of Plato and Demosthenes was viewed as a degradation of the classic Greek by an influential school known as the Atticists, who incessantly castigated the use of *koine* forms by writers (Newton, 2018).

> Atticism is the name of the sweeping attempts to revive the use of the Attic dialect, at the expense of the already established Hellenistic Koine, in speech writing (oratory) and literature, in accordance with precepts derived from the canon of the ten orators and from the main representatives of Old Comedy. The works of the orators were viewed as the epitome of terse, clear, and effective (i.e., "classical") style, while the comic writers' elegant and graceful language was considered a repository of the purest Attic dialect (Kazazis, 2007:1200).

Thus, a rift developed between the everyday spoken language and an archaized written language (Newton, 2018). "It became fashionable to publish manuals of 'good usage' in which the Attic equivalents of *koine* innovations were recommended as models for the student's imitation" (Newton, 2018). On the part of some, this would have led to superiority complexes and arrogance and displays of prideful posturing, pretentiousness, and snobbery.

> The chronological framework of Atticism: the movement's initial phase occurs just before the time of Christ, when its proponents, still fostering primarily literary aspirations, established a beachhead in the rhetorical schools, which had already been initiated in it, and completely short-circuited creative prose writing. Its high point (in its expanded version, as a language movement *par excellence*) coincided with the so-called Second

Sophistic movement (a term coined by Philostratus), from the final years of the first century AD . . . (Kazazis, 2007:1200).

Atticism waged war against the acquiescent style of contemporary rhetoricians and its crude sounds and extolled the ancient linguistic glory (Kazazis, 2007:1202). The general prevalence of Atticism was such that not a single writer of the first century AD escaped its influence (Kazazis, 2007:1203). Because the biblical author Luke's writing style is more polished and classical than that of Matthew and Mark, there is the suggestion that some parts of his Gospel are also in Atticistic Greek (Sandmel, 1978:260). Those, who customarily used a more rhetorical and flamboyant style, felt more comfortable in the Atticist camp and so adopted those Attic conventions (Kazazis, 2007:1204).

A pointed criticism of Atticism by a Greek philosopher of the first century was, "What is the value of Atticism, when the words are as if shrouded by darkness and the intervention of others is needed to bring their meaning to light?" (Kazazis, 2007:1204). That's a pretty telling statement if we keep the background of 1 Corinthians 14 and the Epiphanius thesis in mind.

It's well documented that an Atticizing effect was achieved through the wide circulation of specialized Atticist lexica by Tryphon and Irenaeus into the first century, and subsequent to that by lexica of Harpocration, Pollux, and Moeris, with no shortage of anonymous "rhetorical" lexica, compiled either according to writer or work (Kazazis, 2007:1205).

The Epiphanius text, at the center of this book's thesis, and cited in the first chapter, refers to the use of Attic, Aeolic and Doric Greek, which squares with the ancient tradition to the first century (Karali, 2007:392). There was no uniformity and indeed a competitiveness. Even as late as the first century AD and beyond, there was a jockeying for pre-eminence among the various dialects with their multiple variants. Added to that dynamic was the Atticism, still widely promoted in the first century AD, which reinforced a more flamboyant rhetorical style (Kazazis, 2007:1204). Hence, the previous Greek-dialect maps referenced above would be no contradiction with the Greek dialect depiction of the first century AD or the Epiphanius thesis.

As a newly re-established city, with opportunities to be upwardly mobile, Corinth was like a magnet to draw a diversity of peoples and languages. It's very significant that Corinth was almost at the center of where various Greek dialects converged.

With this backdrop, it's likely that in Paul's Corinthian surroundings of the first century AD, he had to be diplomatic about the competing Greek dialects, without appearing to favor a particular dialect to prevail in the translating within the congregational meetings. He didn't want to alienate these different groups.

The Apostle Paul wanted to establish beneficial guidelines for the Hebraic Jews, Hellenistic Jews and Gentile Greeks to learn the Hebrew Older Testament and grow in their new-found faith. The use of the Hebrew language and Greek dialects was an issue, but mutual edification was the primary concern of the Apostle Paul.

3.6 ROMAN INFLUENCE ON CORINTHIAN ASSEMBLY

The city of Corinth's dominant Roman influence is indicated by a vast majority of its public inscriptions which appear only in Latin (Millis, 2010:38–53). "Latin was the language that belonged to the western side of the Mediterranean and the Romans" (Ong, 2016:169).

Latin-speaking migrants from Italy who settled in the eastern provinces of the Roman Empire in the first century AD were referred to as *Italikoi, Italoi or Rhomaioi* according to the epigraphical evidence (Souris & Nigdelis, 2007:899). These *Italikoi* settled in mainland Greece, the Aegean islands, and on the coast of Asia Minor, engaging mainly in trade and banking, in increasing numbers, after the Roman civil wars ended, when Emperor Augustus stabilized the political situation throughout the empire (Souris & Nigdelis, 2007:899).

The other large group of Latin-speaking migrants were veterans of the Roman army or groups from the lower social classes of Rome and other cities on the Italian peninsula, who were sent to colonize pre-existing Greek cities like Corinth, Patrae, Pella, Alexandria, Antioch, Cremna, Lystra in Asia Minor and Philippi in the Balkans (Souris & Nigdelis, 2007:900). In all these colonies, the Latin language of these incoming migrants gradually gave way to Greek, but not until the beginning of the second century AD (Souris & Nigdelis, 2007:900).

Of the surviving, public dedicatory inscriptions in Corinth from the time period of Emperor Augustus to Nero (27 BC–68 AD), 73 are in Latin, with only 3 in Greek (Kent, 1966:18–19). This disparity is probably because it reflected Corinth's social and governing elite (Meeks, 1983:47) and the fact that Latin was the official language in the city, Corinth being a Roman colony and the capital of the senatorial province of Achaia (Kent, 1966:18; Engels, 1990:67–74).

Corinth was typical of pre-existing Greek cities, with Roman colonists settling there in large numbers, as a consequence of which Latin became widely used as evidenced in the colony's resolutions and dedications to the emperors, to officials and to Roman deities (Souris & Nigdelis, 2007:900). In Corinth, Greek was limited to epitaphs of those of Greek origin and to dedications to particular eastern deities (Souris & Nigdelis, 2007:900). In Corinth, "The predominance of Latin began to decline perceptibly in the second century [AD], especially from Hadrian's time" (Souris & Nigdelis, 2007:900).

Rome's Latin language reached all the way over to the land of Israel as evidenced by Latin words in the Gospels (Ong, 2016:169).

Safeguarding and transmitting one's ancestral customs was a core value in Roman society (Goodman, 1996:4–6). This is what protected the Judaean and Jewish institutions and customs because they were regarded as reaching far enough back into antiquity. Under the umbrella of ancient Judaism, the Apostle Paul and the Christ-believer congregations were initially shielded to a degree (Acts 18:12–17). This Roman protection played out in that Acts account in favor of Paul and the Corinthian group of Christ-believers (Acts 18:12–17), with broader, positive legal precedent for similar Pauline-planted congregations throughout the Roman Empire.

"Jews frequently appealed to Rome in order to counter attempts by municipal authorities to undermine their status" (Levine, 2005:134). This is seen in Acts 25:11 when Paul, a Jew, but in this case even more importantly, as a Roman citizen, makes that significant pronouncement, "I appeal to Caesar" immediately after the Roman Governor Festus suggested that Paul appear in Jerusalem for trial (Acts 25:9). As the reader, we already know that the previous Roman Governor Felix left Paul languishing in prison for two years "to do the Jews a favor" (Acts 24:27). When the change-over to the new Governor Festus occurred, narrator Luke tips us off that, like his predecessor, Festus was "wishing to do the Jews a favor" (Acts 25:9). Paul realized he'd not receive a fair trial if conducted by Festus, especially if transferred to Jerusalem. Thus, Paul utilized that ancient, cherished right of a Roman citizen and exercised his right of appeal to the Emperor (Acts 25:11).

The Earliest View of New Testament Tongues

In Acts 16:37, Paul and Silas, having Roman citizenship (cf. Acts 22:28), apparently had the right of a public hearing and protection against a scourging. Paul draws attention to these rights, when he replied to the policemen of the chief magistrates, by saying, "They have *beaten us in public without trial*, men who are Romans."

The Corinthian Christ-believers were also affected and unfortunately influenced by the Roman culture surrounding them, which drew specific rebukes from Paul as he directed a counter-cultural message against these osmotic and negative influences. Competitively litigating in the Roman courts was the mood of Corinth to which Paul forcefully objected that it should not be occurring between Christ-believers (1 Cor 6:1–8).

The surrounding Greco-Roman culture had the societal-shaping "patron/client" dynamic which the Apostle Paul assiduously avoided in Corinth (cf. 1 Cor 9:18). Paul didn't have a financial-sponsoring patron to whom he was beholden, as he didn't want accusations of ulterior financial-greed motives levelled against him.

Roman women enjoyed relative independence compared to those of many other ancient cultures (Cantarella, 1987:140–141). By the time of 44 BC (Johnston, 1999:33–34), in a "free" marriage, being more the custom, a woman remained under her father's authority, when she moved into her husband's home, but there she did not have to conduct her daily life under her father's surveillance and her husband had no legal power over her (Frier and McGinn, 2004:19–20). So, in Roman marriage structures, women had a subordinate rank. However, though the broader Roman society didn't permit women to attain official political power, it allowed them to be involved in business (Frier and McGinn, 2004:461).

In the New Testament, Lydia, from Thyatira, is an example of a successful Roman businesswoman, a seller of purple fabrics, whom Paul and his mission team met in Philippi. After Paul preaches by the Philippian riverside, Lydia, a worshipper of God, comes to faith in the Lord Jesus and immediately becomes a friend and hostess of Paul. Lydia and her whole household were baptized, and a group of believers began meeting in her house (Acts 16:15, 40). By hosting the new believers in her home, Lydia likely became the group administrator and helped shepherd the group in its early days. Because of her previous experience as an effective leader and entrepreneur, Lydia would have easily slipped into these new roles. The Philippian congregation became generous partners with the

Apostle Paul in the propagation of the gospel, and Lydia would have undoubtedly played a central role in that respect (Phil 1:3–5).

The Roman political system allowed the involvement of citizen men only—as voters, politicians, representatives, and magistrates, with many women having "citizen rights" but none having the vote, irrespective of their wealth or their standing in Roman society (Bauman, 1992: 8, 10, 15, 105). There would have been nothing preventing women from persuading their husbands or the men in their lives and thus exercising indirect political influence. From the last decades of the first century BC onward, opportunities for women, slaves and freedmen increased, which allowed them to exercise influence behind the scenes (Bauman, 1992:8, 10, 15, 105). In the book of Acts, Luke alludes to such when he refers to "women of prominence" (Acts 13:50) and "leading women" (Acts 17:4).

The fact that women in Roman society who were well off, ran businesses and the affairs of a large household which included extended family and servants and slaves, may be the cause of the misunderstandings that developed when similar women of status hosted a gathering of new believers in their home. This would have been perceived as a private gathering and not a public event or venue wherein the women would have been more discreet and circumspect in one's speech and actions, especially to avoid causing offense. It may have been perceived that the unobtrusiveness required in the public square was not incumbent in their own domestic situation where guests were present. Therefore, the hostess woman and her female peers may have judged it not imprudent to "let down their hair" figuratively and literally. This may be the dynamic in 1 Corinthians 14.

To say whether the idol worship issue in Corinth was specifically a Roman influence is outside the pale of this book's thesis. At most, we can say that the idol worship was a Greco-Roman influence, which took a notable amount of space in Paul's exhortative correspondence, specifically subsumed in 1 Corinthians chapter 8 and chapter 10. Only if there was Emperor worship can we categorize it as a singular Roman religious influence. There very well may have been some pressure in respect to imperial worship in Corinth. However, in Paul's two canonized letters to the Corinthians, there are no clear-cut statements or strong allusions in that regard, so conjecture will be avoided.

At a minimum, it's safe to say that Corinth and the Corinthian congregations/house gatherings were affected by Roman language, law, and culture, as in the examples above.

3.7 DELPHINE ORACLE INFLUENCE ON CORINTHIAN ASSEMBLY

No doubt pagan forces were hard at work to disrupt the spiritual growth of the Christ believers at Corinth. However, to identify those specific pagan forces and to determine to what degree they influenced that congregation, has been a matter of contentious scholarly debate over the past 120 years. Early in the last century, the proponents of the History of Religions school promulgated the view that Christ believers of the first century AD were significantly influenced by the Hellenistic mystery religions (Hatch, 1890). These Gottingen academics promoted the concept that Christianity was mostly a product of its time with Christians borrowing and adapting ideas from the culture(s) around them to create their message and construct their claims about Christ. In a similar vein, Reitzenstein (1978; first published in 1910) sought to establish the direct dependence of early Christianity on Hellenistic, Mandaean, and Iranian mythology and ritual. Some years later, Clemen (1931:342) asserted that primitive Christianity acquired concepts and rites from the mystery sects.

Schweitzer (1950:189) contended that Pauline Christianity was not influenced by the mystery religions. Subsequently, Metzger (1968:11) went further when he wrote that "it is not only possible but probable that in certain cases the influence moved in the opposite direction" with the Greco-Roman cults imitating the new Christ movement in order to stem their losses.

The major Greco-Roman cult, which would have been known to the Corinthian Christ believers, was that of Apollo, for whose worship there were several temples in Corinth and the famous shrine at Delphi, not so far distant (Broneer, 1951:84). The slave girl who harassed Paul and his companions in Philippi, on their way to Corinth, had the spirit of a "python" (Πύθωνα/*Pythōna*; Acts 16:16–18). Bruce (1954:332) describes the Philippian slave girl "as a person inspired by Apollo," the god particularly associated with the giving of oracles, who was worshipped as the 'Pythian' god at the oracular [Apollo] shrine of Delphi. Apollo was especially associated with oracles (Bruce, 1954:332). The Oracle at the Apollo shrine in Delphi was a woman who was much in demand by people who wished to have their fortunes told (Bruce, 1954:332).

It was argued that unintelligible *glossolalia* was displayed in the Dionysus and Cybele mystery religions and at the famous Delphi Apollo shrine (Forbes, 1995:162). However, the Delphine Oracle, who was always a woman, uttered speech that was *intelligible* (Forbes, 1995:162). In summarizing his search for ecstatic and unintelligible speech in the Hellenistic world prior to the Christian era, Forbes (1995:168) emphatically states that the speech of the woman, named Pythia, the Oracle of Apollo at Delphi, "was neither 'ecstatic' nor unintelligible" but was commonly cryptic and obscure in archaic and poetic form. The "enthusiastic" worship of Dionysus and Cybele included ritual and invocation which was also *intelligible* (Forbes, 1995:168).

In view of the evidence that Forbes marshalled as to the intelligibility of the Delphine Oracle, it's difficult to then argue convincingly that the supposed counterpart speech in the Corinthian assembly of Christ believers was unintelligible. From this perspective, the Delphine Oracle influence on the Corinthian Assembly appears to be negligible, as not only was her speech intelligible (Forbes, 1995:168), but in response to the questions put to her, she cryptically told the fortunes of the petitioners (Bruce, 1954:332). Predicting the futures of congregational members is not reported anywhere as part of the normative or expected congregational life among the Christ believers in Corinth.

3.8 LOW LITERACY INFLUENCE ON CORINTHIAN ASSEMBLY

It is estimated that during the first century, in the Roman Empire, only 10–15% of the population was literate (Hezser, 2001:23). This means that the public reading of Scripture was a vital necessity. Chancey (2005:143; cf. Gamble, 1995:4) proposes literacy rates as low as 10 percent in the Roman Empire, with the possibility of it being higher in the urban areas. Harris (1989:328-330) makes the case that in the Greco-Roman period, only a small percentage of the population could read and write. This aspect of the culture of that time points to the reason for the *glōssai* (languages/tongues) dilemma in 1 Corinthians 14 and serves to support the Epiphanius thesis that *glōssa* (singular) or *glōssai* (plural) means earthly language/languages.

Dr. Luke hints at the degree of literacy or lack thereof in first-century Israel, in recording the comment on the education level of no less than the Apostles Peter and John, two initial leaders of the Christ believer movement: "Now as they observed the confidence of Peter and John and understood that they were uneducated and untrained men, they were marvelling . . . (Acts 4:13). Mind you, this may simply reflect the elitism of the Judaean rulers, elders, scribes and those of high-priestly descent interrogating these two disciples of Jesus (Acts 4:5–6). A similar comment was made of Jesus in John 7:15 where some Jews were marvelling at Jesus' articulate teaching: "The Jews therefore were marvelling, saying, 'How has this man become learned, having never been educated?'" So, again it could indicate the snobbery of the Judaean upper class leaders toward those who hadn't the formal training of their rabbinical schools. It is interesting to note that this characterization was never made of the Apostle Paul, even by his most virulent enemies, because Paul had been trained in the rabbinical school of the esteemed Gamaliel. Even a skeptical Roman Governor Festus paid a backhanded compliment to Paul when he said to Paul, "Your great learning is driving you mad" (Acts 26:24).

According to Luke 4:16–20, Jesus could read. However, we have no clear indication to what degree his disciples were literate. However, in conjecturing the ideal on literacy for Jews, Seltman (2015:18) asserts that:

> A significant feature distinguishing the Jews of this time from other people amongst whom they lived was their much higher literacy rate. Jewish men had to be ready to read aloud in the synagogues a portion of the Torah or the Prophets every Sabbath and by the time of Jesus the vast mass of ordinary Jewish men had been literate for, perhaps, a thousand years. Women were expected to be able to read at least enough to enable them to fulfil their religious duties and to deal with things connected with marriage, menstruation and so forth.

Perrot (1988:149) emphasizes that ". . . the biblical traditions were committed to writing, that was surely to have them read, and publicly at that. Writing calls for reading and in ancient times reading was done out loud before a group."

In view of the high illiteracy of the first century AD (Chancey, 2005:143; Gamble, 1995:4), it makes sense for the Apostle Paul to tell his protégé Timothy to "give attention to the *public* reading of *Scripture*" (1 Tim 4:13). It is therefore also logical for John in writing his revelation, to say, "Blessed is he [singular] who reads and those [plural] who hear the words of the prophecy . . . " (Rev 1:3). In other words, in that first-century low-literacy context (Chancey, 2005:143; Gamble, 1995:4), only a few "read" and most would have to simply "hear" the words of the Hebrew Scriptures.

Justin Martyr (c. 90–c. 165 AD), also known as Justin the Philosopher, was an early Christian apologist and philosopher (Hanegraaff, 2012:20; Wagner, 1994:158). Justin Martyr (ANF, Vol. 1, *The First Apology of Justin*, Chapter 67, p. 186) refers to this public reading:

> And on the day called Sunday, all who live in cities or in the country gather together to one place, and the memoirs of the apostles or the writings of the prophets are read, as long as time permits; then, when the reader has ceased, the president verbally instructs, and exhorts to the imitation of these good things.

In addition, even if a person could read, there was the huge problem of access to the Scriptures. Many western world twenty-first-century persons project their contemporary experience back into the first century AD. In the present western world a person has ready access to multiple versions of hard-copy and electronic versions of the Bible. We can project it via Power Point in college and seminary classes and Sunday church services. The reality is that ordinary first century AD persons did not own a copy of a portion of the Bible, let alone the whole Bible, and this would not change for more than 1500 years until the invention of the printing press.

Richards (2004:169–170) emphasizes that the production of letters and books in the first-century world was a costly task. The cost of papyrus and a professional scribe for the Apostle Paul's First Epistle to the Corinthians would have been an expense of approximately \$2,108 US dollars in 2004 AD currency (Richards, 2004:169). The 2.45 denars scribal labor cost (unskilled workers in Paul's day earned a half denar per day) would be per copy (Richards, 2004:169). The assumption is for the scribe/secretary to do an initial draft and revision on reusable material, for which Paul would not be charged papyrus material cost, and then a final copy would be scribed for sending, plus a retained copy made for Paul's notebook, as a consequence of which Paul would be charged labor on four copies (Richards, 2004:169).

To those questioning the expense of a scribe/secretary, it must be stressed that, in keeping with the first century AD, Paul would not have "written" out his own letters to the Diaspora congregations of Christ believers. "It is difficult for modern Westerners to separate literacy from the ability to write" because to us "literacy" implies knowing how to read and write (Richards, 2004: 161). The typical literate person of the first century could write, but often only slowly (Richards, 2004:161). As Richards (2004:162) aptly puts it:

> Ancients who were literate often had no particular skill with handwriting. Like modern calligraphy, they considered it a separate skill only somewhat related to literacy. The art of scoring paper, mixing ink, sharpening reeds, and writing beautifully upon the rough surface of a sheet of papyrus, perched upon one's knees were the trained skills of a secretary.

"The author's own writing [Paul's] at the end of the letter often demonstrated that his own handwriting was much inferior to that of the secretary" (Richards, 2004:162). The Apostle Paul, in a self-effacing manner, refers to this in Galatians 6:11 when he writes, "See with what large letters I am writing to you with my own hand" (cf. 1 Cor 16:21; Rom 16:22; Col 4:18; 2 Thess 3:17; Phlm 19).

Of significance here in the matter of "signing" a letter is that the ancient writer did not sign his personal name in a distinctive cursive script to authenticate the letter, as we moderns do (Richards, 2004:162). The first-century author would authenticate the letter in one of three ways:

> (1) the use of a seal (signet) pressed in clay, or (2) a summary of the letter's contents in the author's own handwriting at the end of the letter, or (3) a word of farewell in the author's own handwriting at the end of the letter (Richards, 2004:171).

The Apostle Paul used the latter two options for authenticating his letters as particularly evinced in the respective closing sections (Rom 16:22; 1 Cor 16:21; Gal 6:11; Col 4:18; 2 Thess 3:17; Phlm 19). In Paul's authenticating the Second Epistle to the Thessalonians, he especially draws attention to his own handwriting at the conclusive greeting and notes that "this is a distinguishing mark in every letter; this is the way I write" (2 Thess3:17).

In the ancient world, only the very wealthy and institutions like government archives and the few existing libraries could afford scrolls and manuscript collections. An example of a person with access to wealth would have been the Ethiopian Eunuch who, according to Acts 8:26–35, did not even have in his possession the entirety of the Hebrew Scriptures, but just the scroll of Isaiah. The book of Isaiah, as the Ethiopian Eunuch had, could mount to a cost of approximately 1,100 US dollars, for the parchment alone, in 2004 AD (Richards, 2004:168).

All this to say that it is quite understandable that the copies of the Hebrew Scriptures were held in trust by the synagogue or Christian community. The Jerusalem Temple would have been the primary place where the sanctioned copies of the Hebrew Scriptures were stored.

> Problems related to the transmission of the text and authenticity of various books of the Bible were examined in the Temple; copyists and correctors sat in the Temple and worked to supply books *to those who needed them in the land of Israel and in the Diaspora* [italics emphasis added]. There was a bible in the Temple called 'the book of the court' on the basis of which books were corrected" (Safrai, 1976:905).

Synagogues possessed collections of the Hebrew Scriptures, as shown when Jesus read from the Isaiah scroll provided to him in the Nazareth synagogue (Luke 4:16–17). However, it may be that a synagogue did not even have all the scrolls of the Tanakh (the Older Testament). Typically, individuals did not own these Hebrew Scriptures. Sometimes a very rich person might own some of the scrolls of the Tanakh (Older Testament) as in the above-mentioned case of the Ethiopian Eunuch (Acts 8:26–35).

The Corinthian assembly of Christ believers in the first century AD lived in an oral culture. The vast majority of people of that era were functionally illiterate and relied on the few who could read. Pertinent to this, Runesson (2014:272) comments, in respect to the synagogue context that "public reading and teaching of Torah on Sabbaths is the most prominent. Anyone who had acquired reading skills was allowed to read and expound portions." We know that there were some literate believers within the Corinthian assembly, as Paul alludes to that in 2 Corinthians 1:13: "For we write nothing else to you than what you read and understand..."

We have a very interesting and insightful request made by Paul to Timothy that sheds some further light on this issue. The Apostle Paul requests of Timothy, "When you come bring the cloak which I left at Troas with Carpus, and the books, especially the parchments" (2 Tim

4:13). The cloak was probably requested because Paul was cold in the dank prison in Rome from where he wrote this letter. The "books" may have been copies of Paul's own letters to the congregations he planted. "Ancients kept copies of their own letters for several different purposes. That Paul retained copies of his letters seems a matter of course to scholars of Greco-Roman letter writing" (Richards, 2004:161). However, the most important thing on Paul's mind was "the parchments." Ryrie (1960:246) writes that:

> Although papyrus was the common material used for writing, parchment was reserved for important and precious documents, like the Scriptures. The parchments which Paul was calling for, then, were his own personal copies of Old Testament books and perhaps some New Testament fragments. These had undoubtedly been carefully collected over the years and were probably annotated in the margins by his own hand.

Regarding the wording "especially the parchments" (μαλιστα τας μεμβρανας; Latin *membrana*) in 2 Timothy 4:13, Robertson (1931:632) observed: "These in particular would likely be copies of Old Testament books, parchment being more expensive than papyrus." In the holy city of Jerusalem, Paul was "educated under Gamaliel" (Acts 22:3) who taught the Law and was respected by all the people (Acts 5:34), so it is understandable that Paul would have acquired personal copies of the scrolls of the Hebrew Scriptures.

Even if the Apostle Paul mostly cited the Greek Septuagint, in one of its recensions, is not to say that the Corinthian assembly which Paul left behind used only the Greek Septuagint in one or several of its recensions. If the initial converts were drawn from a "Hebrew" synagogue of Judaean ex-patriots, rather than a Greek-using Hellenistic synagogue, and because there was an unspiritual jockeying for superiority and the clash of ungodly egos, there very well may have been the use of one of the Hebrew versions of the Older Testament in the spawned assembly of Christ believers. A set of the Hebrew scrolls may have been brought over by the converted Corinthian synagogue leader Crispus (or later by the successor synagogue leader Sosthenes of Acts 18:17, if also converted and the same person acknowledged as Paul's co-author in the preface of Paul's first canonical letter to the Corinthians in chapter 1 and verse 1).

Jews of some financial means were known to personally own scrolls of the Hebrew Scriptures and Levine (2005:416) indicates

CULTURAL ANALYSIS

that, in the literary and epigraphical material, an ἀρχισυνάγωγος/ *archisynagōgos* (synagogue ruler) was generally a person of financial means. In addition to being a financial patron (Levine, 2005:416), the ἀρχισυνάγωγος/*archisynagōgos* (synagogue ruler) was the one in charge of worship (Acts 13:15).

3.9 CONCLUSIONS

As seen in section 3.1, with the early believers being regarded as a sect of Judaism ("the Way"), at this early stage of development, it's very likely that the assembly of Corinthian Christ believers had this self-perception as well, with the essential differentiating concept that the Corinthian Christ believers had recognized in Jesus the long-promised Messiah, while their close-at-hand synagogal counterparts had not come to that recognition, as yet. It would make sense that these newly formed groups of believers in Jesus would be significantly susceptible to influence from the motherland and Jerusalem, in particular, in that the Messiah and Saviour in whom they believed was a Jewish Galilean who lived, taught, died and rose again there. Neither would it escape their notice that the central book referenced, by the deified Jewish Jesus whom they worshipped and their Jewish church planter Paul, was the Hebrew Scriptures.

For the Jews and Jewish proselytes, "Hebrew would still have remained as the Jewish religious, linguistic symbol and identity marker in the first century CE" (Ong, 2016:183; so also Spolsky, 1997:138 and Joosten, 2017:44–49, 62).

In section 3.2.1 we learned of the rich Hebraistic background and training that the Apostle Paul constantly utilized and in section 3.2.1.1 we learned that the recipients of the Corinthian letters must have been quite familiar with Jewish worship and Older Testament teaching in order to understand the plethora of Hebrew Scripture stories, allusions and inferences which Paul wove into the two epistles to them and which formative influences were reinforced by the half a dozen or more Jewish associates of Paul's who helped develop this Corinthian assembly.

The archaeological/epigraphical evidence cited in the 3.3 "synagogue" section above seems to point to a Hebraic background, which Hebraic cultural trappings would likely be carried over by the initial nucleus in forming the fledgling Christ assembly and have some bearing on the congregational dynamics thereafter.

The Earliest View of New Testament Tongues

Also one may suppose that from such a "synagogue of the Hebrews" at Corinth, the custom of Scripture reading in Hebrew would have migrated over to the Christ assembly (cf. Perrot, 1988:155) and that "the Septuagint translation (or variations thereof) may have been used after the Hebrew reading" (Levine, 2005:159) in the participatory mode of the Pauline Christ assembly in Corinth (cf. 1 Cor 14:26; Sanders,1999:7; 1992:202; Idelsohn, 1932:16). 1 Timothy 4:13–15 highlights Paul's emphasis that, in the pattern of the synagogue, there should be the public reading of the Hebrew Scriptures and explanation of same as a core component in the meetings of Christ believers as part of a "fixed order" of their congregational services in first-century Corinth (1 Corinthians 14:40).

This Jewish DNA, as delineated in section 3.3, would understandably and inevitably have a bearing on the congregational life in Corinth in the years ahead.

In section 3.4, as was pointed out, in the Western Diaspora, of which Corinth was a part, with its Greek and Latin dominating, and the use of Hebrew being less common, an individual with some facility in Hebrew would more easily stand out and would impress others not conversant in the original language of the Older Testament.

In section 3.5, we found that the Epiphanius text squared with the ancient tradition, from approximately 700 BC to the first century BC of classifying the many Greek dialects into three basic groups, namely Attic-Ionic, Aeloic and Doric (Karali, 2007:392) and even as late as the first century AD and beyond, there was a jockeying for pre-eminence among the various Greek dialects still surviving (Bubenik, 2007:482).

With this backdrop, it's likely that in Paul's Corinthian surroundings of the first century AD, he had to be diplomatic about the competing Greek dialects, without appearing to favor a particular dialect to prevail in the translating within the congregational meetings.

Section 3.6 drew attention to the diverse Corinthian ethnic groups, such as Greeks, Jews, Egyptians, Syrians, Anatolians, and Phoenicians (Engels, 1990: 70–71), with Doric Greek being the predominant dialect in Corinth (Kent, 1966:18; Engels, 1990:67–74).

In Section 3.7, we concluded that the Delphine Oracle influence on the Corinthian Assembly, appears to be negligible, as her speech was intelligible (Forbes, 1995:168).

Consonant with the oral culture, low literacy (Chancey, 2005:143; Gamble, 1995:4) and inaccessibility to the Older Testament Scripture scrolls as detailed in section 3.8, hearing the reading and explanation of the Hebrew Scriptures would take on added significance.

There appears to be nothing in this chapter that undermines the unique Epiphanius proposition that the γλώσσαις-speaking in 1 Corinthians 14 was a controversy around the use of the Hebrew Older Testament Scripture and classic Greek dialects in the assembly and the need to interpret into the dominant Greek dialect, so others could be edified. Most sections in this chapter directly or indirectly connect with the thesis of Epiphanius, and those sections which divulged the primacy of the Hebrew language in religious settings and the competitiveness of the classic Greek dialects and resurgence of the elevated Greek classical language, known as Atticism, still being widely promoted in the first century AD, particularly point to the viability of the Epiphanius thesis.

Thus far, the Epiphanius thesis has been shown to be linguistically sound and culturally relevant.

4

Historical Analysis of "Language/Languages"

4.1 POST-APOSTOLIC TIME UNTIL 1516 AD

THIS CHAPTER WILL CONSIST of an historical analysis to assess whether the Epiphanius thesis is explicitly or indirectly contradicted, and if so when, why and by whom. Thus, there will be a targeted culling through the post-apostolic time until 1516 AD, the Reformation period (1517–1648 AD), the post-Reformation time (1649–1905 AD), the modern period—Azusa until the Third Wave (1906–1980 AD) and right up until the present time (1980ff AD), to locate relevant references to γλῶσσα/γλῶσσαι, to gain insight on the meaning of the term(s). In pursuing this chronological, historical analysis, support for the Epiphanius thesis or counter argument may be found, or it may be determined that periods of it are not greatly germane one way or other.

As we shift into the post-apostolic era, it is important to first note that in the apostolic era γλῶσσαι (*glōssai*—plural, meaning "languages/tongues") is only mentioned in two of the earlier books of the New Testament. Dr. Luke refers to γλῶσσαι (*glōssai*—languages/tongues) in his book of Acts. Aside from one use of the term γλῶσσαι, in Romans, where it clearly denotes the organ in the mouth, after 1 Corinthians, the Apostle Paul wrote twelve or more epistles and never again mentioned γλῶσσαι (*glōssai*—languages/tongues). Peter, James, and Jude never

HISTORICAL ANALYSIS OF "LANGUAGE/LANGUAGES"

brought up the subject of γλῶσσαι (*glóssai*—languages/tongues). When the Apostle John uses the terms γλῶσσα/γλῶσσαι (*glóssa/glóssai*) in the book of Revelation, he is clearly referring to language/languages in the normal, earthly sense. However, was there a resurgence of this topic after the New Testament apostolic period?

In this first subsection, there'll be a survey, in chronological order, of what the leaders of the post-apostolic age, 101 AD to the fifth century AD, had to say about γλῶσσα/γλῶσσαι (*glóssa/glóssai*—languages/tongues). In the second subsection, in chronological sequence we'll move through the Middle Ages (late fifth century to the late fifteenth century AD). Then in sequence, there'll be subsections on the Reformation period, the post-Reformation era, the modern times, and right up to the present.

Burgess (1976:16), an Assemblies of God scholar, laments that on this "tongues" matter,

> Pentecostal historians have shown the same aversion to the primary records, with the result that the same stories are repeated again and again—usually without question—and mistakes once made are perpetuated and often compounded.

Burgess (1976:26) also complains of "the inadequacy of the primary records" and how research "effort cannot be expected to yield much data about the layman or the lesser clergy." Burgess (1976:26) re-emphasizes "the need for a study of the primary materials in every period of the history of Pentecostalism, even when our evidence is limited and not entirely credible."

Burgess (1976:18) then goes on to write of discovering Catholic hagiographic ["excessively flattering"] texts (i.e., *Acta sanctorum*—the "Deeds of the Saints," *Analecta Bollandiana, Bibliotheca hagiographica Latina*) and "additional primary *evidence for the outpouring of the Holy Spirit during the Middle Ages* [italics mine] in the publications of certain leading religious orders." Notice that Burgess (1976:18) calls it "additional primary *evidence for the outpouring of the Holy Spirit*" and not primary evidence for γλῶσσαι (*glóssai*—languages/tongues). Burgess (1976:18–19) lists *Monumenta historica Societatis Jesu* and the *Annales minorum*, which is concerned with the Franciscans, and the *Monumenta ordinis Fratrum Praedicatorum historica*, produced by the Dominican order. A note of significant caution should be added here, insofar as reading of this hagiographical material, thus far, appears to

The Earliest View of New Testament Tongues

strain credulity, as possible fact appears to be larded with liberal measures of fiction.

Finally, Burgess (1976:19) recommends, to the historian of medieval Pentecostalism, the inquisitional records and the separate private letters of ecclesiastical leaders regarding heretical charismatics, published by church historians. Although Burgess emphasizes the importance of primary records to his Pentecostal brethren, he indicates no examples of "tongues" in the "primary records" he touts, so we glean no evidence from him on this particular aspect.

For "primary records" research, Burgess (1976:19) also recommends *Migne's Patrologia Latina* and the *Monumenta Germaniae historica*. The *Migne's Patrologia Latina* formed one half of *Migne's Patrologiae Cursus Completus*, the other part being the *Patrologia Graeco* patristic and medieval Greek works. Much of this material can be acquired, without cost, through Christian Classics Ethereal Library (CCEL) http://www.ccel.org/ in English translation.

After an extensive survey, of the primary material, in the volumes of *Migne's Patrologia Graeca*, Blosser and Sullivan (2022: Kindle Location p. 196) report that,

> Of the thirty-four or more passages explicitly referencing the gift of tongues by ecclesiastical writers in the period spanning upwards of the first thousand years of Church history, only seven are popularly cited in support of the new definition [unintelligible non-linguistic vocalizations]. These include Irenaeus, *Against Heresies* (1.13.3), Origen, *Against Celsus* (7.8–9), Eusebius, *Ecclesiastical History* (5.16), Tertullian, *Against Marcion* (5.8), Epiphanius, *Against Heresies* (48.4), Chrysostom, *Homily 29 (on 1 Corinthians)*; and Clement of Alexandria, *Stromata* (1.431.1). The selection is tendentious, to say the least.

In launching into this section, it's also necessary to expose some serious flaws in definition of terms. Williams and Waldvogel's (1975:105) coverage of the "tongues" topic in *The Charismatic Movement* is misleading when it says that "Paul himself had listed glossolalia and its interpretation as only two of many gifts of the Spirit . . ." *Glossolalia* is actually not a term used in the New Testament by the Apostle Paul or any other writer, and was first coined in the English by theological writer, Frederic William Farrar, in 1879 AD (Oxford English Dictionary, 1933:232). The Williams and Waldvogel (1975:105) article is also seriously defective in that they blend into their definition of *glossolalia* (non-earthly language) disparate concepts, even including "swift linguistic acuity" and para-psychological communication. In this manner, making their definition of the non-biblical term *glossolalia* to be a catch-all that goes even further to incorporate *xenolalia* (instantaneously and miraculously given, foreign earthly languages, previously unlearned) and known earthly languages, is singularly unhelpful.

Presumptuousness in regard to definition is quite exhibited in Hunter's (1980:125) statement, at the beginning of his journal article on this subject, when he writes:

> In view of the association of prophecy with tongues-speech in the book of Acts, and since one form of tongues-speech is listed among the charismata enumerated in 1 Cor 12:8–10, wherever the term charismata or various gifts listed in 1 Corinthians 12 are in evidence, especially prophecy, it will be considered to indicate the possibility of the presence of tongues-speech.

Undermining Hunter's (1980:125) position is his previous admission that, "It is difficult to establish objective criteria for determining the presence of tongues-speech where no explicit claim is made regarding its presence or absence."

Other proponents of modern-day "tongues" have this very elastic definition of it. Assemblies of God writer Frodsham (1941:253–262) was one such enthusiast when he lists a number of individuals, from the post-apostolic age and subsequent, who spoke in "tongues," but then his own description sometimes divulged that it was a supposed description of known, earthly languages, miraculously instilled in the speaker and understood by the hearers. Sometimes Frodsham was referring to an incomprehensible language. Sometimes it was a reference to an individual in an ecstasy (Frodsham, 1941:257) or a trance (Frodsham, 1941:262). This kind of omelette description is not helpful to understanding the γλῶσσαι (*glōssai*) of the Corinthian apostolic assembly. Frodsham (1941:256) seems very credulous, to the point of gullibility, about every report of "tongues-speaking" of whatever description or no description and seems to show no discrimination whether it's fantastical stories of a person miraculously and instantaneously speaking numerous, previously unlearned, earthly languages or someone speaking in an incomprehensible language, with no attempt at interpretation, nor singling out persons with a natural aptitude for learning languages.

The Earliest View of New Testament Tongues

In his unquestioning enthusiasm, Frodsham gleaned his stories from exaggerated hagiographical and secondary sources and from the *Darkness to Dawn* fictional tale by Dean Farrar, who apparently had "contemporary authority" to reference "the persecuted Christians in Rome speaking and singing in unknown tongues" (Frodsham, 1941:254). Frodsham (1941:256) refers to Francis Xavier's stupendous language ability and glowingly remarks that Catholic Jesuit order Xavier was "a truly converted man and most remarkable missionary" (Frodsham, 1941:255). Frodsham (1941:253–262) naively recited his exaggerated and secondhand sources and accepted them all uncritically. Frodsham (1941:253–262) indiscriminately cites his post-apostolic examples as support for *glossolalia* ("speaking in tongues") as defined by The Encyclopedia Britannica (1941:254).

4.1.1 Post-Apostolic time until 500 AD

As we turn to find out what the Apostolic Fathers say on the matter of γλῶσσα/γλῶσσαι (*glōssa/glōssai*—languages/tongues), it is important to note their uniform silence on the subject. The most remarkable instance of this silence is with Clement of Rome (c. 35–c. 99 AD). Clement was bishop of Rome in the late first century AD, holding office from 90 AD to his death in 99 AD (Chapman, 1908:13, 16). Clement is considered to be the first Apostolic Father of the Church (Chapman, 1908:12–13). Clement (Lake, 1912; ANF, Vol. 1, *First Epistle to the Corinthians, Clement of Rome*) writes a pastoral letter to the church at Corinth, from where this γλῶσσαι (*glōssai*—languages/tongues) problem surfaced in its infancy. This γλῶσσαι (*glōssai*—languages/tongues) was a significant problem which the Apostle Paul had to address in his first canonical letter to the Corinthian congregation, yet not so many years later, γλῶσσαι (*glōssai*—languages/tongues) does not even get a passing mention by Clement of Rome in his letter to this same congregation (Lake, 1912; ANF, Vol. 1, *First Epistle to the Corinthians, Clement of Rome*). The focus of Clement's letter was the insurrection of some younger men against the elders of the congregation (Lake, 1912; ANF, Vol. 1, *First Epistle to the Corinthians, Clement of Rome*).

Rogers (1965:135) tenders that the wide geographical coverage of the Apostolic Fathers makes their silence on γλῶσσαι/*glōssai* even more significant, with Clement writing from Rome to Corinth; Ignatius of

HISTORICAL ANALYSIS OF "LANGUAGE/LANGUAGES"

Antioch writing to the churches of Ephesus, Magnesia, Tralles, Rome, Smyrna, Philadelphia; Polycarp, bishop of Smyrna, writing to those at Philippi; and Hermas possibly writing from Rome.

It is important to recognize that there is a very telling gap of close to 100 years from the writing of Corinthians/Acts to the first known mention (about 160 AD), by any church figure, of γλῶσσαι/*glōssai* (languages/tongues), subsequent to the Apostolic Age. It is also significant that these first recorded remarks which we have on the issue were by Irenaeus, the Gentile bishop of what is now Lyons, France, far removed from the Judean culture at the time of the first Christian Pentecost and the writing of the first canonical Corinthian epistle. Irenaeus, whose words on the matter appear to have been misconstrued, would have been without an indigenous knowledge of how important the Hebrew language was to the Temple ritual and to the first believers in Jesus who were all Jewish, as noted in the first several sections of chapter 3 of this book. By the middle of the second century AD, the number of Gentiles in the Church swamped the number of Jews. The Gentile and Greek domination would have decimated the Hebrew language ethos held by the first-generation believers in Judea and to which the Diasporan pilgrims to the major Jewish festivals were also exposed prior to the 70 AD destruction of the Jerusalem Temple. In respect to the book of Acts Pentecost account, Gentile Church Father, Irenaeus, may not have fully appreciated that Hebrew was ingrained as the "holy language" for a number of centuries and all other earthly languages were viewed as just that—"other languages" (cf. Acts 2:4).

The testimony of Irenaeus (c. 130–c. 202 AD), bishop of what is now Lyons, France, is quite important because his statement on the subject has been pointed to as evidence, by Pentecostalist Frodsham (1941:253), among others, for the existence of *glossolalia* (term not found in the Bible), in the sense of ecstatic languages in the non-normative, non-earthly sense, in the centuries after the Apostles. Therefore, we need to look at the original sources and we continue with Irenaeus (Roberts et al, 1885:531, Vol. I).

Based on the report of Eusebius, in the original Greek, Irenaeus ambiguously writes that:

> In like manner we do also hear many brethren in the Church, who possess prophetic gifts, and who through the Spirit speak all kinds of languages, and bring to light for the general benefit

the hidden things of men, and declare the mysteries of God . . . (Roberts et al, 1885:531, Vol. I).

Though no complete version of Irenaeus' *Against Heresies* in its original Greek survives, the full ancient Latin version, of the third century, is widely available. Any full Greek text of Irenaeus' *Against Heresies* is at least a partial reconstruction from the Latin and in any event uses the Greek word γλώσσαις/*glōssais* and the Latin term *linguae*. Therefore, it would beg the question to definitively translate it as "tongues" (with the presumption of *glossolalia*, as in a non-earthly, angelic/heavenly language for public or private use), when "languages" in the ordinary, earthly sense would be the normative understanding for the Latin term *linguae*.

Editor Coxe, on the above English version of Irenaeus' *Against Heresies* has a footnote that the old Latin has the perfect tense "*audivimus*" (Roberts et al, 1885:531, Vol. I), which, according to Rogers (1965:139) is better translated "have heard" instead of the English translation "we do also hear" (Roberts et al, 1885:531, Vol. I). Warfield (1953:25) writes that "Irenaeus' youth was spent in the company of pupils of the Apostles . . . " so may have been simply reporting what he'd heard (past tense) as a youth, "of many brethren in the Church . . . who through the Spirit spoke all kinds of languages." By 177 AD, Irenaeus was in Lyons in Gaul (southern France) where he was a presbyter under Pothinus. After the martyrdom of Pothinus, Irenaeus became bishop of Lyons (Schaff, 1889:749, Vol. II).

In the context of the surrounding sentences, it seems that Irenaeus is inferring that, in conjunction with prophetic gifts, earthly, foreign languages were, as Irenaeus says in the next clause, to "bring to light for the general benefit the hidden things of men," and declaring "the mysteries of God" (Roberts et al, 1885:531, Vol. I). This sounds like Irenaeus had the Apostle Paul on his mind as it parallels the gospel "mystery" terminology of the Apostle Paul (Eph 1:9; 3:3,5; 6:19; Col 1:26 27; Rom 16:25–26; 1 Cor 4:1). The Irenaeus' citation and Pauline references refer to a truth being brought "to light" and now made manifest/revealed.

In Irenaeus' sentence immediately prior to the one under discussions, Irenaeus' mention of γλώσσαις (*glōssais*/languages) actually, rather pointedly, indicates that Irenaeus had Paul specifically in mind, when he writes: "For this reason does the apostle declare, 'We speak wisdom among them that are perfect,' terming those persons 'perfect' who have received the Spirit of God, and who through the Spirit of God do speak in all languages, as he [Paul] used Himself [sic] also to speak" (Roberts et al, 1885:531, Vol. I). Assuming the antecedent "the apostle" [Paul] is less awkward in the flow of the sentence, rather than the capitalized "Himself," jarringly intimating that the Holy Spirit singularly "used . . . also to speak" in all languages. Understood this way, in harking back to the Apostle Paul's personal claim in 1 Corinthians 14:18 to "speak in γλώσσαις/glōssais more than you all," opens the door to Paul there intending earthly languages which he spoke (i.e., Hebrew, Aramaic, the Syriac dialect, Latin, *koine* Greek and Greek dialects).

Irenaeus appears to be under the impression that those with the prophetic gifts were speaking in more than one foreign language, reminiscent of the Apostle Paul who spoke in various γλώσσαι/glōssai (languages/tongues) during the time period of 1 Corinthians 14. Irenaeus here writes of many brothers speaking in languages "πολλῶν ἀκούομεν ἀδελφῶν . . . γλώσσαις" (*pollōn akouomen adelphōn . . . glōssais*). Irenaeus, and others of his day, had heard of "brethren in the Church," who possessed the προφητικὰ χαρίσματα (gift of prophecy), and who were also enabled, through the Spirit, to "speak all kinds of γλῶσσαι" (earthly languages). It may also be intended that the totality of brethren (plural) spoke various ("all kinds") of languages.

It is admitted that Irenaeus had a close association with Bishop Polycarp of Smyrna and would thereby have derived much of his knowledge of Christian doctrine (Rogers:1965, 139). *Glossolalia* (non-earthly languages) did not play a part in Polycarp's writings (Rogers, 1965:139). It is also noteworthy that Irenaeus does not say that he spoke in *glossolalia* (non-earthly languages) or (*xenolalia*), nor does he classify those close to him as having done so, for he uses the plural "we have heard" (Rogers, 1965:139).

Irenaeus, in his written work, (ANF, Vol. 1, *Irenaeus, Against Heresies*, Book III, Chapter 12, p. 429-436), discourses on the Acts 2 Pentecost account and other passages in Acts, but gives no indication that a *glossolalic* (non-earthly) or *xenolalic* (supernaturally bestowed, earthly) language was functioning in his day.

It may be conjectured that Montanism (c. 170ff AD) is the theological antecedent to the modern Pentecostal/Charismatic movement. Montanus had been a priest of the mother goddess Cybele (Walker,

1970:56). However, there does not appear to be any explicit indication that Montanus and/or his immediate followers spoke in *glossolalia* (non-earthly languages). Eusebius conveys a third-party description of Montanus: "He began to be ecstatic and to speak (*lalein*) and to talk strangely (*xenophein*), prophesying contrary to the custom which belongs to the tradition and succession of the church from the beginning" (Eusebius, 1926:474–475; i.e., *Eusebius: The Ecclesiastical History*, Book 5, Chapter 16, Paragraph 7, p. 474–475; cp. NPNF, Series 2, Vol. 1, Book V, Chapter 16, Paragraph 7, p. 231). The term for languages/tongues, γλῶσσαι/*glóssai*, is not in the Eusebius Greek text. Furthermore, Eusebius makes no connection between Montanist ecstasy and γλῶσσαι/*glóssai*.

It is instructive that the divisive and insurmountable controversy precipitated by Montanism was their "new prophecies," which failed, and being delivered in a wild, raving manner under the claim of being the mouth-piece of the Holy Spirit (Paraclete), with the presumption of superseding apostolic revelation, and non-conformity to the Scriptures, was judged to be demonic and caused Montanism to be declared heretical (Schaff & Wace–Eusebius, 1890 [1995 Reprint]: Book V, Chapter XIV, 229–239). It was not about *glossolalia* (non-earthly "tongues" or angelic/heavenly "tongues" for public or private use), as the Montanists never made any such claims. Montanism seems to have been condemned both for the style and the content of its prophecy. The "prophecies" of Montanus and his female protégés, Priscilla and Maximilla, were not fulfilled, so based on Deuteronomy 18:20–22, they are false prophets, and not ones to be emulated nor claimed as forerunners.

Next, we turn to an important Latin ecclesiastical writer, Tertullian (c. 155–c. 220 AD), who became an exponent of Montanism. A close examination of Tertullian's Latin writings indicates that his supposed, vaunted support for *glossolalia* (non-earthly language) seems to be overstated. The Ante-Nicene Fathers, Volume 2, *Against Marcion*, Book V, Chapter VIII, page 446–447, contains the supposed Tertullian proof-text on "tongues."

For full context, here below is the pertinent passage (ANF, Vol. 2, *Against Marcion*, Book V, Chapter VIII, p. 446–447):

> Now compare the Spirit's specific graces, as they are described by the apostle, and promised by the prophet Isaiah. "To one is given," says he, "by the Spirit the word of wisdom;" . . . . to another divers kinds of *tongues* [italicized emphasis mine, and

HISTORICAL ANALYSIS OF "LANGUAGE/LANGUAGES"

underlying Latin is *linguarum*], to another the interpretation of *tongues* [italicized emphasis mine, and underlying Latin is *linguarum*];" . . . . When he mentions the fact that "it is written in the law," how that the Creator would speak with other *tongues* and other lips [italicized emphasis mine, and underlying Latin is *linguis* in this allusion to Isaiah 28:11], whilst confirming indeed the gift of *tongues* [italicized emphasis mine, and underlying Latin is *linguarum*] by such a mention, he yet cannot be thought to have affirmed that the gift was that of another god by his reference to the Creator's prediction.

Tertullian does not say that the "tongues" are unintelligible, and furthermore, the underlying pivotal word Tertullian uses in *Against Marcion* (ANF, Vol. 2, *Against Marcion*, Book V, Chapter VIII, p. 446–447) is the Latin word *linguae* or derivatives (normally understood to mean "languages"). Part way through the above passage, Tertullian alludes to Isaiah 28:11 where the prophet says that the Lord would speak in a foreign [Assyrian] language to his people, Israel and Judah, and that the gift of *linguae* fulfilled this prophecy. This circumscribes Tertullian's perspective on the gift of *linguae* to that of foreign languages. However, he doesn't elaborate whether it is a natural or supernatural ability to speak in foreign languages, and so it doesn't give a complete picture.

In Book V, *Against Marcion*, Tertullian is surveying the Apostle Paul's epistles and drawing attention to the apologetic value found in each one (ANF, Vol. 2, *Against Marcion*, Book V, Chapter I–XXI, p. 429–474). At the end of Chapter VIII, Tertullian challenges Marcion to replicate these gifts as displayed by the Apostles but doesn't indicate that he has known or seen anyone who manifests the *linguae* gift in his time (ANF, Vol. 2, *Against Marcion*, Book V, Chapter VIII, p. 446–447).

It can't be denied that the Latin Father Tertullian took the position that many *charismata*, like *donum curationum* (giving a cure), *prophetia* (prophecy), *distinctio spirituum* (discerning of spirits), *interpretatio* (interpretation), and *linguae* (languages/tongues) were being exercised in his day. However, Tertullian never indicated whether this was a learned foreign language(s), miraculously speaking an unlearned, earthly, foreign language (defined as *xenolalia*), or yet something altogether different. Tertullian matter-of-factly stated that *linguae* was extant without any elaboration.

Novatian (c.200–c. 258 AD), who also wrote in the Latin, pointed to the existence of *linguae* (languages/tongues): "This is he who places prophets in the church, instructs teachers, directs tongues [*linguae*/languages], gives powers and healing... and arranges whatever other gifts there are of *charismata*" (ANF, Vol. 5, *A Treatise of Novatian Concerning the Trinity*, Chapter XXIX, p. 641). Present tense notwithstanding, this Novatian description reads like it's no more than a recounting of the New Testament Scripture passages. Also, here we have no elucidation whether it was *xenolalia* or a special God-given aptitude for languages or a non-earthly language to which Novatian was referring.

Ambrosiaster (2009:183) writes of these two previous men, "Knowledge is no good if love is absent. Both Tertullian and Novatian were men of no small learning, but because of their pride they lost the fellowship of love and, falling into schism, devised heresies, to their own damnation."

Origen (c. 185–c. 253 AD) quotes the virulent, anti-Christian, heathen philosopher Celsus' portrayal of prophecy, in which the concluding sentence of the description has been latched onto as supposed inference of *glossolalia* (non-earthly languages): "To these promises are added strange (*agnōsta*), fanatical (*paroistra*), and quite unintelligible words (*panta adēla*) ["indistinct sound"] of which no rational person can find the meaning; for so dark are they, as to have no meaning at all; but they give occasion to every fool or impostor to apply them to suit his own purposes" (ANF, Vol. 4, *Origen Against Celsus*, Book VII, Chapter IX, p. 614). In the foregoing Greek quote, there is the crucial omission of the Greek term for "languages/tongues." Nowhere in this Greek Origen text is the term γλῶσσαι/*glōssai* found.

Origen (ANF, Vol. 4, *Origen Against Celsus*, Book VII, Chapter X, p. 615) regarded the "prophecies" to be understandable, as he says of Celsus, "If he were dealing honestly in his accusations, he ought to have given the exact terms of the prophecies." Therefore, Origen assumes that the statements of the contemporaneous so-called "prophets" were in intelligible language and he accuses Celsus of dishonesty in his describing them as "dark" and without "meaning" and castigates Celsus for not providing any of the names of the so-called "prophets (ANF, Vol. 4, *Origen Against Celsus*, Book VII, Chapter XI, p. 616). Origen (ANF, Vol. 4, *Origen Against Celsus*, Book VII, Chapter XI, p. 616) also emphasizes that "Celsus is not to be believed when he says that he has heard such men prophesy; for no prophets bearing any resemblance to the ancient prophets have appeared in the time of Celsus."

HISTORICAL ANALYSIS OF "LANGUAGE/LANGUAGES"

In reading this Celsus passage, it must also be remembered that Celsus was a virulent opponent of Christianity and therefore his hostile outsider view, as reported by Origen, will likely be inaccurate. In fact, Origen calls the account of Celsus "a piece of pure ostentation" (ANF, Vol. 4, *Origen Against Celsus*, Book VII, Chapter IX, p. 614). Moreover, in the immediately preceding paragraphs of chapter 8 in setting the context, Origen pre-emptively and bluntly says of Celsus that "his statement is false" on the matter (ANF, Vol. 4, *Origen Against Celsus*, Book VII, Chapter VIII, p. 614). It must also be recognized that Origen is not here attempting to explain the γλῶσσαι issue of 1 Corinthians 14.

Origen (2001:85), in his Commentary on the Epistle to the Romans, sheds some helpful light on his more exact views on this subject.

> *Commentary on the Epistle to the Romans chapter 1:13, Book 1, Chapter 13, paragraph 6.*
> At this point it must be asked in what sense the Apostle is a debtor to Greeks and barbarians, to the wise and foolish. For what had he received from them which would cause him to be indebted to them? In my opinion he has become a debtor to the various nations because, through the grace of the Holy Spirit, he had received the ability to speak in the tongues of all the nations, as he himself says, "I speak in more tongues than all of you." [1 Cor 14:18] Accordingly, since a person receives the knowledge of tongues not for his own sake but for the sake of those to whom he is supposed to preach, he becomes a debtor to all those, the knowledge of whose language he has received from God.

Origen's comment on Romans 1:13 points to this gift being given to fulfil the obligation to preach the gospel in the various languages of all the nations. We know Origen to be wrong if he literally means that Paul "had received the ability to speak in the tongues of all the nations [each and every]," because Acts 14:11–12 indicates that Paul appeared to not understand the multitudes, who in the Lycaonian language loudly attributed the miracle he performed to the incarnated gods "come down," naming Barnabas as Zeus and Paul as Hermes. Only later when the priest of Zeus had brought out garlands and oxen, to the city gates, to offer sacrifice with the crowds to Paul and Barnabas, did the two missionaries figure out the colossal, blasphemous error (Acts 14:14).

Beginning as a young child, Paul had been learning the Hebrew, the Aramaic, the Syriac dialect, *koine* Greek, the various Greek dialects

The Earliest View of New Testament Tongues

and probably the Latin in his adolescent years. As these languages of Paul were learned languages and not typically termed *xenolalia*, Origen's comment on Romans 1:13 must be taken as a generalization of God being the bestower of all good gifts (James 1:17).

The Epiphanius (c. 288 or 310–c. 403 AD) text is potentially insightful for explaining the γλῶσσαι/*glṓssai* problem at Corinth. The text is customarily credited to *Epiphanius (c. 310–c. 403 AD; according to Bartolocci born in 288 AD)*, the Romaniote Jewish Bishop (consecrated approximately 365 AD) of Salamis, an ancient Greek city-state on the east coast of Cyprus (Jewish Encyclopedia, 2023:Epiphanius). Salamis and Paphos on Cyprus are places where Paul spent time on his first missionary journey.

The passage is one of the clearest and most logical by a church father on the Pauline address to the divisive Corinthian γλῶσσαι/*glṓssai* problem (Thomassen & van Oort, 2009:349–351). The relevant words of the text are in the Epiphanius Panarion, Book I, Section III, Heresy 42 beginning at Scholion 13 and 21. This Epiphanius text refers to the classic Greek dialects of Attic, Aeolic and Doric Greek which were in contrast to the lower-style, levelled, common *koine* Greek, also known as Alexandrian or Hellenistic, spoken in the New Testament era. This Epiphanius text, on the divisive Corinthian γλώσσαι problem, is not referring to a non-earthly, ecstatic phenomenon nor being miraculously and instantaneously given a previously unlearned, earthly, foreign language. It is clearly referring to known, learned, earthly languages.

Pachomius (c. 292–c. 348 AD) was the founder of cenobitic monasticism in Egypt, which emphasized uniform communal monastic living rather than solitary hermitic asceticism (NPNF, Series 2, Vol. III, *Jerome and Gennadius, Gennadius. Lives of Illustrious Men, Pachomius the presbyter-monk* Chapter VII, p. 387 and footnote 4; Schaff, History of the Christian Church, Nicene and Post-Nicene Christianity, *The Rise and Progress of Monasticism*, § 38. Pachomius and the Cloister life). Pachomius would have known the Egyptian language, but apparently never learned Greek or Latin (Pachomius *et al.*, 1981:51–52). Allegedly, however, to take the confession of a visitor from the West, Pachomius prayed earnestly for three hours to be able to communicate with this Roman visitor, and was supposedly given the gift of *all* human languages (τὰς γλώσσας τῶν ἀνθρώπων "the languages of men") and was able to speak fluently in Greek and Latin with the visitor (Pachomius *et al.*, 1981:51–52). In answer to his prayers, a letter supposedly had come from heaven into his right hand, and reading it, Pachomius "learned the speech of all the languages" (ἔμαθεν πασῶν τῶν γλωσσῶν) (Pachomius et al., 1932:154–155). In this mythical, hagiographical story, *xenolalia* and real earthly languages is what is portrayed.

While in Phrygia, Hilary of Poitiers (c. 310–c. 367 AD) wrote *De trinitate* (*On the Trinity*), the first work in Latin to do with the Trinitarian controversies. Hilary of Poitiers, who became the Bishop of Poitiers, France, plainly described the miracle as foreign languages in *On the Trinity* (NPNF, Series 2, Vol. 9, Book VIII, Section 25, p. 144), in the following words: "And we learn that all this prophecy was fulfilled in the case of the Apostles, when, after the sending of the Holy Spirit, they all spoke with the tongues of the Gentiles." Hilary understood tongues to be earthly languages. Interestingly, "the tongues of the Gentiles" covering the Roman Empire were Greek and Aramaic (Beare, 1963:237; Haenchen, 1971:169; Neusner, 1965:10; Bruce, 1988:55; Hengel, 1980:115).

In the *Book of Diverse Heresies*, the Bishop of Brescia, Filastrii/Filastrius (1889:63), who died about 397 AD, claims that although the knowledge of languages had been lost [at Babel] 2700 hundred years earlier, after the Ascension, as in the Acts of the Apostles, the Holy Spirit conferred that knowledge again so the Apostles and others could preach Christ to the Gentiles. In that passage there's mention that it is the grace and virtue of angels to know the languages of all men (Filastrii, 1889:63). In other words, Filastrii's conception of "angelic language" is not that angels were able to speak their own separate and different language but that angels had the unique ability to speak all human languages.

Ambrosiaster (Kinzig, 2012:69), also known as Pseudo-Ambrose, is the unknown author of the *Commentary on Thirteen Pauline Letters* (except Hebrews) in Latin, written in Rome during the time of Pope Damascus (c. 366–c. 384 AD). The so-called Ambrosiaster (2009:181) commentated on 1 Corinthians 12:28 in the following manner:

> Teachers are those who instructed boys in the synagogue in reading and writing, a practice which has come down to us in the church as well. . . . It may be one's gift from God [*donum sit Dei*] to be able to speak many languages. The grace of God [*gratia Dei*] may also give people the ability to translate from one language to another.

The Earliest View of New Testament Tongues

Ambrosiaster's reference to received synagogue customs, fits with the research laid out in the previous chapter 3 of this book and also coincides with the thesis of Epiphanius which intimated synagogue precedent. The above Ambrosiaster comment on 1 Corinthians 12:28 affirms the God-given ministry to speak many earthly, foreign languages and the grace of God to translate same. Although Ambrosiaster obviously refers to various earthly languages here, but supernatural, miraculously instantaneous *xenolalia* is not the impression we get from this Ambrosiaster passage.

Ambrosiaster (2009:185), in his elucidation of 1 Corinthians 14:5, appears to understand the 1 Corinthians 14 practice of tongues to refer to earthly, foreign languages.

Ambrosiaster (2009:185), on 1 Corinthians 14:11, explains that "Paul is saying that people should not appear as strangers to one another by using unknown tongues [*linguae*, Latin plural for "languages"], but in the search for harmony should rejoice with a shared joy in a common understanding."

Ambrosiaster (2009:185), on 1 Corinthians 14:14, adds further description in remarking that, "Latin speakers sing in Greek and enjoy the sound of the words but do not understand what they are singing." Again, in this depiction, Ambrosiaster is pointedly referring to earthly, foreign languages.

Ambrosiaster (2009:186), is very plain about what he understood the Apostle to mean in 1 Corinthians 14:18, when he elucidates that Paul "here attributes to God the fact that he speaks in the language of them all."

Ambrosiaster (2009:186) sketches his perception of the Corinthian situation, in his paraphrase of the Apostle Paul in 1 Corinthians 14:19, where "Paul says that it is better to say a few things clearly than to make a great speech which nobody can understand"—an obvious reference to the pride and pretension of some who addressed the Corinthian congregation. Ambrosiaster (2009:186) goes on to describe the precipitating cause of this posturing, by explaining on 1 Corinthians 4:19 that:

> These people were descendants of Jews who used either Aramaic or Hebrew in their books and sacrificial rites, hoping to be admired for it. They gloried in the names of Hebrews because of the merit of Abraham ... In imitation of these people, preferred to address the congregation in an unknown tongue, just as some Latin-speakers prefer blessings to be in Greek.

HISTORICAL ANALYSIS OF "LANGUAGE/LANGUAGES"

This description is remarkably similar to that of Epiphanius who lived from 310 to 403 AD (according to Bartolocci born in 288 CE; Jewish Encyclopedia, 2023:Epiphanius) which period of time overlaps these Ambrosiaster (Pseudo-Ambrose) writings (c. 366–c. 384 AD). The convergence of "Hebrew in their books" and speakers preferring "Greek" adds credibility to the Epiphanius thesis.

The Ambrosiaster passages, taken as a whole, do not tend toward *xenolalia* and definitely do not offer any support for a *glossolalic* non-earthly language/tongue.

Gregory of Nazianzus who was born approximately 330 AD (McGuckin, 2001:3), died about 389 AD (McGuckin, 2001:371ff) and was Archbishop of Constantinople for a short time (McGuckin, 2001:311ff). Gregory's Oration "On Pentecost" in an English translation (NPNF, Series 2, Vol. 7, Oration XLI, Section 15, p. 384) has the passage, which triggered the long-running debate, as follows. Gregory does not cite 1 Corinthians 14 nor comment on the problematic γλῶσσαι/*glõssai* issue there.

The big controversy stirred up by this Gregory was whether the Acts 2 account of Pentecost was a miracle of speaking or hearing. After raising the hypothetical, Gregory of Nazianzus inclines to it being a miracle of speaking because in Acts 2:13 it was the speakers "who were reproached for drunkenness, evidently because they by the Spirit wrought a miracle in the matter of the tongues" (NPNF, Series 2, Vol. 7, Oration XLI, Section 15, p. 384).

Witherington (2015:30) remarks:

> Sometimes the issue has been muddied by the suggestion that there were two miracles involved—the disciples spoke in angelic tongues, but each person heard it in their native human languages. Alas, the Greek grammar is against this suggestion. The phrase 'in their native language' modifies the verb 'speaking' in verse 6, not the verb "hearing."

What we do definitively discern from these comments of Gregory's is the glaring omission of any reference to ecstatic speech or non-earthly language. To Gregory, there were only two options—it was either a miracle of speaking or hearing earthly, foreign languages. Gregory makes no mention of a *glossolalic* phenomenon in the church of his day based on Acts chapter 2. Gregory of Nazianzus has no comment of note on 1 Corinthians 14. After his speculative writing and stirring up "a hornet's nest," Gregory indicated his position on the matter and logic for it, and then moved on.

Bishop of Milan, <u>Ambrose</u> (c. 339–c. 397 AD), remarks on I Corinthians 12 and the Mark 16:17 longer disputed ending (NPNF, Series 2, Vol. 10, Book II, Chapter 13, Section 150–152, p. 134). Therein, Ambrose infers that tongues (language/*linguae* in his native Latin) was a grace bestowed on some and led off paragraph 152, by saying, "In like manner we have heard also above concerning the Holy Spirit, that He too grants the same kinds of graces" and Ambrose again enumerates healings, divers kinds of tongues (*genera linguarum*), and prophecy. By this wording, the distinct impression one gets is that Ambrose hadn't personally experienced these three graces or seen them in operation, but he had heard about the Holy Spirit dispensing these three graces. In these paragraphs attributed to Ambrose, we glean no insight as to whether the grace of *linguae/linguarum* (languages) granted was *xenolalia* or an exceptional God-given acuity for languages.

John <u>Chrysostom</u> (1984:53–54), who lived from approximately 347 to 407 AD and served as the Archbishop of Constantinople, wrote in a homily *On the Incomprehensible Nature of God*:

> For the disappearance of prophecy and the silencing of tongues raises no difficult problem. These charismatic gifts served us preachers for a time and have now ceased. But their passing can do no harm to the word we preach. See how now, at least, there is no prophecy nor gift of tongues. Still this did not hinder or thwart the preaching of piety.

The nature and definition of tongues is spelled out quite concisely by Chrysostom in Homily 35 in his *Homilies on First Corinthians* (NPNF, Series 1, Chrysostom Volumes, Vol. 12, Homily XXXV, p. 208–209):

> At this point he makes a comparison between the gifts, and lowers that of the tongues, showing it to be neither altogether useless, nor very profitable by itself. For in fact they were greatly puffed up on account of this, because the gift was considered to be a great one. And it was thought great because the Apostles received it first, and with so great display; it was not however therefore to be esteemed above all the others. Wherefore then did the Apostles receive it before the rest? Because they were to go abroad every where. And as in the time of building the tower the one tongue was divided into many; so then the many

tongues frequently met in one man, and the same person used to discourse both in the Persian, and the Roman, and the Indian, and many other tongues, the Spirit sounding within him: and the gift was called the gift of tongues because he could all at once speak divers languages.

Chrysostom's Homilies on I Corinthians, particularly Homilies 29–36, make it clear that he believed the Apostle Paul had in mind foreign, earthly languages. In Homily 35 on 1 Corinthians 14:10, Chrysostom wrote: "*There are, it may be, so many kinds of voices in the world, and no kind is without signification:* i.e., so many tongues, so many voices of Scythians, Thracians, Romans, Persians, Moors, Indians, Egyptians, innumerable other nations" (NPNF, Series 1, Chrysostom Volumes, Vol. 12, Homily XXXV, p. 210).

The two preceding passages of Chrysostom provide some enlightening context for the commonly controverted quotation of his from Homily 29 on I First Corinthians (NPNF, Series 1, Chrysostom Volumes, Vol. 12, Homily XXIX, p. 168):

> *Now concerning spiritual gifts, brethren, I would not have you ignorant. Ye know that when ye were Gentiles, ye were led away unto those dumb idols, howsoever ye might be led.*
> This whole place is very obscure: but the obscurity is produced by our ignorance of the facts referred to and by their cessation, being such as then used to occur but now no longer take place. And why do they not happen now? Why look now, the cause too of the obscurity hath produced us again another question: namely, why did they then happen, and now do so no more?

In other words, by his day (c. 347–c. 407 AD), the well-informed and much-travelled Chrysostom had not heard of certain supposed apostolic gifts being exercised in his time, which leads one to conclude that they were not functioning at that time.

Severian who was Bishop of Gabala until about 403 AD (NPNF, Series 2, Vol. 3, *Gennadius. Lives of Illustrious Men, Severianus the bishop*, Chapter 21, p. 2609), on 1 Corinthians 14:28 commented, "The person who speaks in the Holy Spirit speaks when he chooses to do so and then can be silent, like the prophets. But those who are possessed by an unclean spirit speak even when they do not want to. They say things that they do not understand" (Severian, 2006:141).

On 1 Corinthians 14:10, Severian (2006:137) wrote, "There is no language without meaning because all languages are human." On

The Earliest View of New Testament Tongues

1 Corinthians 14:19, Severian of Gabala (2006:139) comments that, "Paul wants to speak with a clear mind and in a normal language."

Jerome (c. 347–c. 420 AD) tells the legendary account of a monk, Saint Hilarion from Gaza, who, in an exorcism of a demon from an officer of Emperor Constantius, encountered *xenolalia* (NPNF, Series 2, Vol. 6, *Treatises, Life of St. Hilarion*, Section 22, p. 308). That demon-controlled attaché of the Emperor spoke flawless Syriac when he only knew French and Latin (NPNF, Series 2, Vol. 6, *Treatises, Life of St. Hilarion*, Section 22, p. 308).

Augustine of Hippo (c. 354–c.430 AD), one of the greatest theologians of the Western Churches, oft denied the existence of tongues-speech in his day. Augustine was a very prolific Latin author in terms of written works that still survive.

In a homily on 1 John 3:23, Augustine declares that, "These were signs adapted to the time" (NPNF, Series 1, Augustine Volumes, Vol. 7, Ten Homilies on the First Epistle of John, Homily VI, Section 10, p. 497–498):

> In the earliest times, "the Holy Ghost fell upon them that believed: and they spake with tongues," which they had not learned, "as the Spirit gave them utterance." These were signs adapted to the time. For there behooved to be that betokening of the Holy Spirit in all tongues, to shew that the Gospel of God was to run through all tongues over the whole earth. That thing was done for a betokening, and it passed away.

Augustine also expounded (NPNF, Series 1, Augustine Volumes, Vol. 7, Lectures on Gospel of John 7:37–39, Tractate XXXII, Section 7, p. 195):

> How then, brethren, because he that is baptized in Christ, and believes on Him, does not speak now in the tongues of all nations, are we not to believe that he has received the Holy Ghost? God forbid that our heart should be tempted by this faithlessness. Certain we are that every man receives: but only as much as the vessel of faith that he shall bring to the fountain can contain, so much does He fill of it. Since, therefore, the Holy Ghost is even now received by men, some one may say, Why is it that no man speaks in the tongues of all nations? Because the Church itself now speaks in the tongues of all nations. Before, the Church was in one nation, where it spoke in the tongues of all. By speaking then in the tongues of all, it

signified what was to come to pass; that by growing among the nations, it would speak in the tongues of all.

In addition to understanding the tongues of the New Testament era to be earthly languages, Augustine, was of the view that, in his day, as a corporate entity, the Church's expansive reach was such that it now encompassed all *linguae* (languages/tongues), therefore it effectively spoke "in the tongues of all nations." Christian congregations existed throughout the then-known world and consequently the church spoke in all those diverse languages. Thus, a native-born Mandarin speaker attending an English-speaking church could be said to speak in tongues. Augustine's thinking was that the Pentecost event was prophetic of this new universal reality in his time.

Cyril of Alexandria (c. 370–c. 444 AD) was the Patriarch of Alexandria from 412 to 444 AD (NPNF, Series 2, Vol. III, *The Ecclesiastical History of Theodoret,* Book V, Chapter XXXV, p. 154 and footnote 2).

Attributed to Cyril of Alexandria (Migne, 1863:Vol. 74, Section 25, Col. 757–759) is the following exposé, translated from the Latin:

> And indeed at the beginning not all of them comprehended the meaning of these things. For after they had begun to speak in tongues to strangers, turning the gift of the divine Spirit into insolence and ostentation, they began unworthily to teach the multitudes about the holy prophets and to instruct them in the doctrines of the gospel . . .

Cyril acknowledges that even at the outset, at Pentecost (Acts 2), not everyone could figure out what was happening. However, subsequently, some of those impressed with being able to speak in γλῶσσαι/*linguae* to strangers perverted the gift by their insolence and ostentation as they taught sacred things in an unworthy manner. This parallels the Epiphanius understanding of the climate in the Corinthian church that instigates Paul's rebukes in chapter 14.

On 1 Corinthians 12:9, Cyril of Alexandria commentates: "ποίων δὲ πνευμάτων, εἴρηται πρότερον. Διδόναι γε μὴν καὶ ἑτέροις ἰσχυρίζεται τὸ εἰδέναι γένη γλωσσῶν, καὶ μέν τοι καὶ ἑρμηνείας" (Migne, 1859:Vol. 74. Col. 888), which I translate as "Regarding the spirits, mentioned earlier, he [the Apostle Paul] assuredly emphasizes that it is granted to others who are strong in knowing various languages and indeed interpretation also." Here Cyril is obviously referring to intelligible, earthly, foreign languages. Non-earthly languages or modern-day *glossolalia* is not even hinted at.

Cyril of Alexandria expounding on 1 Corinthians 14:5 says, "ἐκτὸς εἰ μὴ διερμηνεύῃ, τουτέστιν, εἰ μὴ ἔχοι τινὰ τὸν ἀεὶ προσεδρεύοντα καὶ τοῖς μυσταγωγουμένοις ["initiate" https://morphological_el.en-academic.com/264849/μυσταγωγουμένοις] διερμηνεύοντα" (Migne, 1859:Vol. 74. Col. 892), which I translate as "Except, unless he interprets, to be specific, if he doesn't have someone who habitually sits by and for the initiate interprets." This scenario seems to suggest a mature believer closely alongside, assisting a new believer to understand the basics, the terminology, and the rituals of the Christian faith, particularly when the public speaker is reading the Older Testament Scripture in an unfamiliar language or expounding in a language unfamiliar to the new devotee.

Cyril of Alexandria appears to link 1 Corinthians 14:10 with traveling preachers of the day who regularly visited congregations throughout the vast network of Alexandrian churches (Sullivan, 2020). This vast domain of churches would have had many different peoples and language groups, so being able to speak in various languages would be necessary for these preachers to teach and lead in prayer in these various congregations (Sullivan, 2020). Cyril appears to have viewed the traveling preacher's polyglot ability as a necessary and naturally acquired one to meet the needs of the extensive and lingually diverse church communities (Sullivan, 2020).

Cyril (1872:293–294), premised on 1 Corinthians 14:10, directs that, "Εἰσεφοίτων ἐν ταῖς ἐκκλησίαις τινὲς τῇ τοῦ Πνεύματος ἐνεργείᾳ πεπλουτηκότες τὸ δύνασθαι γλώσσαις λαλεῖν.... τοῦτο διδάσκει ὁ Παῦλος ὅτι ἐὰν μή εἰσιν οἱ ἀκούοντες ἐπιστήμονες τῆς γλώσσης, ᾗ διαλέγοιτο ὁ τὸ χάρισμα ἔχων, οὐδὲν ὄφελος ἐκ τοῦ πράγματος· μυρία γάρ εἰσιν ἔθνη καὶ πολλαὶ γλῶσσαι τῶν ἀνθρώπων." which I translate as, "Traveling preachers in the churches, who are fully energized (endued) by the Spirit should be able to speak in languages.... This is what Paul teaches, that if the listeners are not students (i.e., knowledgeable) of the language, which the gifted one has chosen [to speak], there is no benefit from the thing (situation); for there are thousands of nations and many languages of men" (For insights on meaning of Εἰσεφοίτων, see Sullivan, 2020, notes on the Cyrillian catena on I Corinthians 14:10). Cyril seems to regard the traveling preacher's acumen with various languages as acquired, but enhanced by the Spirit's enabling, and vital to the nature of fulfilling the Great Commission in the Alexandrian church sphere of influence.

Cyril of Alexandria (1872:293–294) in further comment, built off 1 Corinthians 14:10, instructs that "Δεῖ δὲ οὖν ἄρα τοὺς διδάσκειν ἑτέρους ἐθέλοντας τὸν συνήθη τοῖς ἀκροωμένοις ἐρεύγεσθαι ["belch out" https://morphologia_gr_en.en-academic.com/702565/ἐρεύγεσθαι]   λόγον." which I translate as, "Moreover, of necessity, therefore, those willing to teach others, should accommodate ("hearken to") the locals ("dwelling") in expressing the word(s)." The visiting preacher/teacher should address the assembled auditors in a language they readily understand.

Cyril of Alexandria's understanding of the Apostle Paul, in the 1 Corinthians 14 context in particular, is that γλῶσσαι/glṓssai is a reference to earthly, foreign languages learned by those with an aptitude for same and not some kind of non-earthly, private prayer language.

Although it was not known when Pope Leo I the Great was born, he died in 461 AD (Britannica, 2023:St. Leo I). Pope Leo I held the same view that Augustine did, that as a corporate entity, the Church's expansive reach was such that it now encompassed all *linguae* (languages/tongues), therefore it effectively spoke "in the tongues of all nations" (NPNF, Series 2, Vol. 12, The Letters and Sermons of Leo the Great, Sermon LXXV, On Whitsuntide, I, Section II, p. 190).

Theodoret of Cyrrhus/Cyrus (c. 393–c. 466 AD) became a monk and from 423 AD the Bishop of Cyrrhus in Syria (Chadwick & Edwards, 2012:1457). In respect to 1 Corinthians chapter 12, verse 1 and verse 7, Theodoret (2006:117) wrote:

> In former times those who accepted the divine preaching and who were baptized for their salvation were given visible signs of the grace of the Holy Spirit at work in them. Some spoke in tongues which they did not know and which nobody had taught them, while others performed miracles or prophesied. The Corinthians also did these things, but they did not use the gifts as they should have done. They were more interested in showing off than in using them for the edification of the church. . . Even in our times grace is given to those who are deemed worthy of holy baptism, but it may not take the same form as it did in those days.

From this quote of his, when Theodoret writes of the Corinthians "showing off," he obviously would have agreed with the sentiments of Epiphanius on this γλῶσσαι/glṓssai matter.

Thus, in the church from 100 AD to the middle of the fifth century AD, the evidence, above, does not indicate that γλῶσσα/γλῶσσαι, when referenced by the various writers, would fit the category of *glossolalia*. Rather it could fit the category of *xenolalia* or a special God-given grace/acuity for languages.

The term *xenolalia* comes from the Greek words *xenos* "foreign" and *lalia* "language," and means "a foreign language." *Xenolalia* occurs when a person miraculously speaks an actual earthly language, in ordinary human speech, intelligible to those who know the language but foreign to those who don't. *Glossolalia* is defined as non-linguistic vocalizations, non-earthly language or an angelic/heavenly language for public or private use. Burgess (1976:19) defines *glossolalia* as "ecstatic utterance in an unknown tongue." Burgess (1976:19) adds the category of *heteroglossolalia*, "a phenomenon in which each person hears his own language when the speaker is communicating in his native tongue." Some would simply call this "the miracle of hearing the language" rather than "the miracle of speaking the language" as with *xenolalia*.

To reiterate, in a study of church history thus far, to the middle of the fifth century AD, there is no indication of, nor examples of, nor a theory posited of "tongues-speaking" being a non-earthly, angelic/heavenly language for public or private use, i.e., *glossolalia*.

4.1.2 500 AD until 1000 AD

As we now chronologically come into the Middle Ages (late fifth century to the late fifteenth century AD), there is little reliable evidence in either East or West of any type of "tongues-speaking" and even proponents of *glossolalia* (non-earthly languages) admit that (Williams & Waldvogel, 1975:69).

Kelsey (1968:47) acknowledges that "all, or nearly all, tongue-speaking in the medieval church was limited to the ability to speak in a foreign language in the course of missionary activity." He (Kelsey, 1968:47) conjectures that was so, because "of a church ban on speaking in and interpreting an unknown language, a ban found in the *Rituale Romanorum* in a section describing characteristics of the demon-possessed." Kelsey (1968:46) also admits in respect to the medieval era that "almost nothing is said about the religious emotions accompanying the utterance, or about ecstatic speech."

Hinson (1967:56) also acknowledges that,

> From the early fifth century through the entire medieval era, evidences for tongue speaking are scanty at best. In Western Christendom, these are confined mostly to accounts of the ability to speak foreign languages which had not been learned. The surprising thing, in view of the general credulity of the medieval era, is that there are so *few* reports.

Burgess (1976:17) chides his Pentecostal brethren and others who just parrot secondary sources:

> We read that certain medieval mendicants, Waldensians, and Albigensians spoke in tongues, but we are left with no identification of individual recipients and with few details . . . We read that St. Stephen, Jean of St. Francis, Martin Valentine, and Jean of the Cross spoke in tongues, but of these there is no additional identification. In fact, we are even left in doubt as to whether Jean of the Cross was male or female!

Hinson (1967:56) reports that, "We have the most complete record in J. J. Gores' *Die christliche Mystik*." However, there is the difficulty of accepting such accounts because of the unreliable witnesses in the hagiographical exaggerations in the campaign to have the person declared a saint by the Catholic Church (Hinson, 1967:56–57). The various persons supporting prospective individuals for beatification or sainthood apparently had no qualms about relating fanciful anecdotes to that end, even when it contradicted the direct testimony of the idealized person (Hinson, 1967:57). In any event, these suspect stories were of individuals supposedly receiving the "gift of (foreign) tongues" (Hinson, 1967:56).

The titles of these hagiographical books (with names like "*Legenda Sanctorum*," "*Legenda Aurea*," "The *Legend of the Three Companions*," "*The Golden Legend*") engender a considerable skepticism because of their mythical and legendary nature.

4.1.3 1000 AD until 1516 AD

Michael Psellos was born about 1018 AD and is believed to have died in 1078 AD (Britannica, 2023:Michael Psellus). Psellos (1989:292–297) commentates on Acts chapter 2, and makes it plain that, from his perspective, what occurred at Pentecost was speaking in foreign languages which the speakers didn't know previously.

The person of Hildegard of Bingen (c. 1098–c. 1179 AD) must be touched on briefly, because some authors appeal to her as one who spoke in "tongues." Kelsey (1968:47) intimates that, in the annals of the Church, after Pachomius in the fourth century AD and following, there was a void of 800 years to the twelfth century. Hildegard was thereafter the first one reported to have spoken in "tongues" (cf. Burgess, 1976:21). However, Higley (2007:20) emphatically states:

> Given Hildegard's similar interest in structure and taxonomy, her Lingua has little if anything to do with *glossolalia* . . . Glossolalia has a different and complicated background: it is the spontaneous utterance of vocables that has no semantic content, hence none of the components by which language, natural or otherwise, produces reference and meaning.

Higley (2007:39) sees the sharp distinction between *glossolalia* (non-earthly) and Hildegard's invention of a language, for the nuns of her convent, is that "the essentially oral, performative, and spontaneous nature of glossolalia is not replicated in the written and thought-out nature of [Hildegard's] *glossopoeia* [the making of languages] where meanings can be rationally applied to words and parts of words." After much comparative work, Higley (2007:43) says, "My preference, then, is to return the term *glossolalia* to its more conventional meaning—free vocalization inspired by an *alienatio mentis* [Latin "alienation of mind"]—and to substitute the word "*glossopoeia*" [constructed language] for what Hildegard is doing: inventing a *glossary* of nouns copied from a German *summarium* with meaningful elements in them that she translates."

Hildegard's *ignota lingua* (unknown language), with its concocted alphabet of 23 letters, has much in common with the invention of personal and fictitious languages that we see in subsequent centuries (Higley, 2007:50). Hildegard's vocabulary list of a thousand words is systematized in a way that *glossolalia* (non-earthly, "alienation of mind") is not (Higley, 2007:111).

Burgess (1976:17) refers to Waldenses (late twelfth century to the present) and Albigenses (twelfth to thirteenth century, southern France) speaking in "tongues," but acknowledges that we are left with no identity of individuals and without details, so after a personal search, from a scholarly perspective that elusive suggestion will have to be set aside.

Thomas Aquinas, of noble family, was born in the early days of 1225 AD (Conway, 1911:1) and deceased on March 7, 1274 AD (Conway, 1911:102). Aquinas says some rather profound things in his writings. On the subject of languages/tongues (*linguarum*), translated from the Latin, Aquinas (2023) in section 729 of 12-2 on 1 Cor 12:7-11, as reported by his friend Reginaldi de Piperno, wrote:

> But the faculty of speaking persuasively consists in being able to speak intelligibly to others. . . . to another is given various kinds of tongues [*genera linguarum*], namely, in order that he be able to speak in diverse languages [*diversis linguis*], so that he will be understood by all, as it says of the apostles in Ac (2:4) that they spoke in various languages [*variis linguis*].

We derive a further clue, about Aquinas' (2023) understanding of languages/tongues, in section 760 of 13-1 in respect to 1 Cor. 13:1-3, when he wrote:

> The Corinthians had a great desire for the gift of tongues [*donum linguarum*], as will be shown in chap. 14; therefore, beginning with that he [Paul] says: I have promised to show you a more excellent way; and this is, first of all, clear in the gift of tongues [*donum linguarum*], because, if I speak in the tongues of men [*linguis hominum*], namely, of all, i.e., if I should have the gift through which I could speak in the languages of all men [*linguis omnium hominum*] . . . .

Aquinas (2023) in section 814 of 14-1 on 1 Cor. 14:1-4, made this interesting comment:

> In regard to the second it should be noted that because there were few in the early Church assigned to preaching faith of Christ throughout the world, the Lord enabled them to proclaim the word to more people by giving them the gift of tongues [*linguarum*/languages], by which they could all preach to all. Not that they spoke in one language [*lingua*] and were understood by all, as some say, but that they spoke the languages [*linguis*] of different nations and, indeed, of all. Hence the Apostle says: "I thank God that I speak in the language [*lingua*] of all of you," and in Ac (2:4) it says: "They began to speak in other tongues [*variis linguis*/various languages], as

> the Spirit gave them utterance." Furthermore, many received this gift from God in the early church. But the Corinthians, being inquisitive, were more desirous of this gift than the gift of prophecy. Therefore, when the Apostle mentions here about speaking in a tongue [*lingua*/language], he means an unknown language [*ignota lingua*] not interpreted; as when one might speak German to a Frenchman without an interpreter, he is speaking in a tongue [*lingua*/language].

Aquinas (2023) in section 831–832 of 14-2 on 1 Cor. 14:5–12, provides additional clarification:

> First, therefore, he says: The languages of the world are many and diverse, and anyone can speak in whichever one he wants; but if he does not speak precisely, he is not understood. . . . But if I do not know the meaning of the language. Here he shows their uselessness. And this is what he says: "If I have spoken in all tongues," but did not know the meaning of the words, I will be a foreigner (barbarian) to the speaker, and the speaker a foreigner (barbarian) to me. Note that barbarians according to some are those whose idiom completely disagrees with Latin.

Aquinas (2023) in section 842–843 of 14-3 on 1 Cor. 14:13–17, stresses the earthly, liturgical Latin ecclesiastical language, "unknown" to the assembled faithful:

> . . . the gift of tongues, even in public prayer, which is when a priest prays in public, where he sometimes says things he does not understand and sometimes things he does understand.

In that era and for many years thereafter, Latin was the supposed "sacred" language, used by the clerics in religious ceremonies, not even always understood by the priest delivering the word. Even when he didn't understand the Latin (Aquinas, 2023, section 843 of 14-3, 1 Cor. 14:13–17), the priest or reader by rote recitation was to "give a blessing in the spirit, i.e., in a tongue not understood" (hence speaking in an *unknown tongue* or as the Lain would have it *lingua ignota*). The *unknown tongues* issue—of the church service not being conducted in the understandable vernacular language of the people—was to be one of the crucial grievances of the Reformation, against the Catholic hierarchy, in the centuries ahead. This is the background of the phrase *unknown tongues* inserted by translators of English Bibles in the years to come, without warrant in the underlying Greek text. It is not a reference to non-earthly language nor angelic/heavenly "tongues," but a reference to the uncomprehended Latin language.

According to Aquinas (2023), section 843 of 14-3, on 1 Cor. 14:13-17, the responsive "Amen" was to be in unison chanted by the congregational persons even when they didn't understand what was being said ("who supplies the place of the ignorant man" *quis supplet locum idiotae*). The *idiota* is the one "who knows only the tongue in which he was born" (Aquinas, 2023, section 843 of 14-3, 1 Cor. 14:13-17). "As if to say: you will say what he should say there to the ignorant man; for what he should say there is Amen" (Aquinas, 2023, section 843 of 14-3, 1 Cor. 14:13-17). In other words, the Christian lay person, who didn't know the Latin language, was to be coached as to when to say "Amen."

Aquinas (2023) in section 848 of 14-4 on 1 Cor. 14:18-22, which I translate from the Latin, says:

> "I [Paul] give thanks," as if to say: I don't denigrate the gift of languages/tongues as if lacking it, because I have it. Therefore, he [Paul] says: "I give thanks." And lest it be understood that they all spoke the same language, he [Paul] says, "I speak the language of all of you" (Acts. 2:4 "The Apostles spoke in various languages").

Aquinas (2023) in section 867-868 of 14-5 on 1 Cor. 14:23-26 follows up from noting "another has a tongue" (*alius linguam habet*) and "another has an interpretation" (*alius interpretationem*) to acknowledge that they can be derived "from human talent."

In the Summa Theologica of Thomas Aquinas (1947), "Pertaining to Speech, under Question 176 "Of the Grace of Tongues—(1) Whether by the grace of tongues a man acquires the knowledge of all languages?" in Objection 3," Aquinas makes a very novel assertion:

> I answer that, Christ's first disciples were chosen by Him in order that they might disperse throughout the whole world, and preach His faith everywhere, according to Matthew 28:19, "Going . . . teach ye all nations." Now it was not fitting that they who were being sent to teach others should need to be taught by others, either as to how they should speak to other people, or as to how they were to understand those who spoke to them; and all the more seeing that those who were being sent were of one nation, that of Judea, according to Is. 27:6, "When they shall rush out from Jacob [*Vulg.: 'When they shall rush in unto Jacob,' etc.] . . . they shall fill the face of the

world with seed." Moreover those who were being sent were poor and powerless; nor at the outset could they have easily found someone to interpret their words faithfully to others, or to explain what others said to them, especially as they were sent to unbelievers. Consequently it was necessary, in this respect, that God should provide them with the gift of tongues; in order that, as the diversity of tongues was brought upon the nations when they fell away to idolatry, according to Gn. 11, so when the nations were to be recalled to the worship of one God a remedy to this diversity might be applied by the gift of tongues.

Continuing on in Reply to Objection 3, stating his agreement with Augustine (Tract. xxxii in Joan.), Aquinas understood the *donum linguarum* (gift of languages/tongues), as having long before passed from individuals to the corporate ecclesiastical body by his blunt statement that "no one speaks in the tongues of all nations, because the Church herself already speaks the languages of all nations."

In summarizing the foregoing, Aquinas viewed the gift of tongues (*donum linguarum* in Latin) to be earthly, foreign languages as demonstrated by the above examples. In Aquinas' writings, there is no indication of non-earthly nor angelic/heavenly languages nor a private prayer language (i.e., *glossolalia*).

Aquinas' *Lectures on I Corinthians* indicates the problematic issue of the Corinthian congregation to be the utilization of an earthly, foreign language and the attendee not comprehending because it wasn't their first language (Aquinas, 2023, section 863 of 14–5, 1 Cor. 14:23–26).

Aquinas' perspective on the gift of tongues, as in its initial form, was that it was no longer required. The rapid growth and geographic spread of the Church meant that by Aquinas' day, multilingual speakers and accompanying interpreters had replaced miraculously endowed speakers.

In Aquinas' Summa Theologica (1947, First Part of the Second Part, under Question 51, "Of the cause of habits, as to their formation," Article 4 "Whether any habits are infused in man by God?"), Aquinas asserts that God can produce the effects of second causes, directly (cf. 1947, First Part, Question 105, Article 6), for example, by implanting the habit of traditional study to acquire languages/tongues (*linguae*).

> He infuses into man even those habits which can be caused by a natural power. *Thus He gave to the apostles the science of the*

Scriptures and of all tongues, which men can acquire by study or by custom, but not so perfectly [italics emphasis mine].

This Aquinas insight would mean that, in this immediately preceding scenario depicted, God needn't suspend the laws of nature, in the Acts chapter 2 Pentecost event, but the attainment of the additional language(s) would still be supernatural. It's a more ready recognition of God's injection into the human sphere on a regular basis.

After a careful assessment of passages marshalled by Pentecostal/Charismatic proponents in support of non-earthly "tongues-speaking" from the writings of Irenaeus, Origen, Eusebius, Tertullian, Epiphanius, Chrysostom, and Clement of Alexandria, in the volumes of Migne's Patrologia Graeca, Blosser and Sullivan (2022:Kindle Location p. 196) report that,

> A key problem is that none of these passages includes a single reference to the term glóssa (γλῶσσα), meaning "language," except for a hopelessly-obscure sentence from the Tertullian text. Furthermore, passages from the same writers, and numerous others, which do refer to the term *glóssa* and suggest (or explicitly state) that "tongues" are human languages are overlooked or omitted. The attempt to harness these seven Patristic texts in support of the revisionist, Higher Critical, and Pentecostal-Charismatic understanding of "tongues," is steadfastly contradicted by the vast majority of other Patristic and later texts, concerning which the silence of contemporary scholarship is deafening.

The writings of the church fathers reflect an understanding of the γλῶσσαι/*glóssai* at Pentecost as either spoken or heard foreign languages (Roberts et al, 1885; Lake, 1912; ANF, Vol. 1, *First Epistle to the Corinthians, Clement of Rome*, etc.). These church fathers, in the context of Acts 2 and 1 Corinthians 12–14, were not aware of an interpretation of γλῶσσαι/*glóssai* as ecstasy (nor *glossolalia* which is not a word in the Greek New Testament). Tertullian (c. 155–c. 220 AD), who became a Montanist in his later days, upon closer examination does not explicitly support γλῶσσαι/*glóssai* as an unintelligible, non-earthly language nor an angelic/heavenly language for public or private use (Tertullian, 1972). Augustine relates that Tertullian left the Montanists, founding a new sect named Tertullianists, but through the agency of Augustine was reconciled to the Catholic congregation of Carthage (Schaff, 1910b:421).

The Earliest View of New Testament Tongues

Even Pentecostal historian, Harold Hunter (1980:135), concedes that "When the [church] fathers clarified the nature of the tongues-speech being practiced they most usually specified them as being xenolalic."

Notably, the Church Fathers linked their comments about "foreign languages" for evangelism propulsion to the book of Acts and not to the γλῶσσαι/glōssai of 1 Corinthians 14.

4.2 REFORMATION PERIOD (1517–1648 AD)

Francis Xavier lived from 1506 to 1552 AD (Britannica, 2023:Francis Xavier). In Butler's *Lives of the Saints* (1938:5997; cf. Bartoli & Maffei, 1889:340–341)), in respect to Francis Xavier's Japanese mission he "set himself to learn Japanese (so far from having the gift of tongues with which he is so often credited, he seems to have had difficulty in learning new languages)." Schurhammer (1977:448) refers to Xavier's own admission in a letter from India:

> I am alone here among these people without an interpreter. Antonio is ill in Manapar. Rodrigo and Antonio are my interpreters. From this you can see the life I am leading and the exhortations I am able to give, since the people do not understand me and I understand them even less.

As to Francis Xavier knowing all the languages of India and preaching without an interpreter, Schurhammer (1977:448) footnotes: "But this letter shows that these claims are exaggerated." As a matter of fact, Francis "could not even think of learning the difficult Tamil alphabet with its numerous characters and combinations" (Schurhammer, 1977:308).

Based on the foregoing and his own writings, it is highly questionable whether Francis Xavier had the "gift of tongues" in any sense, at any time, as his own admission, from his own correspondence, is that he struggled with language learning (Venn, 1862:88–90).

Martin Luther (c. 1483–1546 AD) is a seminal figure of the Protestant Reformation. Martin Luther (Bergendoff, 1958:142) alleged that the Apostle Paul was, in 1 Corinthians 14, primarily concerned with the role of preaching and the listening and learning of the congregation. The German Luther used 1 Corinthians 14 to elaborate his position on preaching in the vernacular:

> Who ever comes forward, and wants to read, teach, or preach, and yet speaks with tongues, that is, speaks Latin instead of German, or some unknown language, he is to be silent and preach to himself alone. For no one can hear it or understand it, and no one can get any benefit from it. Or if he should speak with tongues, he ought, in addition, to put what he says into German or interpret it in one way or another, so that the congregation may understand it (Bergendoff, 1958:142).

Luther insisted that the Scripture reading and teaching and preaching, in the believer's assembly, be in the vernacular language or translated into same, using 1 Corinthians 14 to support his position. The cure for the Epiphanius diagnosis of the Corinthian malady is remedied by Luther's prescription on 1 Corinthians 14.

John Calvin, born July 10, 1509, in Noyon, Picardy, France, and deceased May 27, 1564, Geneva, Switzerland (Britannica, 2023:John Calvin), was a leading French Protestant reformer. His commentaries on the book of Acts and Apostle Paul's epistles to the Corinthians are enlightening to the topic of "speaking in tongues" as understood in Calvin's day.

A brief excursion into those writings of Calvin clearly demonstrate that he viewed "tongues" as earthly, foreign languages. In commenting on 1 Corinthians 14:5, Calvin (1573:368) asserts that this "knowledge of languages is more than simply necessary" and "the use of a foreign tongue is seasonable" as long as we "have an eye to this as our end—that edification may redound to the Church." Therefore, Calvin in all the Acts and 1 Corinthians passages does not posit the "gift of tongues" (earthly, foreign languages) for evangelism but rather for edification. This supports the Epiphanius view that the gift of languages (γλῶσσαι/ *glōssai*) was to be used in the normal course of teaching Corinthian congregants and bringing spiritual understanding to those new believers. That Calvin believed it was being used in the ancient Corinthian congregation for "ostentation and display" (1965:318) also parallels the understanding of Epiphanius.

George Williams (1962:133, 443), in his work on "The Radical Reformation," remarks that among *the Anabaptist Brethren* "*Glossolalia* broke out.*" However, with his scant three words only on these two pages in his almost thousand-page book, Williams does not define what he means by this term nor describe what it looked like, nor in extensive search is anything more determinative located.

4.3 POST-REFORMATION (1649–1905 AD)

George Fox, born July 1624 (Fox, 1952:1; Fox, 1909:65), deceased January 13,1691 AD (Fox, 1909:578), and the early Quakers have sometimes been referred to as tongue speakers, but "this has never been authenticated, nor was it apparently claimed by Fox or any of the early leaders" (Kelsey, 1968:55; cf. Fox, 1909). In respect to the early Quakers, "quite possibly manifestations of revival were confused with tongue speech" (Kelsey, 1968:55). The most that can be found is a statement by an early Quaker, who died young, a man named Edward Burrough (1634–1663 AD), who reported that at their meetings "our tongues loosed" and "we spake with new tongues, as the Lord gave utterance" (Fox, 1659:13). We have no detail beyond those few words and no other similar Quaker description that can be located to ascertain exactly what Burrough meant.

The Shakers and Ranters have been cited as evidence for *glossolalia* but neither group were Christians in any biblical sense, as from their very beginnings, heretical doctrine and practices unequivocally exclude them from this category (Edgar, 1996:215–216).

During the lengthy reign of Louis VIV (1643–1715) and the 1685 revocation of the Edict of Nantes, French Huguenot Protestants having lost all religious freedom and civil rights, some would have practiced their faith in secret, some fled the brutal persecution by leaving France, and eventually some resisted politically (Williams & Waldvogel, 1975:75). The resisters in France's Cevennes mountains were known as Camisards, which name derives "from the peasants' smocks that the Camisards wore" as in the French word *camiso* meaning "shirt" plus French *-ard* (Merriam-Webster Dictionary, 2023).

The Camisard Prophets "claimed that they were directly inspired by the Holy Spirit" (Williams & Waldvogel, 1975:75). Out of that dreadful period of persecution of France's Huguenots, in 1688 AD, the first remarkable report was of a wool-carder's young daughter, Isabeau Vincent, though knowing only their native *patois* [Occitan dialects], prophesying for hours in "perfectly cultivated French" (Hinson, 1967:60).

Occitan (Provençal) is spoken by people in southern France and is part of the Romance language family, which includes French, Italian, Spanish, Portuguese, and Romanian. Today, all Occitan speakers use French as their official and cultural language, but Occitan dialects are still used for everyday purposes (Britannica, 2023:Occitan language).

HISTORICAL ANALYSIS OF "LANGUAGE/LANGUAGES"

The book "*Les Prophètes Protestants,*" is a reprint of the book entitled "*Le théatre sacré des Cévennes*" or alternately titled in English "*Narrative of the various wonders newly operated in this part of the province of Languedoc.*" It was written by Francis Maximilian Misson, originally François Maximilien Misson (c.1650–12 January 1722 AD), who was a French author and travel writer, and who had been a judge in the "chamber of the edict" in the Parlement de Paris (British Museum, 2023: Francis Maximilian Misson). Born in Lyons, he left France in 1687, after the 1685 revocation of the Edict of Nantes, and settled in London (British Museum, 2023: Francis Maximilian Misson). He was actively involved throughout his life in the affairs of the French church in London, promoting the "French prophets" of the Cévennes, especially through his written works (British Museum, 2023: Francis Maximilian Misson). This French book, *Les Prophètes Protestants*, has a preface and notes by Ami Bost.

The original eyewitness accounts by Camisards are in French but translated into English below (Misson, 1847:139–141).

Jean Vernet, a refugee to England, from France, testified in London, that in 1693 AD amid the Camisard persecutions, to his great surprise, he had first heard his mother, in repeated episodes over several years, speak only French, which she'd never uttered a word in before (Williams & Waldvogel, 1975:76). The eyewitness account is reported in the book, *Les Prophètes Protestants* (Misson, 1847:139–140), wherein this Jean Vernet, of Bois-Châtel, in the Vivarais [region in the southeast of France on the river Rhône], in a deposition on January 14, 1707, declared the following:

> My sisters received the gift some time after my mother received it; one at the age of nineteen, and the other at eleven . . . . She spoke only French during the inspiration; which caused me great surprise the first time I heard it; *for never had she tried to say a word in that language, nor will ever have done since, to my knowledge*; and I'm *sure she wouldn't have done it when she wanted to*. I can say *the same* of my sisters. All three made great exhortations to the amendment of life; and in my private individual, as I was a little libertine, they urged me strongly to govern myself with more wisdom.

Vernet remarked that when these pronouncements were made, "my mother or my said sisters were in ecstasy" (Misson, 1847:140).

The Earliest View of New Testament Tongues

Les Prophètes Protestants goes on to report (Misson, 1847:140) of a Jacques Keboux, "After the greatest agitations, he began to speak and he made great exhortations to repentance."

Another remarkable occurrence, which happened among the Camisards, was the ability among toddlers to deliver exhortations in flawless French (Williams & Waldvogel, 1975:76; cf. Misson, 1847:152–154). What's notable about these descriptions is that there was no need of translation, as the listeners gathered around understood what was said (Misson, 1847:140–141).

These and a number of other depositions are reported in the subsequent pages (Misson, 1847:1–196) of *Les Prophètes Protestants*, a reputedly credible and original source. These examples suffice to demonstrate that the Camisard manifestations would more accurately be labelled "prophesying" as the duress-induced speeches under "inspiration" and in "ecstasy" by men, women, young children and toddlers "were to urge repentance" (Misson, 1847:143) and "predicted the ruin of the Antichrist and the deliverance of the Church" (Misson, 1847:143) in the French language which they hadn't previously spoken or at a much better level of fluency in the view of the reporter. There is also one reference to "foreign language" which may or may not have been French (Misson, 1847:154), followed by the speaker explaining himself.

It seems that various writers have mistaken prophetic-type fervor or a trance-like state or terrorized hysteria for some form of "tongues" and then the error has been compounded by yet other writers undiscerningly repeating the statement, without checking the original sources (Burgess, 1976:17; Schaff, 1882:237; Randall, 2009:Kindle locations 17, 246, 764, 849, 1211, 1602, footnotes 125–128, chapter 3; Frodsham, 1941:254, 255, 258; Hinson, 1967:59; Kelsey, 1968:52–54; MacArthur, 1992:234). For example, Catharine Randall (2009:Kindle Locations 847–853) in *From a Far Country: Camisards and Huguenots in the Atlantic World* tells of one of the few women to testify for the *Théâtre Sacré* (on March 15,1707), a Marie Chauvain, a widow from Provence, who supposedly claimed that after witnessing one of her seasonal, teenage workers prophesy, she herself began to speak in tongues. Readers can judge for themselves that there is nothing in the entire account that indicates "tongues," by referring to the full French version of the actual deposition in the pages Randall attributes as her source (Misson, 1847:176–178). This eyewitness account also incidentally exposes the fact that some of the Camisards were exposed to the more cultured French language when they worked as seasonal laborers down in the valleys for French orchard owners. This is to say that some of the Camisards had at least been around the related French language and may have subliminally and unconsciously absorbed some of the language as younger minds might be quicker to do.

In 1539, the Edict of Villers-Cotterêts, established French as the official language in France's administrative and justice systems, which propelled the French language dominance, leading to the decline of Occitan and other regional languages (Britannica, 2023:Edict of Villers-Cotterêts; Cite langue francaise, 2023:Ordinance of Villers-Cotterets).

Many of these "minor" prophets were young people, both guys and gals, with most of them illiterate and only speaking the Occitan dialects, which is why it surprised some that they should prophesy in French (Musée protestant, 2023:The Bible in times of persecution . . .). The Occitan dialects share some features with the French language and have a number of common and cognate words and word order similarities. The Scriptures most widely available among the Protestants in France were French language versions of the Bible (Musée protestant, 2023:sixteenth-century translations of the Bible into Latin and French). These young people prophesying in French can be explained by their in-depth knowledge of French biblical texts, and an outstanding oral memory (Musée protestant, 2023:Prophetic Movement). These young people had memorised the verses of the Bible when it was read out loud in French (Musée protestant, 2023:The Bible in times of persecution . . .).

The subconscious mind surfaces that which resides deep in the psyche when under great duress as the Camisards tragically were. Anderson (1979:19) makes this point: "Cryptomnesia, in the context of this discussion [*xenoglossia*], is the ability to recall in trance a language that one has heard or seen but never consciously committed to memory. Cryptomnesia requires a deep state of dissociation . . . " Samarin (1972:115) also affirms that some alleged cases of *xenoglossia* (previously unspoken earthly languages) might be explained by cryptomnesia which is defined as something coming to the fore in the conscious mind which was stored in the "hidden memory" or a language one has been exposed to coming to the surface under certain kinds of stress. Certainly, the Camisards were under incredible stress and dread and the adrenalin must have been flowing pretty much non-stop.

In these personal Camisard accounts there is no indication of a non-earthly, angelic/heavenly language for public or private use. In other words, *glossolalia* (non-earthly) as in the modern-day, common Pentecostal/Charismatic experience was not in their purview. It was rather a seemingly miraculous expression of the French language, foreign to some of the speakers or an enhanced French language ability to others of these mostly uneducated and illiterate, horrendously persecuted Protestants. The inhumanity and brutality of the Catholic Church and their agents made it a very dark day in the life of professed Christianity. What is notable about all the Camisard occurrences is that there is no expectation or need of translation/interpretation, as the listeners understood what was said.

After the genocidal actions against the Camisards began to diminish, in 1730 AD, prophetic utterances became increasingly common among a faction of the Catholic Jansenists. The broader Jansenist body promoted the doctrine of grace as put forward by Augustine. The Jansenists had a grievance against Pope Clement XI's *Unigenitus* (1713 AD) condemnation of their Augustinian beliefs (Ott, 1912).

In the later stages of the Jansenist movement (1727ff AD) within the Roman Catholic Church, strange and fervent, convulsive activity centered around the tomb of a revered, ascetic, Catholic Jansenist deacon, Francois de Paris (June 30, 1690 AD–May 1, 1727 AD), at the Saint-Medard Catholic Church Cemetery in Paris (Mathieu, 1864:1–491; cf. Kreiser, 1978:173–177). Those invoking the intercession of the deceased Jansenist deacon for a cure would lie on his grave, and some would thrash around in spasms and convulsions there, creating quite the spectacle (Mathieu, 1864:199–200; cf. Kreiser, 1978:173–177; Strayer, 2008:245). Some later confessed that they had faked the convulsions because they had seen others do it (Kreiser, 1978:211–212).

The grave-side cult of the deceased Jansenist Francois de Paris intensified around his relics (wood from his bed, wool from his mattress, his clothes, his hair, his fingernails) (Mathieu, 1864, 2009). Among many other strange reports, there was also an account of dirt from the grave site of Francois de Paris in a wine suspension which supposedly effected a healing (Mathieu, 1864, 2012 "l'usage d'un vin tenant en suspension de la terre enlevée au tombeau du diacre Pâris n'avaient fait que préparer"). The stories are very peculiar (Mathieu, 1864).

After a civil ban on gathering at the tomb of the revered Catholic Jansenist deacon, Francois de Paris who had deceased on May 1, 1727 AD (Kreiser, 1978:89), and the closure on January 29, 1732 AD of the Saint-Medard Catholic Church Cemetery in Paris (Kreiser, 1978:243–244),

HISTORICAL ANALYSIS OF "LANGUAGE/LANGUAGES"

within a year, many turned to a quasi-millenarian eschatology introduced into *convulsionary* circles, at that time, by Jansenist priests and theologians (Kreiser, 1978:244-245). Clandestine conventicles developed throughout Paris and beyond (Kreiser, 1978:250ff, 278).

In preparation for these cell meetings, and in imitation of the ascetic, Jansenist Catholic deacon, Francois de Paris, some endured extended periods of intensely subduing one's bodily desires, sleep deprivation, and excessive fasting "which no doubt help to account for some of the ecstatic experiences" (Kreiser, 1978:255). At some point in the meeting, as religious enthusiasm predictably heightened, contagious, convulsive seizures began to occur, where "They thrashed about on the floor in a state of frenzy, screaming, roaring, trembling and twitching" (Kreiser, 1978:256). Some archival reports indicate that about three quarters of the convulsionists were women (Kreiser, 1978:259). The ability to have convulsions became a prestigious status symbol among them (Kreiser, 1978:258).

These contagious, convulsive seizures were often accompanied with vocal utterances (Kreiser, 1978:268):

> Some of this "speech," serving perhaps as a form of prayer, consisted of little more than unintelligible mutterings and a steady stream of incomprehensible exclamations. In other cases, it involved equally incoherent screaming and roaring, howling and yelling. Still other convulsionaries spent these periods of "inspiration" making utterly obscure pronouncements that were without any particular logic, sequence, or theme.

Extremist cells of the Jansenists continued to engage in brutal, torturous, sadomasochistic practices (Strayer, 2008:269) and even conducted crucifixions, the last of which was documented in 1788 AD (Strayer, 2008:282).

The Paris cult manifestations of "unintelligible mutterings, incomprehensible exclamations, incoherent screaming, roaring, howling and yelling" have been too conveniently sanitized by those who want to portray it as examples of acceptable precedents of modern day *glossolalic* "tongues." The context, taken as a whole, was not honourable as these bizarre cultists followed the extreme ascetic lifestyle of their exemplar, the Catholic deacon, Francois de Paris (Strayer, 208:250-251, 258). Francois de Paris wore a metal plate with wires to cut into his flesh and a spiked metal belt and beat himself with an iron-tipped lash until the blood ran down his back (Strayer, 208:238). These and other macabre self-torture devices understandably weakened him, so that he died before his 37th birthday of "religious suicide" (Kreiser, 1978:88–91). The roots determined the fruit.

While still on the European continent, figuratively speaking, we need to look in on the eighteenth-century Moravians. Their earthly protector and eventual resuscitator, Nicholas Zinzendorf was born May 26, 1700 (Hamilton, 1900:17) and lived until May 9, 1760 AD (Hamilton, 1900:159). In 1722 AD, this Count Zinzendorf began to allow Moravian refugees, from Bohemia and Moravia in the Czech Republic, to live on his Saxony estate in Germany and they established a village, which they named Herrnhut (Hamilton, 1900:26–27). In 1727 AD, there was the outbreak of a revival with a visitation of the Holy Spirit which restored unity to the community which had become divided into factions (Hamilton, 1900:38–39).

There is no mention of "tongues" or *glossolalia* in their Moravian Catechism (Moravian Church, 2020:1–55) nor in the much older "Doctrinal Position of the Moravian Church" (Hamilton, 1900:592–601). There is no mention of "tongues" in the many articles on Zinzendorf (e. g. Appletons', Vol. 6, 1889:661; Britannica, 2023:Zinzendorf; Schattschneider, 1998:762; MacCulloch, 2009:744–7; etc.).

In an extended account, in the *Memoir of Count* Zinzendorf, of the religious revival at Herrnhut on August 13, 1727, and in the months leading up to it and thereafter, there is no mention of "tongues" (*glossolalia*) or anything closely approximating it (Pond, 1839:38–53, 126–138). Those making claims for historic Moravian "tongues" don't cite any primary sources. It appears to be another case of "aversion to the primary records, with the result that the same stories are repeated again and again—usually without question—and mistakes once made are perpetuated and often compounded" (Burgess, 1976:16).

In the late eighteenth century, Edward Irving (August 4, 1792– December 7, 1834 AD), a Scotch Presbyterian clergyman came on the scene. The Irvingite "tongues" episodes are an important saga for the modern *glossolalia* (a non-earthly, angelic/heavenly language for public or private use) narrative, as Irving is often dubbed as the forerunner of modern Pentecostalism. It appears that our Epiphanius thesis on γλῶσσαι (*glōssai*) is impacted insofar as proponents of Irvingite-era "tongues" quickly shift into advocating that the experience was different than the Pentecost event recorded in Acts 2 and that the "tongues" needed translation, unlike the book of Acts occurrences where no translation was called for.

The chain of events was instigated in 1830 via the Campbell family in the Glasgow vicinity of western Scotland who had experiences of "tongues" (Oliphant, 1862:129). It was initially thought to be earthly, foreign languages, but gave way to instead being "a supernatural sign and attestation of the intelligible prophecy" as Oliphant (1862:206) reports that:

> Mary Campbell herself expressed her conviction that the tongue given to her was that of the Pelew Islands, which, indeed, was a safe statement, and little likely to be authoritatively disputed; while some other conjectures pointed to the Turkish and Chinese languages as those thus miraculously bestowed. Since then opinion seems to have changed, even among devout believers in these wonderful phenomena; the hypothesis of actual languages conferred seems to have given way to that of a supernatural sign and attestation of the intelligible prophecy...

Sometime after these incidents, Irving assented to special morning prayer meetings in the vestry for an "outpouring" (Miller, 1878:67, Vol. 1), which, because of overflow, transitioned into the Regent Square Church auditorium where, not wanting to restrain the Spirit, he allowed "prophesying" and "tongues" in the early morning meetings (Miller, 1878:68, Vol. 1). "Thenceforward the prophets had their way with him" (Miller, 1878:69, Vol. 1). Soon, the exercise of "the gifts" were permitted in the Sunday morning services (Miller, 1878:70, vol. 1) and shortly thereafter "at all services, without reserve" (Miller, 1878:71, Vol. 1) at Irving's Regent Square Church in London. This eventually, being the issue beneath the surface, got him deposed from that church and subsequently was the unstated reason for his being defrocked in 1833 as a minister of the Church of Scotland (Britannica, 1911:855).

The outburst of "tongues" occurrences that eventuated were presumed to be caused by the Holy Spirit and termed by Irving as *unknown*, whereas much to Irving's consternation, an attender, George Pilkington, who assumed himself to be a language aficionado asserted that on a certain occasion they were languages of English, Spanish and Latin (Pilkington, 1832:21–40). Irving had Pilkington called to a special meeting, at which he was bluntly told, "You cannot interpret by human understanding; interpretation must be given by the Spirit" (Anon., 1832:32–33).

The Earliest View of New Testament Tongues

Irving was evasive, having initially, in 1825, said that the gift of tongues at Pentecost were for the promulgation of the gospel to all nations (Irving, 1825:57). By 1828, Irving admitted that the γλῶσσαις (*glōssais*/languages) of the Acts 2:4ff Pentecost event was the miraculous ability to speak in a foreign language but the speakers could not comprehend the language(s) nor could their hearers unless the gift of interpretation then came into play (Irving, 1864:558). It was simply channelled through them with their own mind suspended, and was the indication of intimate communion with God, but the gift of interpretation needed to be then exercised to complete the sequence (Irving, 1864:558). This *unknown tongues* was a new definition without precedent in the annals of church history. Various versions of the English Bible were by then using the word *unknown* as an adjective of γλῶσσαι/*glōssai* (languages/tongues) in the Apostle Paul's 1 Corinthians letter, but discerning readers would have understood that the word "*unknown*" was placed in italics to show that it was not derived from the original Greek text.

Nevertheless, without historical support, as surveyed thus far, the novel concept proposed by Edward Irving proved to be the precursor of the modern "tongues" movement and its definition of a *glossolalic* non-earthly, angelic/heavenly language for public or private use.

In January of 1834, his last year on earth, being minutely obedient to the explicit commands of his newly established, independent Newman Street Church apostles and prophets, Irving was sent on a mission to a church with "an evil spirit" in Edinburgh (Oliphant, 1862:370–371). "From this mission, he returned very ill," brought on by "the griefs and disappointments which encompassed him" and "the chill of this wintry journey" (Oliphant, 1862:371). His doctors urged rest and warm weather, but he had been issued authoritative orders by the Newman Street Church prophets that he was "to do a great work in his native land" of Scotland (Oliphant, 1862:374–375). So with the directive of his spiritual superiors at his Newman Street Church (Oliphant, 1862:375), and free from their "apostolic" and "prophetic" censure and rebuke (Oliphant, 1862:375), starting out in September of 1834, Edward Irving made his last journey to his home country and there a few months later succumbed to tuberculosis/consumption (Hannan, 2017) that Lord's Day, December 7, 1834, at the age of 42 (Oliphant, 1862:402–403). The fact that Jesus Christ did not return in 1864, as Irving had predicted, further tarnished his reputation (Britannica, 2023:Edward Irving) nor did it help that, a Mr. Baxter, one of Irving's most active and urgent prophets, came to the conviction that they "had all been speaking by a lying spirit, and not by the Spirit of the Lord" (Oliphant, 1862:420).

By the time of 1878, the *unknown tongues* were a thing of the past in the Catholic Apostolic Churches which formed as a consequence of Irving's ministry (Miller, 1878:239, Vol. 2).

So, the truism seems to hold that from the Apostolic Fathers until the second quarter of the nineteenth century, there is nothing that compares with the Irvingite-era of "tongues" which was the immediate precursor to the modern-day version of "tongues" (i.e., non-earthly *glossolalic* "language").

At the same time as the Irvingite narrative was evolving in the United Kingdom, the new Mormon (LDS) sect in the United States was experiencing "tongues" by its adherents and notably by a zealous convert Brigham Young (June 1, 1801–August 29, 1877 AD), which was then decreed by their "prophet" Joseph Smith (December 23, 1805–June 27, 1844 AD) as the language of Adam (Smith, 1902:296–297, Vol. 1). Joseph Smith soon received the "gift of tongues" also (Smith, 1902:296–297, Vol. 1). Thereafter, Joseph Smith, the founder of Mormonism, taught his followers to speak in "tongues" in this way: "Rise upon your feet, speak or make some sound and continue to make sounds of some kind and the Lord will make a tongue or language of it" (Samarin, 1972:53).

Copeland (1991:13) writes that,

> ... during the mid-1800s, speaking in tongues was so commonplace in the LDS and RLDS churches that a person who had not spoken in tongues, or who had not heard others do so, was a rarity. Journals and life histories of that period are filled with instances of the exercise of this gift of the Spirit.

Copeland (1991:20) further emphasizes that,

> From 1833 to 1836, speaking in tongues became a [Mormon] church-wide phenomenon. The 'language' spoken was often identified as the language of Adam. Because speaking in tongues was generally regarded as a sign of the truthfulness of the restored gospel rather than as a tool to be used in spreading the gospel in foreign lands, it generally took the form of glossolalia rather than xenoglossia.

The Earliest View of New Testament Tongues

Some of the particular animosity toward Mormons regarding "speaking in tongues," can be attributed to opponents hearing it exhibited by Mormon children (Copeland, 1991:20–21). Thus, unsurprisingly, there were many in the outside community who were skeptics, and some became so within their own Mormon ranks.

According to Copeland (1991:18), on March 8, 1831, Joseph Smith received the only revelation in the Doctrine and Covenants dealing specifically with gifts of the Spirit: "And again, it is given to some to speak with tongues, And to another is given the interpretation of tongues. And all these gifts come from God, for the benefit of the children of God" (D&C 46:24–26).

Copeland (1991:20) writes that at the March 1836 dedication of the Kirtland Temple, speaking in "tongues" was plentiful and Joseph Smith, in his dedicatory prayer, pled: "Let it be fulfilled upon them, as upon those on the day of Pentecost; that the gift of tongues be poured out upon thy people, even cloven tongues as of fire, and the interpretation thereof" (D&C 109:36).

Samuel Hawthornthwaite was an elder among the Mormons in the Hulme Branch in Manchester, England, in 1850, at a time when the growth of the British LDS church was reaching its peak. Samuel, in a meeting, spoke out a memorized Latin piece, purporting it to be "tongues" which an eager Mormon immediately and incorrectly interpreted (Hawthornthwaite, 1857:86–93). At that point in the history of Mormonism, there was an assumed need for the interpretation of those *glossolalic* "tongues" which on the surface seemed more aligned with 1 Corinthians 14 and different than Acts 2 Pentecost and the other Acts occurrences where no translation appeared to be needed or called for.

Copeland (1991:22) detects a decided shift on the understanding and practice of Mormon "tongues" in the mid 1800s.

> Between 1837 and 1899, though the [LDS] Saints continued to speak in the Adamic language, Church leaders emphasized the utility of speaking in foreign languages, or xenoglossia.... William Clayton's 1840 missionary journal is filled with instances of speaking in tongues (Allen and Alexander 1974, see entries for 7 Feb.; 29 May; 12,13,14, 27 June; and 6 Oct. 1840).

Today, the Seventh Article of Faith of the Mormons (LDS) states: "We believe in the gift of tongues, prophecy, revelation, visions, healing, interpretation of tongues, and so forth" (Copeland, 1991:13).

HISTORICAL ANALYSIS OF "LANGUAGE/LANGUAGES"

Some investigators discount this religious aspect of "tongues," instead considering *glossolalia* to be a normal, though uncommon, human behaviour (Copeland, 1991:14). Carlyle May (1956:75-96) of Harvard University, in an extensively documented *American Anthropologist* journal article entitled *A Survey of Glossolalia and Related Phenomena in Non-Christian Religions*, showed "that *glossolalia* and similar speech-phenomena occur in various forms during shamanistic rites of the New, and especially of the Old, World."

Gromacki (1967:5-10) notes that frenzied speech (*glossolalia*) occurred among the ancient Greek and early Phoenician religions, the Greco-Roman mystery religions, Islam, and in the paganism of the Eskimos, Tibetans and Chinese. *Glossolali*a has been a common practice among many pagan groups, witch doctors and the demonically possessed right up to the present (Kildahl, 1974:76; Copeland, 1991:14; Rose, 1979:170).

4.4 MODERN PERIOD—AZUSA UNTIL THIRD WAVE (1906-1980 AD)

Events related to Charles Parham and Azusa Street in Los Angeles, California, are the next "tongues" occurrences that loom large on the radar.

Charles Fox Parham was an independent evangelist in the early twentieth century (Parham, 1930:23-28). The doctrine of initial evidence—that the baptism of the Holy Spirit is evidenced by speaking in "tongues"—was his major contribution to the modern "tongues" movement (Blumhofer, 1993:56). At Parham's urging, a black student of his, William Seymour, went to Los Angeles, California to conduct revival meetings which in due course congregated at a rented building on Azusa Street (McClung, 2006:5). The resulting Azusa Street Revival has become the seminal public image for at least the type of Western Pentecostalism which began to spread over the globe.

Parham believed "tongues" to be the miraculous speaking in a foreign language previously unknown by the speaker for the purpose of preaching the gospel. Charles Parham's wife, Sarah, writes a biography wherein she confirms that her husband's view was that it was foreign languages (Parham, 1930:62, 116-117, 163). From neither of Charles or Sarah Parham, do we get an impression that "speaking in tongues" was a *glossolalic* non-earthly, angelic/heavenly language for public or private use (Parham, 1930:1–452).

William Seymour had been heavily influenced by Parham's ministry in Houston (Blumhofer, 1993:55). Parham funded and sent Seymour to Los Angeles, California, to collaborate in the work there with Lucy Farrow, a black woman who had been the cook at Parham's Houston school (McClung, 2006:5). When Parham, Seymour's "Father in this gospel of the Kingdom," came to Los Angeles and the Azusa Street mission, he had a falling out with Seymour, over what Parham perceived as the fanaticism and "unteachable spirit and spiritual pride" that he observed there (Parham, 1930:163). Parham judged the Azusa meetings as led by Seymour as having "hypnotic influences, familiar-spirit influences, spiritualistic influences, mesmeric influences, and all kinds of spells, spasms, falling in trances" (Parham, 1930:168).

Parham clearly believed that "tongues" was not to be a "jabbering and sputtering, speaking in no language at all" (Parham, 1930:163). Charles Parham believed it was the miraculous speaking of an earthly, human language, previously unknown to the speaker, given for the purpose of evangelism and missions, extinguishing the need for missionaries to learn foreign languages and thus expediting the spread of the gospel (Blumhofer, 1993:52). Hunter (1980:135) states that, "it was Charles Parham who remained the outspoken critic of tongues that were not xenolalic."

Faupel (1996:97) writes of the conviction by Pentecostal, Wesleyan and Evangelical leaders that the gift of tongues would be restored as "missionary languages" to enable the rapid evangelization of the world before the end of the church age.

Those expectations were soon shattered by harsh disappointment (Faupel, 1996:99; Anderson, 2006:109). S. C. Todd, of the Bible Missionary Society, investigated mission stations in China, India, and Japan where Pentecostals came "expecting to be able to preach to the natives of those countries in their own tongues" and by their own confession, he discovered that "in no single instance have they been able to do so" (Faupel, 1996:99).

In The Christian Alliance and Missionary Weekly on "The Gift of Tongues," Editor A.B. Simpson (1892:98) had instructed:

> Certainly we do expect, in every case where it is claimed by humble believing prayer, a supernatural assistance in acquiring

the native language, and we should not be surprised in any case to hear of the direct bestowal of the power to speak an unknown tongue.

Six years later, in a weekly sermon for publication, entitled "The Worship and Fellowship of the Church," Rev. A. B. Simpson (1898:126), the founder of what much later became the C&MA denomination, of which I am a member, had mellowed his perspective thus:

> This surely settles the question. If more is needed to be said it would be sufficient to add that the apostle preached the Gospel to the people among whom he moved through the Greek, Latin, and Hebrew languages which he had himself acquired, and on one or two occasions his audiences were surprised to find that he could speak their language through the large and liberal culture which he had received. . . .
>
> In our own day there is the same strained and extravagant attempt to unduly exaggerate the gift of tongues, and some have even proposed that we should send our missionaries to the foreign field under a sort of moral obligation to claim this gift, and to despise the ordinary methods of acquiring a language.

By April 4, 1908, we get a further picture of the evolved position of the C&MA in A.J. Ramsey's exegetical study on speaking with "tongues" in *The Christian and Missionary Alliance* periodical where he makes the point that the speaking "with tongues" at Corinth was different from the speaking "with other tongues" in Jerusalem on the day of Pentecost (Ramsey, 1908:9).

This disappointment of not acquiring miraculous missionary languages to circumvent years of difficult language learning precipitated a crisis—either straightforwardly admit they were wrong or revise their convictions. The entrenched Pentecostalists reverted to revisionism and shifted it to mean primarily a non-earthly, angelic/heavenly language for public or private use. They were ironically and incidentally helped in this redefinition by German historical-critical scholars. The historical-critical method, which is also known as higher criticism, involves a methodology of probing the Bible with a secular, non-supernatural worldview, negating the possibility of fulfilled prophecy and the miraculous.

In the first half of the nineteenth century, these German historical-critical scholars, who had an aversion to the supposed miracle of *xenolalia*, were reclassifying speaking in tongues as *glossolalia*, meaning unintelligible utterances out of an ecstatic state beyond earthly language (Neander, 1900:11). The German historical-critical scholars were thus defining "speaking in tongues" as a psychological state rather than a miracle of earthly language and this new definition has been virtually the universal position taken in commentaries, theological word study books (TDNT/Theological Dictionary of the New Testamenty, DNTT/Dictionary of New Testament Theology) and Greek linguistic dictionaries (Thayer, BDAG and its earlier editions, Louw & Nida, etc.) ever since. August Neander (1900:11), who died in 1850 AD, was the leading proponent of this redefinition, and this new thinking then made its way into the English vocabulary (1879ff AD) through the influence of men like Frederick Farrar (Oxford English Dictionary, 1933:232) and Philip Schaff (1910a:230).

August Neander (1900:11) pointedly writes of 1 Corinthians 14 that "the apostle is there treating of such discourse as would not be generally intelligible, proceeding from an ecstatic state of mind which rose to an elevation far above the language of ordinary, earthly communication." Neander (1900:12-17) then, in liberal theological fashion, imposes that view back into the Acts passages attempting to prove that even the Pentecost event was *glossolalic* unintelligible utterances out of an ecstatic state, beyond ordinary language, violating even his own acknowledged "natural laws of exegesis" when he "attempt[s] to explain the clearer passages by the more obscure" (Neander, 1900:11).

Farrar (1880:97), who lived from 1831 to 1903 AD, also vigorously denied that the tongues of the Acts 2 Pentecost account had anything to with earthly, foreign languages: "Pentecost, does not contain the remotest hint of foreign languages. Hence the fancy that this was the immediate result of Pentecost is unknown to the first two centuries, and only sprang up when the true tradition had been obscured." Farrar (1880:97-104) goes on at great length to denigrate the belief that it was earthly, foreign languages in effect at Pentecost as intimated in Acts 2:9-11. Farrar was quoted affirmingly by Pentecostalist writers (Boddy, 1914:88-89).

Philip Schaff, who had embraced the German historical-critical mode, was a darling of certain Pentecostal writers (Bartleman, 1980:77, 167). Pentecostalists were also enamoured with two other leaders who had embraced the German historical-critical mode, namely the writers of *The Life and Epistles of St. Paul* (1863), W. J. Conybeare and J. S.

Howson, who are quoted favourably on the new "tongues" definition by Pentecostalists (Bartleman, 1980:77; Boddy, 1908:4). <u>Conybeare and Howson's</u> (1863:401–402) newly conjured-up definition of *glōssai*s at Pentecost (Acts 2) was that it was not foreign languages, but an ecstatic trance whereby the believer was constrained by an irresistible power to pour forth his feelings of thanksgiving and rapture in words not his own and which meaning he was usually ignorant of.

The irony is that, back in that era, Pentecostalism was very suspicious of higher education (Wacker, 2001:73ff) and few of their pastors and Bible teachers had education beyond elementary or junior high equivalency (Wacker, 2001:199–212; Anderson, 1979:100–110, 291–295). In any event, incongruously, rationalistic, anti-supernatural, historical-critical scholarship provided the support for the Pentecostalist's redefinition to *glossolalia* (primarily a non-earthly, angelic/heavenly language for public or private use) and thus the contradictory heritage of the otherwise conservative and fundamental Pentecostalism. Having to redefine their novel experiences forced Pentecostalists to concur with rationalistic, anti-supernatural, historical-critical scholarship on this issue.

According to Pentecostal historian Vinson Synan, by 1981 there were estimates of 75,000,000 Pentecostals and Charismatics worldwide, with millions of Roman Catholics included in that number (Bartleman, 1980:xxiv). Synan reported that in 1975 over 10,000 Roman Catholics gathered in St. Peter's Cathedral in Rome to celebrate the Pentecost season and at the climax of that service thousands are reported to have spoken and sung in "other tongues" (Bartleman, 1980:xxiv). At a similar Pentecost service in England's Anglican Canterbury Cathedral in 1978, "tongues" broke out among the assembled (Bartleman, 1980:xxiv).

The Charismatic movement which launched the newly defined "tongues" (i.e., *glossolalia*, non-earthly, angelic/heavenly "tongues" for public or private use) into non-Pentecostal churches is usually identified with the 1960 announcement by Dennis Bennett, priest of St. Mark's Episcopal Church in Van Nuys, California, that he had been baptized in the Holy Spirit and had spoken in "tongues" (Hyatt, 2002:2). The penetration of modern-day "tongues" into the Roman Catholic Church began at a retreat, from February 17–19, 1967, attended by professors and grad students from Duquesne University in Pittsburgh, Pennsylvania (Hyatt, 2002:177).

The Epiphanius thesis on γλῶσσαι (*glōssai*) agrees with Ramsey in the foregoing (1908:9) that the speaking "with tongues" at Corinth was different from the speaking "with other tongues" in Jerusalem on the day of Pentecost because in 1 Corinthians 14, in order for the assembled believers to be edified, there was the need for translation of these unfamiliar languages/tongues, unlike in the Acts chapter two Pentecost and the other Acts occurrences where no translation was required or called for. The hearers understood what was being said (Acts 2:4–11; 10:46; 19:6).

The Acts occurrences were to confirm, to skeptical Jews, God's gracious inclusion of additional groups by his Holy Spirit. In the first-century AD Corinthian congregations, when translated, the γλῶσσαι (*glōssai*) was meant to be primarily for the edification of the assembled believers.

4.5 PRESENT TIME (1980FF AD)

In 1983, C. Peter Wagner, then professor of church growth at Fuller Theological Seminary School of World Missions, referred to a Third Wave of the Holy Spirit's work that was already stirring in the conservative, evangelical churches (Hyatt, 2002:180). Speaking in *glossolalic* "tongues" commonly occurs in the Third Wave environments (Hyatt, 2002:180).

Morton Kelsey (1968:218) remarks that in gathering the information and surveying the history of *glossolalia* in the present time, there are reportedly positive aspects and negative aspects and even dangerous aspects to the experience. Some claim psychological and emotional benefit from this *glossolalia* (1968:219ff) which linguists call "free vocalization" inspired by an *alienatio mentis* [Latin "alienation of mind"] (Higley, 2007:43). Butler (1985:86) concludes that in many cases it is simply a psychological event with no supernatural origins.

On the dangerous side, occult researcher Kurt Koch (1980:206–210) records several cases where he claims that he had to cast out demons which first possessed a person when he/she spoke in "tongues" (*glossolalia*). Ex-charismatic C.S. Butler (1985:99) records an incident of a man who wanted to receive "speaking in tongues" the supposed evidence of "baptism" with the Holy Spirit—"I let my mind become quite blank and began yielding myself to the external power outside myself that seemed to be pleading for full control of me. At once a feeling of paralysis began to numb my feet. It soon affected my legs . . . I became alarmed. 'This thing is coming upon me from beneath . . . ' Without a moment's hesitation, I cried out, 'May the blood of Christ protect me from this thing!' At once it vanished and I was normal again."

To reiterate, from post-apostolic times to the second quarter of the 1800s, γλῶσσαι (*glōssai*) meant real, earthly, foreign languages, whereas the modern-day "tongues," known as *glossolalia*, is defined as primarily non-earthly, angelic/heavenly languages for public or private use.

Thorough studies have found no evidence that this *glossalalic* phenomenon in the present time has either the form or the structure of human speech (Faupel, 1996:101). Anderson (1979:16ff) cites a number of studies where tape recordings of *glossolalia* have been thoroughly assessed by linguists who found no correspondence to traditional human languages and that modern-day "speaking in tongues is incoherent, repetitive syllabification having neither the form nor the structure of human speech" (Anderson, 1979:16–17).

A study analysing the tape-recorded "tongues" of more than sixty persons in Southern California demonstrated that not one person spoke a word of any known language and that when the same tape of any given individual was "interpreted" by several persons claiming the "gift of interpretation," the interpretations were all different (Anderson, 1979:16–17).

Professor William J. Samarin of the University of Toronto's Department of Linguistics did an extensive study of modern-day *glossolalia* ["tongue-speaking"] and concluded that, in the hundreds of examples he studied in his travels across the world, all lacked several essential elements of languages: grammar, syntax, vocabulary, etc. (Samarin, 1972:104-9). After over a decade of systematic research in various Christian denominations, Samarin unequivocally rejected the idea that modern day *glossolalia* or ecstatic utterance is some currently spoken foreign language of this world and came to the conclusion that modern-day *glossolalia* is a "pseudo-language" (Samarin, 1972:234–235) and a "façade of language" (Samarin, 1972:128). As a result of his study, he defined *glossolalia* as "A meaningless but phonologically structured human utterance believed by the speaker to be a real language but bearing no systematic resemblance to any natural language, living or dead" (Samarin, 1972:2).

In regard to fakery, manipulation or self-inducement with "tongues-speaking," Kildahl (1974:74; cf. Kildahl, 1972:2–5) lays out the sequence:

> There are five steps in the process of inducing someone to speak in tongues.... From a psychological point of view, the first step seems to involve some kind of magnetic relationship between the leader and the one who is about to attempt to speak in tongues. Second, the initiate generally has a sense of personal distress—usually involving a profound life crisis. Third, the initiate has been taught a rationale for understanding what tongues-speaking is. Fourth, the presence of a supporting group of fellow believers enhances the possibility of eventually speaking in tongues. Fifth, somewhere in the process there is an intense emotional atmosphere.

Kildahl, above, proposes that the phenomena of "tongues" is commonly linked to peer pressure and self-expectation. Charismatic/Pentecostal leadership promotes the concept of their members/adherents speaking in "tongues;" many congregants anticipate other members will eventually speak in "tongues;" and most of the members themselves expect to speak in "tongues." Some Charismatic/Pentecostal churches offer specific seminars to encourage attenders to speak in "tongues" (Kildahl, 1972:2–5; cf. Hunter, 1976:188). Neil Babcox (1985:64–65), an ex-charismatic, reports how he learned to speak in "tongues" and gained fluency through practice. A linguist reports that he's been able to teach a class of students to speak in "tongues," without reference to religious beliefs (Kildahl, 1974:76). Even if not consciously aware of it, as Samarin (1972:74) remarked, "the tongue speaker is the product of considerable instruction."

Faupel (1996:108), at the time of his writing, stated that his Wesleyan church denomination questions "whether it [*glossolalia*] reflects New Testament practice. The primary reason given is the conviction that biblical tongues were actual languages while the contemporary phenomenon is not." At the conclusion of his academic article on the subject, Weaver (1973:23) concludes that "The present day phenomenon of Christians claiming to speak in tongues has some other explanation than that it is a continuation of the New Testament practice of the gift."

Williams and Waldvogel (1975:64) add a nuance to the long-held historic understanding of γλῶσσαι (*glóssai*) being real, earthly, foreign languages, by suggesting that, as an alternate to it being an instantaneous attainment of a previously unlearned, earthly language, it may be an acquisition by "swift linguistic acuity." This would be a little closer to the Epiphanius thesis that 1 Corinthians chapter 14 is not referring to

HISTORICAL ANALYSIS OF "LANGUAGE/LANGUAGES"

a non-earthly or ecstatic phenomenon nor being instantaneously given a previously unlearned, earthly, foreign language, but the γλῶσσαι (*glōssai*) conflict in Corinth was a problem of pompous people using Hebrew and Greek dialects in elevated manner to pridefully posture as superior to others in the assembly.

4.6 CONCLUSIONS

It is crucial to recognize that there is a very telling gap of close to 100 years from the writing of Corinthians/Acts to the first known mention (about 160 AD), by any church figure, of γλῶσσαι/*glōssai* (languages/tongues), subsequent to the Apostolic Age. It is also significant that these first recorded remarks, *circa* 160 AD, were ambiguous and were by Irenaeus, the Gentile bishop of what is now Lyons, France, far removed from the Judean culture at the time of the first Christian Pentecost and the writing of the first canonical Corinthian epistle. Irenaeus, whose words on the matter appear to have been misconstrued, would have been without an indigenous knowledge of the importance of the Hebrew language to the Temple ritual and to the Jews. By the middle of the second century AD, there was a loss of the Hebrew language ethos held by the first-generation believers and to which the Diasporan pilgrims to the major Jewish festivals were also exposed prior to the 70 AD destruction of the Jerusalem Temple. The Gentile Church Father, Irenaeus, does not acknowledge that Hebrew had been ingrained as the "holy language" for a number of centuries and that all other earthly languages were viewed as just that—"other languages" (cf. Acts 2:4). Had Irenaeus recognized this vital socio-linguistic fact, this first post-apostolic pronouncement, at about 160 AD, may have been clarified and thus altered the trajectory of comments thereafter on the matter.

Overlapping the life span of the Romaniote Jewish Bishop, Epiphanius, the writings of Ambrosiaster, are the mother lode in terms of aligning with the Epiphanius position on γλῶσσαι/*glōssai* in 1 Corinthians 14. In referring to the pride and pretension of some who addressed the first-century Corinthian assembly, Ambrosiaster (2009:186) described the precipitating cause of this posturing being their Jewish descent.

This description is remarkably similar to that of Epiphanius who lived from approximately 288 or 310 AD to 403 AD (Jewish Encyclopedia, 2023:Epiphanius), which period of time overlaps these

The Earliest View of New Testament Tongues

Ambrosiaster (Pseudo-Ambrose) writings (c. 366–c. 384 AD). The convergence of "Hebrew in their books" and the speakers' "Greek" preferences buttresses the Epiphanius thesis.

Ambrosiaster's (2009:181) reference to received synagogue customs, fits with the research laid out in the previous chapter 3 of this book and also coincides with the Epiphanius thesis which intimated synagogue precedent. The whole context of any one of the Ambrosiaster passages does not support a glossolalic non-earthly language/tongue but does support the thesis of Epiphanius in respect to γλῶσσαι/*glóssai* in 1 Corinthians 14.

Bishop Severian of Gabala remarked that the "tongues of men" are "human languages" (Severian, 2006:137), which we learn, which don't come to us naturally (Severian, 2006:128), and "Paul wants to speak with a clear mind and in a normal language" (Severian, 2006:139).

It is intriguing that in that early church era, the writings of Epiphanius, Ambrosiaster and Severian, of the same time period, all predicated a similar view of the type and origin of languages/tongues under discussion in 1 Corinthians 14, with some significant geographic spread between these three proponents.

Cyril of Alexandria (Migne, 1863:Vol. 74, Section 25, Col. 757–759; similarly Theodoret of Cyrrhus, 2006:117) acknowledges that subsequent to the occurrence of Pentecost in Acts 2, some of those impressed with themselves being able to speak in γλῶσσαι/*linguae* to strangers perverted the gift by their *insolence* and *ostentation* as they taught sacred things in an unworthy manner. This parallels the Epiphanius understanding of the climate in the Corinthian church that instigates Paul's rebukes in chapter 14.

Cyril of Alexandria's understanding of the Apostle Paul, in the 1 Corinthians 14 context in particular, is that γλῶσσαι/*glóssai* is a reference to earthly, foreign languages learned by those with an aptitude for same, which fits the Epiphanius thesis (Cyril, 1872:293–294; Cyril of Alexandria (Migne, 1859:Vol. 74, Section 30, Col. 888).

Aquinas (2023, section 867–868 of 14-5) acknowledges that "tongues" and "interpretation" can be derived "from human talent." This point of view would harmonize with the Epiphanius thesis.

The views of Martin Luther (Bergendoff, 1958:142) have a very close affinity to the Epiphanius thesis on 1 Corinthians 14, and Luther's insistence that there be translation, into the vernacular language of the auditors, is based on what he understands to be the Apostle Paul's stance on 1 Corinthians 14.

Calvin (1573:372), like Epiphanius, similarly understands the Corinthian problem to have been their "foolish ambition" to show off, "eager to obtain praise and fame." That Calvin (1965:318) believed some in the ancient Corinthian congregation were using earthly, foreign languages for "ostentation and display" parallels the Epiphanius understanding.

Calvin posits that earthly, foreign languages are for edification to bring spiritual understanding to new believers. This supports the Epiphanius view that the languages (γλῶσσαι/*glóssai*) were to be used, with translation, in the normal course of teaching Corinthian congregants.

It is significant that *glossolalia* (a non-earthly, angelic/heavenly language for public or private use) is nowhere alluded to, nor hinted at, nor found in the Apostolic or post-Apostolic Fathers, nor in the major Reformers.

The modern redefined Pentecostal-Charismatic "private language of prayer and praise" or their "public expression of heavenly language" does not appear to be the traditional doctrine of post-apostolic church history but a novelty introduced in the modern era which would actually make it "discontinuous" and not part of "continuationism," at least in respect to γλῶσσαι/*glóssai* (Blosser & Sullivan, 2022: Kindle Location p. 282).

It appears that our Epiphanius thesis on γλῶσσαι (*glóssai*) is viable since from the apostolic era to at least the second quarter of the 1800s there has been found overwhelming evidence that γλῶσσαι/*glóssai* was regarded to be real, earthly languages. The open question then is how was that language(s) acquired? Was it uniformly instantaneous, on-the-spot, in-the-moment acquisition?

In addition to Epiphanius, at a minimum, Ambrosiaster, Cyril of Alexandria, Augustine, Pope Leo I, Theodoret of Cyrrhus, Aquinas, Calvin and Luther, all used wording in their writings on 1 Corinthians that indicated the γλῶσσαι/*glóssai* or *linguae* (languages) could be a more natural-appearing acquisition.

Thus far, the Epiphanius thesis has been shown to be linguistically sound, culturally relevant, and historically viable.

5

Contextual and Exegetical Analysis of γλῶσσαι (glóssai)

THE FRUITS OF RESEARCH from previous chapters 2 (Linguistic Analysis) and 3 (Cultural Analysis), understandably, must of necessity, influence this chapter 5. However, only if the chapter 5 findings are not in contradiction with the foregoing will it lead us to a final defensible conclusion.

We find three references to the use of γλῶσσαι (glóssai—languages/tongues) in Acts (2:4, 10:46, 19:6). There are about 18 references to γλῶσσα/γλῶσσαι (glóssa/glóssai, language/languages) in 1 Corinthians chapters 12, 13, and 14. Over-all, in these Corinthian epistolary passages, in the Apostle Paul's treatment of γλῶσσαι (glóssai—languages/tongues), he indicates that the possession and use of this particular ability had potential for modest value in the early Church. There is also the one occurrence of the term γλῶσσαι (glóssai) in the disputed ending of Mark 16:9–20. Seven of the eight γλῶσσα/γλῶσσαι (glóssa/glóssai) uses in Revelation are conceded by all to simply mean "language/languages" and the eighth is a reference to the organ of speech.

The first manifestation of speaking in γλῶσσαι (glóssai), in the New Testament, occurred at Jerusalem on the day of Pentecost, ten days after Jesus' ascension, when the waiting disciples were baptized with the Holy Spirit (Acts 2:4ff). As a result, Jews originating from the Diaspora heard in their birth languages (Acts 2:8) the preaching of the wonderful works of God (Acts 2: 1–11). It appears that the effect of this

Pentecost language-speaking was to disseminate the gospel message to the different parts of the Roman Empire and beyond, that the Messiah had come in the person of Jesus the Nazarene, attested by miracles, wonders and signs, and though crucified, had risen from the dead and ascended to the right hand of the Father as the triumphant Lord, whereupon he sent the promised Holy Spirit.

Schiffman (2015:53) makes the point that the Dead Sea Scrolls tell us about the apocalyptic messianism of the time and "the expectation of an assumed-to-come redeemer and numerous other motifs found in Qumran apocalyptic tradition [which] have left their mark on the rise of Christianity . . . " This was part of the context of Acts 2.

Secondly, the Holy Spirit subsequently came on the half-Jew Samaritans through the laying on of hands by the Apostles Peter and John (Acts 8: 14–18), but with no mention of "speaking in γλῶσσαι/glōssai."

Thirdly, approximately 7 to 8 years after Pentecost, a baptism with the Holy Spirit with a notable manifestation of "speaking in languages" (γλῶσσαι/glōssai) occurred in Caesarea, when the first Gentiles, Cornelius and his household, were received into the Body of Christ (Acts 10: 43–47; 11:15; cf. Acts 8:26–39 for the competing tradition of the Ethiopian eunuch being the first Gentile conversion). One should well ask the question, "Why did it take more than 7 years after Pentecost for Jesus' Judean followers to go to all nations as Jesus commanded in Matthew 28:19?" Was there lingering prejudice? The Apostle Peter seems to admit as much in his opening words to the assembled Gentiles of the household of Cornelius (Acts 10:34–35).

Fourthly, the Apostle Paul laid hands on the disciples of John the Baptist at Ephesus and the Holy Spirit came on them and they ἐλάλουν τε γλώσσαις καὶ ἐπροφήτευον/elaloun te glōssais kai eprophēteuon—"prophesied" in "languages" (Acts 19: 6).

The Spirit came upon these groups of believers in these four instances subsequent to Pentecost (Acts 8:14–18; 10:43–47; 19:6). These groups appear to be representative.

Of a hermeneutic nature, one must ask, is the book of Acts prescriptive literature or descriptive literature? It appears that, mostly, the book of Acts is descriptive literature and tells us what happened. In some instances, it gives us examples of what to do or think and, in other cases, what not to do nor think. The writer of Acts appears to have polemic (Dunn, 1996:xi–xii) and apologetic (Dunn, 1996:xiii) intentions as well. It has theological themes also (Dunn, 1996:xi–xii, xixff).

The Earliest View of New Testament Tongues

The Acts narrative describes the movement of Jesus' followers during the first several decades after his Ascension. It is a book recording the beginnings of the Church. It can't be assumed that it is a textbook of itemized instructions for living. Because an event or instance occurred in a narrative account doesn't mean it should necessarily continue to occur. The following questions make the point. Must we pray at 3 p.m. every day because Peter and John prayed at that hour (Acts 3)? Must we have all possessions in common with all other Christians in the pattern of the initial Jerusalem community of believers (Acts chapters 2 and 4)? Must we travel by boat as the Apostle Paul did on his missionary journeys, as recorded in Acts?

When proceeding from interpretation to application, narratives require us to be cautious. Narratives can be helpful in illustrating doctrine, but we're on safer hermeneutical ground when the New Testament epistles enunciate it.

To ensure a sound hermeneutic in addressing the Acts passages, one must also acknowledge the transitional character of the book of Acts (Pohl, 1982:17). It is a book recording the transition from the Older Testament to the Newer Testament, from the Age of Law to the Age of Grace—the Church Age (Pohl, 1982:17).

Some claim that Romans 8:26 refers to the "gift of tongues" and argue that speaking in "tongues" need not always be intelligible speech, but that it may consist of words incomprehensible to the ordinary person. The claim is that these are possibly "glossolalic" utterances and human emotional "groanings which cannot be uttered" (Garland, 2003:716,717; Osborne, 2004:216 and Thiselton, 2000:985–988). Fitzmyer (2008:510, 516) categorically exposes the fallacy of this view, when he states that, "the 'ineffable sighs' of Romans 8:26 are not human sighs, but those of the Spirit, which is the source of all genuine Christian prayer, whether uttered by charismatics or eggheads; those sighs have nothing to do with glossolalia." A careful, objective reading of the text determines that the "groanings" are not done by a person on earth, but by the Holy Spirit to God on behalf of a Christian who is at a loss of what to pray for in many situations. This is not a defensible text for the practice of modernistic, non-earthly *glossolalia*.

From here, as we proceed to contextual and exegetical analysis of particularly relevant passages, it will bear on those verses, phrases, and words most germane to the Epiphanius thesis, while not omitting those which seem harder to harmonize with his thesis.

CONTEXTUAL AND EXEGETICAL ANALYSIS

5.1 CONTEXTUAL/EXEGETICAL ANALYSIS OF ACTS 2 EVENT (JERUSALEM JEWISH RECIPIENTS)

The first question to ask of the Acts 2:1-4 text is: Was it just the twelve Apostles or was it the 120 disciples who spoke in γλῶσσαι (*glṓssai*)? It is widely held that all 120 believers (Acts 1:15) spoke in γλῶσσαι (*glṓssai*) on the day of Pentecost (Geisler, 2019, 198). Against that traditional view, some argue that the γλῶσσαι (*glṓssai*) speakers on the day of Pentecost were just the twelve Apostles, based on the following details, as listed by Geisler (2019:198-200):

> (1) Before the day of Pentecost, the baptism of the Holy Spirit was promised only to the Apostles (Acts 1:2-5). *[However, Peter is plain to state in Acts 2:39 that the promise of the gift of the Holy Spirit is "for you and your children, and for all who are far off, as many as the Lord our God shall call to Himself."]* (2) The church was "built upon the foundation of the apostles and prophets" (Eph 2:20). *[Although the Apostles were authenticated on that day, this wouldn't have to exclude the 120 followers from receiving the promised Holy Spirit.]* (3) The closest prior antecedent for the words "they" and "them" in Acts 2:1-3 is to the newly reconstituted group of twelve Apostles of Acts 1:26. *[However, this contention of closest prior antecedent is undermined by Acts 1:15, which indicates that the issue of replacing Judas was raised by Peter within the larger group of 120 and "they" in Acts 1:23 (proposing), Acts 1:24 (praying), Acts 1:26 (picking) can be understood as still referring to the 120]* (4) Responding to the accusation that "they" had too much wine was "Peter, taking his stand with the eleven" (Acts 2:14). *[This point leaves some ambiguity because it could be that the other eleven stood in solidarity with Peter to defend the entire group of 120 γλῶσσαι (glṓssai) speakers against the charge of being inebriated so early in the day.]* (5) The bewildered Jewish onlookers alleged that the γλῶσσαι (*glṓssai*) speakers were Galileans (Acts 2:7) which would presumably be accurate in respect to the Twelve (cf. Acts 1:11), but inaccurate in describing the whole group of 120, which included Jerusalemites, Judeans and possibly even Diasporan Jews who had weeks earlier become believers in the resurrected Jesus as the Messiah and stayed on the 50 days from Passover. *[However, as the onlookers were wrong about Jesus' disciples being drunk (Acts 2:13) at this 9 a.m. hour of morning prayer, they could well have been wrong on this matter, if they derisively presumed*

The Earliest View of New Testament Tongues

that because Jesus was a provincial Galilean, all his followers must have originated in Galilee also.]

Also, when the Apostle Peter delivered his Pentecost sermon (Acts 2:14–36), he links what had just occurred with the words of Joel and twice specifically refers to "prophesy" by "sons and daughters" (Acts 2:17) and "both men and women" (Acts 2:18) to emphasize that the Holy Spirit would empower common people of both genders and young and old with bold, authoritative, inspired speech. This would point to a more diverse crowd (Bruce, 1954:68; Marshall, 1980:73) than just the 12 Apostles, "with other languages" (Acts2:4) "speaking of the mighty deeds of God" (Acts 2:11). There was some sense in which the "last days" had been inaugurated. The calamitous events predicted in the second segment of Joel's prophecy, as cited by Peter in Acts 2:19–20, did not occur on that day, but seemed to be reserved for the future, although the sun turning to darkness in the early afternoon of Jesus' crucifixion may have been a partial fulfilment of the first clause of Acts 2:20 (Ger, 2004; 46).

So the traditional view that all 120 believers (Acts 1:15) spoke in γλῶσσαι (*glōssai*) on the day of Pentecost is not refuted and the relevant prior antecedent for the words "they" and "them" in Acts 2:1–3, in the fuller context, appears to be the larger group of 120 referred to in Acts 1:15 (cf. also Acts 2:23, 24, 26 "they" being the group of 120). Peterson (2009:132; so Schnabel, 2012:113 and Dunn, 1996:24) affirms that, "Despite the prominence of the Twelve in the preceding chapter, it is likely that those gathered together included the 120 disciples mentioned in 1:15."

It is important to recognize also that Galilee was an international crossroads and thus a multi-ethnic area, with the immediate environs east and west, being Greek or non-Jewish in ethnicity. So Galilean Jews were probably conversant in Greek, Aramaic, and dialects of same, and possibly Latin as major Roman centers, like Tiberius, had been established in Galilee.

The fishermen, whom Jesus strategically chose, in addition to being fluent in Aramaic, would have had at least a working acquaintance or better with Greek to interact with the fishers from the other side of the Sea of Galilee (i.e., Sea of Tiberius, Lake Gennesaret), which was a Greek-settled territory, called the Decapolis (Ten Cities). Furthermore, it is likely that the fishermen, whom Jesus chose as his disciples, were

CONTEXTUAL AND EXEGETICAL ANALYSIS

functional in Latin as the Roman administration of Roman puppet ruler, Herod Antipas the Tetrarch of Galilee and Perea, had commercialized the Galilean fishing industry as a source of taxation (Hakola, 2017:124–126; cf. Wilson, 2006:527 and Marzano, 2013:102–110).

Another particularly relevant question to ask at this point is, "Where did the circumstances of Acts chapter 2 occur?" If occurring in the temple, then a crucial socio-linguistic factor could explain some of the events that occurred. Acts 2:2 recounts: "Suddenly there came from heaven a noise like a violent, rushing wind, and it filled the whole house where they were sitting." Schnabel (2012:113) inserts that, "Luke's readers would assume this was the 'upper room' of 1:13," but we're left at a loss as to "why" Schnabel would assume that Luke's readers would necessarily assume this scenario. Schnabel (2012:114) ultimately concedes that "The gathering of the crowds mentioned in vv. 5–6 is not given a location." Schnabel (2012:114) points out that the "term οὐρανός [ouranos] in Acts 2:2 can mean 'sky,' particularly when used in the singular" which might more likely suggest an outdoor setting. This might indicate they were in a walled enclosure of some kind, open to the sky (οὐρανός/ouranos), such as a decent-sized courtyard. Zerhusen (1995:126) suggests the Temple area.

On this note, there is good precedent for "the house" being the Temple. Beale (2005, 64–66) proposes that the Pentecost Acts 2 events occurring in the Temple precincts is a distinct possibility. In the account of Solomon building and dedicating the Temple in 1 Kings chapters 5 to 9, there are numerous references to it being "a house," "the house" or "the house of the Lord." In fact, in the First Book of Kings alone, the word "house" is used over fifty times for Temple.

When Moses finished the construction of the tabernacle, "the cloud covered the tent of meeting, and the glory of the Lord filled the tabernacle" (Exodus 40:34), and after Solomon completed building his temple, "the cloud filled the house of the Lord ... [and] the glory of the Lord filled the house of the Lord" (1 Kgs 8:10–11). The Exodus 40 and 1 Kings texts have a similar ring to Acts 2:2–3: "there came from heaven a noise like a violent, rushing wind, and it filled the whole house where they were sitting and there appeared to them tongues as of fire distributing themselves." The passage parallel to 1 Kings 8:10–11, found in 2 Chronicles 7:1 describes it as "fire came down from heaven ... and the glory of the Lord filled the house ... and they worshipped and gave praise to the Lord saying, 'Truly He is good, truly His lovingkindness is everlasting.'" Acts 2:11 reads: "we hear them ... speaking of the mighty deeds of God."

The expression of God's presence "filling the house" or "the house of God" occurs frequently elsewhere also (2 Chron. 5:13–14; 2 Chron. 7:2; Hag. 2:7; Isa. 6:1, 4; Ezek. 10:3–4; 43:5; 44:3), so it was not an uncommon way of speaking about God's presence in the Temple.

The Older Testament allusions point to the likelihood that "house" in Acts 2:2 refers to the Temple, which also makes sense in that this was the place in Jerusalem during Pentecost where thousands of individuals would be gathered (Exod 23:16–17, 19; Num 28:26–21). When the crowd, which would have been scattered through the various Temple courts, Solomon's Portico, and the Royal Stoa, heard the extraordinary "sound," they probably would have come running to the area where Jesus' followers were congregated. This would allow space for several thousand listeners (cf. Acts 2:41). Luke 24:52–53 notes that right after Jesus' ascension, the disciples "returned to Jerusalem with great joy, and were continually in the temple, praising God."

A Hebrew concordance shows that the Temple is referred to as *habayit* (the house) many times in the Older Testament (1 & 2 Kgs, 1 & 2 Chr, Ezra, Neh, Ps, Eccl, Isa, Jer, Lam, Ezek, Dan, Hos, Joel, Amos, Mic, Zeph, Hag, Zeh, Mal). In the post-exilic period, Ezra, Nehemiah and Malachi wrote of the Temple as "the house of God," and "the Lord's house," at least 20 times.

The Greek Septuagint translation of the Hebrew Older Testament Scriptures translates the Hebrew word *habayit* (the house) as the Greek οἶκος/*oikos* (as in Acts 2:2, "the whole house"—ὅλον τὸν οἶκον/*holon ton oikon*), which is also the Greek term used a number of times in the Newer Testament in reference to the Temple (Matt 12:4; 21:13; 23:38; Mark 2:26; 11:17; Luke 6:4; 11:51; 13:35; 19:46; John 2:16, 17; Acts 7:47, 49), not to mention numerous times in Apocryphal books (e.g., Bar 1:8; 2:26; 1 Esd 6:26; Jdt 9:1, 13; 1 Macc 7:37; Tob 14:5, etc.) and Josephus (1852:176–180, i.e., Ant. Book 8, ch. 2, para. 6; ch. 3, para. 2, 3, 7; ch. 4, para. 3). Elsewhere, Luke refers to the Temple by the term ἱερόν (*hieron*), with the forms ἱερῷ (*hierō*) and ἱεροῦ (*hierou*) also being used at other places in the Newer Testament. In any event, the several prior Lukan references above demonstrate that the term "house" (οἶκος/*oikos*) is part of Luke's language usage for the Temple and coupled with the predominate Older Testament precedent and the typological parallels in this momentous event, a good case can be made for this Acts 2 seminal event occurring in the Jerusalem Temple.

On the question of where Acts 2:1ff takes place, Bock (2007:94), citing Haenchen, categorically states, "It is not at all likely to be the temple, as the term οἶκος (*oikos*, house) appears in verse 2. Luke always refers to the temple (twenty-two times) as τὸ ἱερόν (to hieron; Haenchen 1987: 168n1)." That's not completely correct as Bock seems to have overlooked the above noted several verses in Luke, the verses in Acts and as importantly the verses in Mark which is probably a source for Luke, where in these verses "house" (οἶκος) is a definite reference to the Temple. Bock (2007:94) is quick to qualify that "It is a public place, however, as a crowd quickly is drawn to the event." Bruce (1988:51) suggests that after the sound and light show recedes, the disciples move into the streets. The big question that naysayers must face is, "Where would a devout Jew be, for the 9 a.m. hour of prayer, on the Day of Pentecost, in Jerusalem, as soon as the Temple gates opened?" The most reasonable answer seems to be: "Not in a private residence, not in the street, but in the Temple precincts, gathered with other devout Jews to celebrate this most important festival!"

Although some might question whether the description of Jesus' followers "sitting" in the "house" in Acts 2:2 synchronizes with the Temple setting, there are corroborating biblical references which refer to individuals sitting in the Temple courts (Matt 26:55; Luke 2:46; John 8:2; 2:14) or at its different gates (1 Sam 1:9; Acts 3:10). Acts 2:2 does picture the disciples as sitting. It doesn't say that they then got up and hustled out into the Jerusalem streets on their way to the Temple. There's nothing to later indicate that the Apostle Peter in Acts 2:14 had relocated from where he was in Acts 2:2. The Acts 2:14 verse recounts that Peter "taking his stand with the eleven, raised his voice" and addressed the gathered crowd. The crowd was probably not at a private house, but rather they were likely in the Temple precincts, at the 9 a.m. time of prayer, where a "devout" Jew would be on the special day of Pentecost.

After Pentecost, Acts 2:46 reports that, "day by day continuing with one mind in the temple . . ." They were meeting in the Temple courts and continued that pattern. Several chapters later and after some time elapsed, Luke reports that the Temple continued to be a focus of the ministry of the Apostles (Acts 5:42). Luke 24:53 records that after Jesus' ascension to heaven, the disciples "were continually in the temple, praising God," so the Acts reports of the Temple being a place of ministry (Acts 2; 5:42) only continued a pre-Pentecost pattern. Pentecost occurred only ten days after Jesus' ascension and they had been told to stay in Jerusalem "until you are clothed with power from on high" (Luke 24:49), because "you shall be baptized with the Holy Spirit not many days from now" (Acts 1:5). In obedience to Jesus' command, they remained in Jerusalem, and spent time at the Temple, although the housing accommodation of the eleven Apostles was in an upper room elsewhere (Acts 1:13; cf. Rev 21:25).

In that period, it is assumed that a large residential room measured 180 square feet (Kennedy & Reed, 1963:402). If one were to err on the very generous side in that day, a large room of 300 square feet in Jerusalem would likely have been satisfactory for the eleven apostles to sleep and store a few possessions, but not adequate for 120 seated, as Acts 2:1 requires (Germano, 2002). For that, one needs to allow a minimum of 6 square feet per person totalling 720 square feet, which is well over double the size of a large residential room in Jerusalem in the first century AD, and even at that, when the group began speaking in foreign languages (Acts 2:4–6), drawing a crowd of several thousand, with whom they engaged, an upper room of 720 square feet would have been preposterously insufficient (Germano, 2002). Pervo (2009:59) notes that "One hundred twenty is a large number for a house."

The massive Temple courts had ample space for the devout 120 disciples and their families (Acts 1:15) to congregate, once the gates opened at 9 a.m. for the first hour of prayer (cf. Acts 2:15), to be seated in readiness for the commencement of the Pentecost Day services and to be immediately accessible to thousands of Jews and proselytes (Acts 2:6ff) gathered for the festival (Germano, 2002). The deliberate symbolism, so important to the Judean culture, of the Spirit of God coming down to the Temple precincts, not unlike the Tabernacle (Exod 40:34–35) and Solomon's Temple (2 Chr 7:1–2), was thus also fulfilled.

In the three times I've been in old Jerusalem, I've noticed how very narrow the streets are. If the Acts 2 scene occurred in or adjacent to some private residence in old Jerusalem, in order to accommodate Peter's audience, which exceeded three thousand, the lines would have stretched for miles, and a few hundred yards down the twisting, narrow street they would have been out of earshot of Peter's preaching. Besides, at 9 a.m. in the morning, "devout" Jews (Acts 2:5) would surely have been at the Temple for the time of morning prayer on this very special day.

What is also telling is that in subsequent Acts references, the disciples Peter and John, being devout, were at the temple gates (Acts 3:2) at the hour of prayer (Acts 3:1—in this case the ninth hour, i.e., 3 p.m.) and proceeded to Solomon's portico, which was a covered colonnade running the length of the east side of the outer court of the Temple. Acts 5:12 also records the Apostles being "with one accord in Solomon's portico." It was the place where their Master, Jesus, was accosted by Jews wanting him to deny or acknowledge that he was the Messiah (John 10:23), so it's not surprising that his followers would assemble in the same place.

Because of the centrality of Jerusalem, the Temple, and the regular feasts to Judaism, Jews from near and far travelled to Jerusalem for the major festivals. The largest celebration was Passover in which the population of Jerusalem swelled significantly. The next in order of importance was the Feast of Pentecost which was 50 days after Passover. The majority came from Judea and nearby territories and countries.

Joachim Jeremias (1988:71) pointed out that most of the Jews in Jerusalem for Pentecost would have come from within the near region: "The greatest number of visitors to Jerusalem have always come from within Palestine." Safrai (1975, 326–27) concludes the same: "On each of the three festivals many tens of thousands went up from the land of Israel and the Diaspora. Most, of course, came from the Land of Israel, on whose inhabitants the precept was regarded as chiefly binding. Of these, moreover, the majority came from nearby Judea and Idumea." Elsewhere Safrai (1976:900) wrote: "of course the greatest number of pilgrims were from Palestine. Of these the largest number came from nearby Judea and Edom. The sundry testimonies and traditions which tell of whole cities going, refer primarily to Judea." There's a similar description of how, at Herod's death in 4 BC, "on the eve of Pentecost . . . a countless multitude gathered from Galilee and Idumea, from Jericho and Peraea east of Jordan; but they could not equal in number and enthusiasm the native population from Judaea itself" (Josephus, 1982:133 [War, Book 2, para. 42–43]).

Therefore, it's not at all odd for Judea to be mentioned in the list of Acts 2:9–11. Judea represents not only a notable portion of the pilgrims, but the largest percentage of them. This make perfect sense in that, when Canada's annual Farm Show is held in Regina, Saskatchewan, more of those in attendance come from my home province of Saskatchewan than from any other province, but there are those who come from other western provinces and some from elsewhere in Canada and in North America and beyond. It's more suitable for people the closer they are to Regina, Saskatchewan.

In the first century AD, for the feast of Pentecost in Jerusalem, those from the territories surrounding Judea would have been represented in disproportionate numbers. Therefore, most of the speakers of the "other tongues/languages" and the majority of the Acts 2 audience would have been Judeans, Idumeans, Pereans and Galileans. In Peter's Acts 2 message, he starts in referring to the "Men of Judea" (2:14) and the inhabitants of "Jerusalem" (2:14) and then addresses the "Men of Israel" (2:22), launching into his impassioned sermon about "Jesus the Nazarene, a man attested to you by God with miracles and wonders and signs which God performed through Him in your midst, just as you yourselves know" (2:22). Undoubtedly, if they witnessed these things, they must have been living in the land of Palestine when these miracles, wonders and signs occurred. Peter singles out no Diasporan group but only Judeans, Jerusalemites and Israelites which signals the preponderance of them.

The native languages of the crowd consisted in large part of those from the adjacent territories. This means that the "other tongues" of Acts 2:4 must have included Aramaic and Greek, which were the native languages of Judeans, Idumeans, Pereans and Galileans.

However, a number of distant Diasporan Jews came to the pilgrim festivals also. Because of the considerable time commitment and challenges of travel all that distance to Jerusalem, many Diasporan Jews and proselytes remained in Jerusalem for the fifty-day period between Passover and Pentecost. This was the only period on the Jewish festival calendar when Jerusalem would be packed with so many visitors from abroad (Ger, 2004:41). For that reason, it was strategic for spreading, to all parts of the Roman Empire, the news of Jesus' crucifixion, resurrection and the remarkable events at this particular Pentecost (Ger, 2004:41).

As we saw in the previous chapter 4 historical analysis, the interpretation of Acts 2 most held is the *xenolalic* language-miracle interpretation. However, Pervo (2009:69) candidly remarks, "To proclaim an event as a miracle is to embrace an interpretation of the event. Other views are possible."

According to this *xenolalic* language-miracle view, when the disciples spoke "other tongues" (Acts 2:4) they were miraculously speaking languages they had never learned. This view presumes that the large crowd of Judeans and Diasporan Jews in Acts chapter 2 spoke a variety of languages that the disciples were unable to speak, so the situation needed a language miracle. Reflective of this presumption is Schnabel's (2012:109) comment that the power of the Holy Spirit "made the disciples speak in languages they had not learned (2:4–11)." This is all the more striking in that Schnabel (2012:109), in his translation of this passage, of the Acts 2:9–11 list, acknowledges that these are places, not languages, yet has no hesitation to enumerate "fifteen or so languages" previously unknown to the disciples who were speaking (Schnabel, 2012:110). Similarly, Peterson (2009:134) remarks that, "The other tongues (*heterais glōssais*) on this occasion were intelligible languages different from their own . . . Suddenly delivered from the limitations of their Galilean speech. . ." Peterson doesn't enlighten us as to how he knows, from the immediate context, that the "intelligible languages" were "different from their own" or even what were the "limitations of their Galilean speech."

If the speakers were only "Galileans," it is safe to say that those "Galileans" were probably conversant in Aramaic and Greek, which would have been the languages spoken by the crowd which Peter addressed as Judeans, Jerusalemites and Israelites (Acts 2:14, 22). As a minimum, these "other languages" of Acts 2:4 must have included Aramaic and Greek, because Diasporan Jews aside, for the moment, there is a consensus, as pointed out in the previous sections, that these were the native languages of Palestinian Jews (i.e., Judeans, Idumeans, Pereans and Galileans), the overwhelming majority of the assembled listeners (Schnabel, 2012:117). That these "other languages" (ἑτέραις γλώσσαις/*heterais glōssais*) of Acts 2:4 were unfamiliar and foreign to the speakers is not stated in the verses nor required!

On Acts 2:4, Dunn (1996:25) advocates "That the experience also involves *glossolalia* is again a common feature of such experiences, *glossolalia* understood as automatic speech, or articulation without conscious manipulation or monitoring of speech patterns." Dunn doesn't tell us where he derives this *glossolalia* assumption from, out of the text before us, nor from where he derives that precise definition, although Dunn (1996:27) later adds that it must have been "an ecstatic experience" because "those who had been filled with the Spirit gave the impression of being drunk" (Acts 2:13). Dunn (1996:25) writes that "Elsewhere in the New Testament it is understood to be unknown, probably angelic language," citing I Corinthians 13:1 and 14:2, 9—both passages subject to considerable debate. Dunn (1996:25) confusingly continues, "But only Luke (Acts 2:6, 11) presents *glossolalia* as speaking in known foreign languages." This latter statement of his seems to be a contradiction with his own above definition and at odds with how *glossolalia* is generally defined as unknown, non-earthly expressions. Dunn's above Freudian slip that Acts 2:6, 11 is "speaking in known foreign languages" seems contradictory to a *glossolalic* or *xenolalic* interpretation and more akin to the learned, earthly languages of the Epiphanius thesis.

Intriguingly, the text of Acts 2: 1–13 does not actually refer to any particular languages. The Acts 2:9–11 list is of geographic regions or the people associated with those geographic regions (Rackham, 1901:22–24). The list is not of individual languages but is often so misconstrued. Not to be overlooked is that these are all specified as "Jews" (Acts 2:5) and "Jews and proselytes" Acts 2:10–11. It is not a reference to Gentiles of those listed geographic regions.

Luke's language of Acts 2:5a (Ἰερουσαλὴμ κατοικοῦντες Ἰουδαῖοι/ *Ierousalēm katoikountes Ioudaioi*) is more properly understood as "Jews [now] living in Jerusalem" who originated from somewhere in the Diaspora but, to use a modern phrase, "made *aliyah*" to live out their days in the land of their forefathers. In Acts 1:19a, 2:9b and 2:14b, 4:16, 13:27, etc., the same Greek verb (κατοικέω/*katoikeó*) is used, which seems to reinforce that these Jews had settled down and were permanently dwelling in Jerusalem. They weren't just "home for the holidays." They were inhabitants of Jerusalem (BDAG, s.v. κατοικέω [*katoikeó*], §1 & 2).

This may mean that as settled immigrants now residing in Jerusalem, they had occasion to be more frequently reminded of the expectation of the Hebrew holy language use in religious settings and in prophetic pronouncements, in contrast to their profane Greek or Aramaic birth language from their Diasporan country of origin.

Acts 6:9 again mentions some of these Jewish resident returnees who had settled down in the land of their forefathers but who originated from Cyrene, Alexandria, Cilicia and Asia. Acts 6:1 refers to some Jewish believers who were returnees as Hellenistic Jews.

We only know for sure that those from Rome, both Jews and proselytes, in the Pentecost crowd (Acts 2:10) were ἐπιδημοῦντες/ *epidēmountes* those in "transit," in other words "visitors" (BDAG, s.v. ἐπιδημέω, §1 & 2). Suffice to say, many Diaspora Jews returned to Jerusalem to reside there permanently (Marshall, 1980:70; so also Bock, 2007:103).

Luke's rhetorical flourish of "devout men, from every nation under heaven" cannot be taken, in an absolute sense, to mean each and every nation across the globe—he missed Canada, Iceland and others—but rather in a relative sense to denote the whole circumference of God's chosen people spread abroad in the then-known world and fundamentally to underline "the universal scope of the witness" (Schnabel, 2012:124; Pervo, 2009:66).

When Acts 2:4 refers to ἑτέραις γλώσσαις (*heterais glōssais* i.e., "other languages"), which languages are in mind? Which languages did the "Jews ... devout men, [originating] from every nation under heaven" (Acts 2:5) normally converse in? Bock (2007:106) views the variety of languages spoken by the 120 disciples as matching the nationalities of Diaspora Jews now permanently living in Jerusalem.

To the question of which "other" languages are in mind, the geographical regions and people-groups noted in Acts 2:9–11 give us the clear answer. The groups of people and geographical regions noted in Acts 2: 9–11 basically coincide with both the eastern and western Diaspora. Bickerman (1985:93) stated that there was "a linguistic and cultural split between the two halves of ancient Jewry: the Jews in the Greek and graecised lands in Africa and Asia Minor, and the Jews in the Aramaic world, which reached from Jerusalem to Babylon and Ecbatana." The eastern Diasporan Jews spoke Aramaic as their mother tongue, whereas the western Diasporan Jews spoke Greek as their mother tongue and were also referred to as Hellenistic Jews.

Eastern Diaspora Jews from Parthia, Media, Elam, and Mesopotamia spoke Aramaic. As well, the Jews from Arabia likely spoke Aramaic, because Arabic was heavily based on Syriac, which was a dialect of Aramaic. Those western Diaspora Jews from Cappadocia, Pontus, Asia, Phrygia, Pamphylia, Egypt, Libya, and Crete, spoke Greek. Cyrene was a Greek colony, so its people would have obviously spoken Greek. Jewish Pentecost visitors and proselytes from Rome would have spoken Greek and Latin.

Thus Aramaic, Greek, and Latin were the common languages of Jews and proselytes present from abroad on the Day of Pentecost. The vast majority of those gathered on Pentecost would have been from the Roman province of Judaea (6–135 AD, which encompassed Samaria,

Idumea and up to the Galilee, who would have spoken Aramaic, Greek and some level of Hebrew.

Beare (1963:237) remarks that, "taken literally, there was no need for so many languages; and Jews born abroad would not normally be taught the language of Elamites (if it still was spoken anywhere) or of Persians or Libyans and so forth. They would speak a dialect of Aramaic, or the common Greek, or perhaps both." In the midst of his *xenolalic* commentary on Acts chapter 2, Schnabel (2012:118) makes a puzzling confession that, "most of these diaspora Jews would have understood either Aramaic or Greek or both and would thus not have 'needed' a [language] miracle."

Knox (1948:83) writes: "In reality it is most unlikely that any Jew of the Dispersion would have understood such native dialects as survived in the remoter regions of the Middle East, since the Jews of the dispersion were almost entirely city dwellers." Schnabel (2012:111–120) does some good work in the historical records to determine the places where the Diasporan Jews resided in that era and he lists all cities, attesting that the Diasporan Jews were city dwellers, thereby giving indirect support to Knox's assertion that the Jews of the Dispersion, as urbanites, would not have understood any non-urban, remote, erstwhile dialects nor would such defunct dialects have been the "language to which we were born" (Acts 2:8). The language of all Schnabel's (2012:111–120) listed cities was either Aramaic (Eastern Diaspora) or in the Western Diaspora, it was Greek (Haenchen, 1971:169; Neusner, 1965:10; Bruce, 1988:55; Hengel, 1980:115; Kistemaker,1990:220; MacArthur, 1994:178; Sevenster, 1968:82).

As an analogy to Acts 2:8, even though two of my children were born in an area where Plautdietsch was spoken, that doesn't make it their native language into which they "were born," being as I have never spoken it and don't understand it and they've never spoken it nor understand any of it. It has never been the language of our home.

Haenchen (1971:169) asserts: "The Jews in the regions enumerated did in *fact* speak either Aramaic or Greek." Neusner (1965:10; cf. also Bruce, 1988:55), in respect to the eastern Diasporan Jews, vouches that their native language was Aramaic.

In respect to western Diasporan Jews, Hengel (1980:115) asserts, "The pilgrims who came to the feasts in Jerusalem from the West brought their Greek *mother tongue* [italicized emphasis mine] to Jerusalem." In respect to the Hellenistic Jews of Acts 6, who had previously resided in the western part of the empire, Kistemaker (1990:220; cf. also MacArthur, 1994:178) acknowledges that "their *native* [italicized emphasis mine] tongue was Greek." Sevenster (1968:82), after considerable work on inscriptions of Judaism in the first century AD, pronounces the supremacy of Greek among the western Diasporan Jews in the centuries around the beginning of the Christian era.

The ascendancy of the Greek language spawned the Septuagint, the Greek translation of the Older Testament Scriptures. This further proves that Greek was the native tongue of the Diasporan Jews from the West.

All this evidence, of the native/birth languages of the Diasporan Jews being Greek and Aramaic respectively, creates an unconquerable problem for proponents of the *xenolalic* language-miracle theory. The phrase, "in our own language to which we were born" (Acts 2:8), which the advocates of the language-miracle view thought conclusively proved their case (Gundry, 1966:299–307; Gundry, 2010; MacArthur, 1994; Hodge, 1860; Busenitz, 2006:61–78; *et* al.), actually, is their Achilles heel (Zerhusen, 1995:122).

After first using the term γλώσσαις (*glōssais*) in Acts 2:4, in the following verses 6 and 8, the Greek term διαλέκτῳ (*dialektō*) is used, which the current standard lexicon (BDAG, s.v. διάλεκτος) defines as "language of a nation or region" which squares with the remarks of the foregoing commentators. Right after listing the geographical areas in Acts 2:9–10 (Rackham, 1901:22–24), author Luke summarizes in Acts 2:11 with the phrase ἡμετέραις γλώσσαις (*hēmeterais glōssais*—"in our languages/tongues"). Of the 6 occurrences of διάλεκτος/*dialektos* in the New Testament, all in the book of Acts (Acts 1:19; 2:6, 8; 21:40; 22:2; 26:14), διάλεκτος/*dialektos* and γλώσσαις/*glōssais* are used interchangeably, with no distinguishable difference, so the use of διάλεκτος/*dialektos* is unlikely to indicate that there is a *xenolalic* language-miracle meaning in Acts 2.

Peterson (2009:136), in keeping with the commentators above, remarks: "Jews from the east would have known Aramaic and Jews from the west would have known Greek," and then continues "but what they heard was in their native language or local dialect." Peterson doesn't tell us what those native languages or local dialects were and appears to assume that each listed geographic region had a distinct language, which begs the question of what these local Judeans and Diasporan Jews actually spoke from their birth, if different than Aramaic or Greek.

To reiterate, the text of Acts 2: 1–13 does not refer to any particular languages. The Acts 2:9–11 list is of geographical areas (Rackham, 1901:22–24). The list is not of individual languages.

It would be helpful in the debate if the *xenolalic* language-miracle proponents were able to marshal linguistic evidence from the first century AD to substantiate which, if any, native languages, other than the Aramaic and Greek, that the Diasporan Jews spoke from their birth. Up until now, language-miracle (*xenolalia*) proponents have never done this and merely conjecture that the Diasporan Jews spoke "local languages" other than Aramaic and Greek. This is unproven speculation. The *xenolalic* language-miracle proponents have never yet identified what those alternate "local languages" are and even more crucially would then have to establish that the hypothesized "local language" was spoken by any of the Diasporan Jews as their mother tongue from birth.

Regarding Acts 2 γλώσσαις (*glōssais*), Cremer (Cremer, 1895:163) makes this shrewd remark in his definition: "We must not, however, conclude that this gift consisted in speaking in foreign languages which had not been learned; the account is given from the standpoint of the hearers mentioned in vv. 8–11." One ought not to speculate on the minds of the speakers, when the text is explicitly informing us about the minds of the hearers.

Hebrew, Greek, Latin, the three languages of the inscription on the cross, along with Aramaic were media of communication throughout the Roman empire. Therefore, the number of "other languages" (Acts 2:4) spoken need only have been two or at the most three, namely Greek, Aramaic and the lesser likelihood of Latin.

At this juncture, it is important to interject that, in his message to the massive crowd on the day of Pentecost, the Apostle Peter spoke in only one language and the Jewish crowd of several thousand easily comprehended what he said (Acts 2:14ff). The Acts text doesn't say which language he spoke on that day, but the greater likelihood is his use of the Greek language which was the supra-regional *lingua franca* in the Near East during the time of the first-century Roman Empire. It would have been less likely that it was the Aramaic which was receding and very doubtful that it was Hebrew which was utilized in Judea proper by the educated Jews, and in the Jewish religious settings there and abroad. Latin was a Roman administrative language and occupied a smaller niche in the Empire.

CONTEXTUAL AND EXEGETICAL ANALYSIS

A relevant observation (from Acts 2:7, 8ff, and 11–13) is that the disciples comprehended precisely what the throngs of listeners were responding to their languages-speaking (Zerhusen, 2020b). There would have been "a miracle of hearing" if the disciples had so exactly understood the responses of amazement and mockery, if the assembled crowd had expressed their dismay in many foreign languages which the disciples never learned, but on the contrary, there is no hint of a miracle on this point (Zerhusen, 2020b). The disciples understood exactly what was being said of them because they spoke the same few languages as the assembled crowd, confirming that there was not the great language diversity as typically conjectured (Zerhusen, 2020b).

On the premise that the Temple, the religious/liturgical centre of the Jewish nation, was the place where the events of Acts 2 happened, and since the native languages of Diasporan Jews at the Temple at the Festival of Pentecost were either Aramaic or Greek, then an over-looked socio-linguistic factor explains much of what follows in the account (Zerhusen, 1995:118–130).

In this regard, which language(s) were the Diasporan "other languages" being compared with? As noted previously, in chapter 3, in the first century AD, in Judea proper, the Hebrew language was used to some degree in every-day speech by the religious leaders and better educated, but specifically used in religious ceremony and Temple ritual. Aramaic and Greek were the "other languages" being contrasted with Hebrew, which functioned to a degree in everyday life, but was singularly the language of religious life in the Jerusalem Temple precincts.

The Hebrew language had a very exalted position in the Temple and religious ritual and Judean culture. Kaplan (1972:192) explains how Hebrew did not succumb to the encroachment of other languages "but retired to the inner sanctuaries of Jewish life, where it continued not as the esoteric language of a few pedants, but as the medium in which the most vital interests of the people found expression." Birnbaum (1964:316) stated the reverence of the Jewish people "that Hebrew is God's language in which he gave us the Torah. It was the Hebrew language in which the prophets expressed their lofty ideas and our fathers breathed forth their sufferings and joys." During the first century AD, Hebrew was "known as the לְשׁוֹן הַקֹּדֶשׁ (Leshon Hakodesh), the Holy Tongue, as contrasted with other languages … " (Segal, 1927:2; similarly Engelbrecht, 1996:302 and Joosten, 2017:44–49, 62).

The Earliest View of New Testament Tongues

Rabin (1976:1008) explains an important pattern in multi-lingual environments, in the first century AD, called *diglossia,* in which "the same community uses two different languages in its innercommunity activities, their use being regulated by social conventions." One of the languages is referred to as the lower (L) and is "spoken in ordinary everyday life by everybody" (Rabin, 1976:1008) and the upper (H) "is employed in formal speech, on formal occasions, in writing, in religious activities, and the like" (Rabin, 1976:1008; similarly Haidir *et al.*, 2019:60; Yule, 2020:241).

In a particular circumstance, only H is appropriate and in another only L, and one cannot overestimate the importance of using the right language in the right circumstance (Ferguson, 1959:328, 329; Hengel, 1989:8). "An outsider who learns to speak fluent, accurate L and then uses it in a formal speech is an object of ridicule" (Ferguson, 1959:329; see Rabin, 1976:1008). Haidir *et al.* (2019:60) write, "If either dialect [L versus H] is used in inappropriate situations, their speakers sometimes can be pointed out, mocked, scorned, or ridiculed by others."

The "higher" (H) language has greater prestige than the "lower" (L) language and is usually believed to be more beautiful, more logical, and better able to express important thoughts (Ferguson, 1959:329; so also Haidir *et al.*, 2019:60). This view is even generally held by speakers whose command of H is quite limited (Ferguson, 1959:329). Many speakers of a language where *diglossia* is a factor characteristically prefer to hear a speech in H even though it may be less intelligible to them than it would be in L (Ferguson, 1959:329). Sometimes the supposed superiority of H is connected to religion. "The proponents of H argue that H must be adopted because it connects the community with its glorious past or with the world community and because it is a unifying factor as opposed to the divisive nature of the L dialects" (Ferguson, 1959:338–339). There also may be an insistence that the H language has divine sanction (Ferguson, 1959:339), which was the case with Judeans in the first century, who believed that Hebrew was "the לְשׁוֹן הַקֹּדֶשׁ (*Leshon Hakodesh*), the Holy Tongue, as contrasted with other languages ... " (Segal, 1927:2; similarly Engelbrecht, 1996:302 and Joosten, 2017:44–49, 62).

The pioneering *diglossia* linguist Ferguson (1959:330; cf. Yule, 2020:241) wrote of the literary heritage connected to an H language: "In every one of the defining languages there is a sizable body of written literature in H which is held in high esteem by the speech community."

Haidir *et al.* (2019:60) write that "many society members assume that only literature and poems with the H variety are actually the literary works of a nation." Because the *Tanakh* (Older Testament) and particularly the *Torah* (Pentateuch) was first written in Hebrew, it has always been venerated by the Jewish people.

L is learned by children in the "normal" way of learning one's mother tongue, whereas the learning of H is chiefly accomplished by means of formal education (Haidir *et al.*, 2019:60; Ferguson, 1959:331). As a result, the speaker has a fluency in L that he almost never achieves in H (Ferguson, 1959:331), The ordinary Diasporan Jew would have been comfortable with his mother tongue (L), be that Aramaic or Greek, but on the other hand Hebrew (H) was for the better educated (cf. Lyons, 1981:281–285).

Lyons (1981:281285) notes that in all instances the contrast between the H and L forms is more than the variance between their nationality's different dialects.

Latin use among Roman Catholics is an example of H language, whereas the local vernacular of the country is the L language for Roman Catholics. Some of my Catholic acquaintances have preferred the Latin mass, although I didn't get the impression that they actually understood much non-liturgical Latin.

The heroic William Tyndale was strangled and then burnt at the stake for violating the Roman Catholic *diglossia* of his day because he dared to translate the Bible into English. Martin Luther faced opposition when he wrote works of theology in the vernacular German.

Diglossia happens in the Muslim world with the Koran in Arabic being the H language and all translations are considered interpretations, thus the L language. With Hinduism, Sanskrit is the H language and other than Sanskrit would be the L language. With Judaism, Hebrew is the H language and Greek, Aramaic, Latin, etc. are the L languages.

Carter (1969:43) in describing the Jewish *diglossia* in Acts chapter 2, responds to the objection that the vast crowds of the dispersion wouldn't have come to the Feast of Pentecost if they had known they would just get a "one-language Hebrew observance" in the Temple precincts. Carter (1969:43) responds that attendance was mandatory for every Jewish male at the three feasts of Passover, Pentecost, and Booths (Exodus 23:17; cf. Deuteronomy 16:16) in order to "appear before the Lord God," if such was within his ability. Carter (1969:43) makes the point that religious worship is an even greater influence on men than religious language. Besides maintaining that the Feast of Pentecost involved "a one-language observance" (worship in Hebrew), Carter (1969:43) thus counters the argument that the Diaspora Jews—who may have had a more limited understanding of Hebrew—would not "get much from a one-language observance."

In this regard, in Acts 2, "It is important to remember that the languages spoken by co-religionists in a restricted context, limited in vocabulary and subject matter and probably peppered with Hebraisms, Aramaisms and other religious loanwords common to many of the languages, were probably more mutually intelligible than might appear at first sight" (Blanc, 1994:355). Using the correct language (H, the "Holy Tongue," Hebrew) for the liturgy at Pentecost was vitally important for its legitimacy.

Other scholars, like Gustaf Dalman, have concluded that a Judean *diglossia* existed in the first century AD. Dalman (1929:27) discussing the special place of the Hebrew language among the Judeans, affirmed: "As the 'holy tongue' (*leshon ha-kodesh*), 'God's language' since the creation of the world, the language of Adam, of Abraham, of Joseph, and of the Law, Hebrew was still held to be the real language of Israel." Dalman thus recognised that Hebrew was the H language (the "high" language of Israel). Hengel (1989:8) acknowledged that Hebrew was the H language, with Aramaic and Greek as the L languages: "While Aramaic was the vernacular of ordinary people, and Hebrew the sacred language of religious worship and of scribal discussion, Greek had largely become established as the linguistic medium for trade, commerce, and administration." Daniel-Rops (1962:305) wrote that "after the return from Babylon . . . . Hebrew becomes 'the language of holiness,' *leshon ha-kodesh* . . . The Law was read in Hebrew in the synagogues; prayers were said in Hebrew, both privately and in the Temple. The doctors of the Law taught in Hebrew."

With *diglossia* existing among first-century Judeans, we confirm what was meant by "other tongues" in Acts 2:4. "Among first-century Judeans, the religious language, *leshon ha-kodesh* ("holy language"), Hebrew, was the language which both Judeans and Diasporan Jews expected to hear in the temple liturgy, during the feast of Pentecost" (Zerhusen, 1995:126). "Instead of *leshon ha-kodesh*, the disciples of Jesus, inspired by the Holy Spirit, began speaking in 'other tongues' (i.e., languages other than Hebrew). The speakers spoke Aramaic and Greek, languages they knew, languages that were simultaneously the native languages of the crowd assembled in Acts 2" (Zerhusen, 1995:126).

With this as the background to the events of Acts 2, how does this relate to the phrase "as the Spirit was giving them utterance" (Acts 2:4)? The Greek text of Acts 2:4 doesn't say that those filled with the Holy Spirit were supernaturally given "other tongues" to speak. Zerhusen (1995:126) initially translates: "They began to speak in other tongues as the Holy Spirit *was giving (eididou) utterance (apophtheggesthai)* to them." The verb ἐδίδου (*edidou*—third person singular) is in the imperfect, active, indicative signifying ongoing, continuing action in the past. The other verb in question is ἀποφθέγγεσθαι (*apophtheggesthai* is present middle or passive) and it is in the infinitive mood. Bruce (1952:82) says it refers to "weighty or oracular utterance" and lists as examples, in the Septuagint, the use of "prophesying" in 1 Chronicles 25:1 and of "soothsaying" in Micah 5:12. Pervo (2009:63) asserts essentially the same and adds "loud, clear, and emphatic speech." Haenchen (1971:168) emphasizes that it means speech "in a solemn or inspired way, but not ecstatic speech." Marshall (1977:357) denotes that, "it indicates a solemn, weighty, or oracular utterance." Zerhusen (1995:126) glosses it as "the kind of authoritative, weighty, important speech characteristic of a prophet or similarly inspired person." Pervo (2009:63) states that "solemn speech" in "other languages" is the best translation.

The Greek term ἀποφθέγγεσθαι (*apophtheggesthai*) occurs but three times in the Newer Testament (Acts 2:4, Acts 2:14, Acts 26:25). In Acts 2:14 Peter "taking his stand ... raised his voice and declared [ἀπεφθέγξατο/*apephthenxato*] to them ... " We ought not to speculate that the Apostle Peter is given a new language in Acts 2:14; when instead, in the straightforward meaning and grammatical construction of the two Greek words (ἐδίδου ἀποφθέγγεσθαι), his speech is described as bold, authoritative, and inspired by the Spirit. The word translated "declared" ἀπεφθέγξατο (*apephthenxato*) is the same term used in Acts 2:4, in a statement about the Spirit giving them "utterance." Peter's core gospel speech had a prophetic nature and was no less a Spirit-inspired "utterance" than the immediately-prior speaking in "other languages" by the 120 disciples (Peterson, 2009:139). The previously vacillating and fearful Peter's speech was bold, authoritative, inspired and clear. Peter's impassioned speech seems to have presumed a good understanding of the Older Testament, on the part of his audience (Acts 2:16ff).

The Earliest View of New Testament Tongues

In Acts 26:1–32, Paul makes his defense before King Agrippa II. King Agrippa, while listening to Paul's defense, responds: "Paul, you are out of your mind! *Your* great learning is driving you mad" (Acts 26:24). Paul emphatically replies: "I am not out of my mind . . . but I utter [ἀποφθέγγομαι/*apophthengomai*] words of sober truth" (Acts 26:25). In this third and last instance of this Greek term, Paul's manner of speaking is emphasized. *Apophthengomai/* ἀποφθέγγομαι seems to refer more to *the manner of speaking*, and the content of the speech is incidental to that. In each of the three above Newer Testament instances, the person's speech is bold, authoritative, inspired and there is clarity and understanding.

It is also significant to note that when Peter delivers his Pentecost sermon (Acts 2:14–36), he nowhere refers to a miracle of in-the-moment, supernaturally bestowed languages, unfamiliar to the speakers, heard by the vast crowds just previously. This omission is telling! You would think that had such a stupendous thing just occurred, it would at least have rated a passing mention. However, the Apostle Peter does link what had just occurred with the words of Joel and twice specifically refers to it as "prophesy" (Acts 2:17, 18). Pervo (2009:80) notes that Luke effectively ignores the remarkable language occurrence "by subsuming it under the rubric of prophecy."

"In OT times, the regular consequence of a person's possession by the Spirit of God was prophecy (e.g., Nu. 11:26–29; 1 Sa. 10:9–10; 2 Sa. 23:2; Is 61:1–3), and this was the specific outcome of the Spirit's advent on this [Pentecost] occasion too" (Peterson, 2009:134). In respect to being "filled with the Holy Spirit," Peterson (2009:133) reiterates that it can "refer to the special inspiration of a person for prophetic utterance, for preaching, or for testimony to Christ in some other way (Lk. 1:41, 67; Acts 4:8, 31; 13:9; cf. Lk. 12:11–12)." Peterson (2009:133) adds that "Acts 2:4 speaks of a filling specifically for inspired utterance." The wind, fire, and inspired speech of Acts 2:2–4 were regarded in Older Testament tradition to signify God's presence (Ezek 37:9–14; Exod 3:2–5; 13:21; 24:17; 40:38; 1 Enoch 14:8–25; Num 11:26–29; cf. Matt 3:11; Luke 3:16).

Consonant with the foregoing, Zerhusen (1995:126) offers the following amplified translation of Acts 2:4: "They began to speak in other languages [than Hebrew] as the Spirit kept giving *bold, authoritative, inspired speech* to them." As a caveat, "prophesy" in the New Testament is always in the normal, earthly language of the recipients, with 1 Corinthians 14 being the prime support for that (1 Cor 14:3, 4, 5, 6, 24, 39).

This meaning of ἀποφθέγγεσθαι (*apophtheggesthai*) synchronizes well with Peter's response to the allegation of drunkenness. Because it's at the 9 a.m. hour of prayer, Peter says it's too early for the speakers to be drunk. Furthermore, inebriation generally, and inversely, causes a person's speech to be slurred and not weighty and authoritative.

So, again, to the question, "Why would the bystanders think they would be drunk if the speakers just spoke languages like Aramaic and Greek?" Admittedly, the amazement of the hearers seems not to be at the content of the utterance, but rather at the languages they spoke and at their manner of speaking. How is this accounted for if the speakers merely spoke Aramaic and Greek?

Agreed—it was the languages they spoke and their bold manner of doing so and maybe only secondarily the content of magnifying God. If one has ever been to a sporting event like Canadian/American football, it's typical of inebriated spectators to do brash, unconventional things. With the "alcoholic spirits" imbibed, inhibitions are cast off and with the normal conventions discarded, people do bold things. Some of these things would definitely be considered rude and some actions even obnoxious, all because of the "intoxication of distilled spirits." In this Acts context, if there was a centuries-old, intensely-held convention to only speak Hebrew in the Pentecost Temple liturgy praising God, and if bona fide prophetic utterances were perceived to be only uttered in Hebrew, it would be audaciously busting out of deeply ingrained religious and Temple conventions to be prophetically speaking and magnifying God in the profane languages of Greek and Aramaic. Therefore, it was a mixed response—some were amazed and perplexed and some mocked that the disciples must have had too much sweet wine (Acts 2:12–13).

Luke seems to be making the point that Jews originating from all over the then-known world are now back in Jerusalem and he indicates the particular regions which they originated from, that is to say west of the Holy Land, where the Jews spoke Greek from their mother's wombs and east of the Holy Land, where the Jews spoke Aramaic from birth.

Linguistic analysis, as far as can be determined, surfaces no research that these Jews originating from the Western and Eastern Diaspora spoke any other language from birth than Greek and Aramaic. The Jews originating from the Diaspora had lived in urban centers (Knox, 1948:83) and even if eventually proven that there were remote rustic dialects, not yet extinct, still used to some extent, in these named regions, it would have to be proven that the urban-dwelling Jews spoke that language(s) from birth. The illusion is that because there were these different regions listed in Acts 2:9–11, that there must be a different and distinct *native language* for each listed region and that it was spoken by the urban Diasporan Jews living there. That presumes too much.

In respect to the legitimate question: "What would be the significance of the Spirit giving them utterance, if it was just Greek and Aramaic which these disciples were speaking on Pentecost in the Temple precincts?"

The Apostle Peter, in citing the prophecy of Joel (2:28–32), refers to a time when the Spirit would be poured out on God's people regardless of their gender, age or social category (Joel 2:29). Common people, and not just prophets and kings, would have remarkable experiences of the Spirit. The phrase "will prophesy" found only once in the Joel 2:28–32 passage is repeated a second time in Peter's inspired Acts 2 speech (Acts 2: 17 and 18) probably to emphasize that the Holy Spirit would empower common people with bold, authoritative, inspired speech. Zerhusen (1995:126) makes a good pre-emptive point when he writes: "Some may object that by denying the *xenolalic* language-miracle interpretation the miraculous is being denied in Acts 2. This is not true because the prophesying by the 120 disciples of Jesus is *inspired* speech." Pervo (2009:63–64) suggests that "Luke chose to view the phenomenon as intelligible prophecy out of a desire to dissociate the Christian movement from hostile criticism (and, possibly, to discourage Christians from venerating unintelligible ecstasy)."

In defining "prophesying," it is noteworthy that only a small proportion toward the end of each Older Testament prophetic book was "predictive" prophesying, that is, "foretelling" their future good fortune if they returned to the Lord. A fair bit of each prophetic book was "forthtelling" (telling forth the Word), specifically chastising the Israelites for disobedience to Torah and exhorting them to obedience. A major part of every prophetic book was magnifying the greatness and awesomeness and sovereignty of God and his past deliverance. This magnifying, exalting, and extolling God is explicitly part of Acts 2 and 10 and implied in Acts 19.

This significant Pentecost event of Acts 2 was the beginning of the fulfilment of Jesus' prediction (Luke 12:11–12; Luke 24:45–49; Acts 1:4–8; cf. Matt 10:17–20; Mark 13:11; Luke 21:12–15) that common people, like the disciples of Jesus, would speak out powerfully by the enabling of the Holy Spirit. The book of Acts serves as a chronology of this bold, authoritative, inspired speaking by common believers before rulers, authorities, Governors and Kings. Post-Pentecost that boldness was exemplified by the "uneducated and untrained" Peter and John before the High Priest and rulers and elders and scribes, as they were "filled with the Holy Spirit" (Acts 4:8) and exhibited "confidence" (Acts 4:13). When Peter and John were released and reported the proceedings to their brethren, the pursuant prayer meeting asked that the Lord's servants would be granted to speak his word "with all confidence" (Acts 4:29) and subsequently they again "began to speak the word of God with boldness" (Acts 4:31) and "with great power . . . giving witness to the resurrection of the Lord Jesus" (Acts 4:33). That's where the supernatural miracle is—timid men and women, normally cowed by their peers and the earthly powers that be—boldly, authoritatively, under the inspiration of the Holy Spirit, with supreme confidence proclaiming the resurrection of Jesus the exalted, ascended Messiah (Acts 2:31–36) and "the mighty deeds of God" (Acts 2:11; cp. Luke 2:25–38 and the prophetic pronouncements of Simeon and Anna at the Temple when the infant Jesus was presented to the Lord).

Even after his bold, Holy Spirit anointed preaching on that Pentecost, Peter frequently needed to be emboldened by the Holy Spirit. He still showed traces of fear and cowardice. Peter was still quite tentative about going to the Gentile Cornelius and so the Spirit urged him to go without "misgivings" (Acts 10:29; 11:12). Peter showed cowardice in withdrawing from table fellowship with Gentiles at Antioch (Gal 2:11–14). Peter continued to need his backbone strengthened by the enabling of the Holy Spirit all along the way! Whenever the New Testament believers came under attack, they gathered together in prayer asking for "boldness" (e.g., Acts 4:29, 31, 33: cf. Acts 4:8, 13), not asking that they could speak in "*glōssai*."

We need to approach this Acts 2 Scripture passage from a first-century AD Judean perspective, not from a modern, western world perspective nor with any other set of cultural lenses.

The "devout" Jews "from every nation under heaven" had gathered in "the holy land" in "the holy city of Jerusalem" at the "the holy place" of the Temple expecting to hear God magnified by the trained "holy men" in the liturgical Hebrew "holy language" on the special "holy day" of Pentecost (Zerhusen, 1995:127). Instead, what do they hear but common, untrained persons "speaking of the mighty deeds of God" (Acts 2:11) in the profane "other tongues" of Aramaic and Greek. It was anticipated that those professing to speak with solemn, weighty, religious authority would utilize the high language of the Judean society, which was Hebrew.

How rude could these Judean Galilean rubes get? Flouting, so flagrantly, these serious cultural restraints was reprehensible and outrageous. Talk about bursting deeply-held religious and social conventions! The Holy Spirit "enabled" (Acts 2:4 NIV) the disciples to overcome severe cultural restraints.

Some marvelled and some ridiculed (Acts 2:7, 12, 13). The immense Jewish crowd expected to be hearing the praises of God on the lips of priests in "the holy tongue" (*leshon ha-kodesh*), "God's language," which was the Temple language (the high or H language) even though some of it would not be understood by them. They were "bewildered" (Acts 2:6) and "amazed" and in "great perplexity" (Acts 2:12) when they heard common, ordinary people *boldly, and authoritatively* speaking of the mighty resurrection deeds of God in their mother tongues (Acts 2:8–11), which were Greek and Aramaic (Bickerman, 1985:93; Beare, 1963:237; Haenchen, 1971:169; Neusner, 1965:10; Bruce, 1988:55; Hengel, 1980:115; Kistemaker, 1990:220; MacArthur, 1994:178), rather than Hebrew.

Some of the onlookers, who were appalled at this behaviour, mocked them by accusing them of being drunk ("full of sweet wine" Acts 2:13). They thought that only inebriated people could be so insensitive as to flagrantly and boldly contravene firmly and established rules of devoutly-held, centuries-old, religious and societal convention. There is the appearance of a grain of truth here, as like an inebriated person, Jesus' disciples cast off their inhibitions, under the inspiration of the Holy Spirit, and, without shame, violated seemingly insurmountable Judean religious conventions embedded in the Judean *diglossia* with its long-held and deeply-held sacred/profane distinction. It is more than interesting, and probably a throw-back to this auspicious occasion, when the Apostle Paul writes, "And do not get drunk with wine . . . but be filled with the Spirit" (Eph 5:18).

Up until now the repeated references to "Jews," "Judaea," "Jews" (Acts 2:5, 9, 11) reinforced the ethno-centric message and not its universal potential (Dunn, 1996:27). However, from this point on, instead of keeping God's great news curtailed to the Hebrew language, the profane languages became sanctified, as the norms, expectations and barriers of the Judean *diglossia* were breached with the "other languages" of Greek and Aramaic. All languages and their dialects could be used to carry this marvellous message.

One could rightly ask, "Why would the 'other languages' then be confined to Greek and Aramaic?" Well, those were the languages covering the then known Roman world, so with that greatly enlarged ambit, the good news was going out in the vernacular languages well beyond the parochialism of the Hebrew language central to the Temple cult. It didn't have to cover off every single language spoken in the world, then or future, to make that point. It obviously omitted the mention of many languages in Asia and Africa and the lesser-known parts of the globe and did not even list all the geographic regions of the world and thereby entirely missed all the languages throughout the continents of the Americas, Australia (Oceania), and Antarctica, to name a few exclusions.

The Holy Spirit freed them of certain inhibitions, and they began to do what the Lord had commanded in the Great Commission. Even though they were in the Temple, they disregarded a significant cultural taboo and spoke of the mighty deeds of God in the low languages (L) which they knew and had in common with the other Pentecost pilgrims.

A text critical issue to look at is the inclusion of Ἰουδαίαν (Ioudaian/Judea) in the middle of Acts 2:9. As Metzger (1975:293) indicates, "It involves the curious anomaly that the inhabitants of Judea should be amazed to hear the apostles speak in their own language (ver. 6)." Metzger (1975:293) also pre-emptively dismisses the claim that this surprise would be because the dialect of the Galileans differed from the dialect used in Judea.

So, what would be the reason for the Judeans to be amazed at this speaking of their own language? A most natural answer to that question may well be that the devout Judeans were as shocked as those Jews who originated in the Diaspora at the insolence and apparent utter rudeness of upending the centuries-old, intensely-held tradition of speaking the holy language, Hebrew, in the Temple precincts. Instead, these 120 were boldly, authoritatively, prophetically making pronouncements in the low languages (L), that is their everyday profane languages of Greek and Aramaic, rather than the expected high language (H), in of all places, the Temple, on Pentecost Day no less.

This first-century Judean cultural context may be the key to solving not only the riddle of Acts 2 but also the subsequent Acts 10 and Acts 19 accounts of γλῶσσαι (glōssai—languages/tongues).

The Earliest View of New Testament Tongues

One final point to touch on in the Acts 2 passage has to do with the Greek language having two different words for "another" or "other" (Acts 2:4). The two words are ἄλλος (allos) and ἕτερος (eteros). One of the glosses in the BDAG lexicon (s.v. ἄλλος, §2A) is "different in kind" with examples of 1 Corinthians 15:39ff, where it speaks of flesh of different animate beings. The BDAG lexicon (s.v. ἄλλος, §2A) under "different in kind" also notes 2 Corinthians 11:4 where ἄλλος (allos) and ἕτερος (eteros) are used interchangeably and also suggests Galatians 1:6–7, where ἄλλος (allos) and ἕτερος (eteros) are also used interchangeably.

In his older lexicon, Thayer (1889:29) indicates that the Greek term ἄλλος (allos) typically means "another," presumably of the same kind, while ἕτερος (eteros) "involves the secondary idea of difference of kind" or framed another way ἄλλος (allos) "denotes numerical in distinction from [the] qualitative difference" of ἕτερος (eteros). From there, the incorrect trajectory based on the older Thayer lexicon was to note that Acts 2:4 and 1 Corinthians 14:21 describe these "other languages" not as ἄλλος (allos) languages but ἑτέραις (eterais) languages, which might lead a person to say, "Therefore these languages are not natural languages, but are a different kind, different in their very nature and origin. They are ecstatic, non-earthly tongues." Yes, it is to be admitted that the "other languages/tongues" (ἑτέραις γλώσσαις/eterais glōssais—Acts 2:4) on the day of Pentecost, were different, but, rather, in the manner as described above! The Greek and Aramaic languages were viewed as "profane" as compared with the "sacred" Hebrew language. The Greek and Aramaic were regarded as in a different category. They were viewed as lower languages (L) and Hebrew as the higher (H), the "holy tongue," (לְשׁוֹן הַקֹּדֶשׁ leshon ha-kodesh), but all were still recognized as earthly languages.

If "difference of kind" is the meaning of ἑτέραις (eterais) in Acts 2:4, the concept of the Judean *diglossia* is further supported. Nevertheless, there remains the challenge raised by more recent lexicographers than Thayer. Blass *et al.* (1961:160, §306) indicate that ἕτερος (eteros) is only one of two surviving dual pronominal adjectives and is not always used in a consistent manner and has had its territory encroached upon by ἄλλος (allos). As above, BDAG too (s.v. ἄλλος, §2A) notes that ἄλλος (allos) like ἕτερος (eteros) can also "pertain to that which is different in type or kind from other entities." Robertson (1934:748–749) also cites examples where ἄλλος (allos) may be equivalent to "different" which concept therefore can't be dogmatized to be the sole domain of ἕτερος (eteros).

CONTEXTUAL AND EXEGETICAL ANALYSIS

Buchsel in TDNT (Kittel, 1964, vol. 1:264) writes that even in ancient Greek, it is very difficult to make a distinction between ἕτερος (*eteros*) and ἄλλος (*allos*) and in the Hellenistic and New Testament eras even more so. Buschel cites a number of passages where they are used interchangeably (Kittel, 1964, vol.1:264). Robertson (1934:748) cautions not to make too much of the concept of "different" with ἕτερος (contra Thayer) and insists that the term does not necessarily involve the "secondary idea of difference of kind." All the immediately preceding noted lexicographers, in their respective citations above, allow for ἕτερος (*eteros*) the "idea of difference of kind." Yet, as Robertson (1934:748) puts it, "That is only true where the context demands it." To uniformly assume the "idea of difference of kind" with every occurrence of ἕτερος (*eteros*) in a Greek New Testament or Septuagint concordance would lead to some pretty bizarre conclusions.

On that note, the Acts 2 context does not demand the notion of non-earthly languages, as instigated in the nineteenth century, but, in fact, sets it aside, because the passage is definitive that the ἑτέραις γλώσσαις (*eterais glōssais*; "other tongues") of Acts 2:4 are the mother tongues of the assembled crowd, as divulged in the subsequent verse of Acts 2:8 ("to which we were born"), which we have deduced to be Greek and Aramaic. The text of Acts 2 is clear that it's actual earthly languages.

In respect to Acts 2, Pervo (2009:64) concludes:

> The primary difficulty for those who claim that this account describes either *glossolalia* proper or *xenoglossia/xenologia* is the text, which speaks neither of unintelligible, ecstatic speech (*glossolalia*) nor of speech in foreign languages unknown to the speaker (one type of *xenoglossia*) but describes what the audience *heard*.

The events of Acts 2 follow right on the heels of the command issued by Jesus in Acts 1:8 to be his "witnesses both in Jerusalem, and in all Judea and Samaria, and even to the remotest part of the earth." The first apostolic witness was in Jerusalem to local, regional and Diasporan Jews, in effect to the whole Jewish nation worldwide, to which the Apostle Paul's *modus operandi* would also adhere, as expressed in Romans 1:16, "The gospel . . . is the power of God for salvation to everyone who believes, to the Jew first and also to the Greek." Let the mission begin!

5.2 CONTEXTUAL/EXEGETICAL ANALYSIS OF ACTS 10 EVENT (CAESAREA GENTILE RECIPIENTS)

Luke's reporting of this event makes it plain that the experience at Caesarea, as understood by Peter, parallels that of the earlier Pentecost. Luke does not indicate that the Pentecost event of Acts chapter 2 involved non-earthly languages nor supernaturally imparted earthly languages. Unless one approaches Acts 10 with either of those presumptions, the pivotal Caesarea event needn't have involved non-earthly languages nor supernaturally imparted earthly languages either. The amazement (Acts 10:45) was not because there was anything odd about the outburst of languages exalting God, but rather the amazement of Peter's accompanying six Jewish believers was because Gentiles had astoundingly received the gift of the Holy Spirit.

The Acts 2 and Acts 10 passages appear to be parallel in all significant aspects. The two clinching phrases follow in the book of Acts: "As I began to speak, the Holy Spirit fell upon them, just as he did upon us at the beginning" (Acts 11:15) and "If God therefore gave to them the same gift as he gave us" (Acts 11:17) make clear that Peter did not intend a different kind of γλῶσσαι/glōssai (languages) than experienced by the Jewish believers on the day of Pentecost. The argument is repeated a third time at the Jerusalem conference (Acts 15:7-8). It would have been a significantly less convincing case to present to the leadership of the Jerusalem believers if the outpouring of the Holy Spirit on the Gentiles was substantially different than their own encounter.

Like the context of Acts 2, the Acts 10 event was also multi-lingual. Acts 10:1 indicates that Cornelius was an officer in charge of 100 men ("centurion") part of a larger Italian "cohort." comprised of about 480 soldiers (Goldsworthy, 2016: 137, 443). It would be safe to conclude that Cornelius was from Italy and spoke the Latin language of Italy plus probably also the dominating and wide-spread Greek of that Roman era. By the time the Apostle Peter arrived at Caesarea, the devout, God-fearing (Acts 10:2-3) Cornelius "had called together his relatives and close friends" (Acts 10:24). In addition to Latin and likely Greek, some in this group of Italians would probably have also spoken some Aramaic and Hebrew due to that need in the environment in which they were posted. In any event, it appears that, from the moment Peter and his six Jewish companions arrived, they readily conversed with Peter. Peter's native languages would have been Aramaic and Hebrew, and as a fisherman from the Galilee, engaging with Roman authorities, he had to have a working knowledge of Greek and an acquaintance with the rudiments of Latin.

This group of God-fearing Italians have a providential life-changing encounter observed by a group of Messianic Jews. While Peter was still preaching the miraculous life, death, resurrection and forgiveness of sins through Jesus (Acts 10:34–43), the Holy Spirit fell upon Cornelius and his gathered relatives and close friends (Acts 10:44), and in response, this large household, in gratitude, commenced speaking in languages (γλώσσαις/*glōssais*) and magnifying/extolling (μεγαλυνόντων/*megalynontōn*) God (Acts 10:46).

Pervo (2009:63) notes that Acts 10:46 uses the expression (μεγαλυνόντων τὸν Θεόν/*megalynontōn ton Theon*) evocative of Acts 2:11, which Peter had identified in his follow-up speech as "prophecy." Where Acts 10:46 states that the relatives and close friends of Cornelius were "speaking with language/tongues and exalting God," Pervo (2009:63) argues that it is unlikely that the καὶ ("and") is sequential but rather that "the conjunction either records simultaneous activity or is explanatory." These Gentile believers were, in "languages" "prophesying." Pervo (2009:282) asserts that in respect to these "languages," the context shows that it means "foreign languages."

As those of the extended household of Cornelius celebrated being "saved" (cf. Acts 11:14) having been granted "repentance *that leads* to life" (cf. Acts 11:18), they declared the greatness of God, and Peter's accompanying six Jewish compatriots (cf. Acts 11:12) were amazed "because also on the nations the gift of the Holy Spirit has been poured out" (Acts 10:45 literal translation). Peter and his companions must have comprehended some of the languages because in author Luke's report they clearly understood what was being said (Acts 10:46). Therefore the "speaking" must have been in earthly languages as these Jewish onlookers ("circumcised believers" Acts 10:45) marvelled at these spontaneous declarations of the greatness of God in more than one language.

Even if there was a language or two unfamiliar to these accompanying Jewish brethren, they'd heard and understood enough to know the content was praise of God, a clear sign of the presence of the Holy Spirit within them, just like in Acts 2 "at the beginning" (cf. Acts 11:15). Because the parallel was plain and "on the nations the gift of the Holy Spirit has been poured out," Peter called for the concomitant of water baptism (Acts 10:47, 48). The Apostle Peter recognized that these Gentiles were genuinely converted, and he knew he could not resist the work of God (Acts 11:17). What's notable here is that there were seven witnesses, all Jewish, to this epoch-making event (Peter plus six "circumcised" brethren). In this connection, Bruce (1990:269) references "the seven witnesses sometimes required in Egyptian documents, and the seven seals attached to a will in Roman law (cf. Rev. 5:1)."

Luke does not regard the event at Caesarea as a different phenomenon of non-earthly languages, but instead it was clearly reminiscent of the Acts 2 Jerusalem Pentecost. This connectedness means that interpreting γλώσσαις (*glóssais*) as various earthly languages is the most logical understanding of the Acts 10 event. Schnabel (2012:505) agrees that it is various earthly languages, but, consistent with his *xenolalic* view of Acts 2, posits Acts 10:46 as speaking "in unlearned languages, praising God." Schnabel (2012:505) allows that Hebrew or Aramaic may have been among the languages which Cornelius or some of his friends miraculously spoke and languages which Peter and his six Jewish compatriots would have understood. Despite several Western textual witnesses (Metzger, 1975:381) qualifying γλώσσαις (*glóssais*) with one or another adjective, such as ἑτέραις (other) or Latin *linguis variis* (in various languages) reminiscent of Acts 2:4, Bock (2007:401) is not sure that the γλώσσαις (*glóssais*) entailed other languages.

On Acts 10:46, Pervo (2009:282) suggests that in respect to the γλώσσαις (*glóssais*), "the response is unusual, presumably ecstatic, but of sufficient intelligibility to indicate that God was being praised."

That the languages spoken were understood by those who heard them is significant. In the account of Peter's preaching in Caesarea we read (Acts 10:45, 46), "that on the Gentiles was poured out the gift of the Holy Spirit. For they heard them speak with tongues [languages γλώσσαις/*glóssais*]" (Ramsey, 1908:7–8).

> To the careful student this passage raises the question: Does the phrase, "with tongues" [γλώσσαις/*glóssais*] in this case, mean the same thing as the phrase, "with other tongues" [ἑτέραις γλώσσαις/*heterais glóssais*] in Acts ii. 4? In both places the same word in the original . . . may be used to indicate a language, when so qualified as to make such reference necessary, or when the context or other conditions show that such was the intention of the writer. The case which we are examining seems clearly to belong to this class. (1) The writer having

previously described so fully ... in the second chapter [of Acts], would naturally make briefer mention of its recurrence, and would be understood as referring to a similar manifestation without going into detailed explanation and careful qualification. Had the writer meant to describe a different kind of phenomenon, while using the same word in the same piece of writing, we should have expected him to use some qualifying conditions to differentiate it. (2) Peter's reference to this incident, in Acts xi. 15-17. is almost, if not altogether equivalent to an affirmation that the speaking "with tongues" [γλώσσαις/ glóssais] at Caesarea was essentially the same thing as speaking "with other tongues" [ἑτέραις γλώσσαις/heterais glóssais] at Jerusalem ... (3) When the disciples at Ephesus received the Holy Spirit, they also "spake with tongues" [γλώσσαις/glóssais] (Acts xix. 6). The argument of "(1)" above applies in this case also, and, if "the tongues" [γλώσσαις/glóssais] at Caesarea were languages, it is quite certain that "the tongues" [γλώσσαις/ glóssais] at Ephesus were languages (Ramsey, 1908:7-9, 17).

5.3 CONTEXTUAL/EXEGETICAL ANALYSIS OF ACTS 19 EVENT (EPHESUS DIASPORA RECIPIENTS)

The Apostle Paul had a standing invitation to return to the Ephesian synagogue when he returned from his sending congregation in Antioch of Syria. So, on his return to Ephesus, he meets these certain men. At the end of this Acts 19:1-6 account, we learn that it was twelve men. In tracing God's dealings with Israel, the number twelve has always been especially significant. These men confess their affiliation with John's baptism (Acts 19:3), so as John's message was for the nation of Israel (Matt 3; Mark 1:1-11; Luke 3:1-22; John 1:19-37), and these twelve men had responded to John the Baptizer's appeal, it stands to reason that they have a Jewish background. Further emphasizing the Jewish context, Luke notes that immediately after the event of Acts 19:1-7, Paul entered the Ephesian synagogue, which became his place of ministry for the next three months—his longest recorded ministry in such a setting. Ephesus is the main city of Asia and therefore a major beachhead into that continent.

Paul is here shown as filling in the theological pieces that were missing in the teaching of John the Baptist. Based on the new comprehensive truth which Paul presented, these twelve men received the gospel message and underwent believer's baptism, and after the laying on of Paul's hands, they received the Holy Spirit.

Dunn (1996:256) asserts that Paul viewed these twelve men as unconverted. F.F. Bruce (1988:385) argues that, because Luke uses the term μαθητάς, (*mathētas*/disciples) without any modifier, that it must be understood that these were Christian disciples. Witherington (1998:570) has refuted this argument, asserting that Bruce has not taken into account the wider context in which Luke tells us that these "disciples" of John the Baptist have a confession that is not consistent with a true believer's profession. They aren't yet aware of Jesus' redemptive work and the gift of the indwelling Holy Spirit. As the Apostle Paul says elsewhere: "If anyone does not have the Spirit of Christ, he does not belong to Him" (Rom 8:9; 1 Cor 12:3, 13; Gal. 3:2; 1 Thess 1:5–6; Titus 3:5). One is not a Christian if he or she does not have the Holy Spirit residing within (Dunn, 1996:255; likewise Marshall, 1980:305 citing non-Pauline verses of John 3:5; Acts 11:17; Heb 6:4; 1 Pet 1:2; 1 John 3:24; 4:13 also). That foundational theological axiom is synchronous with the tense of the Greek verb here in Acts 19:2, where in the matter of the reception of the Holy Spirit, Paul used the verb πιστεύσαντες (from *pisteuó*/to believe) in the aorist active participle form, indicating contemporaneous action, not subsequent action. What this means is that the Apostle Paul assumed that the believing and receipt of the Holy Spirit was to occur simultaneously (Dunn: 1996:255). This is best translated in coincident construct, "Did you receive the Holy Spirit simultaneously upon belief?" (Acts 19:2). Ger (2004:252) draws attention to the incorrect translation of the King James Version, "since you believed," which has been the basis of much erroneous doctrinal teaching.

So, the Apostle Paul leads this fourth and last representative group from the Older Testament economy to faith in Jesus Christ, followed by immediate water baptism in the name of Jesus. As Paul laid hands on these twelve new Jewish believers, he witnessed the obvious working of the Holy Spirit, in their magnifying, praising, and giving thanks to God in their various earthly languages, while his ministry companions looked on.

Schnabel (2012:789) explicitly translates in Acts 19:6 as "they spoke in unlearned languages" despite "unlearned" having no textual support. The consensus Greek text simply has γλώσσαις (*glōssais*), which Schnabel does translate correctly as "languages," but there is no adjective meaning "unlearned" linked to γλώσσαις (glōssais) in the generally accepted Greek text. Interestingly though, the Western text, had "other" as a modifier of γλώσσαις (glōssais) and, as to those languages, added "and they knew them, which they also interpreted for themselves," which Metzger (1975:470) ascribes to "scribal embroidering of the Alexandrian text."

The relationship between γλώσσαις (glōssais) and ἐπροφήτευον (eprophēteuon/prophesying) in Acts 19:6 appears similar to that of Acts 2. In Acts 19:6b, the "languages" (γλώσσαις/glōssais) seem to be inseparably tied to "prophesying" (ἐπροφήτευον/eprophēteuon), "the latter [prophesying] being given understandably in the former [languages]" (Baxter, 1981:52). In other words, the "languages" (γλώσσαις/glōssais) may be understood as the medium of "prophesying" (ἐπροφήτευον/ eprophēteuon) and not two different aspects. Through the instrumentality of their various known, earthly "languages" (γλώσσαις/glōssais), the twelve new Messianic converts were "prophesying" (ἐπροφήτευον/ eprophēteuon). "Prophecy" was the content of what they were "speaking in languages." Pervo (2009:63) notes that Acts 10:46 uses a phrase evocative of Acts 2:11, which Peter had identified in his follow-up speech as "prophecy." Pervo (2009:63) then goes on to argue that, in both Acts 10:46 and Acts 19:6, it is unlikely that the καὶ ("and") is sequential but rather that "the conjunction either records simultaneous activity or is explanatory."

In Acts 19:6, the Greek (ἐλάλουν τε γλώσσαις καὶ ἐπροφήτευον/ elaloun te glōssais kai eprophēteuon) would thus be understood to mean that they were prophesying in languages and not indicating two different features. Pervo (2009:463) suggests here that Luke may have desired his readers to understand that "tongues" means foreign languages. This is the view of Blass *et al.* (1961:254, §480 (3)), who view the word "other" as assumed, and not necessary to include, because it being superfluous with the obvious linguistic antecedents in Acts 10:46 and 1 Corinthians 14:21 (cf. also Acts 2:4).

With this scenario, for Jewish Paul and his likely Jewish travel companions to have understood that these twelve were prophesying in foreign languages, means that they understood the languages and therefore another reason to logically conclude that they were earthly languages, within their repertoire of known languages.

Even if there was a language or two unfamiliar to Paul and these accompanying, likely Jewish brethren (Conybeare & Howson, 1863:145;

The Earliest View of New Testament Tongues

cf. Acts 19:29; 20:4; Rom 16:21; Gal 1:2; Col 4:10-11, 14), they'd heard and understood enough to know the content was praise of God, a clear sign of the presence of the Holy Spirit within them, just like in Acts 2 "at the beginning" (cf. Acts 11:15). In the Acts 19:1-6 account, it was the Jewish Paul and his likely Jewish travel companions who saw the evident ingress of the Holy Spirit. In all instances in Acts it was a measure of doubt on the part of Jews that was addressed. The earthly languages (γλώσσαις/glōssais) in Acts were primarily confirmatory for the onlooking Jews, as the recipients of the Holy Spirit magnified God.

One of the overlooked passages in defining prophesying is 1 Chronicles 25, where it describes the choirs and singing and instrumental music in the temple and the ministry role of the chief musicians, who with their lyres, harps, and cymbals "prophesied in giving thanks and praising the Lord" (1 Chr 25:3). This service was shaped "according to the words of God" (1 Chr 25:5) and this service was to be done "to the Lord" (1 Chr 25:7).

In the book of Acts, of the four representative groups being embraced by the Holy Spirit (Acts chapters 2, 8, 10, 19), three of the passages refer to the speaking of γλώσσαις (glōssais/languages) with Acts 2:17-18 and Acts 19:6 mentioning "prophesy/prophesying" explicitly. Furthermore, as a definer of Acts 2:17-18, in the Pentecost account, Acts 2:11 has the language speakers telling "the great deeds of God" (μεγαλεῖα/megaleia) and at the conversion of the Caesarean Gentiles in Acts 10:46 they "magnify" God (μεγαλυνόντων/megalynontōn). Both the foregoing Greek words derive from μέγας (megas). I think it's safe to assume that this "prophesying" in Acts 19:6 is another way of saying that they are praising God for his *greatness* and *great deeds* in a multilingual way. Pervo (2009:63) notes that Acts 10:46 uses the expression (μεγαλυνόντων τὸν Θεόν/megalynontōn ton Theon) evocative of Acts 2:11, which Peter had identified in his follow-up speech as "prophecy" (Acts 2:17, 18).

Regarding Acts 19:6, Loisy (1920:273) doubts that the author Luke differentiated between the two terms of γλώσσαις (glōssais/languages) and ἐπροφήτευον (eprophēteuon/prophesying). In this instance, they were inseparable. In γλώσσαις (glōssais/languages), these properly baptized twelve Diasporan Jews were ἐπροφήτευον (eprophēteuon/prophesying) "the great deeds of God" (cf. Acts 2:11 μεγαλεῖα τοῦ Θεοῦ/megaleia tou Theou; see also Acts 10:46). Relying, in part, on his previous description of similar events (Acts 2 and 10), with efficient authorial economy of words, Luke doesn't feel the need to go into quite the same level of detail. "Items of the same name and description, which have no statements of explanation, but are assumed to be recognized by the readers, are normally considered to be the same" (Edgar, 1996:150).

It seems important for the writer Luke to emphasize that the universal gospel (Pervo, 2009:66) is inexorably advancing, and God by his Spirit is breaching the language barriers. Speaking in various languages was to show that "Jews, Gentiles, and Samaritans were all equal in the church" (MacArthur, 1994:42). Acts 15:8–9 makes very clear that there is no distinction. "The church, which had embraced Jews, Gentiles, and Samaritans, now gathered in the last group: Old Testament saints" (MacArthur, 1996:166). Those adherents of John the Baptist's ministry "were a transitional group, whose full incorporation into the church needed to be openly demonstrated" (Peterson, 2009:533; so also Ger, 2004:253).

These twelve new Jewish converts were the nucleus of the Ephesian church (Bruce, 1954:387). They weren't the only ones who had a serious misunderstanding about John's baptism and believer's baptism, as Aquila and Priscilla had to explain this issue to Apollos also (Acts 18:25f).

It is of note that, after Paul's sojourn of about two years and three months in Ephesus (Acts 19:8–10), he was joined by Luke in Greece by the time of Acts 20:5ff, which can be discerned because writer Luke switches from the third person singular ("he") to the first-person plural ("we" and "us"). By this chronology, it is reasonable to assume that the Acts 19 event of the twelve Ephesian Jews speaking in γλώσσαις (*glōssais*/ languages) was recounted to Luke directly by Paul when they reunited in Greece. Careful investigator and orderly writer from original sources that Luke was (Luke 1:2–3; cf. Acts 1:1–2), with a commitment to pass on to Theophilus an account with certainty (Luke 1:4—ἀσφάλειαν/ *asphaleian*), it would be quite shocking if Luke would not draw to the reader's attention any conspicuous differences in the Acts 2:4ff and Acts 19:1–6 occurrences, if indeed there were. Luke does not indicate any appreciable dissimilarity and uses the same word γλώσσαις (*glōssais*) to describe it, which ought not to be surprising when Luke, in the Acts occurrences, appears to be portraying God's stamp of approval, via the incoming Holy Spirit, on each new group embraced, in order to convince skeptical, onlooking Jews (Acts 2, 8, 10, 19).

The Earliest View of New Testament Tongues

Because of the use of the same γλώσσαις (*glōssais*) terminology by Paul, followed by Luke, what happened in Acts 2, 10 and 19 could not have been inherently different than the Corinthian experience. Pervo (2009:64) acknowledges that "In this matter, as in others, Luke followed Paul's inclination without refinement or qualification."

The nature of γλώσσαις (*glōssais*) in Acts 19:6 and Acts 10:46 is of necessity defined by Acts 2:4ff (cf. Acts 11:15,17 and 15:8) which must in turn be defined by 1 Corinthians 12 and 14, being that Pauline letter was written prior to Luke's Acts of the Apostles, which all drives us to deduce earthly, foreign languages.

Luke details the attributes of Peter in the first part of Acts and draws attention to Peter's preaching, miracles, and his role in witnessing the approval of the Holy Spirit and welcoming three representative groups into the new Messianic community of faith (Diasporan and Palestinian Jews in Acts 2; half-Jew Samaritans in Acts 8; Gentiles in Acts 10). Paul's apostleship conforms to the same pattern with "signs of an Apostle" and laying on of hands in witness to the reception of the Holy Spirit by these Ephesian Jewish believers (cp. Acts 8:15–18 and Acts 19:6; *et al.* cp. Acts 2:22–39 and Acts 13:26–41; cp. Acts 3:2, 4, 6– 8 and Acts 14:8–10; cp. Acts 4:8 and Acts 13:9; cp. Acts 5:1–11 and 1 Cor 5:3; cp. Acts 5:15 and Acts 19:12; cp. Acts 5:19 and Acts 16:26; cp. Acts 5:40 and 2 Cor 11:24; Acts 8:18–24 and Acts 13:6–11; Acts 9:36–41 and Acts 20:9–12; Acts 12:6–11 and Acts 16:25–34). Luke has carefully drawn parallels between Peter and Paul (Dunn, 1996:xiv). Paul had all the traits of an Apostle.

Storms (2019:62) raises an interesting objection to γλώσσαις (*glōssais*) meaning earthly languages in Acts 19:6:

> First, if tongues-speech is always in a foreign language intended as a sign for unbelievers or as an evangelistic tool, why are the tongues in Acts 10 and Acts 19 spoken in the presence of only believers? This is precisely what I mentioned in chapter 2. Again, if tongues is always in an actual human language so it might serve to communicate the gospel to unbelievers, why are no unbelievers present in Acts 10 and Acts 19? Why would the Spirit energize or lead believers to speak in tongues in the absence of the very folk for whom this alleged evangelistic tool is designed?

Storms extracts a bit of a "straw man" here from Paul's 1 Corinthians 14 passage, to make a sweeping application to the Acts passages, when in fact author Luke, in the Acts occurrences, appears to be portraying God's stamp of approval, via the incoming Holy Spirit, on each new group embraced, in order to convince skeptical, onlooking Jews (Acts 2, 8, 10, 19). In the case of Acts 2, it was a mix of amazed/perplexed Jews (Acts 2:12) and mocking Jews (Acts 2:13). In respect to the Samaritans in Acts 8, it was the skeptical Jewish Messianic leadership in Jerusalem who sent Peter and John to check it out. In the event of receiving Gentiles into the fold in Acts 10, Peter wisely took six fellow Jews who would end up being his collaborators in the matter of Gentile water baptism and witnesses of what God had done (Acts 11:12). In the Acts 19:1–6 account, it was the Jewish Paul and his likely Jewish travel companions who saw the evident ingress of the Holy Spirit. In all instances in Acts it was a measure of doubt on the part of Jews that was addressed. Even at that, there was hesitancy by some and dogged resistance by Judaizing elements within the new community of faith for several decades.

Paul was not a solitary traveller, as that wouldn't have been a safe mode. Paul wrote of the "dangers from robbers" (2 Cor 11:26). Travelers took to Roman roads in large groups because there was a constant risk of banditry. Barnabas, Silas, and Timothy were some of the Jewish travelling companions of the Apostle Paul. Paul referred to his fellow companions of Jason, Lucius and Sosipater as his "kinsmen" in Romans 16:21, understood to mean "fellow Jews." Aristarchus, Mark, and Justus were other Jewish travelling companions (Col 4:10–11, 14). Aristarchus and Gaius were specifically called "Paul's traveling companions" in Acts 19:29. A certain Sosthenes was the chief ruler of the synagogue at Corinth (Acts 18:12–17). If this was the same Sosthenes, who later converted and was referred to by Paul as "Sosthenes our brother" and co-author of First Corinthians (1 Cor 1:1–2), then he too was a Jewish travelling companion. Suffice to say, Paul was routinely accompanied by named and unnamed Jewish and non-Jewish compatriots on his missionary journeys (Conybeare & Howson, 1863:145; cf. Acts 20:4, Gal 1:2), and the arrival in Ephesus would have been no exception. Paul had earlier left Priscilla and Aquila there (Eph 18:19). As Paul made it a point to not personally baptize, it was likely his travelling companions or Aquila who did the honors in Acts 19:5, as was the case with Peter's Jewish travelling companions in the Acts 10:48 instance.

For the purposes of Acts 19:1–6, among other things, it is important to note that in the role of an Apostle, Paul laid hands on these twelve disciples of John the Baptist and witnessed the corporate seal by the Holy Spirit of this fourth group, representative of the Older Testament economy, as they praised God in their various earthly languages, while Paul and his ministry companions looked on. These twelve Ephesian Jews were remote disciples of John the Baptist who was the last and greatest prophet of the old economy, yet that greatness fades relative to the high position of every entrant to God's kingdom since Christ's crucifixion, resurrection and the descent of the Holy Spirit (Luke 7:26–28; Matt 11:11).

It was monumental to have these last outliers incorporated into the "one new man" being created in Christ (Eph 2:15). Jews, half Jews, Gentiles, and John's old-era baptizands, all have now been encircled and embraced and endorsed by the Holy Spirit. The earthly languages (γλώσσαις/*glṓssais*) in Acts were primarily confirmatory, as the recipients of the Holy Spirit magnified God. In this latter respect, they appear to be similar to the γλώσσαις/*glṓssais* (languages) of 1 Corinthians 14, where γλώσσαις/*glṓssais* (languages) were used in the modes of prayer, singing, and the prophetic to petition, praise and publicize the greatness of God.

In all these Acts passages, it is reading into the text to presume anything other than the normal straightforward meaning of γλώσσαις/ *glṓssais* as earthly languages and there is a consistency and coherence in reading these three pivotal events this way. It is also telling that these manifestations all occurred in the polyglottal/multilingual regions of Judea, Caesarea, Ephesus and Corinth.

One must keep in mind that Acts was written a number of years after the events it describes and some years after 1 Corinthians. If one accepts the traditional view that Acts was written by Luke, then the description therein of "known, earthly languages," logically speaking, would have been influenced by Luke's lengthy experiences as the intimate travelling companion of the Apostle Paul (Col 4:14; 2 Tim 4:11; Phlm 1:24). What we see explicitly in the book of Acts on the γλώσσαι (*glṓssai*) issue in terms of earthly languages is likely determined by the goings-on in the book of 1 Corinthians. Luke's portrayal in Acts is sound pre-emptive testimony which places the onus to prove otherwise on those who would interpret Paul differently on this important matter (Wright, 1898:286–288).

5.4 CONTEXTUAL AND EXEGETICAL ANALYSIS OF 1 CORINTHIANS 14

Edward Hayes Plumptre (1863:1555) in an article in Smith's Bible Dictionary on γλῶσσαι (glōssai) made a salient point about the chief passages of:

> (1.) Mark xvi. 17; (2.) Acts ii. 1-13, x. 46, xix. 6; (3.) 1 Cor. xii. xiv. It deserves notice that the chronological sequence of these passages, as determined by the date of their composition, is probably just the opposite of that of the periods to which they severally refer.

In other words, the Corinthian epistles were written first, then the book of Acts and then the Gospel of Mark, although there is debate whether Mark was written after or prior to Acts. (Mark 16:17 mentions "new γλώσσαις/glōssais" although, as before noted, the most reliable early manuscripts omit Mark 16:9-20). This writing progression may be an important fact and the earlier written pieces will have had some bearing on how the subsequent passages were written by a collegial author.

Luke, the companion of the Apostle Paul (Acts 16:10-40; Acts 20:5-21:18; Acts 27:1-28:14; Col 4:14; Phlm 24; 2 Tim 4:11), and Paul himself, were likely to use the same word in the same sense, so it is to be expected that they would be consistent in their definition of γλῶσσαι (glōssai). Consequently, the full description of the language speaking at Pentecost "must be allowed to explain the more limited descriptions that occur elsewhere" (Johnson, 1963:311). The onus would be on skeptics to negate the above Scripture passages indicating that Luke and Paul spent significant time together and to conclusively prove that the use of "we" in the Acts passages (Acts 16:10-40; Acts 20:5-21:18; Acts 27:1-28:14) was no more than a literary convention and doesn't mean what it actually says. The skeptic would then also have the burden of responsibility to persuasively articulate why two close companions would use distinctly different meanings for the same Greek word when having a document scribed. In the absence of a clear indication to the contrary, it is likely that the γλώσσαις/glōssais would display itself in the same form at Corinth as at Jerusalem in Acts 2.

Besides Luke in the Acts passages, Paul is the only New Testament author who discusses speaking in γλώσσαις/glōssais (languages/tongues) and he does so only in two places—1 Corinthians 12 and 14.

The Earliest View of New Testament Tongues

To realize how we got into this quandary, at least in part, it is important to recognize that the English word "language" occurs once only in the King James Version of the New Testament and that in Acts 2:6 where it translates διάλεκτος (*dialektos*). Strikingly, in the King James Version, that same Greek term διάλεκτος (*dialektos*) is rendered "tongue" in Acts 2:8 and all other places in the book of Acts (Buchanan, 2012:13). One would have thought that to be consistent, in the same immediate context (cf. Acts 2:6) at least, it would also be rendered "language" in Acts 2:8. However, there is a simple explanation. To the King James translators "tongue" meant "language" in the normal sense of that word, as an earthly language! That is supported in the preface of a King James Bible where it says "translated out of the original tongues," obviously meaning the earthly "languages," of Hebrew and a few chapters of Aramaic for the Old Testament, and Greek for the New Testament. Obviously, the King James version of the Bible was not translated out of some non-earthly, angelic or heavenly languages.

In the four Gospels and the book of Acts, μεθερμηνεύω/ *methermēneuō* (another compound of ἑρμηνεύω/*hermēneuō*) means "translate" (Buchanan, 2012:13). So, rightly in all places in the New Testament,

> modern versions employ 'languages' and 'translate,' whereas in 1 Corinthians 12-14 they [modern translators] have stuck with the KJV 'tongues' and 'interpret' almost certainly because these English terms have acquired special religious significance, which, I submit, was not there in Paul's original Greek" (Buchanan, 2012:13).

In contrast, in Revelation (5:9; 7:9; 10:11; 11:9; 13:7; 14:6; and 17:15), the King James Version has "tongue(s)" but modern versions have generally and understandably moved to the more contemporary word "language" (Buchanan, 2012:13).

Rather facetiously, Buchanan (2012:13) cites the RV (1881), Weymouth (1902), Moffatt (1913), Phillips (1947), the RSV (1952), the NEB (1961, 1970), The Living Bible (1971), the NIV (1973), the GNB (1976), the New Jerusalem Bible (1985), the Revised English Bible (1989), the NRSV (1989), and The Message (2003), as knowing that γλώσσαις/*glōssais* are peculiar "tongues"; and, facetiously put, some have the further information, in text or notes, that the "tongues" were "ecstatic" (a speculation comparable to "*unknown*"!). Buchanan

CONTEXTUAL AND EXEGETICAL ANALYSIS

(2012:13) contends that all of these New Testament versions "derive their choice of English wording from the KJV tradition, not from the Greek. My NIV alone has a small footnote that says 'or languages.'" Buchanan (2012:13) wryly and incisively observes that "commentators read as though approaching the text already debating whether the 'gifts' have ceased or not, and whether glossolalia was ecstatic or not, and then addressing these issues with vigour, without recognizing they had evaded a more fundamental question."

The 1 Corinthians γλώσσαις/*glōssais* matter is different from the book of Acts occurrences, only in that the languages/tongues of 1 Corinthians 14 needed translation, whereas in the book of Acts occurrences, no translation was called for. Also, the 1 Corinthians 14 occurrences, when coupled with translation, are equivalent to prophecy which is valuable for edification and teaching.

The Acts 2 "speaking of the mighty deeds of God" was prophetic according to Peter's sermon citation of Joel 2:28–32. Recounting the mighty deeds of God is part of teaching, evangelism and edification, so contrary to some who postulate that Acts occurrences were only "prayer and praise," there was, at a minimum, indirect teaching as they spoke "of the mighty deeds of God." The Greek expression τὰ μεγαλεῖα (*ta megaleia*) is used in the Septuagint for God's historical actions on behalf of Israel to teach others (Deut 11:2; Testament of Job 51:4; Ps 71:18–19 [LXX 70:18–19]; Sir 17:8; 18:4; 36:7; 42:21; 2 Macc 3:34; 7:17). The sharp distinction between "prayer/praise" and "prophecy/teaching" that some would attempt to make is not in the Acts chapter 2 record.

In beginning this section, we are reminded that the book of Corinthians was authored, not by Paul alone, but jointly with a man named Sosthenes (1 Cor 1:1) and through an unnamed secretary (cf. 1 Cor 16:21). This may be the Sosthenes who took over as leader of the synagogue (Acts 18:17) after Crispus (Acts 18:8). If this be the same Jewish man, Sosthenes, it would be particularly interesting to know which parts of this letter were the major contributions of this converted leader of the Corinthian Hebrew synagogue or heavily influenced by him.

The main point of the letter appears at 1 Corinthians 1:10: "Now I exhort you, brethren, by the name of our Lord Jesus Christ, that you all agree and there be no divisions among you, but you be made complete in the same mind and in the same judgment." This statement can be taken as Paul's response to the various "factions" in the Corinthian

Christ assembly, which information he has via Chloe, and then spelled out in 1 Corinthians 1:12, wherein some within the assembly are saying: "I am of Paul" or "I am of Apollos" or "I am of Cephas" or "I'm of the Christ group" (cf. 1 Corinthians3:1–4:21). Notably, these four "heroes/exemplars" were Jewish, not Gentile.

In the first chapter, Paul makes a very revealing statement that "Indeed Jews ask for signs and Greeks search for wisdom" (1 Cor 1:22).

In the first four chapters of the epistle, Paul's sets "wisdom" on the center stage. The issue of "wisdom" appears to be a major part of the conflict among the Corinthians believers. In 1 Corinthians, the term "wisdom" (σοφίαν/*sophian*) is used seventeen times in contrast to its negligible presence elsewhere in Paul's epistles (once in Romans and once in 2 Corinthians). "Wise" (σοφῶν/*sophōn*) is found eleven times in 1 Corinthians and four times in Romans. Understandably, the Apostle Paul's letters exhibit subject matter of importance to those to whom he wrote. Apparently "wisdom" was a major issue among those at Corinth (Koester, 1990:55–62). This would be a clue that some thought they were wiser than others in the assembly. This supports the Epiphanius thesis. This seems be a pretty good indication of the inflated egos of some and the resulting snobbery and pomposity and prideful posturing as superior to others in the assembly. In these early chapters, one doesn't yet know on what matters in particular this attitude rears its ugly head. One can discern that the problems addressed throughout this epistle revolve around this issue of "wisdom" and "knowledge" or better put "pseudo wisdom" and "pseudo knowledge" whereby individuals are becoming "arrogant" (1 Cor 1:29–31; 4:6, 18, 19; 5:2; 8:1; 13:4). Gardner (2018:531) agrees that "the Corinthians had emphasized the gifts of wisdom and knowledge." In fact, he (Gardner, 2018:36) argues, in common with several commentators, "that the main underlying issue that Paul addresses concerns the possession of wisdom and knowledge" which some of the Corinthian congregants believed gave them a significance and importance, causing spiritual arrogance in them. Paul's message to the Corinthian congregation was that pride should have no place in their shared life nor should appeal to any of God's gifts (Gardner, 2018:36).

In hindsight, we can see that the Apostle Paul was giving a hint of a topic that he'd be addressing at a later point in this letter, when in 1 Corinthians 1:5 he pays them a compliment, "I thank my God always concerning you for the grace of God which was given you in Christ

Jesus, that in everything you were enriched in Him, in all speech and all knowledge ... so that you are not lacking in any gift" (1 Cor 1:4–7a). Paul pays them the same compliment in 2 Corinthians 8:7.

The Greek word λόγῳ/*logō* in 1 Corinthian 1:5 and 2 Corinthians 8:7 (translated "speech") is defined as "language ... i. e. a word which, uttered by the living voice, embodies a conception or idea ... λαλῆσαι πέντε, μυρίους, λόγους, 1 Corinthians 14:19; διδόναι λόγον εὔσημον, to utter a distinct word, intelligible speech, 1 Corinthians 14:9" (Thayer, s.v. λόγος, §1). BDAG (s.v. λόγος, §1) defines it as "A communication whereby the mind finds expression." It's the sense of a thought gathered together in the mind and then expressed in words (Thayer, s.v. λόγος). Reason is involved. What's interesting is that in all the above and other shades of meaning in BDAG and Thayer lexicons, the mind is fully engaged. So, by Paul complimenting the Corinthian believers (1 Cor 1:5) on this "mind-engaged" mode of speech that they exercised, we may have a clue to the kind of "speech" they were exhibiting in their assemblies, howbeit in an inconsiderate, untranslated, and unedifying manner. This also appears to counter the erroneous notion of the mind being inactive in the misapprehended verse 14 of 1 Corinthians chapter 14.

Gill (1746–1748, col 1:5) understands the 1 Corinthian 1:5 λόγῳ/*logō* reference to mean that they could "speak with divers tongues" and "that they were richly qualified to preach the Gospel to others." On λόγῳ/*logō*, Benson (2019:10091) writes of an "ability to speak a variety of languages."

In 1 Corinthians 14: 9 the Apostle is emphatic that a clear intelligible word (εὔσημον λόγον/*eusēmon logon*) should be given and again in 14:19, the Apostle, by personal illustration, is emphatic that he wants them to handle the languages (γλώσσαις/*glōssais*) issue in a mindful manner (λόγους τῷ νοΐ/*logous tō noi*—"words with the mind"). Zerwick and Grosvenor (1996:498), on 1 Corinthian 1:7, note that the χαρίσματι/*charismati* (plural) provided is gifts of grace "for the benefit of the community." God's grace has enriched the Corinthian believers with rational speech and all manner of knowledge (ἐν παντὶ λόγῳ καὶ πάσῃ γνώσει/*en panti logō kai pasē gnōsei*) so that in their corporate life and testimony they are not lacking in any gift (1 Cor 1:4–7).

The Greek word λόγῳ/*logō* and its above delineated meaning is very important to understanding γλώσσαις/*glōssais* (languages) because the term λόγῳ/*logō* appears 26 times in 1 and 2 Corinthians alone compared to 58 times in all of Paul's other epistles. So, the term and its implication, for a fully engaged mind and rational speech, looms large in Paul's two letters to the Corinthians.

CHAPTER 12 AND VERSE 1

It is of interest to note that a Greek word for "gift(s)" (χάρισμα/*charisma*—gift of grace) is not in 1 Corinthians 12:1 nor in 1 Corinthians 14:1, whereas translators slip in this English equivalent, but have it italicized to denote "not in the original Greek," if readers are paying close attention. This particular Greek term for "gifts" (χαρίσματα) is only used as a preface for "healings" and intriguingly in the plural at that (χαρίσματα ἰαμάτων—1 Cor 12:9, 28, 30). Other common Greek words for "gift(s)," such as δωρεά (*dórea*), δώρημα (*dórem*a), δῶρον (*dóron*), or δόμα (*doma*), are not found in the verses of 1 Corinthians12:1 and 14:1.

In 1 Corinthians 12:1, Paul actually writes "Περὶ δὲ τῶν πνευματικῶν" (*Peri de tōn pneumatikōn*). The literal translation could be "concerning spiritual things" (Calvin, 1537:330; Fitzmyer, 2008:456). Fee (2014:638) allows that "both here and in 14:1 the better translation might be 'the things of the Spirit.'" Collins (1999:445, 446) has "spiritual realities." Ekem (2004: 54–74) argues for "spiritual people" as the correct translation for the genitive τῶν πνευματικῶν (*tōn pneumatikōn*) in 1 Corinthians 12:1, indicating that the interpretation of 1 Corinthians 12:1 as referring to spiritual gifts needs "serious rethinking." In leading off in 1 Corinthians 14:1, the Apostle Paul writes "ζηλοῦτε δὲ τὰ πνευματικά" ("desire earnestly the spiritual"). So, despite the likely mistranslation, what we are dealing with in both these chapters is the pursuit of spiritual traits, for the benefit of others, as the overarching priority.

The Holman Christian Standard Bible® (Copyright © 2003 by Holman Bible Publishers) translates "Περὶ δὲ τῶν πνευματικῶν" as "About matters of the spirit." Gardner (2018:526) translates as "Now concerning spiritual people, brothers [and sisters], I do not want you to be unaware" (Περὶ δὲ τῶν πνευματικῶν, ἀδελφοί, οὐ θέλω ὑμᾶς ἀγνοεῖν). He begins by addressing "their concerns about the identification of spiritual people" (Gardner, 2018:526). In 1 Corinthians 2:15, 3:1, and 14:37 Paul writes of spiritual people, and in view of the letter in totality, it seems likely that he refers to people here as well (Gardner, 2018:526). In any event, Fitzmyer (2008:457) is adamant that "*pneumatika* are not simply to be equated with *charismata* ... but *tōn pneumatikōn* embraces not only *charismata* but also other specific endowments of the Spirit."

Based on the principles in Barr's revolutionary book, *The Semantics of Biblical Language*, in concluding an enlightening journal article on χάρισμα (*charisma*), Berding (2000:50) advises that the term "gift" should be dispensed of as the standard translation of χάρισμα and where a more suitable term cannot be found for a particular context, the descriptor "concrete expression of grace" may be utilized. Berding (2000:52) suggests πνευματικά (*pneumatika*) be translated as "spiritual issues" or "spirit matters" and that it should not be equated with χάρισμα (*charisma*). Berding (2000:51) recommends that we teach "that the word χάρισμα (*charisma*) does not inherently mean Spirit-given individual ability" but rather "that χάρισμα generally means a concrete way that God expresses grace." Berding (2000:51) asserts that "Paul's list-passages [1 Cor 12; Rom 12:3-8; Eph 4:11-13; 1 Pet 4:10-11] discuss ministries rather than abilities" and that these ministries are "given by God to members of the Christian community to build that community up in Christ." God is the one who apportions grace and makes the distributions.

Imputing concepts to a word's meaning is a linguistic fallacy known as "Illegitimate Totality Transfer," to use the jargon of James Barr (Ong, 2014:586). According to Ong (2014:586), the English translation "spiritual gifts" is one of those clear cases of such linguistic fallacy.

Hughson Ong (2014:583-592) has written a thorough article in which he "argues that the term 'spiritual gifts' is a theologically loaded English concept that is often used to catalogue certain gifts, abilities, or ministries." Ong's "article employs some basic theories from modern lexical semantics to analyze χάρισμα (*charisma*), πνευματικός (*pneumatikōs*), and πνεῦμα (*pneuma*), the three Greek lexemes that have been rendered as 'spiritual gifts' in English Bibles in Rom 1:11, 1 Cor 1:7, 12:1, 14:1, and 14:12" (Ong, 2014:583). After a careful lexical study of those lexemes χάρισμα (*charisma*), πνευματικός (*pneumatikōs*), and πνεῦμα (*pneuma*), Ong concludes that the term "spiritual gift" is an inaccurate translation in 1 Corinthians 12:1 and 1 Corinthians 14:1, 12 (Ong, 2014:590). Ong (2014:590) chides Fee for asserting that Paul has used these lexemes interchangeably (Fee, 1993:339).

In addition to arguing that the term "spiritual gifts" has been mistakenly and haphazardly used to translate χάρισμα, πνεῦμα, and πνευματικός," Ong (2014:583-584) "also argues that 'spiritual gifts' should be seen and used more broadly to refer to any kind of gift (including eternal life, the ability to remain chaste, gracious favor, etc.) that is of/from the Holy Spirit." Ciampa and Rosner (2010:Kindle Location 13317) also suggest πνευματικῶν (*pneumatikōn*) is much broader in its meaning.

Ong (2014:583–584) concludes that, "the linguistic evidence shows that 'spiritual gifts' seems to be a concept foreign to Paul and that the lexical and contextual meaning of these three Greek lexemes [χάρισμα, πνευματικός, and πνεῦμα] suggest against such a notion."

Ong (2014:584) presents a convincing case "that 'spiritual gifts' is not a technical term, denoting a catalogue of gifts or abilities or ministries. The tone of Ong's journal article (2014:583–592) is that we should view our abilities as God's gracious infusion, enabling Christians to offer those contributions to God in ministering to others. Thus, if talented in languages, use it in service to the body of Christ and humanity, and likewise with talents of administration, leadership, teaching, wisdom and knowledge, to name a few.

The term χαρισμάτων (*charismatōn*) is introduced in 1 Corinthians 12:4 and is seemingly paralleled by διαχονιῶν (*diakoniōn*) in the following verse (1 Cor 12:5) and in the subsequent verse (1 Cor 12:6) by ἐνεργημάτων (*energēmatōn*), with each attributed to a member of the Trinity, in sequence "Spirit," "Lord" and "God." Verse 7 then defines them all as "manifestations of the Spirit" (φανέρωσις τοῦ Πνεύματος/*phanerōsis tou Pneumatos*). Although 1 Corinthians 12:31 uses the word χαρίσματα (*charismata*) in summation, Buchanan (2012:2) asserts that χάρισμα (*charisma*) is not a technical theological term for a defined special role as "given" by God. Buchanan (2012:2) bases his view on the fact that the Romans chapter 12 list includes ordinary discipleship expectations of hospitality, sharing and showing pity. Buchanan (2012:2) also notes that in 1 Corinthians 12, only *healings* (ἰαμάτων/*iamatōn*) is specifically called a gift (1 Cor 12:9), so he prefers the neutral term "functions."

If one goes to the website *https://passioncitychurch.com*, one finds a variety of about twenty areas of ministry that they are looking to hire for. These ministry opportunities range from graphics and video techs to a lighting director, a warehouse specialist, and a social media coordinator. There's quite a range and it won't do to gamely stuff them all into the "helps" category, which seems to be a catch-all for everything that doesn't fit the other terms in the biblical lists, if one holds to a prescriptive recipe of the ministries and operations of the Spirit.

CONTEXTUAL AND EXEGETICAL ANALYSIS

James 1:17–18 indicates that "Every good thing bestowed and every perfect gift (δώρημα τέλειον/*dōrēma teleion*) is from above, coming down from the Father of lights, with whom there is no variation, or shifting shadow [literally *"shadow of turning"*]. In the exercise of His will He brought us forth by the word of truth, so that we might be, as it were, the first fruits among His creatures." The Greek adjective τέλειον (*teleion*) means "complete." Based on erroneous English translations and presumptuous insertions in 1 Corinthians 12–14, we have overly mystified gifts. When in the service of the Lord, piano playing, serving coffee, setting up chairs, setting up and adjusting cameras and sound systems, etc., can be regarded as gifts!

Berding (2000:51) counsels that we urge Christians:

> to get involved in ministry and not wait around until they have figured out what special abilities they do or do not have. You can tell them to dispense with their "spiritual gift tests" . . . [and] stop using the word "gift" and talk about ministries instead. And after you have done all these, you might consider cancelling your Spiritual Gifts Class altogether and start another called "Ministering to One Another."

Bittlinger (1967:70) includes natural abilities in his idea of "gifts" and says, " . . . Paul knew no distinction between natural and supernatural gifts, between ordinary and extraordinary ministries."

God can work *supernaturally through the natural*—through timing, through placement of people, through herbs, poultices and the like, through the insightful diagnosis and the prescribed treatment of a doctor, and "yes" through direct instantaneous intervention (plural "gifts of healing" χαρίσματα ἰαμάτων/*charismata iamatōn*—1 Corinthians 12: 9). To dichotomize supernatural from natural is almost to deny that God created it all, and to separate them rigidly is Platonic dualism (Thiselton, 2000:948ff).

Bittlinger (1967:70) contends that the Apostle Paul viewed all of a Christian's activities as "saturated with the Spirit." For Bittlinger (1967:70), a χάρισμα (*charisma*) means that "a gift is manifested when being set free by the Holy Spirit, my natural endowments blossom forth glorifying Christ and building up His church."

Stott (1976:90–94) would be in basic agreement and holds that χάρισμα (*charisma*) can in some cases "dovetail with natural endowments" (Stott, 1976:93). In such cases the nature of the χάρισμα (*charisma*) is to be perceived "in the heightening, the intensification, the 'Christianizing' of a natural endowment already present, or at least latent" (Stott, 1976:93). Dunn (1975:255) admits that χάρισμα (*charisma*) may incorporate natural abilities.

Koenig (1978:106) offers the caution that Paul "does not seem to care whether we label a given event, act or talent natural or supernatural. He is far more concerned about whether the Spirit's working can be recognized in it and acknowledged."

After examining a sequence of related Greek terms, Carson (1987:33) remarks that "Paul is not concerned to define 'spiritual gift' too narrowly." The Greek word for "service" (διαχονια/*diakonia*) in 1 Corinthians 12:5 "is a general term used in secular Greek for all kinds of work—waiting on tables, the civil service, a collection for the poor" (Carson, 1987:33). "The point is that everyday acts of service must be included under this rubric" (Carson, 1987:34). "One conclusion is unavoidable: Paul tends to flatten the distinctions between 'charismatic' gifts and 'noncharismatic' gifts in the modern sense of those terms" (Carson, 1987:34). The lists in the various New Testament passages mix what some would label "natural" and "supernatural" or "spectacular" and "more ordinary" endowments (Carson, 1987:37). The Apostle Paul makes no such distinctions (Carson, 1987:37). "It is the same God who works all things in all *persons*" (1 Cor 12:6 NASV). Paul would have been comfortable with a mix of so-called natural talent and specific, Spirit-energized endowment (Carson, 1987:37). Lenski (1946:490) judges that some "have a natural basis in natural talents and abilities. The Spirit sanctifies and augments these talents for his high and blessed purpose."

Blomberg (1994:216) comments that it's "likely that any combination of talents, abilities, and endowments, however suddenly given or leisurely cultivated, may qualify as spiritual gifts, if a believer uses them for God's glory and his work in the world." Blomberg (1994:216) notes that the special preparation of Paul for ministry, as a Hellenistic Jew and Roman citizen, makes it hard to imagine that the Apostle would have deemed all his God-given talents, including preaching and teaching (Acts 13:1), as attained only after his Damascus-road experience.

In the Older Testament (Exod 31:3), we read of God having filled Bezalel with his Spirit "in wisdom, in understanding, in knowledge, and in all *kinds of* craftsmanship." Oholiab was appointed to help him and the Lord "put skill" in additional helpers to make the Designer tabernacle, its ornate furniture, the priestly garments, the oils, and incense

(Exod 31:6-11). The latter part of that Exodus 31:6 is an intriguing "effect and cause" scenario when it says, "in the hearts of all who are skilful I have put skill ... "

In addressing the issue of *charismata*, Barclay (1975:108) writes: "The fault of the Church, in modern times at least, is that it has interpreted the idea of special gifts far too narrowly." Barclay (1975:108-109) goes on to say "that the gifts of a man who can work with his hands, are just as special gifts to God" and then he goes on to enumerate "the mason, the carpenter, the electrician, the painter, the engineer, the plumber."

Lenski (1946:510), in respect to "interpretation," writes of the Spirit taking a natural ability and "sanctifying it and employing it for spiritual ends."

Maclachan (2015:931-935) appropriately asks, "Why should not people who are linguistically skilled, either in speaking other languages or in their interpretation, be understood to be endowed in this way by the Spirit of God so that a multi-lingual church such as that at Corinth, can be built up or edified?"

Therefore, based on the biblical evidence and the seeming intentional breadth of meaning in the Apostle Paul's day, it appears to be legitimate that an aptitude for languages, and being multilingual (polyglottal) with fluency, when used for the Lord, would be within the realm of a grace (χάρισμα/*charisma*) from God, and would thus be within the purview of 1 Corinthians chapters 12 and 14.

The lists in 1 Corinthians 12, Romans 12:3-8, Ephesians 4:11-13, 1 Peter 4:10-11 differ from one another, with the lists in Ephesians and 1 Peter being quite short. No one list appears to be comprehensive or exhaustive but rather suggestive. One draws the conclusion that the lists are somewhat descriptive or representative for their respective locale but not prescriptive nor exhaustive. We must resist using 1 Corinthians chapter 12 to 14 in a limiting sense (Koenig, 1978: 94). Some χαρίσματα (*charismata*) might be needed in one church and not in another. New χαρίσματα (*charismata*) may be endowed as different types of ministry are needed in new situations. We serve a creative God. Therefore, we shouldn't presume rigorous uniformity. The lists in Romans, Ephesians and 1 Peter do not mention γλώσσαις/*glōssais* (languages/tongues), which would lead one to believe that there was something unique about the particular ministry needs in the cosmopolitan, multilingual context of Corinth.

CHAPTER 12 AND VERSE 2

Conzelman (1975:206) notes that characterizing the idols as "dumb" is a traditional attribute in Jewish polemic against images (cf. Deut 28:36; Hab 2:18; Ps 113:15; 3 Macc 4:16).

CHAPTER 12 AND VERSE 3

As to the expression "Αναθεμα Ιησους" *(Anathema Iēsous* "Accursed [is] Jesus"), Fitzmyer (2008:455) raises the question of whether such a slogan derived from Jewish opponents of Christianity. Commentators like Cullmann, Derrett, Garland, Moffatt, Schlatter, and Talbert have suggested this, with their chief argument being that "*anathema*" was a curse formula coming from "only Jewish usage" (Fitzmyer, 2008:455; cf. also Deut 21:22–23 "for he who is hanged [on a tree] is accursed of God").

Gundry (2011:Kindle Location 2041) remarks that "as idolatry characterized the pre-conversion past of Gentile Christians, an estimation of Jesus as accursed characterized the pre-conversion past of Jewish Christians."

With this background, it would suggest the continuing, potential impact of unbelieving Jews of the local synagogue from which the core of this Corinthian assembly originated. "Dumb idols" is also a Jewish sentiment of Paul's (cf. Ps 115:4–8; Hab 2:18–19; cf. 1 Kgs 18:26–29).

In 1 Corinthians 12:3, the Apostle Paul launches in with a concise statement about what defines a spiritual person and in particular what confession he/she makes about Jesus, enabled by the Spirit (Gardner, 2018:527). By the Holy Spirit, the spiritual person would acknowledge that "Jesus is Lord." A bonafide confessor of Jesus as Lord has the Holy Spirit, so other Christians, whatever their abilities, can't look down on him (Gundry, 2011:Kindle Locations 2045–2050). It's the "same Spirit" and the "same Lord" and the "same God" (1 Cor 14:4–6) who operates all things in all, dispensing grace. A spiritual person bows the knee to Jesus as Lord of all, in all of life!

CHAPTER 12 AND VERSE 7

These ministries are to produce benefit for the body of believers and therefore are to be desired for nurturing the spiritual health of the

CONTEXTUAL AND EXEGETICAL ANALYSIS

entire congregation, "for the common profiting" (πρὸς τὸ συμφέρον/ *pros to sympheron*). Barrett (1968:284) asserts that it's not for a person's own private use. Erdman (1966:123) emphasizes that "they were designed not for the gratification of the possessor but for the advantage of all believers."

CHAPTER 12 AND VERSE 10

In this verse, the Greek word for "kinds" (γένη/*genē*), in the phrase "kinds of tongues," is the plural of "*genos*," which in BDAG (s.v. γένος, §4) is defined as "entities united by common traits, class, kind" and in Thayer (s.v. γένος, §d) means "the aggregate of many individuals of the same nature, kind, sort, species" (in Matt. 13: 47; 17: 21; Mark 9: 29; Acts 4: 6; Acts 7: 13, 19; 1 Cor. 12: 10, 28; 14: 10). So it would seem, from a Greek vocabulary point of view, Paul could not have combined the many kinds of intelligible earthly foreign languages (γένη γλωσσῶν/ *genē glōssōn*) with unintelligible, non-earthly utterances, for the two wouldn't come under the same classification (Gromacki, 1967:62).

In regard to this phrase γένη γλωσσῶν (*genē glōssōn*—"kinds of languages") in 1 Corinthians 12:10, Thiselton's (2000:936) suggestion of "species" for γένε/*gene* seems to be stretching it, as the noun γένος/ *genos* is routinely translated "offspring" or "family" or "race" which indicates a much closer relationship than "species." There are no New Testament examples where γένε is translated "species." It appears that Thiselton bends the Greek word to align with his presuppositions contrary to the New Testament common usage of γένος/γένους (*genos/ genous*) as "offspring" (Acts 17:28–29; Rev 22:16), "family" (Acts 4:6), "race/birth/nation/countrymen" (Acts 7:19; 2 Cor 11:26; Phil 3:5; Gal 1:14; 1 Pet 2:9; Mark 7:26; Acts 4:36; Acts 18:2, 24).

As Gromacki (1967:62) reminds us, "There are many 'kinds' of fish (Matt 13:47), but they are all fish" and "several 'kinds' of demons in the world (Matt 17:21), but they are all still demons."

Exactly two chapters later than the 1 Corinthians 12:10 γένη γλωσσῶν (*genē glōssōn*—"kinds of languages") phrase, we find 1 Corinthians 14:10, using a synonymous Greek word (φωνῶν/*phōnōn*), with Paul remarking that there happen to be "a great many kinds of languages (γένη φωνῶν/*genē phōnōn*) in the world," where, in context, Paul was undoubtedly referring to normal languages on this earth. The identical word γένη/genē ("kinds") is in the 1 Corinthians 14:10 verse as in 1 Corinthians 12:10. In 1 Corinthians 14:10, it's placed before a synonym of γλωσσῶν (glōssōn), namely φωνῶν (phōnōn). The phrases γένη γλωσσῶν/genē glōssōn (1 Cor 12:10) and γένη φωνῶν (genē phōnōn) (1 Corinthians 14:10) are syntactically and morphologically undifferentiated, synonymous in meaning and utilized in the same context (Busenitz, 2014:76).

Numerous commentators admit that the phrase "kinds of languages" (γένη φωνῶν/genē phōnōn) in Paul's illustration in 1 Corinthians 14:10 is a reference to families of earthly languages (Fee, 2014:736–737; Garland, 2003:637; Kistemaker, 1993:486; Oster, 1995:319; et. al.), but like Oster, all would not necessarily press the analogy "too hard to suggest that he is indicating that tongues are foreign languages" (Oster, 1995:320). Commentators of all persuasions on the γλώσσαις/glōssais issue, have no choice but to acknowledge the 1 Corinthians 14:10 γένη φωνῶν/genē phonon as earthly foreign languages, being the immediately following phrase ("in the world") makes that abundantly clear. Thus, it would seem that the implications of the analogy, which Paul is drawing, cannot be presumed to mean something fundamentally different.

Even though the scope of the missionary travels of the twelve Apostles were covered off by the Greek and Aramaic languages (Beare, 1963:237; Haenchen, 1971:169; Neusner, 1965:10; Bruce, 1988:55; Hengel, 1980:115), Paul knew there were "perhaps (τύχοι/tychoi), a great many kinds of languages in the world" (Τοσαῦτα/tosauta ... γένη/ genē). In the verse (1 Cor 14:10), the Greek word γένη (genē) is where we get our English word "genus" from. A "genus" is a group of related languages in a linguistic family, based on their development and diversification (Dryer, 1989:257–292).

Maybe outside the realm of Paul's exact knowledge, but indeed, "in the world" there are many languages and dozens of "kinds," each known as a "family" of languages. Some kinds/families of languages are: Indo-European, Germanic, Afro-Asiatic, Sino-Tibetan, Semitic, Slavic, Latin, Turkic, Celtic, Amerindian, Mongolic, Japonic, Saharan (Eberhard et al., 2023).

Each family of languages "in the world" has a significant number of common features in vocabulary, syntax, phonology, and morphology. Based on this linguistic principle, Paul could not have combined, under the same classification, "kinds of languages in the world" (1 Cor 14:10) with non-earthly, ecstatic utterances (Gromacki, 1967:62).

"They simply are not related to each other" (Gromacki, 1967:62). In any event, the kinds of φωνῶν (*phōnōn*) are "in the world" (1 Cor 14:10) and need to be speaking sounds of intelligibility that have meaning.

Meyer (1884:283) stated that in his day (1800–1873 AD) most German commentators generally followed the thinking of Origen, and the Church Fathers, taking the kinds of γλῶσσαι (*glōssai*) in this passage as meaning "foreign languages" (Storr, Flatt, Heydenreich, Schulthess, Schrader, Rickert, Maier), and that the majority of them viewed the kinds of γλῶσσαι (*glōssai*) as "unlearned languages." In the nineteenth century, German commentators Schulthess, Schrader, and Christian Friedrich Fritzsche (Nov. Opusc. p. 802) regarded these kinds of γλῶσσαι (*glōssai*) as earthly languages acquired by learning (Meyer, 1884:283).

Garland (2003:714) understands "language" to be the more natural meaning of the Greek term γλωσσῶν (*glōssōn*) and thinks that better explains how they can be categorized into various kinds (γένη). In the face of incomprehensible languages in the Corinthian assembly, in 1 Corinthians 14:21, Paul quotes Isaiah 28:11f which signifies uncomprehended earthly languages. Garland (2003:714) takes this Isaiah quote as pointing to earthly languages in 1 Corinthians 12:10. Forbes (1995:60–61) reminds us that the most common usage of the word γλωσσῶν (*glōssōn*), translated "tongues" here, is in reference to ordinary human languages (cf. also Barnes, 1949:231).

Morris (1958:173) speculates that the γένη γλωσσῶν "appears to have been a special form of ecstatic speech when the person uttering the words did not know what they meant." Morris doesn't explain how he arrived at such a conjecture, because neither this verse nor any other tells us that it is "ecstatic." In fact, none of the Pauline letters contain the Greek word for "ecstatic" nor its cognates. Morris doesn't even attempt to offer any proof that it's unknown to the speaker.

Gundry (2011:Kindle Locations 2088–2092), without justification, says that "'kinds of tongues' means speaking languages that the speaker hasn't learned, and 'translation of tongues' means translating languages without ever having learned them." Where in the context does he get the idea "that the speaker hasn't learned [the languages]" and that of "translating languages without ever having learned them"?

The Holman Christian Standard Bible® (Copyright © 2003 by Holman Bible Publishers) simply translates 1 Corinthians 12:10b as "different kinds of languages, to another interpretation of languages" which isn't using the archaic King James Version term "tongues" which in the King James era meant "languages" anyhow. So, the HCSB (2003) updated to the term "languages" used in modernity without the mystical connotation of "tongues."

On the other hand, Lenski (1946:510), in respect to "interpretation" here in 1 Corinthians 12:10, writes of the Spirit taking a natural ability and "sanctifying it and employing it for spiritual ends."

As to the Greek word ἑρμηνεία (hermēneia), BDAG (s.v. ἑρμηνεία, §1) indicates that, though the term can mean "interpretation," it more probably means "translation" here in 1 Corinthians 12:10 (a meaning found also in Berliner Griechische Urkunden 326 I, 1; II, 15; Papyrus Oxyrhyncus 1466, 3; Sir. prologue 20; Letter of Aristeas 3, 11, etc.; Justin).

Aker draws to our attention the backdrop of Mediterranean culture:

> One really does not speak, then, unless it is understood by others, which is the social dynamic in a Mediterranean society. For one person to do something which relates only to an individual—such as being personally edified and not being concerned about interpreting the tongues and thus edifying the group—is quite shameful in a kinship-oriented society. This social orientation pertained both to Paul and his Corinthian audience.

For the Apostle Paul, the purpose of γλῶσσαι (glōssai—languages/tongues) and all the ministries in the assembly of Corinthian believers were the building up of others in that local body of Christ. The self-gratification of the individual is very much the attitude of the self-centered twenty-first century, western culture. This reading of the Pauline Corinthian epistle through our present-day, western-world lenses is a very unreliable hermeneutic and leads its proponents and followers astray.

The Charismatic/Pentecostal attempt to justify some kind of private, individual enjoyment of γλῶσσαι (glōssai—languages/tongues) is out of synch with the first-century Mediterranean cultural norm and alerts us to why the glossolalia of my Charismatic/Pentecostal friends is possibly a modern-day invention. We ought not to retroject our twenty-first-century self-absorption and self-help mentality back into the pages of the New Testament. If a believer gets a sense of satisfaction from involvement in any ministry, it should be the joy that comes from edifying others. It should be the Master's smile of approval and his "Well done, good and faithful servant ... enter into the joy of your Lord" (Matt 25:21).

CHAPTER 12 AND VERSE 28-30

It is important to note that nowhere is it said in 1 Corinthians chapters 12 or 14 (nor Acts either) that γλώσσαις (*glōssais*) is an ability to speak in a language which one has never studied. Collins (1999:471) acknowledges that "to speak in tongues" or similar phraseology, in ancient literature, "was used of a person who could speak more than one language."

It is also worth noting that not every believer performs each of the functions listed in these verses. In response to Paul's rhetorical questions throughout 1 Corinthians 12:28-30, the obvious emphatic "No" is expected. To the point, not every believer was expected to have the ministry of "languages" (γλώσσαις/*glōssais*).

Again, the Holman Christian Standard Bible® (Copyright © 2003 by Holman Bible Publishers), in 1 Corinthians 12: 28 and 30, translates "various kinds of languages" and "languages" respectively, which avoids the misleading mystique and archaism of the King James Version "tongues" which, back in that English era, meant "languages."

In 1 Corinthians 12:28 it is notable that γένη γλωσσῶν (*genē glōssōn*), which I translate as "kinds of languages," is not referred to as a "gift" (χαρίσματα/*charismata*) as is the case, immediately prior, with χαρίσματα ἰαμάτων (*charismata iamatōn*—gifts of cures).

Near the end of Paul's ministry, apparently he did not use χαρίσματα ἰαμάτων (*charismata iamatōn*—gifts of cures/healings). In Philippians 2:25-27, the Apostle Paul informs us that his fellow worker Epaphroditus "was sick to the point of death" (Phil 2:27). There is no indication in the text that Paul attempted to heal Epaphroditus. If Paul ever possessed the "gift of healing," it is possible that he no longer did at that point. When he wrote to the Ephesians, Paul listed no such gift. Some years later, Paul told Timothy to "use a little wine for the sake of your stomach and your frequent ailments" (1 Tim 5:23). To Timothy he also wrote: "Trophimus I left sick at Miletus" (2 Tim 4:20). Why didn't Paul exercise a "gifts of cures" and heal Trophimus when no doubt Trophimus could have provided considerable assistance in Paul's ministry (Pohl, 1982:85)? Was it that even then the genuine "gift of cures," which initially resided with an apostolic messenger, was diminishing and giving away to the practice of James 5:14ff in which the sick were to call the elders of the church for prayer?

CHAPTER 12 AND VERSE 31

The first part of 1 Corinthians 12:31 could be translated as an imperative or as an indicative (Talbert, 2002:108–109; Fitzmyer, 2008:484; Keener, 2005:107; Garland, 2003:734–735; Thiselton, 2000:1024). A command from Paul to the Corinthians, "But earnestly desire the greater gifts" (χαρίσματα/charismata) harmonizes better with the imperatives in 1 Corinthians 14:1, 39 and in the context is fitting as the summarizing statement on this 1 Corinthians 12 section listing the various ministries God has granted to different individuals for the benefit of the church body (cf. 1 Pet 4:10 "employ it in serving one another, as good stewards of the manifold grace of God").

The Corinthians were not giving proper attention to "differences of ministries" (διαιρέσεις διακονιῶν), "differences of operations" (διαιρέσεις ἐνεργημάτων) and "manifestations of the Spirit" (φανέρωσις τοῦ Πνεύματος) "for the common profiting" (πρὸς τὸ συμφέρον) of the body of believers (1 Cor 12:5–7). The benefit of the congregation is to be the overriding concern and each believer is granted a role to serve others, and no individual has a monopoly (Fitzmyer, 2008:465). The body image of 1 Corinthians 12:12–27 has this in mind, as does Paul's desire that the Corinthians embrace these expressions of God's grace in one another's lives.

In brief, chapter 12 is about kindness and thoughtfulness for each other in general (1 Cor 12:25–26) and considerateness for each other in the specific context of congregational meetings. Chapter 13 is a further extension of this encouragement.

The spiritual functions referenced in this didactic passage (1 Cor. 12) are clearly about the public use in the congregation and outward to the world. These "ministries/services" (1 Cor 12: 5) and "operations" (1 Cor 12:6) and "manifestations" (Greek root "visible" 1 Cor 12:7) are for the healthy functioning of the "body" (1 Cor. 12:12ff and 1 Cor. 12:27ff) and then to drive home that outward orientation (for the "common profiting" of others 1 Cor 12:7), Paul launches into "the love chapter" (1 Cor 13) which ought to govern the use of all these ministries/services and operations and manifestations (visible) for the body. This "more excellent way" is reminiscent of the frequent use of an Old Testament term. The Greek Septuagint version of the Old Testament is replete with hundreds of references (ὁδὸν/*hodon*) to the "way" (Hatch & Redpath, 1983:962–966). So again, we have Paul's targeted Hebrew rhetoric to the Jewish core of this congregation.

CHAPTER 13 AND VERSES 1-3

According to Conzelman (1975: 218), 1 Corinthians chapter 13 is not a digression but a narrative on love derived from Jewish wisdom traditions. Its contents are integrally connected to the preceding and subsequent chapters on πνευματικά (*pneumatika*): the emphasis on προφητείαν (prophecy) and γνῶσιν (knowledge) and the use of γλῶσσαι (languages), and the issue of who is the real spiritual person.

The CSB (Copyright 2017 by Holman) in 1 Corinthians 13:1 translates γλώσσαις (*glōssais*) as "languages" avoiding the archaic and misleading KJV term "tongues."

The lead in to 1 Corinthians chapter 13 is the listing of spiritual ministries deemed important at Corinth, but then Paul properly puts them in their place: "If I speak with the tongues (γλώσσαις/*glōssais*) of men and of angels, but do not have love, I have become a noisy gong or a clanging cymbal. And if I have prophecy (προφητείαν) and know all mysteries and all knowledge (γνῶσιν); and if I have all faith (πίστιν), so as to remove mountains, but do not have love, I am nothing" (1 Cor 13:1-2). Paul emphasizes that these 4 things which the Corinthians highly regard (γλώσσαις/languages, προφητείαν/prophecy, γνῶσιν/knowledge, πίστιν/faith) will all fade away, while "love never fails/ends" (ἀγάπη οὐδέποτε πίπτει; 1 Cor 13:8).

In 1 Corinthian 13:1-3, the Apostle Paul uses ἐάν (*ean*) with the present subjunctive active. From a strict grammar point of view, ἐάν with the subjunctive introduces a condition which may be possible, "supposing that" (Rienecker & Rogers, 1982:431; Zerwick & Grosvenor, 1996:524). In the context, this hypothetical "if" is obviously hyperbolic in respect to, at least, verses 2 to 3, as Paul never "knew all mysteries," never "removed mountains," never "gave all his possessions to feed the poor," (cf. retained personal effects of cloak, costly scrolls, valuable parchments 2 Tim 4:13), nor had he "delivered his body to be burned," as he was at that very moment writing the letter to the Corinthian believers. So, verses 2 and 3 are obviously both hypothetical and hyperbolic—in other words, extreme exaggeration to make a point.

The use of ἐάν (*ean*) can denote that something is realistically within the realm of possibility (1 Cor 14:6, 7, 8, 11, 14, 16, 23, 24, 27, 28, 30, 35, 37, 38). In 1 Corinthians 13:1 we know that Paul did actually speak in "the languages of men" (γλώσσαις τῶν ἀνθρώπων/*glōssais tōn anthrōpōn*), but is it pure hyperbole (as suggested by Fitzmyer, 2008:492; Keener, 2005:108; Perkins, 2012:151; Thiselton, 2000:1033; Carson, 1987:58; Schreiner, 2018:356) in respect to the languages "of angels" (τῶν ἀγγέλων/*tōn angelōn*)?

Hyperbole in respect to angels is also found elsewhere in the Apostle Paul's writings: "But even if we, or an angel from heaven, should preach to you a gospel contrary to what we have preached to you, he is to be accursed!" (Galatians 1:8).

Fee (2014:699) *et al.* remark that the Corinthians, and probably Paul, likely thought of γλώσσαις (*glōssais*) as the actual language(s) of angels based on the *Testament of Job*. This view of that particular passage in the pseudepigraphic *Testament of Job* (Charlesworth, 1983) was already rebutted in the last two paragraphs of chapter 2.1 of this book.

Holladay (1990:92; also Barnes, 1949:241–242) has proposed that by the expression of speaking in human or angelic tongues, the Apostle Paul refers to eloquent oratory, reiterating the theme of wise and lofty speech from chapters 1 and 2 of 1 Corinthians. However, there is a more viable line of thinking to consider.

There are a number of biblical examples of angels speaking to men and women (Gen. 19; Exod 33; Josh 5; Judg 13, etc.), but in all these instances, we are given to understand that they speak in the human language of the recipient (i.e., probably Hebrew in the examples of Hagar, Abraham, Lot, Jacob, Moses, Manoah and his wife, Zechariah, Gideon, Mary and Joseph, the shepherds, Mary Magdalene, Peter, etc.). The angels spoke intelligibly and rationally and not ecstatically.

Orlinsky (1974:426) sketches the Jewish tradition that as the "holy tongue," Hebrew is the language of heaven. Orlinsky (1974:426) supplies a sample of this particular mindset by raising the rhetorical Jewish question of "what other language [but Hebrew] was employed in the Garden of Eden, and before the Fall and Dispersion of Man," which assumption was referenced in the oldest Jewish apocryphal book of Jubilees. Orlinsky (1974:426) illustrates this powerful Jewish sentiment in telling the story of an aged eleventh century monk, who, preparing for the life to come, hurriedly began to learn Hebrew, as he thought that to speak with the angels and saints who had gone before, he would have to speak and understand Hebrew.

The pseudepigraphical book of Jubilees (1917), which presents an angel as relating the story of Genesis 1 to Exodus 12, for Moses' preservation in the Pentateuch (Harris, 1997:273), provides some vital information on these views that circulated in Judaism in the first century BC and AD. In Jubilees (1917), Israel's co-religionists are the angels, as indicated by the highest order of angels, in the book of Jubilees, keeping the Sabbath (2:18, 21, 30) and Feast of Weeks (6:17–18) and bearing the mark of circumcision (15:26–30).

Jubilees had a *hebraeophone* view of heaven (Poirier, 2010:14). Recension A of Second Enoch 23:2 also locates the origin of Hebrew in heaven (Andersen 1983:140). Enoch's angelic guide revealed "the Hebrew language, every kind of language of the new song of the armed troops, and everything that it is appropriate to learn" (Second Enoch 23:2 (ver. A); trans. Andersen 1983:140). The angels speak Hebrew all throughout the Older Testament, even when we get to listen in on their praise of God (Isa 6:3; Ezek 3:12).

Jubilees enthusiastically embraces Hebrew as the angelic language "driven by its author's self-understanding as part of a 'holy remnant'" (Poirier, 2010:14). Jubilees rejects the idea of angels speaking esoteric languages (Poirier, 2010:14). Citations for a competing esoteric *angeloglossy* view (Weitzman 1999:41–42) are later than the book of Jubilees. The earliest cited passage of 2 Corinthians 12:4 is a pretty strained example of esoteric *angeloglossy* (Poirier, 2010:14).

In 12:25–27, the writer of Jubilees (1917:91) indicates that Hebrew had been the universal language until the "overthrow," which is reference to the overthrow of the tower of Babel (cf. 10:26 Jubilees, 1917:82).

This background on this view that circulated in Judaism in the first century BC and AD may be quite helpful to understanding 1 Corinthians 13 and 14. In Jubilees 12:25–27 (Jubilees, 1917:91), written between a hundred BC to the latter half of the second century BC (Harris, 1997:272–273; Poirier, 2010:142), we read:

> And the LORD God said: "Open his mouth and his ears, that he may hear and speak with his mouth, with the language which hath been revealed;" for it had ceased from the mouths of all of the children of men from the day of the overthrow

> (of Babel). And I opened his mouth, and his ears and his lips, and I began to speak with him in Hebrew in the tongue of the creation. And he took the books of his father's, and these were written in Hebrew, and he transcribed them, and he began from henceforth to study them, and I made known to him that which he could not (understand), and he studied them during the six rainy months.

Borst (1957:149) regards this reclamation of the Hebrew language to be a singularly momentous occasion for the author of Jubilees: "*Mit diesem Satz tritt eine neue Vorstellung in die Geistesgeschichte ein*" (translated from the German—"With this sentence, a new idea enters the history of ideas").

Muller (1996:254) likens Abraham's enlightened understanding of the Hebrew language in his father's books with the finding of the Law at the time of Josiah's reform. At the time of the subsequent Joseph story, Jubilees 43:15 (1917:195) states it plainly that at the point when the hero Joseph spoke privately to his brothers, he did so in their familiar language of Hebrew. So, it is insinuated that Abraham must have taught Isaac this Hebrew language, and Isaac taught Jacob and Jacob taught Joseph and his other children and thus the Hebrew language became the language of the Israelites.

Therefore, with this understanding of the sequence of events, the entire nation of Israel actually spoke the "tongue of angels" and consequently in the succeeding generations. Thus, the Hebrew language was also restored as a human language. It was sublime and elevated above all other earthly languages. The Hebrew language was still regarded as special in the time of the Apostle Paul, as we shall see in the pages ahead. Paul's 1 Corinthian 13:1 reference to the *tongue* of "angels" would then refer to the Hebrew language. As Poirier (2010:143) acknowledges "the view that angels speak Hebrew is more widespread within Jewish sources for our period." This was a topic of discussion among the Jews of that time with some Jewish teachers insisting that the language of angels was Hebrew (Robertson & Plummer, 1914:288).

The Jewish sages thought that Hebrew would be the "pure speech" (בְּרוּרָה/*bə-rū-rāh* of Zeph 3:9) in which one day all the people of the world will call on the name of the Lord (Sawyer, 2002:26). They also thought that Hebrew was the "original language of the human race referred to in the Tower of Babel story (Gen. 11:1), since only in Hebrew is the wordplay possible to express the notion of Genesis 2:23 that 'woman' *isha* was created out of 'man' *ish*" (Sawyer, 2002:26).

The pre-eminence of the Hebrew language appears to have been established in the church in the first century. This pride of place for the Hebrew language is seen in a statement of Clement (Bishop of Rome from 88–99 AD) who emphasized that Hebrew was the first language of mankind, "until ever since, only one language holds, Hebrew is beloved of God" (Frankenberg, 1937:39).

The crucial thing to realize at this point is that not only did the Apostle Paul know the Old Testament, but he also knew the special beliefs among the religious leadership of his day and their predecessors. Paul followed the tradition of his contemporaries that the Law was given through angels (Gal 3:19; cp, Acts 7:53; Heb 2:2), despite that view not being recorded anywhere in the Old Testament. In the Old Testament account, it's stated that the law was given by God directly to Moses without angelic intervention, but with the transcendence of God being increasingly emphasized in Jewish circles, the religious tradition arose regarding the mediation of angels in giving the Law, which Paul appealed to (Barclay, 1958:17).

The addition to the Old Testament, that the Law was given 430 years after Abraham, was also part of Paul's repertoire (Gal 3:17). In 1 Corinthians 10:4, Paul supplemented the Old Testament narrative when he used the miracle story of the "rock which followed them" in their Israelite wanderings. As a thoroughly trained Jewish religious leader, Paul knew all these streams of thought and used them polemically. Therefore, Paul would have been aware of the view that held Hebrew as preeminent and the language of angels, so was likely alluding to this here in 1 Corinthian 13:1.

The view that Hebrew was the first language can be disproven. However, that's not the point. As above, the view that Hebrew, as the "first language" was to take precedence, was the intensely-held belief of devout Jews for several centuries BC (Orlinsky, 1974:426; Poirier, 2010:14; Andersen 1983:140; Sawyer, 2002:26).

1 Corinthians 13 seeks to redirect the community's interest to love instead, thus redefining true wisdom and knowledge.

This only verse in the Bible (1 Cor 13:1) which ties angelic tongues with the tongues of humanity, then, actually supplies even stronger proof that the normal gift was understood to be human languages (Ciampa & Rosner, 2010:Kindle Locations 13792–13793, 13805).

The Earliest View of New Testament Tongues

CHAPTER 13 AND VERSE 4

As a prelude to our controversial chapter 14, the matter of bragging and arrogance comes sharply into focus in this verse 4, where it's like we overhear one very revealing side of a phone conversation. "Love is patient, love is kind and is not jealous; love does not brag and is not arrogant." This would support the Epiphanius thesis that the γλῶσσαι/ *glōssai* issue, as with all other conflicts in Corinth, was a problem of pompous people inconsiderately and pridefully posturing as superior to others in the assembly. There was a problem within the Corinthian assembly of spiritual snobbery and the inflated egos of some.

CHAPTER 13 AND VERSE 8

This verse, 1 Corinthians 13:8 (and 1 Cor. 1:28; 2:6; 6:13; 13:8, 10; 15:24, 26) evinces the effect of the Older Testament and Jewish apocalyptic literature, particularly that of the "day of the Lord" (cf. Isa 13:6–13; 65:17; 66:22; Joel 1:15–2:11; 3:14–16; Zeph 1:14–18; Mal 3:2; 4:1–2).

The Apostle said (1 Cor. 13: 8, my translation): "Love never fails; but if prophecies, they will be done away [the Greek verb καταργέω/ *katargeó*, used here, means to be "done away" "nullified" "abolished" "fade away"]; if languages, they will cease [παύσονται/*pausontai*]; if knowledge, it will be done away [καταργέω/*katargeó* is used here again]."

In the phrase, "γλῶσσαι (*glōssai*) will cease" (1 Cor 13:8), the Apostle Paul indicated that this manifestation of the Spirit would at some future day come to an end (παύσονται/*pausontai*). The common verb generally used in the Septuagint for the cessation of speech is this παύω (*pauó*). The Greek verb of καταργέω (*katargeó*) here is found only once in the Septuagint (2 Esd) and not with verbs of speaking, whereas, παύω (*pauó*) is normally found in speaking contexts and once with γλῶσσα/*glōssa* (Ps 33[34]:13; cf. also Gen 18:33; 27:30; Num 16:31; Judg 15:17; Jdt 5:22; 14:9; Job 29:9; 1 Macc 2:23; 3:23). Therefore, based on linguistic precedent, it makes sense that the verb παύω (*pauó*) would be inserted in the middle phrase of 1 Corinthians 13:8, rather than καταργέω (*katargeó*). The different verb παύω (*pauó*) sandwiched between the two usages of καταργέω (*katargeó*) should not be made too much of in the "cessationism" and "continuationism" debate. Prophecies and knowledge "will fade away" (καταργηθήσονται/*katargēthēsontai*). Languages "will cease" (παύσονται/*pausontai*).

Why and when *prophecies* and *knowledge* fade away and *languages* cease are important queries but, because these topics are not the focus of this book's thesis, can only be briefly responded to in these verses.

There are different ways to interpret key expressions in these verses (1 Corinthians 13:8–13), but suffice to say that, as a minimum, προφητεῖαι (prophecy), γλῶσσαι (languages) and γνῶσις (knowledge) will no longer be needed in the new reality of the eventual eternal state (Lias, 1905:149). The commencement of the eventual eternal state would be their *terminus ad quem* (latest possible date). If γλῶσσαι (*glōssai*) refers to normal earthly languages, it would appear that they will be needed until the eventual eternal state. Benson (2019:9957), of a future day, writes: "For one language shall prevail among all the inhabitants of heaven, and all the low and imperfect languages of earth shall be forgotten."

CHAPTER 13 AND VERSE 9

"For we know in part"—as in 1 John 3: 2, "Now we are children of God, and it has not appeared as yet what we shall be. We know that, when He appears, we shall be like Him, because we shall see him just as He is."

As I look back at every stage of my life, I recognize how incomplete my knowledge was. I only knew a "part" (μέρους/*merous*) of the full picture. Even now into my senior years, I realize that I know only a "portion" (μέρους/*merous*) of what there is to know about life and spiritual things. And as one who has preached and predicted (προφητεύομεν/*prophēteuomen*), I am aware that little by little and day by day, I grasp a bit more of spiritual verities to share with others. So, even prophetic/preaching ministry is incomplete and partial, at any point in time, prior to eternity.

CHAPTER 13 AND VERSE 10

1 Corinthians 13:10 indicates that "when the perfect (*teleion* Greek) comes, the partial will be done away."

This clause is amplified by Paul's words, before and after, in 1 Corinthians 13: 9–13. After stating in verse 8 that various manifestations of the Spirit would be rendered inoperative or cease, he explains in 1 Corinthians 13:9 and 10: "For we know in part ("in" is the Greek *ek* meaning "from" or "out of"), and we prophesy in part; but when the perfect comes (Greek *to teleion*, "attaining an end or purpose, complete" "meeting the highest standard"—BDAG, s.v. τέλειος, §1; "brought to its end, finished; lacking nothing necessary to completeness"—Thayer, s.v. τέλειος, §1), the partial will be done away (Greek *katargeo*; brought to an end)." The sense of the word points to the ultimate, not to some intermediate state. Therefore, the phrase "when the perfect comes" (τέλειον/*teleion*), likely refers to entering the eternal state—the new heavens and the new earth (Rev. 21:1; cf. Isaiah 65:17–25).

There has been lots of debate on the precise meaning of the Greek word *teleion*. Thomas Edgar (1996:246) sums up his conclusion in the following insightful words:

> If, as seems apparent in the passage, the *teleion* ["perfect"] refers to the individual's presence with the Lord, this passage does not refer to some prophetic point in history. These factors mean that this passage does not teach when gifts will cease or how long they will last. It serves to remind the Corinthians of the abiding nature of love in contrast to the gifts, which by their inherent nature are only temporal, only for this life.

Put succinctly, Edgar (1996:246) believes that the "perfect" (*teleion*) occurs when the individual believer enters into the presence of the Lord, whether that be at the Lord's return or the believer's passing on to heaven, whichever comes first. When the believer meets the Lord Jesus face-to-face, there will be no need for the spiritual gifts, because "then I shall know fully just as I also have been fully known" (1 Cor 13:12; cf. 2 Cor 5:8–9). Calvin (1573:360), in answer to when that "perfect" will come, says, "It begins, indeed, at death, for then we put off, along with the body, many infirmities; but it will not be completely manifested until the day of judgment." Note that Calvin (1573:360) says that the "perfect" *begins* at death, but its full application is not to that intermediate state.

In other words, without fear of being contradicted, we know that various "spiritual ministries" will fade into complete irrelevance, at a different time for me than my grandchildren, assuming they outlive me and that the Lord doesn't return before I depart this present earthly scene.

CONTEXTUAL AND EXEGETICAL ANALYSIS

CHAPTER 13 AND VERSE 11

The verse says, "When I was a child, I used to speak (possible allusion to prophecies, languages, knowledge) as a child (cp. 1 Cor. 3:1; 1 Cor 14: 20), think as a child, reason as a child; when I became a man, I did away with childish things." This is the same Greek verb καταργέω/*katargeó* as in the previous verse 8, but this time instead of being in the "passive, third person," this same verb here is in the "active, first person" indicating that this was not out of Paul's hands, as to some future time, but in this case he took the initiative to bring on this state of greater maturity in this lifetime, in that he "abolished," from his personal life, immature speaking, reasoning and thinking (cf. 1 Cor 14:8), not so subtly hinting that the Corinthian believers should do likewise.

CHAPTER 13 AND VERSE 12

This verse indicates our partial knowledge in this present age in contrast to that future day of complete understanding, in the presence of our Lord. We have a shadow of this, in Exodus 33:11, where "the Lord used to speak to Moses face to face, just as a man speaks to a friend." God spoke to Moses, not in visions and dreams, as to other prophets, but in perfectly clear communication: "mouth to mouth, even openly, and not in dark sayings [Septuagint: αἰνιγμάτων/*ainigmaton* i.e., not in riddles]" (Num 12: 6–8; cf. Deut 34:10). When God appears, "we shall see him just as he is" (1 John 3:2).

In this verse, "The adverb *then* denotes the last day, rather than the time that is immediately subsequent to death. . . although full vision will be deferred until the day of Christ, a nearer view of God will begin to be enjoyed immediately after death" (Calvin, 1573:362; 1 Cor 13:12).

Circling back to the theme of perfection (τελείοις/*teleiois*) Paul raised in 1 Corinthians chapter 2, in which he juxtaposed the perfect person with the carnal Corinthians, Paul stresses, "For we know in part, and we prophesy in part; but when the perfect comes, the partial will be done away" (13:9–10). Using the metaphors of being a baby and of peering into a blurry mirror, 1 Corinthians 13:11–12 emphasizes the juvenility and incompleteness of current knowledge and wisdom. "Knowledge and prophecy are useful as lamps in the darkness, but they will be useless when the eternal day has dawned" (Robertson & Plummer, 1911: 297).

The Earliest View of New Testament Tongues

CHAPTER 13 AND VERSE 13

1 Corinthians 13 reaches a grand crescendo in verse 13, where the Apostle Paul writes: "But now abide (a triad of graces, in contrast with the temporary triad of προφητεῖαι/prophecy, γλῶσσαι/languages and γνῶσις/knowledge, which would pass away; cf. 1 Cor 13: 8) faith, hope, love, these three; but the greatest of these is love."

5.4.1 Contextual Analysis of 1 Corinthians 14

At the outset of this contextual analysis, it is important to keep in mind the portrait of the synagogue as a place of reading the Hebrew Scriptures and instruction thereto as found in the narratives in Luke and Acts (Luke 4:16–19; Acts 13:15–16; Acts 15:21).

The homily/sermonic discourse was an important part of the Scripture reading ceremony by the first century AD (Mark 1:21, 6:2; Luke 6:6, 13:10; cf. also Matt 4:23, 9:35, 13:54; Luke 4:15; and John 18:20). In view of Luke 4:20, it appears that the sermon could be given by the same individual who read the Hebrew Scripture portion. From the Luke 4:20 occurrence, we get the impression that these follow-up sermons or sermonettes were delivered in the vernacular language of the listeners, since the intent of the sermon was to have a clearer understanding of the Hebrew Scripture passage just read. However, one cannot be adamant about this, and possibly in certain circumstances, translation of the Hebrew Scripture just read would have been required. Nevertheless, one can be dogmatic about the centrality of the Older Testament Hebrew Scriptures and the role it would have played in the meetings of these new believers, the initial core group having come out of the synagogue.

In view of the high illiteracy of the times, with only 10–15% of the population literate (Chancey, 2005:143; Gamble, 1995:4), the necessity of public reading is noted in the New Testament writings (Luke 4:16, Acts 13:15, I Timothy 4:13, Rev 1:3).

Because these new believers and seekers did not have the Hebrew Scripture scrolls in their homes, the public reading and exposition of those Hebrew Scriptures would have taken on paramount importance in their gatherings. Thankfully, this synagogue precedent of reading and interpreting the Older Testament Hebrew Scripture appears to be carried over into the Corinthian assembly of Christ believers. This hints at and may provide part of the solution to the γλῶσσαι/*glōssai* (languages/tongues) dilemma in 1 Corinthians 14.

Based on the Pastoral Epistles, even at this early stage, it is assumed that there would be elders of the church "able to teach" (1 Tim. 3:2) and "able both to exhort in sound doctrine and to refute those who contradict" (Titus 1:9). So exhortative teaching and explanation was presumed to have a central place in their gatherings and the teaching of the Older Testament Hebrew Scriptures to the congregation of Christ believers was specifically entrusted to a group of individuals, namely the elders.

This core component of the public reading of the Older Testament Hebrew Scriptures and explanation of it is further reinforced in Paul's instruction to his protégé Timothy, where he additionally says, "Until I come, give attention to the *public* reading *of Scripture*, to exhortation and teaching" (1 Tim 4:13). Following on in verse 15 of the same chapter, Paul again reiterates that Timothy should "Take pains with these things; be absorbed in them, so that your progress may be evident to all." A responsible reading of this text would indicate that, in the pattern of the synagogue, Paul wanted the public reading of the Hebrew Scriptures to be a core component in the meetings of the Corinthian believers. Very plainly, the reading of the Older Testament and exposition of it was at the core of a Christian congregation's regular meetings (1 Tim 4:13).

Being that the nucleus of each Pauline church was drawn from the local synagogue (Acts 13:42-44; 16:12-15; 17:1-4; 18:4-8; 19:8-10), and in significant numbers at that, it should come as no surprise that the synagogue pattern provided a precedent for the teaching and worship pattern in the newly formed gatherings of believers in Jesus. Bacchiocchi (Geraty, 2013:256) concludes that the synagogue did significantly influence the format of services for Christ believers in the first four centuries.

Justin Martyr (c. 90–c. 165 AD), also known as Justin the Philosopher, was an early Christian apologist and philosopher (Hanegraaff, 2012:20; Wagner, 1994:158). Justin Martyr (ANF, Vol. 1, *The First Apology of Justin*, Chapter 67, p. 186) refers to this public reading:

> And on the day called Sunday, all who live in cities or in the country gather together to one place, and the memoirs of the apostles or the writings of the prophets are read, as long as time permits; then, when the reader has ceased, the president verbally instructs, and exhorts to the imitation of these good things.

The Earliest View of New Testament Tongues

Levine (2005:159) suggests that in the Roman Diaspora "... the Septuagint translation (or variations thereof) may have been used after the Hebrew reading..." "Passages in Philo, Josephus, and the NT (Luke 4:16–21; Acts 15:21; 17:1) refer to the regular reading of Scripture in synagogues in the original languages [Hebrew and some Aramaic] as well as in translation" (Tov, 2008:174). Perrot (1988:155) remarks: "Still one may suppose that in the 'synagogues of the Hebrews' which are mentioned several times in connection with the Diaspora at Rome and Corinth, reading was also in Hebrew."

Even if Paul frequently used the Greek Septuagint, in one of its recensions, that is not to say that the Corinthian assembly that Paul left behind used only the Greek Septuagint in one or several of its recensions. If there was an unspiritual jockeying for superiority and the clash of ungodly egos, there likely was the use of one of the Hebrew versions of the Older Testament by some public readers. After all, the pre-eminence of Hebrew appears to have been established in the church in the first century. This pride of place for the Hebrew language is seen in a statement of Clement (Bishop of Rome from 88–99 AD) who emphasized that Hebrew was the first language of mankind, "until ever since, only one language holds, Hebrew is beloved of God" (my translation from Frankenberg, 1937:39). Clement's view of Hebrew's preeminence was a dominant sentiment in the first-century church.

A set of the Hebrew scrolls may have been brought over by the converted Corinthian synagogue leader Crispus (or later by Sosthenes if he was the successor synagogue leader of Acts 18:17, if also converted and then acknowledged in the preface of Paul's first letter to the Corinthians in chapter 1 and verse 1). Jews of some financial means were known to personally own scrolls of the Hebrew Scriptures. Levine (2005:416) implies that, from the literary and epigraphical material, an ἀρχισυνάγωγος/*archisynagōgos* (synagogue ruler) was generally a person of financial means, and in addition to being the person in charge of synagogue worship, the ἀρχισυνάγωγος/*archisynagōgos* was also a financial patron of the synagogue. Thus, the converted Corinthian synagogue leader Crispus (?or the successor synagogue leader Sosthenes of Acts 18?) may have owned a scroll of the Hebrew Scriptures (Older Testament) which was made available to the newly-formed Corinthian assembly of believers in Jesus.

It is of relevance to remind ourselves of the influence of the first-century Pharisees among the Jewish people. The New Testament Greek word for this group is Φαρισαῖοι. It comes from the Hebrew word פָּרַשׁ which means, "to separate or disperse" or "separated ones." They separated themselves from the heathen and from other influences that intruded into Israel, such as Hellenist philosophies and beliefs. They were actually formed to keep Judaism from assimilating the Hellenist philosophies and beliefs. Therefore, the main body of Pharisees would have likely rejected any Greek texts and particularly eschewed any Greek translations of their Hebrew Scriptures for reading in the homeland Jewish Synagogues during the time of Christ and immediately after that time.

The early Christ-believer movement was comprised of a number who were of the sect of the Pharisees (Acts 15:5), who initially had significant influence in the Jerusalem mother assembly, not always in a positive fashion. The Pharisaic influence extending into the Diaspora may have been part of the reason for a continuing bias to the Hebrew text of Scripture.

This reminder that both the Apostle Paul, and the earliest assemblies of believers, even in the Diaspora, were initially Jewish entities, will help to appropriately shape our understanding of chapter 14 in this first letter of Paul's to the Messianic congregation in Corinth.

Even the Gentile converts likely saw themselves as still connected to Judaism (Lockwood, 2000:490). The Hebrew language and the standing Jerusalem Temple were still important factors. Before the destruction of the Jerusalem Temple in 70 AD, the Hebraistic Jews and Hellenized Jews would still find significance in their ancient language and customs, and Gentiles of Greek background would still have an attachment to their mother tongue, be it Doric, Aeolic or Attic, and so Paul, not wanting to tip his hand, had a tight rope to walk on these identity issues. So, we will want to keep in view the Epiphanius thesis that Hebrew was a major language of instruction in the Corinthian assembly of believers with Paul having to additionally navigate the contentious issue of which Greek language (Doric or other) would be the norm for translation into.

Sullivan (2014) asserts that the Apostle Paul did not name the Hebrew language in the book of 1 Corinthians because of the ethnic tensions between Aramaic Jews/Hellenized Jews who didn't want to lose their historic Jewish language and traditions and Greek converts who had either Doric, Aeolic or Attic language backgrounds. If Paul came down unabashedly on one side or the other, he would have exacerbated

The Earliest View of New Testament Tongues

the tensions, so the best course of action was to lay down some principled guidelines that would supersede the disputable specifics (Sullivan, 2014).

We ought to also keep clearly in mind that in Corinth, at that time, it was not a given that Hellenistic/Alexandrian Greek was the common Greek language in Corinth. To the contrary, the significant place accorded to the Doric Greek dialect in Corinth is seen in the account of first-century orator, Favorinus (Dio Chrysostom, 1946:25, Corinthian Oration 37). So, it was by no means agreed as to which Greek dialect would be the norm for translation into. The Epiphanius thesis that there was a conflict in Corinth between the Doric, Aeolic and Attic Greek dialects is supported by the facts of history.

Having spelled out the need for loving consideration in the face of differences in chapter 13, Paul, in chapter 14, challenges the Corinthian believers to handle the uninterpreted languages issue in that same vein.

The elements of "speaking in a language" (1 Cor 14:13), "praying in a language" (1 Cor. 14:14), giving a "blessing" (*eulogeo* 1 Cor 14: 16), the responsive "amen" (1 Cor 14: 16), a "psalm" (1 Cor 14: 26), invitation to offer a word of "encouragement" (*paraklesin* one of three aspects of prophesying 1 Cor 14: 3; cf. Paul being invited forward by synagogue rulers to offer a "word of exhortation"—*parakleseos* Acts 13:15), a "teaching" (1 Cor 14: 26), all seem to derive from a fixed pattern. Paul's instruction in 1 Corinthians 14:26ff describes that. The converted synagogue leader Crispus would have had a significant influence on the service order. Over all, Paul stipulates that the entire conduct of the Corinthian public congregational service is to be done "with decorum/properly" (εὐσχημόνως/*euschēmonōs*) and following "a fixed order/pattern" (τάξιν/*taxin*)—"But all things must be done properly and in an orderly manner" (1 Cor 14:40).

5.4.2 Exegetical Analysis of 1 Corinthians 14

In researching, it is soon discovered that the dominant view in the commentaries for about the last 145 years is the theory that γλῶσσα/γλῶσσαι (*glōssa/glōssai*) was an ecstatic and non-earthly language. This is in view of the fact that, Farrar, the leading English proponent of this redefinition, caused its rise to prominence in the English world from 1879 AD following (Oxford English Dictionary, 1933:232). Frederick

Farrar (1831–1903 AD), Philip Schaff (1819–1893 AD; 1910a:230), and authors of *The Life and Epistles of St. Paul* (1863), William Conybeare (1815–July 1857 AD) and John Howson (1816–1885 AD), among others, were influenced by the writings of August Neander (1900:11), who lived until 1850 AD.

This redefinition of speaking in tongues was instigated by Neander and other German historical-critical scholars, who had an aversion to the supposed miracle of *xenolalia* (language-miracle), basing their new theory on the speculations surrounding the Delphine Oracle, as well as the Dionysus and Cybele mystery religions (Blosser & Sullivan, 2022: Kindle Location p. 304).

Those presumptions have by now been largely disproven (Forbes, 1995 et al). Neander and other German historical-critical scholars were busy in redefining speaking in tongues as *glossolalia*, meaning unintelligible utterances out of an ecstatic, psychological state beyond earthly language (Neander, 1900:11). This despite the fact that none of the Pauline letters contain the Greek word for "ecstatic" (*ekstatikos*) nor its cognates. This new definition of *glossolalia* has been virtually the universal position taken in commentaries, theological word study books (TDNT/Theological Dictionary of the New Testamenty, DNTT/Dictionary of New Testament Theology) and Greek linguistic dictionaries (Thayer, BDAG and its earlier editions, Louw & Nida, etc.) ever since. By the latter years of the nineteenth century AD, Godet (1890:202) admitted that commentators had generally abandoned the interpretation that γλώσσαις (*glóssais*) consisted of earthly languages. The new, avant-garde meaning was not based on any new linguistic discoveries, but maybe came into vogue because of a presumption of supposedly better understanding the semantic context in which the term was used.

Prior to 1879 AD, in the English world, the Greek-English Lexicons of Parkhurst (1817:132), Groves (1830:126), Giles (1839:154), Pickering (1855:237) and Hamilton (1859:53) defined γλώσσα as "foreign language," "foreign speech," "language, " or "dialect," with none describing it as ecstatic, unintelligible, or a non-earthly language derived from the heavenly orb.

Although I will reference some of the contemporary commentators, I will also turn to earlier distinguished scholars like John Gill (1697–1771 AD), Adam Clarke (1762–1832 AD), Charles Hodge (1797–1878 AD), Albert Barnes (1798–1870 AD), J. B. Lightfoot (1828–1889 AD) and others who lived prior, and thus were not caught up in the new trend, in order to give a more complete, wholistic portrayal. Even Robert Jamieson (1802–1880 AD), Andrew Fausset (1821–1910 AD) and David Brown (1803–1897 AD) seemed more immune to the trending new theory, as their 1 Corinthians 14:5 commentary (1880:767) pointedly rebukes Neander in the following words: "Tongues must therefore mean languages, not ecstatic unintelligible rhapsodies (as Neander fancied): for Paul could never 'wish' for the latter in their behalf."

Thistleton (2000:970), in the main, follows the Neander trend and keeps it pretty broad, based on his understanding "tongues" in the light of his own translation ("species of tongues"). Thiselton (2000:972) pronounced that "Writers who accept that species of tongues may denote more than one of some six 'family resemblances' ascribed to tongues are on more solid ground than those who invest everything in a single category of description." This wide ecumenical and conciliatory stratagem of Thiselton's means that if you're hounded on one of the six "family resemblances" you can retreat to the next—surely one will be right or a hybrid of several will be.

After surveying the six different options (Thiselton, 2000:972–986), in respect to Gerd Theissen's *Psychological Aspects of Pauline Theology*, Thiselton (2000:986) approvingly notes that "Theissen's treatment is the most detailed, incisive, and innovative, and sheds much light on the issues." It is interesting that the viewpoint Thiselton lands on is a psychological approach rife with speculations. Thiselton (200:270, 274) regards these "tongues" as likely the articulation by the Holy Spirit of "the unconscious released in 'Sighs too deep for words'" from Romans 8:26–27. If I might be permitted some psychologizing, I think the Apostle Paul would be dumbfounded at this novel mode and, once recovered from the shock, further intrigued to discover, after all these years, his "triple strategy" was "first, to establish a hierarchy of gifts based on Christomorphic service to others and love for others; second, to 'privatize' glossolalia in the home (as both Theissen and Wire stress); and, third, to encourage prayer for the gift of articulating buried longings, yearning, and emotions" (Thiselton, 2000:988).

Buchanan (2012:13) remarks that Thiselton "is specifically not calling this a divine language, but postulating a human confusion, a mental congestion, affecting the not-so-literate convert." That assessment is even more disturbing.

It appears that the speaking "with tongues" at Corinth was a different thing in one respect from the speaking "with other tongues" in

Jerusalem on "the day of Pentecost." This seems apparent by the fact that, in Jerusalem on the day of Pentecost, the speaking "with other tongues" was speaking other languages that were understood by those who heard them—"we each hear in our own dialect [language]" (Acts 2:8). No interpreter was needed! At Corinth, the speaking in γλῶσσαι (glóssai—languages/tongues) needs a translator/interpreter (1 Cor. 14:2). This contrast is very striking in the Greek text. In 1 Corinthians 14:2, we have "no one understands," whereas in the Acts texts, "hearing" (Acts 2: 6), "hear" (Acts 2:8), and "hearing" (Acts 10: 46) are all translations of the same Greek verb, meaning "to hear and understand what was said" (BDAG, s.v. ἀκούω, §7).

It is interesting to note the circumstantial clue that the untranslated γλῶσσαι (glóssai—languages/tongues) in Jerusalem (Acts 2:4ff), Caesarea (Acts 10:46), and Ephesus (Acts 19:6), created no problem, but in contrast the untranslated γλῶσσαι (glóssai—languages/tongues) at Corinth (1 Cor 14) caused significant trouble and required some stern rebuke and restrictions to be put in place by the Apostle Paul. So, although γλῶσσαι (glóssai—languages/tongues) most likely was essentially the same in Acts and Corinthians, there were different dynamics in the two different contexts. It is ironic and semantically inconsistent that many advocates of *glossolalia* acknowledge that προφητεία (prophecy) is essentially the same in both Acts and 1 Corinthians but insist that γλῶσσαι (languages) is intrinsically different in the two books.

A question to address up front is how many times, in the rest of the New Testament where the term γλῶσσα or γλῶσσαι is found (Luke, Acts, Rom, Phil, Jas, 1 Pet, 1 John, Rev and Mark 7:33, 35), aside from these controverted passages in 1 Corinthians 12, 14 and Acts, do we find an indication of γλῶσσα/ *glóssa* or γλῶσσαι/ *glóssai* being *xenolalia* (miraculously given, earthly languages) or *glossolalia* (non-earthly, heavenly languages)? The answer is that neither *xenolalia* nor *glossolalia* is indicated in the rest of the New Testament, although there has been a pretty standard assumption that the γλώσσαις (glóssais) of Acts 2 is a *xenolalic* language-miracle form. However, the text doesn't say this, but nevertheless it's read into the passage based on certain presumptions.

It is curious that γλῶσσαι (glóssai—languages/tongues) are not even mentioned in Paul's other two passages where, in the case of Romans 12:6–8 and Ephesians 4:11–12, he actually banners those entire but brief listings as χαρίσματα/*charismata* (gifts). If Paul does not even mention it, let alone advertise it as a "gift," to the Ephesian (4:11–12)

The Earliest View of New Testament Tongues

and Roman (12:6-8) churches, it would be fair to suggest that something different is going on in Corinth—that there is a unique dynamic in that cosmopolitan and multilingual city, wherein γλῶσσαι (*glōssai*—languages/tongues) became an issue.

The matter of various competing languages may have been less of a problem in other parts of the Mediterranean, but Corinth was a major crossroads of the Mediterranean world so it's much easier to conceive that believers with different first languages/dialects would contend for their own linguistic background and thus create discord in the assembly.

Ministry can be tremendously satisfying, but here in 1 Corinthians 14 as in the previous 1 Corinthians 12, the purpose of any spiritual ministry is understood to be edifying the body of Christ (1 Cor12:7ff and 1 Cor 14:1-8). As with the ministry of prophesying, or generosity, or leadership, the intent of γλῶσσα/*glossa* (language) ministry is not for one's personal benefit. The objective of these ministries is not to "prophesy" to oneself, or to be "sharing" with oneself, or to provide "leadership" to oneself, or to "show mercy" to oneself (cf. Rom 12:6-8).

Similarly, the γλώσσαις/*glōssais* (languages) ministry is not for practicing privately in one's closet. As noted earlier, Akers (1995:19-20) makes the valid point that privatizing γλώσσαις/*glōssais* (languages) would have been quite contrary to Mediterranean cultural norms of the first century AD. The social dynamic in a first-century AD milieu wouldn't be for a person to speak to oneself, without regard to being heard and understood by others (Akers, 1995:19). Contrary to the attitude of our modern, more self-centered western culture, in that kinship-oriented society, it would have been shameful for a person to speak to oneself with only the goal of personal edification, without the intent of edifying the group (Akers, 1995:20). This informs us of the biblical perspective on the modern notion of private, personal "tongues." It does not appear to be birthed from the embryo of the first-century AD Judean or Mediterranean ἐκκλησία (*ekklēsia*) of believers.

CHAPTER 14 AND VERSE 1

A question to raise in respect to this verse and the Acts and other Corinthians passages is how many times is γλῶσσαι (*glōssai*) specifically labelled as a "gift" (χαρίσματα/*charismata*)? Again, the answer is none. For example, in 1 Corinthians 12:1ff about "spiritual matters," we have only "cures/healings" specified as "gifts" (1 Cor 12:9—χαρίσματα ἰαμάτων/charismata iamatōn). It can't be deduced with certainty that γλῶσσαι (glōssai) is a "gift" per se when it is not so prefaced in either 1 Corinthians 12:10 or 12:30 nor here in 1 Corinthians 14:1. Maybe it would be better dubbed as "a ministry" (1 Cor 12:5) or "an operation" (1 Cor 12:6). Although 1 Corinthians 12 concludes with the appeal to "earnestly desire the greater gifts" (vs. 31), the closest prior antecedent banner for "languages/tongues" in 1 Corinthians 12:10 is "manifestation of the Spirit" (1 Cor 12:7).

It is true that even theologians and academics unconsciously slip into the habit of using the appellation of "gift/gifts" for any other *ability* within the *vicinity*, when the text doesn't tie that descriptor directly to a ministry/service (διακονιῶν/diakoniōn), or operation (ἐνεργημάτων/energēmatōn) or manifestation (φανέρωσις/phanerosis) of the Spirit. The problem with that looser approach and penchant for categorizing is that we get very mystical about it and don't make allowance for God to equip believers in more natural and less dramatic ways.

In Corinthians 14:1, the word πνευματικά (pneumatika "spiritual/s"), in the accusative, neuter, plural adjective form, is better translated "spiritual things" or "spiritual realities" (Collins, 1999:489). This gives it a far wider sense than limiting the πνευματικά (pneumatika) term to specific, so-called "gifts." It broadens the scenario away from a limited focus on "gifts." As previously noted, the similar translation, of "spiritual things" or "spiritual realities," is also more accurate for 1 Corinthians 12:1 where you also don't have "gifts" specified, but also have πνευματικῶν (pneumatikōn) in the genitive, neuter, plural adjective form. The Greek word for "gift" is not used in respect to "prophecy" here in 1 Corinthians 14:1 as it was not in 1 Corinthian 13:2 either. It's simply προφητείαν (prophēteian).

Nowhere in 1 Corinthians 14 (not in verse 1, 12 nor 37) does Paul use the term "gift" (χαρισμά/charisma or δωρεά/dórea) in reference to γλῶσσαι/glōssai. To be precise, the Greek word in the plural form, χαρίσματα (charismata/gifts), does not occur anywhere in 1 Corinthians 14, though all the English versions give that impression "in 14:1, many in 14:14, and some also in page, chapter or section headings—all of them gratuitously" (Buchanan, 2012:2).

It is also of importance to note that there are no references to "heaven" or "angels" in 1 Corinthians 14 (Zerhusen, 1997:142). We would expect some reference to such if *glossolalia* were being practiced by the Corinthian language-speakers (Zerhusen, 1997:142). We have already examined 1 Corinthians 13:1 and excluded angelic languages from another realm.

CHAPTER 14 AND VERSE 2

As emphasized before, Corinth was a city with two seaports with a fluid, mixed, multilingual population. For one of these persons from a different area to most freely worship God, he would use his mother tongue but the congregation may not understand him (Zerhusen, 1997:146).

Hasel (1991:55) states that, "There is one clear and definitive passage in the New Testament which unambiguously defines 'speaking in tongues' and that is Acts 2." Hasel (1991:55) then proceeds to the near uniform agreement that Acts 2 is understood to be "known, intelligible languages." In the continued flow of his systematic approach, in respect to sound hermeneutics, Hasel (1991:55) asks, "Would it not be sound methodologically to go from the known definition and the clear passage in the New Testament to the less clear and more difficult passage in interpretation?" The logical consequence of thus interpreting 1 Corinthians 12–14 by Acts means that this verse two (1 Cor 14) is understood as referring to "known, intelligible languages" (cf. Lenski, 1946:510).

Thomas (2011:30, note 4) writes: "Since Paul does not attempt to explain tongues as anything different from what occurred at Pentecost, it is more likely that tongues were also foreign languages, which in this instance necessitated interpreters..."

Edgar (1996:150) writes: "There is perfect consistency between the terminology and description of tongues wherever they are mentioned in the New Testament. They are always foreign languages; they are one and the same in nature."

Fee (2014:736) admits that "the phenomenon of different languages, would also have been commonplace in a cosmopolitan center such as Corinth." Poythress (1977:133) accepts that: "A Corinthian tongue-speaker might speak in a human language unknown to the whole assembly, but known somewhere in the world." This is to say that many Corinthians did not have the local Greek (possibly Doric Greek) as their mother tongue.

Fitzmyer (2008:510) candidly acknowledges that peculiar, ecstatic phenomena in the Greco-Roman world is never referred to as "speaking in tongues." That right away should tip us off that *glossolalia* ("non-earthly, angelic/heavenly language") is probably not what's under consideration here in 1 Corinthians. Ciampa and Rosner (2010:Kindle Location 15531) footnote that "language" (singular) is an alternate rendering in 1 Corinthians 14:2, 4, 13, 14, 19, 26, 27 (Ciampa & Rosner, 2010:Kindle Location 29095) and they indicate that "languages" (plural) is an alternate rendering in 1 Corinthians 14:5, 6, 18, 22, 23, and 39 (Ciampa & Rosner, 2010:Kindle Location 29103).

Keener (2005:113) writes that contrary to many interpreters today, Paul seemed to believe that this manifestation of the Spirit utilized genuine languages as evidenced by Paul using the term (γλῶσσαι/ *glōssai*) which normally meant "languages" and by his referring to "interpretation" (1 Cor 12:10, 30; 14:5, 13, 26–28). Additionally, Keener (2005:113) acknowledges that in ancient Greek examples of inspired speech, the languages were known to the speaker. Keener (2005:113) complains that pagan parallels for early Christian *glossolalia* are difficult to find. (Forbes, 1995:103–162, would say that pagan parallels are non-existent.) Despite these three admissions, Keener (2005:113) charges on to state that "the languages appear to be unknown to the speaker" and that "this probably makes it comparable to the experience of many modern charismatics."

It is of note that the Apostle Paul doesn't diagnose the psychological, emotional, or mental state of the γλῶσσα/*glōssa* (language) speaker in 1 Corinthians 14:2 or anywhere in the chapter. Therefore, we also should avoid diagnosing the speaker's mental state as is presumptuously done by too many modern lexicographers and commentators when conjecturing an ecstatic condition for the γλῶσσα/*glōssa*-speaker.

After an extensive review of pre-Christian Greek literature, the Hebrew Bible, the *Thanksgiving Hymns* of Qumran, the Mishnah and the Aramaic of the Targums, Engelbrecht (1996:302) judged, that in light of the evidence, the expression "to speak in a tongue" is a semitic idiom, which, thereafter, Paul drew on in 1 Corinthians 14. Engelbrecht (1996:302) also concluded that, "It should also be noted that 'to speak in a tongue' is never used in the sense of 'ecstatic utterance' and . . . consistently refers to the speaking of a foreign language or the holy language, Hebrew."

The Earliest View of New Testament Tongues

As noted before, the Corinthian congregation would have been comprised of Hebraistic-Jews, Hellenized-Jews, and Gentile congregants. The Jewish background and the synagogue traditions were the backdrop. With that framework, Paul desired to maintain some semblance of order so that these various language groups could function beneficially together in their assemblies.

If the approach, to 1 Corinthians 14:2ff, envisions at least one scenario being some Jewish Christians enamored with reading the Older Testament in Hebrew and paraphrastic teaching of same, based on the Jewish synagogal precedent from which the initial converts derived, as detailed in chapter 3 of this book, the situation (German *Sitz im Leben*) is more clearly comprehended.

Calvin (1573:366; also Barnes, 1949:260), on 1 Corinthians 14:2, viewed γλῶσσα/*glōssa*-speaking as speaking in a foreign language/tongue, which "had more of show connected with it, for when persons hear a man speaking in a foreign tongue, their admiration is commonly excited." This sentiment of Calvin's perfectly fits the Epiphanius thesis that the γλῶσσαι/*glōssai* conflict in Corinth was a problem of prideful people using a foreign language (Hebrew) and certain Greek dialects to posture as superior to others in the assembly. This means that 1 Corinthians chapter 14 was not referring to a non-earthly or ecstatic phenomena nor being miraculously and instantaneously given a previously unlearned, earthly, foreign language.

We need to recall that, initially, a great percentage of the congregation of Corinth consisted of Jews, likely out of a Hebraic synagogue, not Hellenistic, based on the archaeological and epigraphical evidence (Powell, 1903:60–61). It is therefore likely that their leaders also followed the custom of using the Hebrew language; namely, that one read the Scripture out of the Hebrew text, another prayed or preached in the Hebrew language, according to the pattern in the synagogue from which they came (Lightfoot (1859:261). The Apostle Paul permitted this, if there were an interpreter, as in the synagogue, because the Hebrew language, "full of mysteries" was very conducive to the edification of the church (Lightfoot, 1859:261).

In commenting on 1 Corinthians 14 specifically, Lightfoot (1859:258) states, "We are of opinion, therefore, nor without reason, that unknown language which they used or abused rather, in the church was the Hebrew" and elsewhere Lightfoot (1859:260) emphasizes that

"The Scripture is not read but in the Hebrew text; yea, as we believe, in the synagogues even of the Hellenists . . . "

The renowned Hebrew scholar, Lightfoot (1859:259), envisions that the individual(s) referred to in 1 Corinthians 14:2ff "spake in the Hebrew tongue, that he either read or quoted the holy text in the original language; and that he either preached or prayed in the phrases of the prophets." It's not an unreasonable inference, in view of all the other Jewish/Hebraic indicators which we have in this text and within the Corinthian congregation of believers.

The use of the Hebrew tongue by those ministering was beneficial and necessary, yet in 1 Corinthians 14:2ff we find that there was some abuse which the Apostle Paul chastises; namely, they used it without an interpreter and therefore not to edification (Lightfoot, 1859:260).

There was the need of translation in the Corinthian assembly because the Older Testament text being originally in the Hebrew was unknown to the common people, the Septuagint was faulty in "infinite places," the first-century AD Aramaic Targum paraphrase/translation of the prophets was inconsistent and Judaized, and the Targum on the law did not yet exist (Lightfoot, 1859:258).

There is general agreement among commentators that the three activities listed in 1 Timothy 4:13—the *public* reading of *Scripture*, exhortation, and teaching—were typical features of a meeting of a first-century congregation of believers (Marshall, 1999:562–563). The Apostle Paul's expected pattern of 1 Timothy 4:13 for the Ephesian congregation is a good comparative for 1 Corinthians 14. Timothy was to end the false teaching in Ephesus and the prescription for doing that was to return to an ordered reading of the Older Testament Hebrew Scriptures, and the application and teaching of it ("*public* reading of *Scripture*," "exhortation," and "teaching"). That sequence would be a prudent assumption for all of Paul's planted congregations. This would keep a congregation away from "strange doctrines," "fruitless discussions," and "myths and endless genealogies which give rise to mere speculations" (1 Tim 1:3–6).

Revelation 1:3 speaks of a blessing for the one who reads. In 1 Corinthians 14:2–4 we learn that "one who speaks in a γλῶσσα/*glōssa* (language/tongue) edifies (blesses) himself." However, if not understood by anyone, he's the only one who is edified (gets "a blessing").

"Blessed is he who reads" is in the singular, and "those who hear . . . and heed" are in the plural—one reader and many listeners (Rev

1:3). Somebody read the Scriptures and everybody else heard in the first-century congregations. The word קְרָא/*qera* "to read" in ancient Hebrew meant "to read out, to read aloud" (Sawyer, 2002:47).

"Glossolalics" often point to the speaking in an "unknown tongue" referred to in the King James Version of 1 Corinthians 14:2. However, in the King James Bible, all of the six occurrences of this expression "unknown tongue" (in 1 Cor. 14: 2, 4, 13, 14, 19, 27) show the word "unknown" in italics, thus indicating that it has no underlying word from the Greek text but was inserted by the translators. Although most other translations do not add the misleading word "unknown" to the text, they nevertheless still follow the lead of the KJV and give the impression that these languages were not known, earthly languages.

If the person who read the Hebrew language text of Scripture publicly did not have ability to explain it to others and did not have a translator/expositor to follow up his reading, the listeners could not be edified. It is possible for a person to comprehend a second language, without being capable of explaining it or expounding upon it.

Cremer (1895:164) remarks that γλώσσαις/*glōssais* in 1 Corinthians 14 "must be taken to mean language" (cf. also Keener, 2005:113). Andrew Fausset (1873:289) writes, "Tongues must therefore mean *languages*, not ecstatic, unintelligible rhapsodies (as Neander fancied): for Paul could never 'wish' for the latter in their behalf." There is no historical evidence for "ecstatic speech" interpreted by a Delphine priest (Witherington, 1995:279). The term "ecstatic" isn't anywhere in 1 Corinthians 12 or 14.

Behm (Kittel,1964, vol. 1:725) also admits that there is not "any support in the sources for the conjecture that Ac.2:3f. led to the early Christian use of γλῶσσα as a technical term for ecstatic utterance."

Kleinknecht (Kittel,1964, vol. 6:345–348) alludes to the notion of "mantic" prophecy and also suggests what he thinks are parallels from the oracular speech at Delphi. Kleinknecht (Kittel,1964, vol. 6:345) cites ancient Greek writers, like Strabo, who state that "The supreme and (historically) most important result of the spirit's working is the giving of oracles." This would appear to be far removed from the Corinthian believers' experience of γλῶσσα/*glōssa* as we have no hint from the Apostle Paul that this was the means by which they could ascertain when to marry, when to plant crops or how to conduct other affairs of their personal lives.

On 1 Corinthians 14:2–39, Hering (1962:50) argues that prophets can control their spirits, whereas those in ecstasy, speaking in γλῶσσαι/ *glōssai*, are in a state of inspiration and lose control. However, the fact that Paul instructs γλῶσσαι speakers to wait their turn (1 Cor 14:27) and constrain themselves in an assembly meeting, similarly to self-controlled prophets, repudiates the idea of out-of-control ecstatic γλῶσσαι/ *glōssai* (1 Cor 14:32).

Martin (1995:98–99), in his discussion of Plato's and Philo's hierarchies of body, soul and mind, writes of the mind [*nous*] being evicted at the arrival of the divine Spirit [*pneuma*] and, with the fading of reason [*logismos*], ecstasy is produced, and frenzy is inspired [*ekstasin kai theophoreton manian*]. While this philosophic discourse is interesting, the Apostle Paul does not appear to so dichotomize and advocates a more wholistic, Hebrew perspective contrary to this Greek Platonic view (cf. 1 Cor 14:15).

Of three definitions for *glossolalia* he puts forward, dismissing "Angelic Language" and "Unknown Human Languages," Johnson (1992:596–600) opts for "Ecstatic Utterance" partly basing it on the Apostle Paul's statement that, if they all spoke in γλῶσσαι/*glōssai* at the same time, the Corinthian assembly could be seen as "raving" and "in a frenzy" (1 Cor 14:23) like all the other Greek cults around them.

Johnson (1992:599) attaches the term "ecstatic" to the Acts 2 event, even though that term is never used in that account by Luke. Johnson (1992:597) also sets aside "Unknown Human Languages" saying that "Acts' other accounts of tongues make no mention of their intelligibility" when, in fact, Acts 10:46 indicates that Peter and his six Jewish associates heard the household of Cornelius speaking in languages and magnifying God (λαλούντων γλώσσαις καὶ μεγαλυνόντων τὸν Θεόν), so it must have been "intelligible" for Peter and his six Jewish companions to know that these Gentile converts were declaring God's greatness.

Although a proponent of "ecstatic utterance" in the first-century AD Corinthian congregation of believers, House (1983:142) admits that it may be that Paul also used γλῶσσα/*glōssa* for "human language" in 1 Corinthians. House (1983:143) acknowledges the legitimate question of "why Paul did not use μάντις/*mantis* when he referred to ecstatic utterance?" It is a significant question being that the non-biblical sources to do with the Greek oracular and mystery religion cults consistently used that term μάντις/*mantis* in reference to ecstatic utterance. That term μάντις/*mantis* is not found anywhere in the Apostle Paul's writings.

The Earliest View of New Testament Tongues

Currie (1965:274–294) researched whether there was any evidence from early Christian writings and contemporaneous non-Christian sources of the late first century and second century which would throw light on what was meant by "speaking in tongues." In his conclusion, Currie (1965:294) summarizes that "the church's experience in the first and especially the second century led Christians to regard with great diffidence dark sayings uttered ecstatically" and his study found "no early, firsthand account of the use of such a gift by a Christian; and if such a phenomenon occurred it could be so easily mistaken for charlatanry, sorcery, or some other magical practice (thus constituting a hindrance to the hearing of the preached Word and bringing ill repute upon the church) that its exercise was kept unpublicized and unrecorded."

Forbes (1995:17–25ff) has convincingly shown that the arguments put forth for ecstatic γλῶσσα/glóssa, in first-century Christian settings, are extracted from Greco-Roman sources without accurately matching the applicable time period, and also being inexact comparables, they are not parallel to the 1 Corinthians discussion.

Gundry concludes his evaluation of "ecstatic utterance" by remarking that:

> We have good reasons, then, to doubt that either Paul or Luke meant 'ecstatic utterance' when referring to speaking in tongues. Indeed, their apparent attempt to distinguish it from ecstatic utterance should make us hesitate to compare Christian glossolalia with ecstatic utterance in Hellenistic religion of the day or with a possible prophetic *ecstaticism* in the Old Testament.

Gundry (1966:299) refers to two salient Old Testament examples of γλῶσσα (*glóssa*) which mean intelligible speech (Greek Septuagint version of Isa 32:4 and cf. Isa 28:24) and which refer to stammering but not ecstasy. Gundry (1966:300) goes on to say that in Acts "Luke intends speaking in tongues to mean foreign languages" and the close association of Luke with Paul makes it very likely that Luke reflects Paul's own understanding of γλῶσσα (*glóssa*).

On 1 Corinthians 14:2ff, Verbrugge & Harris (2008:Kindle Locations 5056–5057) remark that "Speaking in tongues involves speaking in specific languages, not simply ecstatic speech done in syllables that sound like nonsense or gibberish." Verbrugge & Harris (2008:Kindle

Locations 5061–5063) add that there are those who believe that we must demystify the spiritual gift of speaking in "tongues," noting that there are individuals who have a remarkable gift of picking up a foreign language easily and if such individuals use that ability in the service of Christ, it is proper to say that they have the "gift of tongues."

On 1 Corinthians 14:2ff, Schreiner (2018:372) asserts that "human languages are likely in view" adding that "the word *glōssai* refers to human languages, not ecstatic utterances." Schreiner (2018:372) writes:

> In verse 2 Paul reflects on uninterpreted tongues. If a tongue is not interpreted, the tongue is not addressed to people but to God alone, since he is the only one who can grasp the meaning of what is being said. Paul is not necessarily saying here that tongues are restricted to prayer; his point is that the tongue is addressed to God in the sense that no-one else is able to understand what is being said. The reason why no-one understands is because the tongue is not interpreted; thus the lack of understanding does not point to ecstatic utterances.

Fausset (1873:289), on "speaketh … unto God" in this first part of 1 Corinthians 14:2, sensibly states the obvious but necessary, that God "alone understands *all* languages." Likewise, Barnes (1949:260) states that speaking in an untranslated foreign language, "No one could understand him but God" and because the listeners "were unacquainted with foreign tongues … it would be lost upon the church and would be useless." Gill (1746-1748, col 14:2) notes, of 1 Corinthians 14:2a, that "though what he delivers are truths of the greatest importance, they are a mere jargon to others, being unintelligible" because the foreign language is not translated. There is a similar vein of thought in 1 Corinthians 14:9 ("you will be speaking into the air").

Gundry (2011:Kindle Location 2309) asserts that 1 Corinthians 14:2ff is most naturally understood as a person speaking in a language that no one in the assembly understands, with nobody available to translate and thus Paul says that, in effect, the speaker is speaking to our omniscient God (1 Cor 14:2a), who understands all languages.

It is inexplicable how an esteemed Bible scholar, like Fitzmyer (2008:511), can note the supposed contrast in 1 Corinthians 14:2a of λαλῶν γλώσσῃ (*lalōn glōssē* "speaking in languages/tongues") effectively being addressed only to God, whereas prophecy addressed to humans (1 Cor 14:3), without catching the crucial fact that it is *untranslated* languages which are in view, as immediately obvious in 1 Corinthians

The Earliest View of New Testament Tongues

14:5. Fee (2014:726–727), in his presumption of λαλῶν γλώσσῃ (*lalōn glōssē*) being directed toward God alone (1 Cor 14:2), also trips up here in his crucial oversight of the *untranslated* aspect of the languages in the immediate context. Yes, in the absence of others from that particular language group, untranslated languages are only understood by God!

On 1 Corinthians 14:2a, we read the presumptuous comments from Ciampa and Rosner (2010:Kindle Location 15573) that speaking in γλώσσῃ is "understood as prayer" when it's not so said. In rebuttal, of course speaking in translated, earthly "languages" can be in the form of a prayer (1 Cor 14:2, 13–15) or praise (1 Cor 14:16–17) or the expression of a song (1 Cor. 14:15) and because of being translated would rate the Apostle Paul's approval for use in the assembly.

Regarding 1 Corinthians 14:2a, we read perplexing comments, like that of Gardner (2018:591), "As this verse shows, this gift is always directed to God as part of a person's praise or prayer." This inexplicable "reading in" of "a person's praise or prayer" reminds me of the need to apply the succinct hermeneutic adage, attributed to Dr. David L. Cooper (1886–1965), the founder of The Biblical Research Society. Cooper (1947–1949:4) is known for his "Golden Rule of Interpretation" which is: "When the plain sense of Scripture makes common sense, seek no other sense; therefore, take every word at its primary, ordinary, usual, literal meaning unless the facts of the immediate context, studied in the light of related passages and axiomatic and fundamental truths indicate clearly otherwise." This axiom is shortened to: "When the plain sense makes good sense, seek no other sense, lest it result in nonsense." When carefully considered, this "literal interpretation" dictum does not contradict acknowledging literary genre and "letting Scripture interpret Scripture." "The interpreter should . . . conscientiously abide by the plain meaning of the words" (Berkhof, 1960:75). "We must not violate the known usage of a word and invent another for which there is no precedent" (Alford, 1865:298).

Gardner (2018:596; cf. Fee, 2014:662–663), on 1 Corinthians 14:2ff does give as an option "'Tongues' as real languages that are foreign to the one who speaks," but one has to rightly ask, "Where does he or anyone else get the notion that the real languages are foreign to the one who speaks?" That is a presumption not anywhere in the text of 1 Corinthians 14. Why does it have to be a language unknown to the speaker, when in the context of 1 Corinthians 14, it is a language unknown to the hearers (1 Cor 14:2; cf. 1 Cor 14:11, 16–17)? Within context, it can very well straightforwardly mean an "earthly language" that is not foreign to the speaker!

Contrary to Gundry's (1966:302) objection to "the one speaking in a language" (ὁ γὰρ λαλῶν γλώσσῃ) actually understanding what he is saying, if the ὁ λαλῶν γλώσσῃ (the one speaking in a language) is reading the Old Testament Scriptures in Hebrew, he could potentially interpret or look to someone else with greater skill in both Hebrew and the most familiar language of the hearers.

Hodge (1860:281), on 1 Corinthians 14:2, asserts that "he did edify himself, because he understood himself. This verse, therefore, proves that the understanding was not in abeyance, and that the speaker was not in an ecstatic state." It appears that Hodge deduces this based on the subsequent 1 Corinthians 14:5, wherein the hearers are edified when they understand. Therefore, the corollary would be that if the speaker is edified (1 Cor 14:4), before his speaking is even translated, by that previous token he must have understood what he was speaking (i.e., Hodge's equation appears to be: "understanding" results in "edification," therefore in reverse "edification" presumes "understanding"). This formula would be borne out by 1 Corinthians 14:4a also, where the *glōssa*-speaker "edifies himself," therefore presuming "understanding" (Masters & Whitcomb, 1982:50–51). The supportive same-verse parallel (14:4b) is that the "one who prophesies edifies the church" because the understanding of the prophetic word is built up in the listeners. The last part of 1 Corinthians 14:5 also reinforces that the *glōssa-speaker* understands what he's saying, when he's urged to interpret his own speech for the church's edification.

In 1 Corinthians 14:2b, the pronoun οὐδείς/*oudeis* in its cardinal form is used, which on the face of it might give the impression that "no one, none," not even the speaker understands. However, we already know from this very same verse that there is an exception, because it is assumed, by all commentators, that God, mentioned in this verse, understands the speaking. Furthermore, in the immediate context of the following verse 4, it is said that the "one who speaks in a γλώσσῃ/ *glōssē* (language/tongue) edifies himself (ἑαυτὸν οἰκοδομε/*heauton oikodomei*)." The word οἰκοδομέω/*oikodomei* (BDAG, s.v. §3), in a metaphorical sense, means "building up," "strengthening," "benefiting" (cf. 1 Cor 14:17). He is getting "built up/strengthened" in the process of his speaking, before even the translation occurs, and pursuant to that, once they understand, the hearers get the same benefit of being "built up/strengthened" (1 Cor 14:5c). Therefore, it's hard to argue that the speaker doesn't understand what he is saying when he gets the "benefit" of being "built up" and "strengthened" before the translation even takes place. The translation is not for the speaker's "benefit"—he's already received the "benefit" (1 Cor 14:4a). In the broader context of 1 Corinthians 14 then, why do some insist that it's a language not understood by the speaker, when the text seems to be clear that it's rather a language not understood by the hearers?

So, it appears that the οὐδείς/*oudeis* ("no one"), in this verse, is not being used in an absolute or universal sense, but in a relative, colloquial sense (cf. 1 Cor 14:23, 24, 31 for relative "all"). An absolute οὐδείς/ *oudeis* ("no one") means "no exceptions" with scientific precision. A relative sense of οὐδείς/*oudeis* ("no one") is used more flexibly and permits exceptions as explicitly or implicitly indicated in the context (cf. Maclachlan, 2015:Kindle Location 791–795 and 1965–1969). Mark 5:37 would be an example of this where it says, "And He allowed *no one* to follow with Him, except Peter and James and John the brother of James." Here it seems to be first stated quite categorically (οὐδείς/ *oudeis*—"no one"), then subsequently there are given exceptions. Mark 3:27 is another example of this—"But *no one* can enter the strong man's house and plunder his property, unless he first binds the strong man, and then he will plunder his house." A strong opening statement is made and then the qualifier ("unless he first binds the strong man"). Matthew 21:19 follows a similar pattern, with an emphatic negation, followed by the exception—"Seeing a lone fig tree by the road, He came to it and found *nothing* on it, except leaves only." In other words, the relative use of οὐδείς/*oudeis* is context-dependent.

As above, in 1 Corinthians 14:2ff, there are given exceptions in the fuller context. To reiterate, in the first part of this very verse (1 Cor14:2a), we have the first exception, with the inference that God understands, so already οὐδείς/*oudeis* ("no one") can't be taken in an absolute sense. The second exception mentioned above is referred to in 1 Corinthians 14:4a where the *glōssa*-speaker "edifies himself" and is also urged to "interpret" (1 Cor 14:5c) therefore presuming that he "understands." The matter of "understanding" is supported by the same-verse parallel (14:4b) of the "one who prophesies edifies the church" and the assumption that the church members "understand" the prophetic word. Moreover, thirdly, the Apostle Paul allows another member of the congregation to do the interpreting (1 Cor 14:26, 27), which obviously assumes "understanding." Therefore, we have at least three exceptions to the οὐδεὶς/*oudeis* ("no one") of 1 Corinthians 14:2. It appears that, based on the context, the usage of οὐδεὶς/*oudeis* ("no one") can be taken in the relative sense allowing it the flexibility to convey a different nuance of meaning. Also crucially on this point of the relative usage of οὐδεὶς/*oudeis* ("no one") and whether more than three exceptions, even if a handful of people were "understanding" the *glōssa*-speaker, it would be contrary to Paul's emphatic statement that he wants the "ἐκκλησία/church" (i.e., everybody) to be edified (1 Cor 14:5c; cf. 1 Cor 14:4b), which is premised on understanding (1 Cor 14:2b). The stark contrast Paul emphatically presents is "no one," relatively speaking, compared to the entire "ἐκκλησία/church" (1 Cor 14:5c; cf. 1 Cor 14:4b).

If a contrarian wants to press the absolute sense of οὐδεὶς/*oudeis* here, they still have the exception of the *glossa*-speaker understanding himself (1 Cor 14:4a, 5c). Furthermore, with the several dialects and multiple variants noted in chapter 3.5 of this book, it is quite possible that a recent convert praising God in one of these rustic variants would not be understood by anyone else there in the small house gathering of several dozen people. It is not sufficient to say that surely somebody else in the gathering could comprehend a few of the speaker's words, when ample "understanding" and "edifcation" is the desired outcome.

Storms (2019:63–64) raises the above objection on 1 Corinthians 14:2, when he queries:

> If tongues-speech is always a human language, how could Paul say that when one speaks in tongues, "no one understands him" (1 Cor. 14:2)? If tongues are human languages, many could potentially understand, as they did on the day of Pentecost (Acts 2:8–11). This would especially be true in Corinth, a multilingual, cosmopolitan port city that was frequented by people of numerous dialects.

However, in the periodic house gatherings of sixty-five to seventy people (Snyder, 2003:70), the odds would not be high that someone would necessarily understand that foreign Greek sub-dialect(s) or the Scripture read in the Hebrew language. 1 Corinthians 14:2b would only mean that, generally speaking, the assembled listeners could not amply understand the γλῶσσα (*glōssa*) speaker (Gromacki, 1967:63;

cf. Hodge, 1860:279; Thomas, 1978:118; Lockwood, 2000:478; Lenski, 1946:577), without translation/interpretation.

Snyder (2003:299) assessed: "The New Testament Church began as a small group house church (Col. 4:15), and it remained so until the middle or end of the third century. There are no evidences of larger places of meeting before 300 [AD]." Snyder (2003:128) also remarked: "There is neither literary evidence nor archaeological indication that any house was converted into an extant church building. Nor is there any extant church or basilica that certainly was built prior to Constantine."

The New Testament size of a congregation would be the number of people who could be accommodated in a first-century villa (Acts 16:40, 20:20; Rom 16:3–5a, 16:23; 1Cor 16:19; Col 4:15; Phlm 1–2b; Jas 2:3). These Scriptures indicate that early believers assembled in the homes of wealthier members. The owner/host of these larger homes would be well off enough to provide most of the food for the regular "love feasts" (1 Cor 11). First-century Roman villas were big, semi-public buildings with the largest room being larger than in modern houses and the rooms on the street side were often the owners place of business (Snyder, 2003:129ff), so it would have been common for strangers to come into the villa for business purposes. Also, several generations of a family normally dwelt under the same roof, with spacious living rooms built around the courtyard to accommodate this arrangement (Snyder, 2003:129ff). The large area of the central atrium or even larger semi-covered enclosed courtyard would be a suitable place for an assembly of sixty-five to seventy people (Snyder, 2003:70).

Gundry (2010:Kindle Locations 2309–2313) lays out his rationale as:

> The case of a person speaking in a tongue presupposes that nobody with the gift of translation is translating it and that the tongue is a language nobody in the assembly has learned before. Otherwise Paul couldn't say that the speaker is speaking to God, who understands all languages, but not to human beings. "For no one hears [the tongues-speaker]" confirms this presupposition, and "he's speaking secrets" shows that "no one hears" refers to not hearing with understanding.

Technically, ἀκούει/akouei could simply mean "hears," but the chapter context indicates that "the real issue is not whether someone can be heard but whether what is heard is intelligible and therefore can be understood" (Gardner, 2018:591; so also Godet, 1890:266).

CONTEXTUAL AND EXEGETICAL ANALYSIS

On the need to "understand," if in my Alliance church congregation, one of my new Chinese friends is sharing their testimony in the service in Mandarin or Cantonese, I can't be edified unless it's interpreted/translated. Thankfully it is and I am greatly blessed by hearing their conversion story. If there's no understanding of what the person is saying, edification is stymied.

1 Corinthians 14:2 is not a command of the Apostle Paul to speak in γλῶσσα/*glōssa*. It's concessive—meaning that if you do speak in a γλῶσσα/*glōssa* (a foreign language untranslated), the result will be that you will in effect be speaking to God alone, because no one will understand what is being said. Therefore, the presumption throughout 1 Corinthians 14 is that the γλῶσσα (*glōssa*—language) should be addressed to fellow congregants by translation/interpretation (1 Cor 14:5, 13, 16, 17, 26, 27, 28).

Cross-referencing back to Acts 10 and 19 and the impulse of those new believers to automatically praise God in their mother tongues, we see that same impetus here in 1 Corinthians 14—whether that be Hebrew or the Greek Doric dialect or another minority language—people feel moved to praise God in their most familiar native language.

The context does not support this as an extraterrestrial language of angels, but rather untranslated earthly, human languages (cf. 1 Cor 14:10). It's why translation (ἑρμηνείαν/*hermēneian*) is paramount (cf. 1 Cor 12:30; 14:5, 13, 26, 27, 28, 37). The context supports an earthly, human language, in view of Paul's later citation of Isaiah 28:11 (in 1 Cor 14:21), which refers to a not-understood earthly, foreign language, not an extraterrestrial language. 1 Corinthians 14:2b uses the same Greek word (ἀκούω/*akouó*) as in Acts 9:7, when on the Damascus road, Paul's companions heard (ἀκούω) the voice, but Acts 22:9 says "they heard (ἀκούω) not," meaning Paul's companions did not hear *with understanding* (NASV) the voice in Hebrew (Acts 26:14).

Additionally, if it's correct that one of the theological themes of Pentecost was the inversion of Babel (note reference to human language in Gen 11:1, 7), then reading γλώσσαις (*glóssais*) as non-earthly languages, which would only be remotely attainable by some, runs contrary to Luke and Paul's purpose of unifying and edifying the new humanity in Christ.

The latter part of 1 Corinthians 14:2 uses the Greek term πνεύματι ("in spirit") which I take it to mean the human spirit rather than the Holy "Spirit" (Fitzmyer, 2008:511; Héring, 1962:146; 1958; Morris

1958:191; Godet, 1890:266; contra Fee, 1987:656, footnote 22; Kistemaker, 1993:478 and Talbert, 1987:90–91). This meaning of the human "spirit" is the more natural, seeing there is no article nor preposition before the substantive (Godet, 1890:266). Translations that leave the word in lower case ("spirit") include the NIV, NAB, NASB, and KJV. Why would we blame the Holy Spirit here for inducing "mysteries" that create a huge problem? When it's conceded by all that we have a messed-up situation in this chapter, why is it so hard to understand that it's the human spirit involved here and referenced in this verse at the outset? The factor of the flawed human spirit looms large throughout this chapter (cf. 1 Cor 14:4, 5, 6, 9, 12, 14, 16, 20, 23, 33).

Gundry (1966:302) appears to be quite right that in 1 Corinthians 14:2, the term "mystery" doesn't indicate *ecstasy* because "it regularly denotes spiritual truth regardless of the mode of communication." Also Paul said one who speaks in a γλώσση (*glōssē* language) "in spirit he speaks mysteries." On this note, what my *glossolalist* friends can't explain in respect to their version of "tongues," is what's the intent of "mysteries" being spoken to God (cf. 1 Cor 14:2). God created and understands all mysteries, so why would a believer need to tell him about them? They are not "*mysteries*" because they are not translatable but rather *because they are not translated*. When the Apostle Paul says "mysteries" are spoken, this doesn't imply that they are "mystifying" the speaker, but to the contrary, 1 Corinthians 14:4 indicates that the very articulating of them edifies the speaker (Buchanan, 2012:13).

Schreiner (2018:372) contends that "The term mysteries does not denote ecstatic utterances; the words are mysterious and hidden because they are spoken in a language the congregation does not understand." "Speaking mysteries" (λαλεῖ μυστήρια/*lalei mystēria*) is acceptable and can even be commendable (1 Cor 13:2), but being uttered in an earthly foreign language that is not understood nor translated for the comprehension of the assembled is not beneficial.

The Apostle Paul often referred to "mysteries" and spelled out what they were (Rom 11:25, Rom 16:25–26; 1 Cor 2:7, 1 Cor 15:51; Eph 3:3–9, Eph 6:19; Col 1:26–27, Col 2:2, Col 4:3). We're not left guessing what the biggest mystery (μυστήριον/*mystérion*) was. It was that all along God had planned for his tender mercies, in the Messiah, to reach the Gentiles and that they would be on an equal footing with God's original chosen people. So, 1 Corinthians 14:2 is likely not speaking of some Greek, Gnostic, esoteric, mystical knowledge, but the μυστήριον

CONTEXTUAL AND EXEGETICAL ANALYSIS

(*mystérion*/mystery) was likely a clear reemphasis of Paul's "Christ for the nations" theme for the edification of Jewish and Gentile attenders alike, but to which those Corinthians were deprived, if left untranslated. We have mystified the *mustérion* about the Messiah more than we must! As the Apostle Paul powerfully exulted, "this mystery among the Gentiles . . . is Christ in you, the hope of glory" (Col 1:27; Gardner, 2018:591; Fitzmyer, 2008:511; Taylor, 2014:325).

The speaker needs to be communicating in a language that everybody understands or translated to same (cf. 1 Cor 14:5) so they can all be "edified" and not just himself (1 Cor 14:4), as he unfolds the wonderful, previous "mysteries" (μυστήρια/*mystéria*—1 Cor 14:2) of God's Messianic redemptive plan from the Older Testament.

1 Corinthians 14:2 raises the first of several barriers for a *xenolalic* language-miracle interpretion of this chapter. The *xenolalic* position has a challenge in explaining the adjunctive necessity of translation in 1 Corinthians 14, relative to Acts 2, 10 and 19, where translation was not needed.

Finally, an elementary principle of hermeneutics requires that the more plain passage of Scripture explains the more controvertible passage. Acts 2 is the clearer passage, so it's appropriate to have our understanding of Acts chapter 2 inform our interpretation of 1 Corinthians chapters 12 and 14 (Busenitz, 2014:74; cf. also Edgar, 1996:150). "In this case, those who see two different kinds of tongues in the New Testament have arrived at this position on the basis of their theological presuppositions rather than from biblical evidence" (Edgar, 1996:150).

CHAPTER 14 AND VERSE 3

Old Testament prophecy included God's rebukes, encouragement and comfort, which would parallel the purposes of prophecy as delineated by Paul here. Talbert (2002:112) writes that "Early Christians understood prophecy within the church as a continuation or renewal of the prophecy of ancient Israel (e.g., Luke 1–2; 7:26, 39; Acts 2:16–21)." Witherington (1995:282) agrees that "the attempt to parallel Christian inspired speech with Hellenistic oracles and cultic procedure ought to be abandoned."

Lightfoot (1859:262) exposited in regard to ὁ δὲ προφητεύων (*ho de prophēteuōn*—one who prophesies) that the word προφητεύειν (to prophesy) envelopes teaching, revelation and psalms. That would harmonize with 1 Corinthians 14:26, where, in coherence with the overlapping theme, throughout the chapter, of prophecy (προφητεύητε) and translated/interpreted language (γλώσσῃ/*glōssē*), the Apostle Paul delineates the nature of edifying, participatory prophecy as a "psalm, teaching, and revelation" (cf. 1 Cor 14:6).

Lightfoot (1859:262) cross-referenced to 1 Samuel 10:5 where prophesy is taken for singing psalms, or celebrating the praises of God, "You will meet a group of prophets . . . with harp, tambourine, flute, and lyre . . . and they will be prophesying" (מִתְנַבְּאִים/*miṯ-nab-bə-'îm*).

Prophesying is understood by Lightfoot (1859:262) as magnifying and declaring the wonderful things of God, as depicted at Pentecost (Acts 2:11) and in the household of Cornelius (Acts 10:46) but just done in various languages.

CHAPTER 14 AND VERSE 4

In 1 Corinthians 14:4a, it is said that the "one who speaks in a γλώσσῃ/*glōssē* (language/tongue) edifies himself (ἑαυτὸν οἰκοδομε/*heauton oikodomei*)." The word οἰκοδομέω/*oikodomeó* (BDAG, s.v. §3), in a metaphorical sense, means "building up," "strengthening," "benefiting" (cf. 1 Cor 14:17). He is getting "built up/strengthened" in the process of his speaking, before even the translation occurs, and pursuant to that, once they understand, the hearers get the same benefit of being "built up/strengthened" (1 Cor 14:5c). Therefore, it's hard to argue that the speaker doesn't understand what he is saying when he gets the "benefit" of being "built up" and "strengthened" before the translation even takes place. The translation is not for the speaker's "benefit"—he's already received the "benefit." In the context of 1 Corinthians 14 then, why do some insist that it's a language not understood by the speaker, when the text seems to be clear that it's rather a language not understood by the hearers?

Speaking one's mother tongue (i.e., a language foreign to the listeners) can edify the speaker. Gill (1746–1748, col 14:4; so also Clarke, 1967:1117 and Lightfoot, 1859:258ff) on 1 Corinthians 14:4 suggested that it may be "the Hebrew language." Gill (1746–1748, col 14:4) commentates on the phrase "edifieth himself" (1 Cor 14:4) that "his heart may be warmed, his affections raised, his devotion kept up, and he be in a very spiritual and comfortable frame, knowing and understanding what he himself says." Barnes (1949:260–261) assumes a foreign language(s) and on "edifieth himself" remarks that, "His own holy affections might be excited by the truths which he would deliver." Pursuant to that, an ability to speak and translate various languages would be of considerable benefit to a multi-lingual church.

In contrasting the verse two λαλῶν γλώσσῃ (*lalōn glōssē*) and the verse three προφητεύων (*prophēteuōn*), the outcome is that in the verse two instance there is self-edification (cf. 1 Cor 14:4a) and in the verse three situation there is group edification (cf. 1 Cor 14:4b). The only difference in input is *intelligibility* leading to *understanding* (cf. 1 Cor 14:2 with no understanding versus 1 Cor 14:3 the resultant edification, exhortation and consolation). Interpreted γλώσσῃ (i.e., intelligibility) gives the same result of edification based on understanding (cf. 1 Cor 14:5). The converse scenario in 1 Cor 14:6 establishes the same principle—intelligibility to understanding to edification. In the equation, the edification can only come if there's intelligibility and the consequent understanding of what was said.

In Corinth, if there is the unintelligibility of a minority Greek dialect (or Hebrew), not understood by the congregants (whose majority language may be the Doric dialect as explained extensively in foregoing chapter 3.5), then there can be no edification. In short form, if there is no understanding of what the person is saying, edification is obstructed.

The context of 1 Corinthians 14:2 indicates that ἀκούω/*akouo* means what is heard and intelligible and therefore understood (Gardner, 2018:591). The speaker comprehending what he speaks is borne out by the illustration of 1 Corinthians 14:9 ("intelligible speech") and the hypothetical summary of 1 Corinthians 14:17 ("giving thanks well"). How do you know that you're "giving thanks well" (καλῶς εὐχαριστεῖς/ *kalōs eucharisteis*) unless you understand what you're saying?

From a reverse engineering perspective, because of the tight interconnected sequence outlined above, the end result of "edifies himself" (1 Cor 14:4) means that the speaker's "understanding was effectual" and what the speaker said was at least intelligible to himself (Masters & Whitcomb, 1982:50–51). (In the previous exegetical analysis of 1 Corinthians 14:2b, the exceptions to the "no one understands" clause of that verse two were explained.)

Packer (1985:208–209) asserts that:

> It is hard to believe that in verse 4 Paul can mean that the glossolalists who do not know what they are saying will edify themselves, when in verse 5 he denies that the listening church can be edified unless it knows what they are saying. But if in verse 4 Paul has in view tongues speakers who understand their tongues, today's Charismatics cannot regard his words as giving them any encouragement, for they confessedly do not understand their own glossalalia.

Keener (2005:113) wiggles in here that this λαλῶν γλώσσῃ/*lalōn glōssē* (speaking in languages) can be done privately, which is in contradiction of this chapter being Paul's advice for the conduct of the gathered assembly. Similarly, Fee (2014:729) appears to let his Pentecostal bias intrude and states that Paul indicates "tongues have value for the individual, meaning in private, personal prayer" and cites 1 Corinthians 14:14–15 and 18–19, setting aside the scholarly consensus, and his own general view, that this chapter 14 is the Apostle Paul's advice for the conduct of the gathered assembly. This "private, personal prayer" notion accords with Fee's own confession (1976:122) that "in general the Pentecostal's experience has preceded their hermeneutics. In a sense, the Pentecostal tends to exegete his or her experience."

Taylor (2014:325) makes the appropriate point that the Apostle Paul

> insists that intelligibility is essential to edification when so expressed (14:13–17), which raises doubts about incomprehensible private tongues as a means of self-edification. If intelligibility is essential to edification corporately (14:6–19), why would unintelligibility be acceptable privately if Paul is conceding that the one who speaks in tongues edifies himself in a positive sense? In other words, if uninterpreted tongues cannot edify the church, then how can tongues edify the individual privately apart from comprehension?

Chapter 14 and verse 5

The Apostle Paul approves language speaking at the beginning of verse 5 to indicate he is not out-of-hand rejecting foreign language speaking in the assembly, by his chiding in the preceding verses. Paul is only rebuking foreign language speaking if there is no immediate translation. The ability to speak in various languages is generally a huge advantage.

Clarke (1967:1117) views Θέλω (*Thelō*) as a command or "full permission to speak in Hebrew whenever it is proper, and when one is present who can interpret for the edification of the church, provided yourselves have not that gift, though you understand the language." The ability to understand the original Hebrew language of the Older Testament, as by training Paul could, was also a significant advantage, but not, if spoken and left untranslated, in a gathering of those who didn't know that language. Calvin (1573:367) concurs in this opinion, on this verse, indicating that Paul preferred prophecy but left "some place for foreign tongues." Calvin (1573:367) on this same verse writes that "God has conferred nothing upon his Church in vain, and languages were of some benefit."

In commenting on this verse, Calvin (1573:368) also infers the necessary Hebrew and Greek languages, when he severely chastises those who "condemn those languages, from which, as fountains, the pure truth of Scripture is to be drawn."

This position is also supported by 1 Corinthians 14:10–11, which can be seen as a comparison of the foreign languages out on the street with the scenario in the Corinthian assembly. The need for translation/interpretation in the Corinthian congregation corroborates that the nature of tongues there was earthly, foreign languages (Edgar, 1996:149).

The verb διερμηνεύω (*diermēneuō*), here in verse 5, means to explain thoroughly and by implication to translate (BDAG, s.v. διερμηνεύω, §1 & §2). *Diermēneuō* (διερμηνεύω) is composed of the preposition *diá* (διά) which has the sense of "thoroughly across, to the other side," which intensifies the word *hermēneuó* (ἑρμηνεύω—interpret) giving it the meaning of thoroughly interpreting and fully explaining. It is curious that the text uses the intensified form (διερμηνεύω/*diermēneuó*) in 1 Corinthians 14:5 as compared with 1 Corinthians 12:10 ἑρμηνεία (*hermēneia*—"gist of a message, an equivalent meaning"). Could this mean, in this context, a more intensified explaining or expounding of what was said or read? It's also intriguing that Paul here doesn't explicitly mention the Spirit as the source of this intensified interpreting (διερμηνεύω/*diermēneuó*).

In an odd twist, BDAG (s.v. διερμηνεύω, §2) places διερμηνεύω in this verse 5, as well as in verses 13 and 27 (1 Cor 14), under their second category, with the explanatory gloss that it is interpreting "ecstatic speech." In all the Greek texts and variants throughout the New Testament that I have looked at, there is no adjectival "ecstatic" nor such synonym. BDAG appears to have crossed the line into presuppositions and presumptive bias. In fairness, BDAG acknowledges that meaning

§1 is also probable here, with that §1 definition being "to translate from one language to another."

Even Ciampa and Rosner (2010:Kindred Location 15716) admit that, in this 1 Corinthians 14:5, with διερμηνεύω/*dierméneuó* in the context of speaking in tongues or "languages," with the same terms as found in Isaiah 19:18 and Acts 2:4, 11, it would seem to indicate that the first BDAG category would be the more intuitive one in this case, meaning to "to translate from one language to another" (BDAG, s.v. διερμηνεύω, §1). According to (Lockwood, 2000:436; also Gundry, 1966:300), the verb "to interpret" διερμηνεύω (1 Cor 12:30; 14:5, 13, 27; cf Acts 9:36) "simply means 'to translate' from one ordinary language into another."

In rebutting the claim of incoherent ecstatic utterances in 1 Corinthians 14, Davies (1952:230) summarizes that "of the twenty-one instances of the use of ερμήνευειν [*hermēneuein*] and its cognates in the LXX and the New Testament, apart from the seven occurrences in 1 Cor. 12 and 14, one refers to a satire or figurative saying, two to an explanation or exposition, and eighteen have the primary meaning of translation."

Davies (1952:230) goes on to assert that the term διερμηνεύῃ (*diermēneuē* from which we derive "hermeneutics") used by Paul regarding the interpreting of γλώσσαις "carries with it the strong suggestion of translating a foreign language." To further strengthen this claim, Davies (1952:230) also appeals to Paul's quotation (1 Cor 14:21) of Isaiah 28:11–12: "By men of strange tongues and by the lips of strangers I will speak to this people, and even so they will not listen to me" (so also Gundry, 1966:306–307). Isaiah prophesies of the invading Assyrians whose foreign language will be heard by the Israelites, in their streets, because of their rejecting the clear message of God's prophet. Similarly, the Apostle Paul argues that foreign languages are a sign to, as yet, unbelieving Jews of his day. The retribution theme of foreign languages in the Isaiah 28 passage is reinforced in Isaiah 33:19, Deuteronomy 28:49 and Jeremiah 5:15. With such a background, it is logical to assume that the Apostle Paul understood λαλῶν γλώσσαις (*lalōn glōssais*) to mean speaking in foreign languages, "especially as there is no good ground in the text for thinking otherwise" (Davies, 1952:230).

Davies (1952:231) concludes that there is no adequate reason for denying that the Apostle Paul understood λαλῶν γλώσσαις (*lalōn glōssais*) to be that of speaking in foreign languages. "Consequently, there is no conflict between his [Paul's] description and the account in Acts 2, which is a unity" (Davies, 1952:231).

On the term "interprets," Wright (1898:299–300) stated that "as it is contrary to God's usual working to supply supernaturally what can be readily produced by human effort, we should expect it to be assigned to one who understood the language."

At a port city like Corinth, many languages would be spoken, so the "gift of interpreting" may thus have depended on a knowledge of the language, supplemented by the power to speak boldly and acceptably in public (Wright, 1898:300). Lenski (1946:510), in respect to "interpretation," wrote of the Spirit taking a natural ability and "sanctifying it and employing it for spiritual ends."

The Greek verb *herméneuó* (ἑρμηνεύω) is used in Hebrews 7:2 "πρῶτον μὲν ἑρμηνευόμενος Βασιλεὺς Δικαιοσύνης" ("was first of all, by the translation, king of righteousness"; cf. John 1:38, 42; 9:7). However, with the intensification to *dierméneuó* (διερμηνεύω), in Luke 24:27, we have the post-resurrection Jesus falling in step with two men on the way to Emmaus and "beginning with Moses and with all the prophets, He explained to them the things concerning Himself in all the Scriptures." Jesus was obviously doing more than just a word-for-word translation. This implies that the word entails explanation also.

In these foregoing examples, διερμηνεύω/*dierméneuó* is to make clear through explanation or translation, in a known earthly language. These usages must govern the meaning of "interpretation" in 1 Corinthians 12:10 and 14:26, 28 (Gromacki, 1967:62). As with the example of Jesus (Luke 24:47), it was translation and/or exposition into the common language.

Thiselton (1979:15–36) suggests that, because the verb ἑρμηνεύω (*herméneuó*) can be used in Philo and Josephus to mean "put into words," in 1 Corinthians 12–14, "tongues" means "a kind of non-conceptual outlet for a powerful welling up of emotions" rather than "to translate." Along with Carson (1987:81) and Turner (1985:18–19), I find that a chasmic leap and less than convincing. The fact that many of the uses of the *hermeneu*-word group in the LXX and the New Testament (eighteen out of twenty-one) have to do with translation (cf. TLNT 3:312–317) is seen as an argument in favor of γλῶσσαι (*glóssai*) being the ability to speak a foreign language (Collins, 1999:456). Buchanan (2012:13) challenges the Thiselton postulation by questioning "whether it is methodologically secure to argue from an attractive

The Earliest View of New Testament Tongues

possible meaning for 'interpret' to a highly speculative meaning for 'tongues'?"

Therefore, "translation" may refer more to a word-for-word conveyance into another language and "interpret" may refer more to the transmission of ideas (Maclachlan, 2015:Kindle Location 3720).

Although we don't to want to draw a rigid demarcation between "translation" and "interpretation," based on the lexical evidence, it would be going too far to say that "interpretation" doesn't necessitate a connection between words and meaning. Such a supposed dichotomy is used to justify the mode of the "interpreter" in Charismatic/Pentecostal circles who figures that he/she doesn't need to understand any of the syllables issuing forth from the "tongues speaker." Thus, a message can be derived which doesn't come from understanding any actual words. This claim is not based on sound semantics. Kraeger (2010:55) in concluding his historical and exegetical examination of early literature in respect to λαλούντων (speaking) γλώσσαις (languages) is emphatic that interpretation/translation is "not to be confused with any subjectively interpretive methodology."

In any event, in 1 Corinthians 14, the Greek term διερμηνεύω (*dierméneuó*), although having its lexical limits, is probably broad enough to encompass the strict translation of the publicly read Hebrew text of the Older Testament Scriptures but could also include a homily in the Doric Greek, or whatever other consensus, receptor language, that thoroughly interpreted and fully explained the passage.

For the Corinthian situation (1 Cor 14:5b) it would make little sense if the person speaking in "a language," then turns around and translates it—what a waste of everybody's time. However, if he has just read the Older Testament Scriptures in the Hebrew language and then interprets it into the majority language of the listeners, that would make the most sense.

Gundry and others presume too much, to assert that the authentic, earthly languages of 1 Corinthians 12 and 14 are miraculously, magically, spontaneously given in the moment. Scriptures, neither here nor elsewhere, tell us how the languages are acquired. Therefore, it's more responsible to assume the normal process of learned languages. No less in this way, it is an ability enabled by God's Spirit!

According to 1 Corinthians 14:5, speaking in γλώσσαις/*glōssai* (ὁ λαλῶν γλώσσαις), if translated, is tantamount to prophecy (ἐκτὸς εἰ μὴ διερμηνεύῃ). With translation as part of the package, ὁ λαλῶν

CONTEXTUAL AND EXEGETICAL ANALYSIS

γλώσσαις is on par with prophesying and just as "great" (μείζων/ *meizōn*—1 Cor 14:5b).

If the Older Testament prophetic Scriptures were being read in the Hebrew *glōssa* (language) followed by inspired explanation of same in the Greek majority language, that would be prophetic, as the Messianic mysteries would be revealed, showing how Jesus fulfilled those prophecies, even as "the New was in the Old concealed and the Old was in the New revealed!" Calvin (1573:368) understands that when interpretation of earthly, foreign language is added," there will then be prophecy."

This equivalency drawn by Paul her in Corinthians 14:5 is an interesting reflection back to the Acts chapters 2, 10, 19 passages. In Acts 2:11 where there was that first "speaking... in languages the great deeds of God" (λαλούντων ... γλώσσαις τὰ μεγαλεῖα [adjectival] τοῦ Θεοῦ), which was immediately referenced by Peter (Acts 2:17–18) as "prophesying" in fulfilment of the Old Testament prediction (Joel 2:28–32).

When the doors were thrown open to the Gentiles, we have in Acts 10:46, from the same Greek word μέγας (*megas*), this time in the verb form, μεγαλυνόντων is used ("speaking in languages and magnifying God" λαλούντων γλώσσαις καὶ μεγαλυνόντων τὸν Θεόν/*lalountōn glōssais kai megalynontōn ton Theon*), which would also constitute that as "prophesying" based on Peter's foregoing elucidation (Acts 2:17–18). And then very explicitly, in Acts 19:6, the same author Luke reports of twelve men in the "half-way house between Judaism and Christianity" (Johnson, 1963:310) who, when the Holy Spirit came upon them, "they were speaking then in languages and prophesying" (ἐλάλουν τε γλώσσαις καὶ ἐπροφήτευον/*elaloun te glōssais kai eprophēteuon*).

CHAPTER 14 AND VERSE 6

Garland (2003:Kindle Location 13414) makes a peculiar comment on this verse's phrase "if I came to you speaking in tongues" when he says that the implication is that had Paul come speaking in tongues, "he would have had no success as an apostle" and that this thereby rules out the view that tongues refers to speaking in one's native language. Garland seems to miss the point that Paul is referring to speaking in one of his foreign languages not understood by the Corinthians and not translated. Garland (2003:Kindle Locations 13407–13413) seems not to have considered this address to the hypothetical problem Paul

The Earliest View of New Testament Tongues

raised in this verse and the significant obstacle that an untranslated foreign language would have created for the Corinthian believers and the Apostle's intended edifying instruction of them.

Paul sets the example (cf. 1 Cor 14:2) when he writes of the need, for him or anyone, when speaking in languages (γλώσσαις λαλῶν), to benefit (ὠφελήσω/*ōphelēsō*) the Corinthian congregation by way of revelation, knowledge, prophecy or teaching. All of these (revelation, knowledge, prophecy or teaching) are to do with putting on display the Older Testament in relation to the Messianic fulfilment and the "mysteries" now revealed in the gospel to Jew and Gentile alike.

Benson (2019:9965) paraphrases: "Supposing the next time I make you a visit at Corinth, I should address you in a variety of languages which you do not understand; what shall I profit you, who are supposed not to understand me, except I speak to you in a language with which you are acquainted." Barnes (1949:262) remarks that for Paul to speak to the Corinthian believers, out of his array of foreign languages, without interpretation, would be useless.

CHAPTER 14 AND VERSE 9

It is intriguing and puzzling that Fitzmyer (2008:513-514) admits that εὔσημον λόγον (*eusēmon logon*—intelligible speech) "could be illustrated by someone speaking a foreign language that is not understood by those present," but then, without a pause for consideration or explanation, moves right on to say that "more than likely it refers to an inarticulate succession of words that give the impression of language, but are unintelligible to the hearers." This latter highly speculative conjecture is not in the verse or even remotely hinted at therein. Where does he get this, other than from an entrenched presupposition? Maybe he gets it from the notions that speaking in "tongues" involves no one understanding (1 Cor 14:2), that "mysteries" in the S/spirit are being spoken (1 Cor 14:2) and that it entails speaking/singing/thanking "with/in the S/spirit" (1 Cor 14:14-16) in which the νοῦς/*nous* (mind) is not involved (1 Cor 14:14, 19), thus being intrinsically unintelligible (1 Cor 14:9). It's definitely a domino effect. If one begins with the premise that it was *glossolalic,* as most have in the last 145 years, ever since German historical-critical, liberal scholar August Neander (1900:11-17 and his

English protégés, Frederick Farrar and others, then the above-described chain reaction follows.

In response to this, one could understand this speaking "in languages" which "no one understands," with the exception of God and the speaker, as explained above, involving the reading of the prophetic Scriptures in the Hebrew language, and with explanation/homily on same, as well as speaking/singing/giving thanks in whatever minority languages/mother tongues arose, but then translated/interpreted for the edification of the assembled in their home groups or the occasional, larger, whole Corinthian church gatherings.

"This does not imply, as is contended by the advocates of the modern theories, that those who spoke with tongues uttered inarticulate sounds. The opposite of εὔσημον [eusēmon], is not inarticulate, but unintelligible, i. e. what is not in fact understood" (Hodge, 1860:284); therein the need for translation from that foreign language which is not understood.

One would think that this verse 9 clue helps explain the similar comparison in verse 2 (1 Cor 14). The verse 9 statement of "speaking into the air" should demystify the verse 2 reference that the individual speaking in a language [untranslated] does "not speak to men, but to God." Instead of using 1 Corinthians 14:2 to breathlessly define "one who speaks in a γλώσσῃ/glōssē" as charismatic praise or prayer (Gardner, 2018:591), it should be detectable by now that Paul is criticising untranslated earthly languages in the Corinthian assembly, especially with reading the two following verses (1 Cor 14:10–11).

The editor's footnote 809 in Calvin's French Commentaries (Calvin, 1573:366) reads: "*Comme on dit en prouerbe 'Il presche a soy-mesme et aux murailles,'* [As they say proverbially 'He preaches to himself and the bare walls.']"

The Apostle Paul could well have reiterated 1 Corinthians 14:2, but here adds another word picture to reinforce the utter futility of speaking uncomprehendible speech. Yes, God would understand, but that entirely misses the point of edifying fellow believers.

CHAPTER 14 AND VERSE 10

(See also previous commentary on 1 Cor 12:10 in chapter 5.4 of this book.) When the Apostle Paul writes to the Corinthians of "a great many kinds of languages in the world," he may be recollecting his own personal experience in Corinth, for that city was a very cosmopolitan, multilingual place.

At the end of this verse, Paul uses the word ἄφωνον (aphōnon; BDAG, s.v. ἄφωνος, §4) which is figuratively glossed as "without meaning." The same Greek word is used in 1 Corinthians 12:2 in reference to "dumb idols"—in other words "mute, voiceless" idols (BDAG, s.v. ἄφωνος, §2).

Paul stresses here that no language is without "signification" (English Revised Version). In regard to γένη φωνῶν (genē phōnōn), they are for *utility* (Barnes, 1949:264; Fausset, 1873:290). The Greek word φωνῶν (phōnōn) denotes human language at Babel (Gen 11:1, 7). The words of a language "in the world" have meaning because they are intelligible. None (οὐδὲν/ouden) are "dumb, mute and voiceless." This tends to support the concept of intelligible, earthly languages, especially because Paul notes that these languages are "in the world" (ἐν κόσμῳ/en kosmō).

Gundry (1966:306) cites 1 Corinthians 14:10f as clear proof that human languages were what the Apostle Paul had in mind when he inserts the phrase γένη φωνῶν εἰσιν ἐν κόσμῳ/genē phōnōn eisin en kosmō ("a great many kinds of languages in the world"). Carson (1987:83) similarly concludes that the evidence favors the view that Paul thought γλώσσαις/glōssais were real languages and that Paul's understanding would have been shaped by the Acts 2 Pentecost event with no substantial evidence suggesting that Paul thought what occurred in 1 Corinthians was anything different. That Paul uses φωνῶν/phōnōn (1 Corinthian 14:10f) strengthens the argument that it's actual earthly languages in view here, being that the Septuagint parallels Φωνὴ/phōnē with γλῶσσα/glōssa (Gundry, 1966:304–305).

It's interesting that Fee (2014:737) acknowledges: "This analogy also emphasizes the perspective of the hearer. It is not that the different languages do not have meaning to their speakers; rather, they do not have meaning to the hearers . . . . it would be intelligible to the one speaking." However, Fee (2014:737) just can't bring himself to allow that implication for the speakers in the Christ community at Corinth.

What is problematic is Fee's (2014:663) statement that the "use of earthly languages as an analogy (14:10–12) implies that it is not a known earthly language, since a thing is not usually identical with that to which it is analogous." First of all, who says this is an "analogy" and not an "illustration" or some other form of "comparison"? Paul doesn't say this is an "analogy." If it is an analogy, in an analogy there may be several similarities between the two objects being compared. Analogies generally highlight not only the similarities but also the differences between the two things. Paul doesn't do that here. It may be a simile because Paul uses the οὕτως καὶ/*houtōs kai* ("so also") to bracket the example (1 Cor 14:9 and 1 Cor 14:12), which Greek words may have a range of meaning similar to the typical "like" and "as" in similes. By the way, who gets to choose the parallels and discard other seeming implications? In this figure of speech that Paul uses, there may very well be several valid points of comparison. Because of the 1 Corinthians 14:10 phrase "languages in the world," Hodge (1860:284) asserts that "The illustration contained in this verse [1 Corinthians 14:10] goes to prove that speaking with tongues was to speak in foreign [earthly] languages (*contra* Thiselton, 2000:1103; Fee, 2014:737; Meyer, 1884:317).

However, Gundry (1966:306) and Carson (1987:82–83) both think that it was miraculous speaking in unlearned human languages. Aside from their assertions, neither of them address the issue of why in the Corinthian assembly it could not have been "learned human languages" as suggested by Epiphanius. The flaw in their reasoning seems to be that because they erroneously presume that the Acts 2 Pentecost event is a matter of "miraculously speaking in unlearned human languages," they then compound their error by assuming that 1 Corinthians 14 must be also. The Acts 2 text never says it is "unlearned languages" and does not anywhere in that chapter use the term "miraculous," nor does the account require either concept as explained earlier on *diglossia* in chapter 5. The theory collapses, if in fact the Acts 2 text is not referring to "unlearned languages" thereby not requiring the corollary of a "language miracle." It would be circular reasoning to use a flawed premise from the book of Acts to argue for that same phenomenon in 1 Corinthian14.

The close association of Luke and Paul (Wright, 1989:287) and the primacy of Paul writing 1 Corinthians before Luke's Acts is a valid precedential argument which can as easily support "learned languages," which admittedly would be perceived as less exciting and electrifying than the conjectured "unlearned languages."

I am in agreement that the disputed passage of 1 Corinthians 14 is explained by the more clear passage of Acts 2. If Acts 2 is a case of "learned languages," it lends support to the Epiphanius thesis of 1 Corinthians 14 being to do with learned, earthly languages, with the contention being about the reading of the Older Testament texts in the original, but uncomprehended Hebrew language or the use of other minority languages and the resultant acrimony about the need to translate it into whichever is the most understandable Greek dialect among the auditors.

CHAPTER 14 AND VERSE 11

The word δύναμιν (*dynamin*) in this verse is translated "meaning" in many English versions of the Bible. It is the Greek word from which we obviously get the English word "dynamite." The regular translation of this Greek word has to do with "power" (BDAG, s.v. δύναμις, §1–§5). It appears that the Greek word morphs into "strength" and "force" and thereby the migration to "meaning" in this sole instance in the New Testament, which can be slightly misleading, without understanding the background. Suffice to say, that for language to be powerful, to have the capacity to be "effective," it must be meaningful. It has to be understood, and therefore the need for translation. Clark (1975:231) comments on τὴν δύναμιν τῆς φωνῆς (*tēn dynamin tēs phōnēs*) by stating: "The 'power' of speech is intelligibility."

Without translation of the language(s) from "in the world," to others, Paul is a "foreigner" (βάρβαρος/*barbaros*, 1 Cor 14:11). He is a foreigner from the earthly planet, not from some other orb, such as the angelic or heavenly realm, thus we have an argument for the concept of intelligible, earthly languages. The word βάρβαρος/*barbaros* simply means "one of another country" (Hodge, 1860:285), not an extraterrestrial from another globe. "If a man utters incoherent, inarticulate sounds, which no man living could understand, that would not make him a foreigner. It might prove him to be deranged, but not a stranger" (Hodge, 1860:285).

Calvin (1573:372) here writes of Paul's derision for the foolish ambition of the Corinthians chattering in an unknown, untranslated foreign language, "who were eager to obtain praise and fame by this means." This again bolsters the Epiphanius thesis that the γλῶσσαι/ *glōssai* conflict in Corinth was a problem of prideful people speaking in foreign languages, without verbal explanation/translation, and the resulting teaching problem within that Corinthian assembly because of the snobbery and inflated egos of some.

In this verse, the use of "if . . . then" (ἐὰν οὖν/*ean oun*) indicates that the Apostle Paul was well aware that he could not speak and understand all languages (Collins, 1999:499).

CHAPTER 14 AND VERSE 12

Zelotai/ζηλωταί is a noun, which can then be translated "since zealots you are of spirit[ual thing]s" (πνευμάτων/*pneumatōn*). Once again there is no underlying Greek word for "gifts" so that word should be left out of the English translation as it is misleading and those with sharp eyes or bi-focals will notice that "gifts" is in italics. These are in effect interpretive insertions reflecting the translator's bias which can lead the English reader down the wrong path. Buchanan (2012:13) alternately suggests that the plural "spirits" in this verse has the sense of "indulging the instincts of your own spirits."

There is an important insight here in the second half of 1 Corinthians 14:12. The Apostle Paul urges believers to "seek to abound" (περισσεύητε/*perisseuēte*) in spiritual matters. With personal initiative, it is possible to cause a particular ability to excel, even though it ultimately depends on the Holy Spirit. This is another indicator in Paul's letter to the Corinthians that the ministries enabled in us by the Spirit are part of our natural talents which we can nurture through diligent work and formal training (Verbrugge, 2008:Kindle Location 5197). Spiritual functions and personal abilities are often inseparably intertwined.

CHAPTER 14 AND VERSE 13

Mare (1976:278) argues that the γλώσση (*glōssē*) "referred to in 1 Corinthians 14:13–15, 20–25 were also foreign-language tongues—not ecstatic utterances, gibberish, or nonunderstandable erratic variations of consonants and vowels with indiscriminate modulation of pitch, speed, and volume." None of the Pauline letters contain the Greek word for "ecstatic" (*ekstatikos*) nor its cognates.

On this verse, 1 Corinthians 14:13, Gill (1746–1748, col 14:13) suggested that the γλώσση (*glōssē*/language) may be "Hebrew, or any other." Clarke (1967:1117–1118) depicts this to be an individual reading the prophetic declarations in the Old Testament, in the Hebrew tongue, praying to God that he might so understand them himself, and receive the gift of interpretation, to explain them in all their depth and breadth to the assembled.

Some people naively wonder why Paul tells the foreign language-speaker to pray to God for the ability to translate his own language. Translating is a significantly difficult task. "It is sometimes said that there is no task more complex than translation—a claim that can be readily believed when all the variables involved are taken into account" (Crystal, 1989:344). These variables that need to be taken into account, in both the source and target language, are: the particular field of knowledge, social and cultural and emotional connotations, special phrasing, taboos in expression, local and regional expectations, etc. (Crystal, 1989:344).

The verb "to pray" is in the imperative mood, so Paul is commanding the one who speaks in another language to pray for the ability to translate. Here we have an indication that the one speaking in a foreign language and the one translating can be the same person, whereas 1 Corinthian 14:26–27, on the other hand, presents a possibility where someone else present might have the ability to translate and provide intelligibility to the foreign language.

As one grows in facility in a second language, there comes that breakthrough moment where they realize that they can actually translate that language—maybe not very smoothly at first, but comprehensibly nevertheless, with improvement over time, if one applies themself. Obviously, any language-speaker will probably know his or her mother tongue much better than his or her second language. It is worth repeating that the 1 Corinthians texts do not prefix "gift of" but simply read "interpretation" (1 Cor 12:10; 14:26) or "interpret" (1 Cor 12:30; 14:5, 13, 27) and similarly just the term "language/languages" without the mystical, magical connotations.

In this section of verses 13 to 19, on γλώσσῃ (*glōsē*), with the liturgical elements of intercessory prayer, songs of praise, thanksgiving, and the responsive "Amen" (cf. Neh 8:6), Paul clearly has in mind the congregation gathered for worship (Collins, 1999:500). Sung praise of God, a type of communal prayer, was a feature of the Jewish synagogal service and here seems customary of the Christian service of worship also (Collins, 1999:502). These various expressions of worship, joined with teaching, indicate that the format of the believers' meetings was rather like the Jewish synagogue service (Collins, 1999:500).

Thiselton's (2000:1108) statement that "this is not a 'message to the congregation' but an act of praying to God" directly contradicts the immediate and broader context of it needing to be interpreted for the benefit of the gathered congregation. This makes no sense, because why would Paul insist that a private devotional prayer to God be made public by interpretation? In context, 1 Corinthians 14:13ff is not a private, devotional setting nor an application for same as my Charismatic and Pentecostal friends mistakenly assert.

For six terms, I was a federal Member of Parliament in Canada, an officially bilingual English-French country. With my mother tongue being English, for almost two decades I had to use the commendable services of the official House of Commons French interpreters when giving a speech in the Chamber (cf. 1 Cor 14:27). As a Canadian Member of Parliament, I have also been at international forums and United Nations meetings and other settings where I had to speak and listen via translation. So, I do very much appreciate the complexities and intricacies of interpretation/translation.

The Lord can also grace multilingual churches with talented translators/interpreters to mitigate the communication challenge, as he has done with my home Alliance Church.

CHAPTER 14 AND VERSE 14

On the phrase, "For if I pray in a tongue/language," Gill (1746–1748, col 14:14) remarks that most of the Jewish teachers of that era insisted that prayer should be in the Hebrew language and that, among those Jewish believers who could speak Hebrew, this concept may have carried over into the assemblies of Jesus' believers at Corinth, even though the majority of the congregation could not understand it.

Calvin (1573:373) simply says that it appears "that the Corinthians had been in fault in this respect also, that, as they discoursed, so they also prayed in foreign tongues." In answer to the question of what is meant by "praying in a tongue," in 1 Corinthians 14:14, Calvin (1573:374) responds that it means "to frame a prayer in a foreign language." Calvin (1573:374) further writes, on this verse, that it is not credible that any spoke in a language that was to themselves unknown. In commenting on "For if I pray in a language" (1 Cor 14:14), Clarke (1967:1118) assumes it was in the Hebrew language, as they would have framed their prayers using "sentences and sayings" from the Old Testament.

Calvin (1573:375) wants us to notice "that Paul reckons it a great fault if the mind is not occupied in prayer" because, as Calvin (1573:375) says, it's in prayer that we "pour out our thoughts and desires before God" and "as prayer is the spiritual worship of God," it needs to proceed not "merely from the lips" but "from the inmost soul." Calvin (1573:375) ridicules the idea that the tongue of a Roman would pronounce Greek words, "altogether unknown to the speaker, as parrots, magpies, and crows, are taught to mimic human voices." A person's understanding must be conjoined with his spirit (Calvin, 1573:375).

At the outset of these two verses (1 Cor14:14–15), we also need to address an erroneous conception that my modern-day Charismatic/Pentecostal friends may be susceptible to in their interpretation of these verses. As Gardner (2018:606) rightly warns, "Paul does not work with a Platonic dualism. It is not that the 'spirit' is what relates to God and the 'mind' is what relates, unspiritually, to this world." Modern-day Charismatics/Pentecostals need to be careful to avoid being drawn into that heretical trap because "dualistic thinking is entirely alien to Paul's worldview" (Gardner, 2018:606; *contra* Thiselton, 2000:1110). In fact, in 1 Corinthians 14:15, Paul writes of praying conjointly with "spirit" and "mind" which speaks unequivocally against this dualism.

Implying the Apostle Paul's approval of some shade of dualism in this verse 14 would make for a serious misunderstanding contra his personal example in the following verse 15. To imply that one's spirit (πνεῦμά μου/*pneuma mou*) is active in prayer while one's mind (ὁ δὲ νοῦς μου/*ho de nous mou*) is inactive (BDAG, s.v. ἄκαρπος/*akarpos*, §2) could be a dangerous path. Hodge (1860:287) writes that "the Scriptures know nothing of this distinction between the reason and the understanding." The Greek term ἄκαρπος/*akarpos* here in 1 Corinthians 14:14 could just as properly fit under BDAG, s.v. ἄκαρπος, §1, which "literally pertains to not bearing fruit, unfruitful, fruitless" as the speaker's mind is not bearing any fruit in the hearers. In other words, they are not being edified—not being built up in the faith.

Suffice to say, the intent here is the human "spirit," in that verse 14 pointedly refers τὸ πνεῦμά μου/*pneuma mou* (literally "the spirit of me") and it would be the height of insolence to infer that the Spirit of God is owned by a person, if erroneously translating in "my Spirit."

The term "my spirit" can be cross referenced to what the Apostle says earlier (1 Cor 2:11) "For who among men knows the thoughts of a man except the spirit of the man which is in him? Even so the thoughts of God no one knows except the Spirit of God." With this analogy and as we observe the working of the Spirit within the Triune Godhead in the Older and Newer Testaments, we have to acknowledge that the Spirit is the epitome of rationality and reason. The Spirit is the most intelligent Being in the universe. That is the pattern and we are made in the image of God. So then, why would God, in contradiction of his own character, place a premium on irrationality when creating man "in His image"?

A person's "thoughts" are known by his or her "spirit" and God's "thoughts" are only known by the Holy "Spirit." No one knows us like we do, except God, and only God knows himself fully. "Mind" and "spirit" are not independent of one another. "I pray" or "my spirit prays" are saying one and the same thing. They are connected and, in the specific context of 1 Corinthians 14, refer to my prayer in a language known to me but not to others assembled. Collins (1999:501) aptly remarks "Good Jew that he is, Paul cannot dissociate the relationship to God from the relationship with other human beings." As a good Jew, the vertical relationship to God was wholly integrated with the horizontal relationship to fellow man, and therefore the edification of others was indispensable.

In regard to "my mind is unfruitful" (1 Cor 14:14), Gill (1746–1748, col 14:14) avers that "what I say with understanding" because it is not translated "is unprofitable to others, not being understood by them." At the human level, only I know what I am thinking, and nobody else does, unless I choose to divulge my thoughts in the form of understandable words.

On 1 Corinthians 2:11, MacArthur (1984:62) aptly comments:

> Paul compares the Spirit's knowledge of God's mind to a human being's knowledge of his own mind. No person can know another person as well as he knows himself. Even husbands and wives who have lived together for dozens of years, and have freely shared their thoughts and dreams and problems and joys, never come to know their mates as intimately as they know themselves. Our innermost *thoughts*, the deep recesses of our hearts and minds, are known only to ourselves.

The Earliest View of New Testament Tongues

On the phrase "but my mind is unfruitful," Hodge (1860:288) argues that "The words, therefore, must be understood to mean, 'my understanding produces no fruit,' i. e. it does not benefit others." This accords with all that precedes and with the uniform use of the word in Ephesians 6:11, Titus 3:14, 2 Peter 1:8 and Matthew 13:22 (Hodge, 1860:288). The Greek word ἄκαρπος (akarpos) has the meaning of "fruitless, without effect" (Zerwick & Grosvenor, 1996:526). Thayer's Lexicon has "without fruit, barren" and "metaphorically, not yielding what it ought to yield, (A.V. unfruitful): Matthew 13:22; Mark 4:19; destitute of good deeds, Titus 3:14; 2 Peter 1:8; contributing nothing to the instruction, improvement, comfort, of others, 1 Corinthians 14:14" (Thayer, s.v. ἄκαρπος, §2). Using this Greek word, Jude 1:12 speaks of "trees without fruit."

There are only 7 occurrence of the word ἄκαρπος/akarpos in the New Testament. The synoptic passages of Matthew 13:22 and Mark 4:19 may be the most helpful in shedding light on the sense of this word as it relates to the occurrence in 1 Corinthians 14:14. Matthew 13:22 and Mark 4:19 tell of God's "word" being "unfruitful" (ἄκαρπος/akarpos). In these cases, there's not anything wrong with God's "word." God's "word" does not lack generative power, but the soil of the hearer's lives, in which the word falls, is metaphorically inhospitable to growth and hence unproductive. Similarly in 1 Corinthians 14:14, the fault is not with "the mind of me" per se, but rather the metaphorical soil of the listeners, into which the speaker's words fall, and which is infertile because of the language barrier and hence no growth or fruit is produced in the hearer.

Thomas (1978:214–215) advocates for the "active" meaning of ἄκαρπος/akarpos because "it is a word for results and does not apply to the process through which the results are obtained." Thus, the speaker's mind per se is not the focus, but rather the potential benefit derived by listeners (Thomas, 1978:214–215).

"By his understanding being unfruitful is therefore meant, that others did not understand what he said" (Hodge, 1860:288). In the immediate prior verse 13, Paul urges that even prayer in a γλῶσσα/glóssa (language) foreign to the listeners should be interpreted and that, if left untranslated, his mind (νοῦς/nous) "like a barren tree" produces no fruit in the hearers (Barnes, 1949:265–266). On 1 Corinthians 14:14, Robertson and Plummer (1914:312) remark that "The preacher's fruit is to be sought in the hearer's progress, not in his own delight or in their admiration of his gift."

The editor (footnote 827) in Calvin's Commentaries (Calvin, 1573:373) asserts: "Νους, intelligence, mind, seems here to be chiefly used in a transitive sense, to mean what we give another to understand."

The other factor that strengthens the current argument, in respect to 1 Corinthians 14:14, is the dyadic nature of Mediterranean personalities back then. In modern North America, persons are concerned about individual psychology (Malina & Neyrey, 1993:78). In contrast, the Mediterranean person, in the past at least, was anti-introspective and not psychologically minded (Malina & Neyrey, 1993:78).

Replete with references to acting for the good of others, the edification of others and the interrelationship of the members of the body of Christ, the Apostle Paul writes to the Corinthian believers as a dyadic personality. The dyadic personality of Paul in 1 Corinthians 14:14 compels us to understand that Paul was primarily concerned about whether the speaker's communication will produce fruit in others (Zerhusen, 1997:148). Thus, when Paul writes "my understanding is unfruitful," he means that when the understanding of his mind is not intelligibly and intelligently communicated to the hearers, Paul has not enabled others to comprehend the conceptions of his mind and there is unfortunately no benefit to them—Paul's understanding bears no fruit in the hearer. His "understanding is unfruitful."

CHAPTER 14 AND VERSE 15

Lightfoot (1859:264) remarks on Προσεύξομαι τῷ πνεύματι, προσεύξομαι δὲ καὶ τῷ νοΐ (*proseuxomai tō pneumati, proseuxomai de kai tō noi*—I shall pray with the spirit and I shall pray with the mind also) "that is, that I be understood by others." The δὲ καί/*de kai* is not adversative but conjunctive ("and also"), so it's not an "either/or" but rather a "both/and" scenario, meaning "I shall pray with both the spirit and mind together" and "I shall sing with both the spirit and mind together"—not exclusive of one or the other. Fausset (1873:290) holds that "by inference, I will keep silence altogether if I cannot pray with the understanding (so as to make myself understood by others)."

Paul urges the wholistic, integrated "both/and" in 1 Corinthians 14:15 and not the "either/or" approach, because of the conjunctive καί/

kai being a connective/copulative. An adversative interpretation of this particle is not possible (Winer, 1882:545; Buttmann, 1891:364). In 1 Corinthians 14:15, the Greek term προσεύξομαι/*proseuxomai* is a future middle. According to Rienecker and Rogers (1982:435), "The future is assertive or volitive expressing the determined decision of Paul's will" (so Burton, 1955:34; Moulton, 1908:150; Robertson, 1934:874). This means the Apostle Paul has a set determination to utilize both his spirit and his mind in praying and singing and, by inference also, in giving thanks. To conclude the sequence of 1 Corinthians 14:15, the "instrumental of means/dative of means" (Robertson, 1934:533; Moule, 1959:44) indicates the action of the verb "pray" and "sing" is accomplished by the spirit conjoined with the mind. To summarize, the Apostle Paul has a set determination to "pray" and "sing" (and, by inference also, in "giving thanks") and accomplish that by the spirit conjoined with the mind.

The Platonic dualism as preached by some modern-day Charismatics on this verse is not supported in the Greek text nor even in a proper understanding of the English text. "Mind" and "spirit" are not independent of one another. There is no platonic dualism here. Paul's anthropology is wholistic and he pleads that the spirit and mind work together in prayer in a complementary way (Collins, 1999:501). "Paul is saying in v 15 that all worship activities should be 'from the heart' (i.e., 'with the spirit') and also 'intelligibly' (i.e., 'with the mind')" (Zerhusen, 1997:149).

This verb ψάλλω/*psalō* is frequently used in the Psalms (Greek Septuagint) and means "to sing" or "sing praise" accompanied by an instrument or not (Ps 7:18; Ps 9:12; Ps 107:4). Paul, as well, uses the term in quotation of the Psalms or reference to them (Rom 15:9; Eph 5:19; cf. Jas 5:13). The early believers' assemblies sang psalms and hymns of praise and thanksgiving, as part of their regular worship and exaltation of the Lord. Calvin (1573:376) has no doubt, "that, from the very first, they followed the custom of the Jewish Church in singing Psalms." The Jewish influence is here evident again in that prayer and singing Psalms, as elements of the worship service, "were taken over from the synagogue" (Conzelman, 1975:238). The singer, "prayer," and "thanker" (1 Cor 14:15–16) may be having a jolly good time and edified/built up in his/her spirit, but only when the singing or praying or thanksgiving (εὐχαριστίᾳ/*eucharistia*) is translated, into the earthly language of the ἰδιώτου (*idiōtou*) and others assembled, do the listeners know what is said (1 Cor 14:16) and are thereby edified (cf. 1 Cor 14:17).

CONTEXTUAL AND EXEGETICAL ANALYSIS

CHAPTER 14 AND VERSE 16 THROUGH VERSE 17

How does he know that he is praising and thanking God (1 Cor 14:16, 17) and not blaspheming him? The obvious answer is because he understands what he is saying and some others do also.

Cremer (1895:164–165) clarifies that the singular γλώσσῃ/glōssē, in classical Greek, "may denote the power of speech or the gift of eloquence." This tends toward a portrayal, in these verses, of an individual (i.e., a teacher/preacher) powerfully and eloquently speaking to the assembled in a language that some don't understand and particularly deplorable is that the ἰδιώτου/idiōtou (the "untrained," "uninstructed," "unskilled," "ungifted") will not be able to comprehend and affirm with a hearty "Amen" (1 Cor 14:16).

Some of Paul's readers were showing lack of concern for the edification of the assembled believers by praying in an unknown language whereby the "unlearned" could not say "Amen" (1 Cor 14:16–17) to such a prayer (Hodge, 1860:288).

The expression Ἀμήν (Amēn) is also evidence for the dominating influence of the synagogue on the Christian service of worship (Conzelman, 1975:239). Lightfoot (1859:265) comments on Πῶς ἐρεῖ τὸ ἀμήν/pōs erei to Amēn (How will [he] ... say, 'Amen') "It was the part of one to pray, or give thanks,—of all to answer, Amen. They answer Amen after an Israelite blessing." This agreement with what was recited appears to have been a well-accepted Jewish custom of the synagogue, which tradition, along with many other customs of worship, carried over to the congregations of Jesus' believers (Calvin, 1573:376). This responsive "Amen" agreement by the congregation was a Hebrew religious practice reaching all the way back to the Older Testament times (Deut 27:15–26; 1 Chr 16:36, and Neh 5:13; 8:6; cf. Rev 5:14) and for that reason points to a synagogue pattern for the conduct of the believer's assembly in Corinth.

First Corinthians 14:16, in the New American Standard Version, has "fills the place of the ungifted." The English Revised Version translates "filleth the place of the unlearned." The biblehub.com Interlinear has "the [one] filling the place of the uninstructed" which may suit best. In respect to ἀναπληρόω, Thayer (s.v. §1) has "after the rabbinical מְקוֹם מָלֵא to hold the position of anyone." Regarding τόπος/topos, Thayer (s.v. §1) has "any portion of space marked off" or "the condition or station held by one in any company or assembly" (metaphorically s.v. τόπος,

§2a). BDAG, regarding ἀναπληρόω/anaplēróō (s.v. §4), has "outsider" and when adding "τόπος here means a place actually occupied by an ἰδιώτης in the meeting."

Gardner (2018:610) writes, "This [ἰδιώτης] is a person who does not have the technical know-how that the specialist has." In Acts 4:13 this Greek term ἰδιώτης (idiótēs) is translated "untrained" (NASV) and in 2 Corinthians 11:6 "unskilled," whereas in 1 Corinthians 14:16, 23, 24, it is translated "ungifted" (NASV). Lias (1905: 155) understands ἰδιώτης/idiótēs as a reference to "those unacquainted with Christian doctrine and practice." Moulton & Milligan (1930:299) cite examples where the predominant meaning of ἰδιώτης/idiótēs is a "private citizen" as compared with a person of rank or religious officialdom. This may point to there having been official leaders performing some defined functions, such as reading the Hebrew Scriptures or explaining it, at the public services when the believers assembled.

On 1 Corinthians 14:16, Bengel (1873:310–311) writes:

> This was their usual practice even at that time; not only the unlearned, but all the hearers spoke ["Amen"], giving their assent *to him who blessed*. And so also, those who could not speak much adopted the words of others, and declared, that they with their understanding assented to it.—τί λέγεις [*ti legeis*], "what thou sayest") Not only ought he to know, that thou hast said nothing evil, but also what good thou hast spoken.

But if it is not spoken in language that he can understand, how could he say, "Amen"? In Paul's day, it seemed to be a very serious matter for a person to be in a service where prayer was offered but the hearers could not say "Amen" because the prayer was in a language which they did not know.

In regard to "giving of thanks" (1 Cor 14:17), Cremer (1895:164) comments: "the prayers of the synagogues were called 'eulogies,' because to each prayer was joined a *thanksgiving*." As an important aside, on this verse, how does the speaker know that oneself is "giving of thanks" or "blessing" God, unless that speaker understands what oneself is saying? The speakers obviously understand what they themselves are verbalizing (Hodge, 1860:291).

After all this, we get the seeming inflexible comment of second-generation, ordained Assemblies of God minister Gordon Fee (2014:928): "Thus it is often thought to refer here to specific kinds of prayers, such as the blessings in the Jewish synagogue. But that will not work here, of course, since it is the verb for 'praising' in tongues." It seems like Fee had an intransigent premise, so with information to the contrary, he summarily sweeps it aside, notwithstanding the "Amen" agreement custom (1 Cor 14:16) which tends toward a normal, howbeit foreign, earthly language view.

CHAPTER 14 AND VERSE 18

When Paul here states that he spoke in tongues more than all of them (πάντων ὑμῶν μᾶλλον/*pantōn hymōn mallon*), it can be taken as referencing the reality that, out of necessity, he spoke several languages (Hebrew, Greek and likely several dialects of same, Aramaic, inevitably some Syriac from his year-long ministry with Barnabas in Antioch, and possibly some Latin from his unavoidable interactions with Roman authorities over his lifetime).

On 1 Corinthians 14:18, Benson (2019:9945) wrote that "the apostle told the Corinthians that he spake more foreign tongues than they all did." Clarke (1967:1118) wrote of Paul that "he understood more languages than any of them did" and cites "Hebrew, Syriac, Greek and Latin." On 1 Corinthians 14:18, Gill (1746–1748, col 14:18) remarked that the Apostle Paul modestly thanks God for his eminent ability in languages, which Paul frequently made use of in travelling into different countries to preach the gospel to people of different languages.

Benson (2019:9946) also commented that because "the books of the Old Testament being written in Hebrew, a language not then understood by the vulgar, even in Judea, and the writings of the apostles and evangelists being all in the Greek tongue," the interpretation of foreign languages was vital. Every congregation of believers would have had interpreters of foreign languages ordinarily present in their religious assemblies, to translate the Hebrew and Greek Scriptures into the language of the common people (Benson, 2019:9946).

Acts 14:11–12 implies that even if Paul spoke several languages, he certainly was not conversant in all the languages of the people to whom he preached. This is proven because after healing the lame man at Lystra, he appeared to not understand the multitudes who thereupon in the Lycaonian language loudly attributed the miracle to the incarnated gods "come down," naming Barnabas as Zeus and Paul as Hermes because he was the chief speaker. Not until later when the priest of Zeus had brought out garlands and oxen, to the city gates, to offer sacrifice with the crowds to Paul and Barnabas, did the two missionaries figure out the colossal, blasphemous error (Acts 14:14).

Corinth was a thriving seaport metropolis attracting many diverse ethnicities, with many of these converting to the new Judaeo-rooted religion, which didn't require circumcision for the men. It would be unsurprising and natural that they felt an inner compulsion to praise God or give testimony in their mother tongue. As well, many Messianic Jews, for a time, assumed that as Moses was for the Jewish people, likewise Jesus would be solely for them also. So, with this complex, mixed background of the Corinthian assembly of believers, Paul's urging was that the use of their various mother tongues and language preferences be kept in check if no translator was present.

Grosheide (1953:327) alleges that the adverb μᾶλλον/*mallon* in 1 Corinthians 14:18 ("more often than" as Grosheide interprets) infers ecstatic speech. The adverb μᾶλλον can mean "more numerous" as well as "more often" (e.g., Gal 4:27), but the BDAG definition of λαλέω/*laleó* under §2 (s.v. λαλέω, §2) doesn't provide any support for Grosheide's allegation of ecstatic speech.

On this verse 18, Pentecostal scholar, Fee (2014:747–748), writes that Paul's "life of personal devotion was regularly given to praying, singing, and praising in tongues." In presuming to distil this from this verse, Fee has veered off into speculation untethered to this statement of Paul's.

Gardner (2018:610; similarly Carson, 1987:105 and Ciampa & Rosner, 2010:Kindle Location 16093), on this verse (1 Cor 14:18), also makes a statement loaded with assumptions and bias, in his unsupportable conjecture that, "Paul held himself up as a hypothetical example, but now he makes it clear that he really does speak in tongues frequently, while reserving this gift for private use."

It is out of harmony with Paul's prior "edification of the church" argument to assume that he now endorses some kind of esoteric γλῶσσαι/*glōssai* for personal edification. It would be the only one in Paul's 1 Corinthians 12 or other lists which is "self-oriented" and would stand in sharp contradiction to Paul's urging in 1 Corinthians 12:7, 25, 26; 13:5; 14:5, 12, 26. Such use of γλῶσσαι/*glōssai* would be practiced without the support of Scripture.

CONTEXTUAL AND EXEGETICAL ANALYSIS

On 1 Corinthians 14:18, Taylor (2014:70) exposes his presumption, with the statement, "Clearly Paul's statement is hyperbolic, for how could he know that he speaks in tongues more (quantitatively) than others?" However, if Paul was referring to the number of earthly languages (γλῶσσαι/glṓssai) he could speak, knowing the members of this congregation he founded, he could do a quick calculation and assert that his half a dozen or so known languages was more than any one of them could speak or maybe even more than the sum total of the languages represented in the congregation. Some hyperbole might be involved here.

What we can safely conclude from these verses (1 Cor 14:18–19) is that in chiding the Corinthians believers, Paul mentions that he spoke in γλῶσσαι/glṓssai (normally meaning "languages" elsewhere in the New Testament), literally "more than you all" (πάντων ὑμῶν μᾶλλον/ pantōn hymōn mallon). This is a genitive of comparison, which can either be interpreted as qualitative, meaning with richer endowment, or with greater frequency.

The less complicated understanding here, as numerous commentators stated before the modernistic Neander *glossolalic* trend, is that Paul spoke in more foreign languages than the Corinthians, and the grammar may mean more than all of them combined (Benson, 2019:9945; Clarke, 1967:1118; Gill, 1746–1748, col 14:18; Hodge, 1860:292; Barnes, 1949:267).

If I had been tasked with Paul's enormous responsibility, I would surely give thanks to God that he had prepared me from my mother's womb (cf. Gal 1:15) to speak a variety of essential languages to reach the nations (ἔθνος/ethnos). From verse 18, where does Fee, Gardner, Carson, Ciampa and Rosner get the indication that Paul reserved the γλῶσσαι/glṓssai for devotional use?

The text doesn't say that it's a comparison of "public" versus "private" (i.e., narrow "devotional" sphere), rather it is less conjectural to say in "church" (with translation) or keep silent there, possibly relative to "elsewhere," which is broader and more open-ended, allowing the speaking in one's native language in family or personal devotional times, and also out in public settings, as the need required.

It can be naturally assumed that Paul used those languages of Hebrew, Aramaic, Syriac, Latin, and Greek dialects out in the public marketplace, in his bi-vocational leatherworking trade and in his missionary endeavours out on the byways and highways of the Empire

(Thomas, 1978:219; Hasel, 199l:149). This then would mean that Paul could speak in more different languages than all of the Corinthians (Toussaint, 2015:184; Benson, 2019:9945; Clarke, 1967:1118; Gill, 1746–1748, col 14:18; Hodge, 1860:292; Barnes, 1949:267; see also the previous chapter 3.2.1 regarding Paul's other languages). The Apostle engaged in multiple languages outside the believers' assemblies but limited himself therein to beneficially teach.

CHAPTER 14 AND VERSE 19

Paul's ἀλλ' ἐν ἐκκλησίᾳ ("but in the *ekklesia*, I desire to speak ... " 1 Cor 14:19), sets up a contrast with where else he would use his γλῶσσα/ *glóssa* (language of Hebrew, Aramaic, Syriac, Greek, Greek dialects or Latin) outside the *ekklesia*. As remarked on the previous verse, these languages could have been used in his tent-making business transactions, in bartering in the public market place and in interactions with synagogue and public governing officials.

"By the word *tongue* [1 Cor 14:19], to which we add *unknown*, I suppose the apostle always means the Hebrew" (Clarke, 1967:1118). It is reasonable to understand, from this verse 19, that Paul never spoke in his variant earthly γλῶσσαι/*glóssai* (languages), which the Corinthian congregants were not conversant in, as there would be no instructional value (1 Cor 14:19). Paul would not speak in a foreign language when it would be mere display (Barnes, 1949:267).

The term ἐκκλησίᾳ (*ekklēsia*) is clearly referring to the gathered assembly for worship, and that teaching was an assumed component, indicates there was a similarity between the believers' assembly and the Jewish synagogue (Collins, 1999:504).

Baur (1875:279, 280, 286) points out that in 1 Corinthians 8, the Apostle Paul, in discussing the heathen sacrificial feasts and meat offered to idols, said that, out of consideration for others, a believer might abstain from what was perfectly lawful. The Apostle Paul then uses this against his opponents to show that, rather than to his disadvantage, these were acts of voluntary renunciation, for the sake of his apostolic calling. As an Apostle, he had certain rights which he did not avail himself of because of higher considerations (Baur, 1875:279, 280, 286). So too, in regard to showing off his array of languages, Paul would decline that and rather speak five words to benefit the Corinthian congregation than 10,000 words in a foreign language unknown to the Corinthian believers.

Paul unequivocally sets forth his stellar example that he would rather speak five words in a language which they comprehended, than a myriad (μυρίους/*myrious*) of words (λόγους/*logous*) in a language not understood nor translated. He didn't want his mindful (τῷ νοΐ μου/*tō noi mou*) words to be unfruitful (ἄκαρπός/*akarpos*) in those needing instruction (κατηχήσω/*katēchēsō*) in their new-found faith (1 Cor 14:19; cf. 14:14). Parallel to 1 Corinthians 14:15, Paul desired that his activities in a believers' assembly should be intelligible ("with my mind"—1 Cor 14:19). The use of untranslated languages in the assembly not only failed to edify believers; it would repel the unbeliever. Intelligible speech could both edify believers and hold out hope for the conversion of unbelievers (Taylor, 2014:373).

CHAPTER 14 AND VERSE 20

In this verse, we again see that the Apostle Paul is not an advocate of the Corinthian believers putting their minds in neutral or of bypassing their minds, when he says "in your thinking be mature" (ταῖς δὲ φρεσὶν τέλειοι γίνεσθε/*tais de phresin teleioi ginesthe*), contra the misconstrual of those who posit otherwise for the previous annotated 1 Corinthians14:14. Thayer's Greek Lexicon (s.v., §2) defines φρήν/*phrén* as "the mind; the faculty of perceiving and judging: also in the plural" citing this 1 Corinthians 14:20 usage. BDAG defines φρήν (*phrén*) "as the process of careful consideration, thinking, understanding" and also cites 1 Corinthian 14:20. The Apostle Paul values "careful consideration" and "mature thinking," therefore it would contradict his *modus operandi* to countenance bypassing the mind (cf. 1 Cor 14:14). In 1 Corinthians 13:11, in opposition to childishness, the Apostle Paul held up maturity of thought (φρονέω/*phroneó*) and reasoning (λογίζομαι/*logizomai*) as the life stage to move to. Having the mind disengaged was not something the Apostle Paul would have acquiesced to for supposedly mature believers.

There is more than a hint of exasperation leading into this verse when Pauls chides, "do not be children in your thinking," which recalls Paul's earlier rebuke of them for their spiritual immaturity (1 Cor 3:1–3).

Thiselton (2000, 1119) comments that verse 20 is a clear statement of the childish love of display or thoughtless self-centeredness caused by their use of γλῶσσαι/*glóssai* in the Corinthian assembly. As far as it goes, this assessment matches with the Epiphanius thesis that immature Corinthian congregants were displaying vanity and egotism around the use of γλῶσσαι/*glóssai*.

CHAPTER 14 AND VERSE 21

Paul's quote from Isaiah 28:11–12 is not talking about "unintelligible languages," with the meaning of non-earthly languages. Paul has the phrase "strange tongues and by the lips of strangers." The language of the Assyrian soldiers was quite intelligible to one another, but not to the Israelites. Obviously, this Isaiah quote is referring to untranslated earthly languages, something very different from non-earthly languages. The conquering Assyrians' foreign language was not a supernaturally-given language, hence this fact does not weigh in favour of supernaturally-given language in this 1 Corinthians 14 passage either. In fact, at least the spokesperson of the Assyrians was tri-lingual, being able to speak Assyrian, Judean (Hebrew) and Aramaic (2 Kings 18:26–28). So, the Apostle Paul has in mind earthly, foreign languages (Edgar, 1996:141–142).

Since foreign languages are referred to here in verse 21 (ἑτερογλώσσοις/*heteroglōssois*), then the use of αἱ γλῶσσαι (*hai glōssai*) in verse 22 most logically refers to foreign languages (Gromacki, 1967:64). To further support this conception, Gromacki (1967:64) points to the article of previous reference (αἱ/*hai*) and the function of the inferential conjunction Ὥστε/*hōste* ("so then") at the beginning of 1 Corinthians 14:22. If Paul considered γλῶσσαι/*glóssai* to be in a non-earthly utterance, he would not have used the same word twice in these two consecutive verses (1 Cor 14:21–22; cf. also 1 Cor 14:10–11), especially being that the meaning of γλῶσσαι/*glóssai* was plainly established as normal, earthly languages in the first usage (Gromacki, 1967:64). This is also reinforced by the earlier contention that the Apostle Paul wrote 1 Corinthians prior to his close associate, Luke, writing Acts, with Luke giving recipient Theophilus an explanation of γλῶσσαι/*glóssai* as normal earthly languages, whereas Paul takes for granted that his readers know what they are (Lenski, 1946:505).

CONTEXTUAL AND EXEGETICAL ANALYSIS

Paul's major point here seems to be that the outsiders who come into the congregation in the Corinthian context are compared with the "outsiders" sketched by this Isaiah text which Paul references.

Another interesting observation is that Paul just launches into this Older Testament quotation with the assumption that they were already familiar with the Isaiah 28 passage. This points to a substantial contingent of congregants who were Jewish, Jewish proselytes and "God-fearers" who had heard this passage discoursed on before, most likely in the adjoining synagogue.

In the context, in Isaiah 28, the prophet warns God's people, Israel, of impending judgement at the hands of their enemies. Since the people of Israel would not heed the Lord, they were to be taught a harsh lesson by pagans—those who spoke a foreign language (Deut 28: 49; cp. Jer 5:15). This is the contextual significance out of which Paul in 1 Corinthians 14: 20-22 applies Isaiah 28: 11, 12, with its reference to a foreign language, in relation to the contentious "languages" issue in the Corinthian church. The foreign language of Isaiah 28 was not miraculously, spontaneously given. It was learned languages that the Assyrians spoke, which undermines the *xenolalic* language-miracle position of previously, unknown languages. Advocates of *xenolalia* say that the Isaiah 28 passage supports normal, earthly, foreign languages in the subsequent 1 Corinthians verses (14:22f), with which one can agree, but then in the same breath they contend that the γλῶσσα (*glóssa*—language) was previously unknown and miraculously given. Conzelman (1975:234) challenges that with his remark that "Paul's opinion is not that what is said in tongues is unintelligible to the speaker himself."

From Paul's perspective, the other languages were to be a σημεῖόν (*sēmeion*/sign) to the Jewish nation as a whole. We note that in particularizing the Old Testament Isaiah prophecy, the Apostle Paul is faithful to the original text by applying it to "this people" (Jewish nation) but ἑτερογλώσσοις (*heteroglōssois*—other languages) is in the plural (1 Cor 14:21). This rebuke to the obtuse Jews would be by more than one language, as it was in Acts 2, Acts 10, and Acts 19, and here by way of the multilingual Corinthian congregation comprised of Gentile and Jewish believers.

The informed Jews would have been aware of their early tradition that the revelation of the Ten Commandments, on Mount Sinai, to Moses, came in all the languages of the world, because God's Word was not just for Hebrew-speaking Jews (Witherington, 2015:30, 66).

Despite the obtuseness of the majority of the Jews, there would always be a remnant of Jews who believed, as was the case with the formation of the Corinthian congregation out of the local synagogue, and the Apostle Paul was optimistic that additional ones would come to faith in Jesus as the Messiah (1Cor 14:24–25). However, untranslated languages in public worship were incongruous because it created a barrier and unnecessarily placed many of the Messiah's own ethnic people in a situation of confusion and alienation without having had the opportunity to hear the gospel message.

CHAPTER 14 AND VERSE 22

For the Apostle Paul to designate γλῶσσαι/*glōssai* as a "sign" (σημεῖόν/*sēmeion*) implies that they were actual, earthly foreign languages (1 Cor 14:21–22).

When the Apostle Paul uses the phrase, "γλῶσσαι/*glōssai* are for a sign ... to the unbelievers" (1 Cor 14:22), mentioned again in 14:23–25, he is referring to the Jewish people. He refers back to ancient history, where the Israelite people were not believing straight-forward, repetitious truth (i.e., "order on order, order on order, line on line, line on line, a little here, a little there" Isa 28:10–13). Fee (1990:682), in his appraisal of these verses, concludes that "Most likely, Paul is using the word 'sign' in a way that is quite in keeping with his Judaic background, where 'sign' functions as an expression of God's attitude, something that 'signifies' to Israel either his disapproval or pleasure."

Understood in context then, the Apostle Paul is not referring to generic "unbelievers," but to Jewish unbelievers in Corinth, who attended the synagogue next door and were drawn to drop in and check out the assembly meeting at the adjoining house of Titius Justus. There would have been skeptics and doubters and unpersuaded (ἀπίστοις/*apistois*; cf. same Greek term in John 20:27 "doubting Thomas") in that synagogue in Corinth. Sticking tight to the context and application of the original passage of Isaiah 28:11f, understood in this way, the purpose of Corinthian γλώσσαις/*glōssais* was not only for *edification purposes* but also for *evidential purposes*.

In the three Acts events (Acts 2, 10, 19) looked at previously, the γλώσσαις/*glōssais* were to convince the reticent, doubting, skeptical Jews. All the non-Hebrew languages on display in the Corinthian assembly, if translated, should have been enough to convince any recalcitrant Jew that God was doing a work in the world well beyond the favoured Jewish people. However, all these languages, if left untranslated, would only cause confusion and mockery.

Like the unbelieving Israelites, non-believing Jews in Corinth will end up doomed, even if unintentionally, by those speaking untranslated languages. They will be blighted and stay dead in their transgressions because they will spurn the saving grace of the Messiah due to the crazy babblers. If the non-believing Jews, in Corinth, still resisted the prophetic word and its equivalent (translated/interpreted languages), then the panoply of languages was indeed a σημεῖόν (sēmeion) of judgement. It was a clear indication that God was reaching out to all the nations—no more exclusivity.

Jesus' parable about the vineyard is instructive (Matt 21:33–46; Mark 12:1–12; Luke 20:9–19). Israel had rejected God's many prophets and ultimately his Son, Jesus Christ. Jesus pronounced the judgement that the vineyard's owner "will come and destroy these vine-growers and will give the vineyard to others" (Luke 20:16). That decisive judgement took place in 70 AD, when the Romans destroyed Jerusalem and the Jews were dispersed. Their exclusive role was suspended. To accomplish his purposes, God grafted in the Gentiles "until the fulness of the Gentiles has come in" (Rom 11:25). God's gracious invitation was already beginning to go out more broadly ("to the main highways" Matt 22:9), specifically, to the Gentiles (ἔθνει/ethnei—Matt 21:43).

Originally γλώσσαις/glōssais (languages) was for a sign to the unbelieving Jew, but not necessarily a saving sign. In fact, it was a sign of judgement. However, in this case, interestingly, the Apostle Paul does not consign these prospective Corinthian attenders to an inevitable judgement and seems optimistic that exposure to "prophecy" within the assembly would cause them to worship God and acknowledge his presence. According to BDAG (s.v. §1 & §2; page 90), ἄπιστος/apistos can have the meaning of "incredible," "without faith, disbelieving," an example of which is Thomas' incredulity in John 20:27 where Jesus says to him, "... be not unbelieving (ἄπιστος/apistos) but believing (πιστός/pistos)." In others words, he was skeptical and not yet persuaded, which nuance fits the context of the Corinthian assembly where skeptics (ἄπιστοι/apistoi) and uninformed inquirers (ἰδιῶται/idiōtai), in need of instruction and insights, about Jesus and his "incredible" life, death resurrection and ascension, given in prophetic manner derived from the

Old Testament, were welcome (1 Cor 14:23). BDAG (s.v. ἰδιώτης, §1) defines ἰδιώτης as "a person who is relatively unskilled or inexperienced in some activity or field of knowledge" and (s.v. §2) describes such an individual as "one not in the know."

Ford (1986:292) and Sweet (1986:144) argue that ἄπιστος (*apistos*) does not necessarily mean "unbelievers" in today's sense, but rather is a reference to one who is "weak in faith" or who is "non-kosher." Ford (1986:292) suggests that the same meaning might be applicable to 1 Corinthians 14:22; "to those who are lacking full faith in Jesus, probably Jews or proselytes, tongues are a sign as they were in Acts and Isaiah 28:11–12." The γλώσσαις/*glōssais* (languages) were a prophetic sign that the Holy Spirit thereafter made no distinction between Jews, half-Jew Samaritans or Gentiles (Ford, 1986:292). The γλώσσαις/glṓssais (languages) had been effective in producing the intended result of removing doubt in Peter and the other Jewish Apostles as well as the recipients (Ford, 1986:292).

Being that the Corinthian believers' place of meeting adjoined the synagogue, these may well have been curious former Jewish compatriots who slipped over to this new Messianic congregation on a Sabbath, if the Corinthian believers assembled on that day, or on the first day of the week, if that had become the custom by then. The citation about "strange languages" from Isaiah 28:11f would have been particularly *apropos* to such curious but uninformed and skeptical Jews (ἰδιῶται ἢ ἄπιστοι). However, if a string of Gentiles were speaking in some obscure, undecipherable Greek dialect or other remote, rustic native lingo without translation, the attending ἰδιῶται ἢ ἄπιστοι would think that the Corinthians believers were not in their right minds. So, whether these visitors had a lack of instruction or lack of belief at that point in time, they would depart with a negative impression of the Corinthian believers and their Lord. Lamentably, untranslated languages would have become a means of judgement since they drive the uninstructed (ἰδιῶται/*idiōtai*) and doubters (ἄπιστοι/*apistoi*) from the believers' assembly. The congregation of believers should not be alienating the uninstructed (ἰδιῶται/*idiōtai*) and doubters (ἄπιστοι/*apistoi*) but attempting to win them to the Lord (cf. 1 Cor 9:19–22). "The conduct of the assembly, says Paul, is a powerful force in evangelization" (Collins, 1999:507).

Analogously, our local Alliance church has offered a "discovery class" for our Mandarin-speaking friends who have come from

Communist China. Some are investigating the truth claims of Christ and Christianity (ἄπιστοι/*apistoi*) and others are believers wanting instruction (ἰδιῶται/*idiōtai*) in their new-found faith. Our church also has a Sunday morning service, centered around the previous week's English-speaking Pastor's message on video, with live Mandarin translation for the edification of new believers and insightful for seekers.

Moving on in 1 Corinthians 14:22, it is important to note that the latter part of the verse does not actually say that "prophecy *is for a sign* . . . to those who believe." Careful readers will notice that "*is for a sign*" is in italics, which means that it is not in the Greek text, but an insertion by the translator or translating committee of that version. There has been much ink spilt by commentators on this non-existent phrase that, in most of our English Bibles, states that "prophecy *is for a sign* . . . to those who believe" (1 Cor 14:22). Commentators have attempted to explain away this apparent contradictory statement in verse 22 and reconcile this non-existent phrase with the subsequent verse 24 where "prophecy" has immense value in bringing an "unbeliever" to faith. The stark juxtaposition is not there in the Greek text and prophecy can have both *a didactic role* for "believers" and *a salvific role* for "unbelievers."

CHAPTER 14, VERSE 23 THROUGH VERSE 25

Here we pick up on the previous theme of Paul's crusade for intelligibility (1 Cor 14:9), rationality in speech (1 Cor 4:19) and maturity in thinking (1 Cor 14:20). We have, in these verses (1 Cor 14:23–24), the Apostle Paul's decided aversion to believers being perceived, by "uninstructed" (ἰδιῶται/*idiōtai*) and "doubters" (ἄπιστοι/*apistoi*), as being out of one's mind μαίνεσθε (*mainesthe*).

If it be argued that the term μαίνεσθε (*mainesthe*) points to ecstatic unintelligible speech, the rebuttal would be that although ecstatic unintelligible speech was not uncommon in the pagan religions of that era, it was described by other terms like *phtheggomai* and not by the term *glōssa* (Edgar, 1996:126), although, I suppose, some might want to suggest that γλῶσσα/*glōssa* is the distinctive term for a Christian context. "There is no evidence in secular Greek of classic or koine times, nor in pre-Christian Judaism, nor in the biblical Greek of the Septuagint that *glōssa* [γλῶσσα] was used to mean ecstatic unintelligible speech" (Edgar, 1996:126). Based on this, Hodge (1860:248) concludes: "If the meaning of the phrase [*laleo glōssa*] is thus historically and philologically determined for Acts and Mark, it must also be determined for the Epistle to the Corinthians."

These verses (1 Cor 14:23–25) also point to the accessibility of early Christian worship at Corinth, in that non-members could come into the larger, periodic, composite assemblies of all the home groups scattered across Corinth (literally "comes together the whole church together the place"), perhaps for the Lord's Supper, possibly in the villa of a wealthy patron like Gaius (cf. 1 Cor 1:14; Rom 16:23). Such ἰδιῶται/ *idiōtai* and ἄπιστοι/*apistoi* may be Jews or analogous to the Gentile "God-fearers" who frequented Synagogue worship and might be referred to as "seekers" today (Billings, 2014:277). They may have been unconverted spouses or the immediate or extended family of a believer or a guest of the host (Witherington, 1995:283) or a household servant of the host (Collins, 1999:506).

To make his point, the Apostle Paul paints a pretty extreme version here of everyone, in an assembly meeting, speaking in different untranslated languages, at the same time. Paul didn't want even one untranslated language at a time, never mind this picture of a madhouse cacophony of languages all at the same time. "All that the words here require is that all who spoke used foreign languages" (Hodge, 1860:297). Although Paul not approving, if there was just one strange untranslated language at a time, possibly an attending "outsider" could pick out a few understood words, but not even a chance of that with all the competing voices in such a bedlam as Paul portrays.

Paul didn't want the Corinthian believers perceived as being disassociated from their minds. For the pleasing aroma of the gospel (cf. 2 Cor 2:15), it was important that they be perceived as sane. Allegations of insanity would have sabotaged the message of the gospel.

There appear to be considerable mental exertions by those who imagine this is about *glossolalia* (i.e., Fee, 2014:758, 762–767) and then making the complex calculations of how many had the so-called gift of *glossolalia*. Whereas, in a multilingual city like Corinth, with people from all over the Roman Empire asserting their minority mother tongue without translation, one can easily imagine the impression of craziness (μαίνεσθε/*mainesthe*) this would create for visiting outsiders, be they uninformed inquirers (ἰδιῶται/*idiōtai*) or skeptics (ἄπιστοι/*apistoi*).

In respect to "languages" (γλώσσαις/*glōssais*), posing the terms "gift(s)," "gifted" and "gifting" as Fee does (2014:758, 762–767), when there are no such underlying Greek terms in the entirety of 1 Corinthians chapter 14, is vexing. Again, Pentecostalist Fee appears here to be living up to his self-confessed mode (1976:122) that "in general the Pentecostal's experience has preceded their hermeneutics. In a sense, the Pentecostal tends to exegete his or her experience." This rubric needs to be kept uppermost in mind when engaging with Fee's Corinthian commentaries (1987, 2014).

The Apostle Paul seems to here parallel the account of Acts 2. The irregular foreign languages throw the uninformed and skeptics into a confused state of mind (1 Cor 14:23). Uninformed and skeptic individuals coming into the assembly, when all there speak in foreign languages, will cause these *uninformed and skeptics* to think that these Jesus believers are crazy (μαίνεσθε/*mainesthe*), which was the similar reaction of the unbelievers at Pentecost (Acts 2:12–13). However, if the prophetic word is delivered, as Peter did in explaining the import of the irregular languages at Pentecost, the transmission of the truth in comprehendible language will bring repentance (1 Cor 14:24–25). There is a similarity between Acts 2:12–13 and 1 Corinthians 14:22–25. In the case of the Corinthian congregational setting, foreign languages must be translated or else they signify the judgement of God upon those who hear but cannot comprehend. If, by the prophetic word, a person "who knows nothing of the sacred [Hebrew] language, come in and hear things just suited to his own state, he is convicted by all, and he is judged by all" (Clarke, 1967:1118–1119).

CHAPTER 14 AND VERSE 26

The verb συνέρχησθε (*synerchēsthe* "to come together, to assemble"), a reappearing expression in this letter of Paul's (1 Cor 11:17, 18, 20, 33, 34; 14:23, 26), causes us to remember that Paul's emphasis is on the gathering of the body for a worship service. It is not about private devotions.

The shift in focus from evangelizing non-Christians (1 Cor 14:22–25) to edifying believers (1 Cor 14:26), with the less formal and more participatory mode, may indicate that this is a template for the regular smaller home gatherings, whereas the previous verses indicate the periodic larger, more public assemblies of several house-churches combined (Blomberg, 1994:246; Prior, 1985:249–250; also see analysis of the early Christian house-church by Branick, 1989).

In that mult-lingual city, the different elements when they assembled, whether smaller or larger gatherings, were assumed to include someone speaking in a γλῶσσαν (*glóssan* language) and a translation (ἑρμηνείαν/*hermēneian*) of same. This would make perfect sense in a cosmopolitan city of individuals with diverse linguistic backgrounds. Gill (1746–1748, col 14:26), on 1 Corinthians 14:26, offers that different foreign languages were allowed in these gatherings of Jesus' believer and specifies that some who "had knowledge and skill in the Hebrew tongue, could not only pray and sing in that language, and read the sacred text, but could deliver a sermon in it" which of course necessitated "interpreting languages, particularly the Hebrew language."

At the end of this verse, the Apostle reminds his readers that each contribution must be for the edifying of the gathered group; otherwise, if it was only for ostentation and to make a show of their abilities and talents, and to nurture their own pride and vanity, no good end would come of it. This accords with the thesis of Epiphanius.

CHAPTER 14 AND VERSE 27

Lightfoot (1859:266–267) on κατὰ δύο ἢ τὸ πλεῖστον τρεῖς/*kata dyo ē to pleiston treis* ("by two or at the most three") was convinced that the γλώσσῃ/*glōssē* (language) was Hebrew because "They would not be weaned from the old custom of the synagogue as to the use of the Hebrew tongue in their worship, and for the present he indulges them their fancy; and this not vainly, since by the use of that tongue the hearers might be edified, a faithful interpreter standing by." Clarke (1967:1119) likewise, assesses that the language-speaking which Paul is here focusing on is Hebrew, while Gill (1746–1748, col 14:27), on this verse 27, less definitively, names Hebrew.

With all the Hebrew and synogogal background explained in the foregoing chapters and sections, a logical scenario for this verse 27 reference is to one "who speaks in a tongue [language]" as one reading and paraphrastically teaching from the Older Testament Hebrew Scriptures. The translator could be the self-same speaker or another person familiar with both Hebrew and the recipient language, translating it a few sentences at a time. Paul noted the proviso, in 1 Corinthians 14:13, that the person speaking in a foreign language could himself/herself translate it or someone else could ("ἵνα διερμηνεύῃ/*ina diermēneuē*," with the verb διερμηνεύῃ/*diermēneuē* being present, active, subjunctive, and in the third person singular).

The Apostle Paul laid down the assembly guideline of, at the most, three individuals speaking in languages, one at a time. As mentioned before, I had the privilege of serving as a Canadian Member of Parliament for 6 terms and on an overseas trip to Sudan, I recall speaking in a long, rectangular, mud-walled, thatched-roof, packed Episcopal church building. Because my speaking was with the aid of a sequential translator, I had to shorten my content considerably. It may have been this time constraint that the Apostle Paul had in mind when he stipulated a maximum limit of three minority language speakers with the complement of translation.

Fee (2014:928, footnote 659) makes a telling admission: "As with 'tongues,' all of this is functional language. There was no group in Corinth known as "the interpreters of tongues"; the language of 14:5, plus the exhortation of v. 13, tells against such a possibility." This apparent attempt at justification by Fee contra other *glossolalic* advocates would not be necessary with the straightforward view of normal, earthly, but foreign languages. It would be very much "functional" as there would be no need for a group of "official interpreters." As the need arose, with someone anticipating to speak in the believers' assembly in an earthly, minority language, that person would collar a friend or acquaintance to do the job of translation if they themselves didn't feel adequate to the task.

Nevertheless, inadvertently, Fee (2014:928, footnote 659) makes a solid case for demystifying the γλῶσσαι (*glóssai*—language) of 1 Corinthians 12 and 14. Viewing it as "functional" (wording of Fee, 2014:928, footnote 659), rather than an esoteric technical term, better suits the non-*glossolalic* perspective. In 1 Corinthians 12 and 14, ἑρμηνεία (*hermēneia*/translation) is best understood as "function" or "ministry" under the aegis of the Holy Spirit.

Calvin (1573:386) remarks that, to Paul, the translated γλῶσσαι (*glóssai*—languages) were helps to prophecy, as translating the original Hebrew and Greek languages were in Calvin's day.

The Earliest View of New Testament Tongues

CHAPTER 14 AND VERSE 28

Some, like Fee (2014:767), interpret this verse as support for γλῶσσαι (*glṓssai*) as "the language of prayer and praise, directed toward God, ... in the setting of personal prayer and devotion" which a believer uses to edify herself/himself (Fee, 2014:728). Such an interpretation doesn't harmonize with the rest of 1 Corinthians. It can't be a private prayer language if it is to be translated (1 Corinthians 14:13–17), although *glossolalic* proponents try to get around this by saying that it only needs to be translated in a congregational setting. It can't be a private prayer language if uninterpreted γλῶσσαι (*glṓssai*) stands "for a sign ... to unbelievers" (1 Corinthians 14:22). It would appear not to be a private prayer language when the New Testament is clear that the Spirit's manifestations (φανέρωσις/*phanerōsis*) are for the corporate benefit (συμφέρον/*sympheron*), not for self-edification (1 Corinthians 12:7). The Apostle Paul, in 1 Corinthians 12:11 and 12:28–29, is unequivocal that all do not speak in languages (γλῶσσαι/*glṓssai*). How could γλῶσσαι/*glṓssai* be for every believer's private self-edification when the expected answer to Paul's questions (1 Cor 12:30) is that not all believers speak in "languages."

Ciampa and Rosner (2010:Kindle Location 16451) concede that "the whole passage [1 Corinthians 14] is about what should take place during the church meeting" and then, in an argument from silence, go on to speculate, in respect to 1 Corinthians 14:28, that "it is intended to evoke the contrast between what is appropriate at church versus what is appropriate at home."

Conzelman (1975:245) likewise, in unsupported manner, states that, if there is no interpreter, the Corinthian congregant should follow some [conjectured] "rule that he should speak in tongues at home."

Fee (2014:767) remarks on 1 Corinthians 14:28: "Speaking 'to oneself' stands in contrast to 'in the assembly' in the preceding instruction (v. 27), meaning that they should pray 'to God' in this way in private." If Fee's reference (2014:928, footnote 660) to the "dative of advantage," ἑαυτῷ in this verse, is to support his view of doing "tongues" in private (i.e., "personal prayer and devotion"), he is overreaching. The "dative of advantage" doesn't infer anything of the sort (Blass *et al.*, 1961:101, §188 (2)). It simply means that it is in the individual's best interest to "speak to himself and to God" in the assembly when there is no one there to translate for him. Paul doesn't mention doing this at home but only that the speaker must keep silent in the church; and speak to himself and to God (Taylor, 2014:382).

On the phrase "But if there is no interpreter" (1 Cor 14:28), Clarke (1967:1119) writes: "If there be none present who can give the proper sense of this Hebrew reading and speaking, then let him keep silence, and not occupy the time of the Church, by speaking in a language which only himself can understand."

The person who is hoping to speak should know in advance if there is anyone in attendance who knows the language he intends to speak plus the majority language of the assembly well enough to translate for him (Blackwelder, 1971:67). If not, he stays seated and "commune[s] with himself, and with God" (Barnes, 1949:272). Blackwelder (1971:67) notes that the scenario Paul portrays in 1 Corinthians 14:28 could not take place if it was a reference to non-earthly languages, because in the situation of a supposed non-earthly utterance, as typically alleged by my Charismatic/Pentecostal friends, the supposed "interpretation" comes as a special disclosure in the moment, thus the ostensible tongues-speaker could never be certain that he or she should get up and speak. If a person of Charismatic/Pentecostalist persuasion protests that the tongues-speaker always has the Spirit's assurance, in advance, that it's safe to proceed with his or her utterance, then in converse, Paul's prohibitory statement in 1 Corinthians 14:28 is without point, unless the strained argument is attempted that certain congregants are known for having the gift/ability of "interpreting" and are at the ready on a standby basis. Paul doesn't say start in and see if an interpreter is present. He presumes that one should know in advance, which doesn't fit the presumed spontaneity of ecstatic, non-earthly utterances, but better harmonizes with the dynamics of a premeditated, yet tentative, speaking in a foreign, earthly language at the believers' weekly assembly.

In 1 Corinthians 14:28, what seems to weigh against both the view of "supernaturally speaking in unlearned earthly languages" and even the lesser credible "ecstatic or non-ecstatic, non-earthly, angelic/heavenly languages" is the significant question of how an all-knowing, every-where present, all-powerful God could provide the "supernatural, unlearned earthly languages or non-earthly, angelic/heavenly languages" for a particular congregational setting and then botch it up by not giving the needed corresponding interpretational ability to someone present. It makes no sense that God would give a supernatural, unlearned earthly language in the moment but with no one there to do the complementary, instantaneous translation. This seems to imply that the Holy Spirit got mixed up or was short-sighted in giving only one element and not the other requisite ability. Natural, learned earthly languages makes more sense with the inference that a potential foreign language speaker should check out in advance that there was a willing translator available (cf. 1 Cor 14:27–28). This understanding doesn't denigrate the foresight of the Holy Spirit and blame him for some spontaneous spur-of-the-moment "miraculous" speaking in unlearned earthly or non-earthly languages for which there is no matching translation.

As Zerhusen (1997:146) adroitly puts it: "If speaking in languages and translation were miraculous (as some say) then the situation described in 1 Corinthians 14:28 could never occur." Furthermore, if the language-speaker is commanded to "pray that he may interpret [translate]" (1 Cor 14:13) and if interpretation/translation is an unlearned, supernatural ability that the language-speaker or other similarly gifted persons could exercise, then the situation of keeping silent and remaining seated (1 Corinthians 14:28) would never arise because either the language-speaker could interpret or one of the "supernaturally" gifted interpreters/translators on standby could interpret/translate (Zerhusen,1997:146).

Language speaking and translation (1 Cor 12:10–11) needn't take on the aura of miraculous ability, when it can be a straightforward "manifestation of the Spirit" (1 Cor 12:7; like "helps" and "administrations/steersmanship" 1 Cor 12:28) without the mystique. Helping others or providing guidance may not appear striking or extraordinary, but all God's grace gifts are enablements of the Spirit, without necessarily being perceived as spectacular or otherworldly. If some of the "manifestations of the Spirit" are not electrifying, stupendous abilities (e.g., "helps" and "administrations"), then ability in multiple languages (1 Cor. 12:10, 28, 30), while not having a veneer of the miraculous, can also be vital manifestations of the Spirit (Zerhusen, 1997:147). After all, in multilingual Corinth, Paul would have known that the ability to speak various languages and translate them were essential ministries in the congregation and in outreach (Zerhusen, 1997: 147). This addresses the Corinthian problem.

CHAPTER 14 AND VERSE 39

"Therefore, my brethren, desire earnestly to prophesy, and do not forbid to speak in tongues" (NASV and similarly other English versions). In respect to the translation "do not forbid to speak in tongues" (τὸ λαλεῖν μὴ κωλύετε γλώσσαις), Isbell (1975:19) points out several problems which such a translation doesn't solve, the first being "that the Greek text does not contain a simple, uninterrupted phrase such as *lalein glōssais* [λαλεῖν γλώσσαις]." Instead, there is a complete grammatical unit, specifically μὴ κωλύετε (*mē kōlyete*), which appears between the two words λαλεῖν (*lalein*) and γλώσσαις (*glōssais*) which are normally spoken and written closely together (Isbell, 1975: 19). Consequently, a normally simple phrase, λαλεῖν γλώσσαις (*lalein glōssais*) has the entire phrase τὸ λαλεῖν μὴ κωλύετε γλώσσαις broken in the middle by a negative particle and an imperative (μὴ κωλύετε/*mē kōlyete*).

Secondly, there is the meaning of the Greek verb κωλύω. The verb κωλύω (*kólyó*) is not always translated "forbid" in the New Testament. Acts 11:17 provides a clear example of another meaning which the word can convey. The Apostle Peter says there, "If God therefore gave to them [the Gentiles] the same gift as *He gave* to us also after believing in the Lord Jesus Christ, who was I that I could κωλῦσαι/*kōlysai* God?" Peter certainly was not capable of "forbidding" God to offer salvation to the Gentiles, but he could have seemingly "hindered" or "impeded" God's intent by refusal to cooperate (Isbell, 1975: 19). Since κωλύω (*kólyó*) does not always mean "forbid," it is fair to challenge whether that's the intent in 1 Corinthians 14:39.

Arguing for the substantival quality of τὸ λαλεῖν/*to lalein*, based on the nominal quality of the articular infinitive τὸ λαλεῖν/*lalein* and given the fact that λαλεῖν elsewhere in the chapter (1 Cor 14:3, 19) alludes to προφητεύων/*prophēteuōn*, Isbell (1975: 19) contends that it is not incongruous to argue that τὸ λαλεῖν/*to lalein* in verse 39 refers, not to γλώσσαις/*glōssais* (languages/tongues), but to προφητεύειν/*prophēteuein* (prophesy). A resulting translation would be: "So, my brothers, desire earnestly *to prophesy* and to speak, don't hinder/impede [*prophecy*] with languages (γλώσσαις/*glōssais*)." I would understand this to say that, the Apostle Paul, in summary, was making clear that his preceding injunctions were not meant as a *carte blanche*, with complete freedom to act as one wanted, in respect to γλώσσαις (languages/tongues). In the Corinthian assembly meetings, the inordinate use of "languages" and the consequent required translation should not take up so much time that it would dominate the meetings and get in the way of the straightforward prophetic word.

We have no clear indication that the Apostle Paul nor anyone at Corinth was trying to forbid γλώσσαις/*glōssais* (*languages*), so this is a more fitting conclusion to what Paul had argued throughout this entire chapter (Isbell, 1975: 19). Calvin (1573:368) would agree, when on 1 Corinthians 14:5, he asserted "that we must not be so taken up with the use of languages, as to treat with neglect prophecy, which ought to have the first place."

On 1 Corinthians 12:31, Calvin (1573:349) says the fault prevailed among them "that they aimed at show, rather than usefulness. Hence prophecy was neglected, while languages sounded forth among them, with great show, indeed, but with little profit." This supports the view of 1 Corinthian 14:39 that untranslated "languages" were getting in the way of prophecy, and the idea of "hindering," therefore reading the verse as "So, my brothers, desire earnestly *to prophesy* and to speak, don't hinder/impede [*prophecy*] with languages (γλώσσαις/*glōssais*)." The Epiphanius thesis, that prideful Corinthians were displaying vanity and egotism around the ability to speak foreign, earthly languages, is thus supported also.

The first, and preferred, mode of speech for the Corinthian assembly was "prophesying" in a language understood by the audience and the second prominent mode being practiced in the Corinthian assembly was addressing the listeners in an unknown earthly "language" not translated for the benefit of those hearers. This second mode resulted in unintelligibility and frustration and exclusion, whereas the first mode resulted in ordered intelligibility, people being built up, encouraged and consoled, and doubters (ἄπιστοι/*apistoi*) and the uninformed (ἰδιῶται/*idiōtai*) worshipping God in acknowledgement of his presence.

Previously, in 1 Corinthians 14:5, the Apostle Paul spoke of the superiority of prophecy (προφητείαν/*prophēteian*) over untranslated "languages" (γλώσσαις/*glōssais*) because in prophecy the content is implied ("edification and exhortation and consolation" 1 Cor 14:3), whereas important as the various earthly languages are, they are a mode, neutral in themselves, by which to convey content, and if not understood, requiring translation.

Speaking foreign languages is a valuable endowment and has its place (Barnes, 1949:277), with the caveats Paul had already attached in

CONTEXTUAL AND EXEGETICAL ANALYSIS

the prior verses (1 Cor 14:27– 28). With those conditions, in a multilingual congregation, the majority language group must not preclude other language speakers (Maclachlan, 2015:Kindle Location 1039). The Apostle Paul didn't want those brethren shut out and thereby lost to the congregation (Maclachlan, 2015:Kindle Location 1043).

CHAPTER 14 AND VERSE 40

When the Apostle Paul said that everything should "be done properly and in an orderly manner" (1 Cor 14:40), his readers would have understood the significant benefit of prophecy but also how that could be impeded and hindered by untranslated languages. From this understanding of the grammatical construction (1 Cor 14:39), we would derive that the Apostle Paul did not want the pomposity and prideful fixation on various earthly languages to get in the way of the edifying work of the prophetic word. This too would support the Epiphanius thesis.

So, in summary, modern English translations have insistently used "tongues" in 1 Corinthians, but without hesitation used the term "languages" elsewhere in the New Testament (Buchanan, 2012:5). Many translations have added supportive chapter-headings and notes (Buchanan, 2012:5–6). "Tongues" has become an entrenched theological term attracting much discussion and research. Modern Bible translators have almost set the mystical term "tongues" in concrete, with commentators effusively "describing" an esoteric phenomenon at Corinth, despite no audio or video recordings nor clear substantiation of it in the Greek biblical text of Acts or Corinthians. However, approaching the translation of 1 Corinthians chapters 12 to 14 with a *tabula rassa* (erased slate) mindset, in consistency, with the rest of the New Testament, translating γλῶσσαι (*glōssai*) as learned earthly languages, a cohesiveness is achieved and the implications for church life in the present era becomes plain. Edgar (1996:147) aptly concludes that: "In this passage there are no reasons, much less the very strong reasons necessary, to depart from the normal meaning of *glōssa* and to flee to a completely unsupported usage."

The Apostle Paul acknowledged that γλώσσαις (*glōssais*—languages) could be beneficial to the Corinthian congregation in their multilingual setting, but he also laid down guidelines. With the overarching

The Earliest View of New Testament Tongues

principle of edification (1 Cor 14:26) for the assembled: (1) Only two or at the most three would be allowed to speak in languages (1 Cor 14:27a). (2) Each was to take his/her turn (1 Cor 14: 27b). (3) Each language episode was to be translated/interpreted (1 Cor 14: 27c). The one speaking in his mother tongue or a language not known to the assembled, should pray in advance that he could translate/interpret (1 Cor 14:13). If he didn't think he had enough facility in the majority language, he should confirm in advance that someone was there who was willing to translate/interpret whatever he was going to share (1 Cor 14:27). Checking in advance of the meeting is implied, otherwise how would he know whether to begin speaking or keep silent and remain in his place. (4) If there is no interpreter, let him or her keep silent and remain in his/her place in the meeting and mentally express his thoughts to God. (5) Being that a minority language spoken and translated is equivalent to prophecy (1 Cor 14:5–6), it too would be subject to the assessment of others, along with the outright prophecy (1 Cor 14:29). (6) The use of minority languages should not hinder or impede prophecy (see explanation on previous verse 39). (7) "Let all things be done properly and in an orderly manner" (1 Cor 14:40).

Even Grudem (1999:419–420) admits that in the New Testament passages where γλῶσσα or γλῶσσαι (*glōssa, glōssai*) is discussed, "the meaning 'languages' is certainly in view. It is unfortunate, therefore, that English translations have continued to use the phrase 'speaking in tongues,' which is an expression not otherwise used in ordinary English and which gives the impression of a strange experience . . . "

Therefore, rather than produce my own translation for verses of 1 Corinthians 14 to demonstrate the premise, I will, immediately below, utilize the Holman Christian Standard Bible® translation (Copyright © 2009 by Holman Bible Publishers. Used by permission). The 2009 Holman Christian Standard Bible® was one of a few versions where the translation committee was consistent in translating "*glōssa*" (singular) or "*glōssai*" (plural) in the more natural sense to mean "language" or "languages" respectively, and not that of a mystical, esoteric, unearthly expression in the modern Pentecostal and Charismatic perception. Based on my foregoing study, I insert three "strikethroughs" and some square-bracketed info to strengthen the translation, but on the whole, I judge the translation following fairly represents the underlying Greek vocabulary, verbiage and grammatical construction.

CONTEXTUAL AND EXEGETICAL ANALYSIS

1. Pursue love and desire spiritual ~~gifts~~ [things], and above all that you may prophesy.

2. For the person who speaks in another [untranslated] language is not speaking to men but to God, since no one understands him; however, he speaks mysteries in the ~~Spirit~~ [spirit].

3. But the person who prophesies speaks to people for edification, encouragement, and consolation.

4. The person who speaks in another [untranslated] language builds himself up, but he who prophesies builds up the church.

5. I wish all of you spoke in other languages, but even more that you prophesied. The person who prophesies is greater than the person who speaks in languages, unless he interprets so that the church may be built up.

6. But now, brothers, if I come to you speaking in other [untranslated] languages, how will I benefit you unless I speak to you with a revelation or knowledge or prophecy or teaching?

7. Even inanimate things producing sounds—whether flute or harp—if they don't make a distinction in the notes, how will what is played on the flute or harp be recognized?

8. In fact, if the trumpet makes an unclear sound, who will prepare for battle?

9. In the same way, unless you use your tongue for intelligible speech, how will what is spoken be known? For you will be speaking into the air.

10. There are doubtless many different kinds of languages in the world, and all have meaning.

11. Therefore, if I do not know the meaning of the language, I will be a foreigner [in English "a barbarian." To a Greek, a "barbaros" was anyone who did not speak Greek], and the speaker will be a foreigner to me.

12. So also you—since you are zealous in matters of the spirit, seek to excel in building up the church.

13. Therefore the person who speaks in another [untranslated] language should pray that he can interpret.

14. For if I pray in another [untranslated] language, my spirit prays, but my understanding is unfruitful [to others].

15. What then? I will pray with the spirit, and [conjointly] I will also pray with my understanding. I will sing with the spirit, and [conjointly] I will also sing with my understanding.

16. Otherwise, if you bless with the spirit, how will the uninformed person say "Amen" at your giving of thanks, since he does not know what you are saying?

17. For you may very well be giving thanks, but the other person is not being built up.

18. I thank God that I speak in other languages more than all of you;

19. yet in the church I would rather speak five words with my understanding, in order to teach others also, than 10,000 words in another [untranslated] language.

20. Brothers, don't be childish in your thinking, but be infants in evil and adult in your thinking.

21. It is written in the law: By people of other languages and by the lips of foreigners, I will speak to this people; and even then, they will not listen to Me, says the Lord.

22. It follows that speaking in other languages is intended as a sign, not for believers but for unbelievers. But prophecy is not [primarily (see vs. 24)] for unbelievers but for believers.

23. Therefore, if the whole church assembles together, and all are speaking in other [untranslated] languages, and people who are uninformed or unbelievers come in, will they not say that you are out of your minds?

24. But if all are prophesying and some unbeliever or uninformed person comes in, he is convicted by all and is judged by all.

25. The secrets of his heart will be revealed, and as a result he will fall facedown and worship God, proclaiming, "God is really among you."

26. What then is the conclusion, brothers? Whenever you come together, each one has a psalm, a teaching, a revelation, another language, or an interpretation. All things must be done for edification.

CONTEXTUAL AND EXEGETICAL ANALYSIS

27. If any person speaks in another language, there should be only two, or at the most three, each in turn, and someone must interpret.
28. But if there is no interpreter, that person should keep silent in the church and speak to himself and to God . . . .
39. Therefore, my brothers, be eager to prophesy and to speak, and do not ~~forbid~~ [hinder/impede *prophecy* with] speaking in other languages.
40. But everything must be done decently and in order.

Another helpful translation worth a read is the one done by Buchanan (2012:11–13) where he is fair with the underlying Greek text. By being consistent in translating "*glōssa*" (singular) or "*glōssai*" (plural) in the more natural sense to mean "language" or "languages" respectively, he too gives us a helpful portrayal of what was probably going on the Corinthian assembly context. Although seemingly unaware of the Epiphanius thesis, Buchanan's work does lend support to aspects of it and certainly does not undermine it.

5.5 CONCLUSIONS

Luke connects the Jerusalem Pentecost with the conversion at Caesarea of Cornelius and his household members, who, according to Acts 10:46, magnify God in γλώσσαις (*glōssais*—languages) under the eye of the Apostle Peter and his Jewish compatriots ("circumcised believers" Acts 10.45). Twice more in the book of Acts, the Apostle Peter ties the momentous event at Caesarea as closely as possible with the inceptual Pentecost event at Jerusalem (Acts 10:47; 11:15; 15:8), otherwise it would not have been very convincing for the Jerusalem leadership of the new Jesus movement if the reception of the Holy Spirit by those first Gentiles had not similar authentication as their own experience at Pentecost (cf. Acts 11:15–17 "just as upon us at the beginning"). The members of the household of Cornelius magnified/praised God in various languages (Acts 10:44–47), as also did the 12 Jewish converts at Ephesus (Acts 19:6).

The skeptical Jews were the ones who needed to be convinced that this was genuine in respect to the Samaritans (Acts 8:4–25), the Gentile conversion scenario (Acts 10) and the twelve Jewish men at Ephesus (Acts 19:1–7). The latter occurrence would also have been an authenticating sign for the "unbelieving" Jews of the Ephesus synagogue, which Paul, immediately thereafter, spoke in for about 3 months (Acts 19:8).

So in the four representative events of Pentecost, Samaria, Caesarea and Ephesus, skeptical/unpersuaded Jews (ἀπίστοις/*apistois*; cf. John 20:27) were the ones who needed to be convinced that these were genuine workings of God by his Holy Spirit. Jews were present on all these occasions and, explicitly at Pentecost, Caesarea and Ephesus, there was the harmonization of "languages" as a sign for the Jews, whereas the Greeks seek "wisdom" (1 Cor 1:22). These were attestations that the Lord had incorporated all believers into the universal body of Christ (1 Cor 12:13).

What is of note is that Peter in his address, recorded in Acts 2, makes not even the slightest allusion to a supernatural bestowal of the languages just spoken by the 120 disciples. Peter seems not to be surprised, as if the languages just spoken by the 120 were previously unknown to them. He doesn't launch into a making a point about the supernaturalness or miraculousness of the languages spoken. This weighs in favour of the various languages that the 120 disciples there spoke being familiar to them, as in Greek and Aramaic (and possibly dialects of same and maybe Latin). These languages encompassed the then known Roman world and would have been the languages well known to these Diaspora Jews from the cradle (Acts 2:8).

So, we can assert with relative certainty that γλῶσσαι (*glṓssai*), as utilized by the first-century AD Messianic believers, was regarded as non-supernatural, learned earthly languages, in keeping with the Epiphanius thesis.

The Epiphanius thesis has been shown to be linguistically sound, culturally relevant, historically viable, contextually consistent and therefore exegetically preferable.

6

Translation Analysis of Any Shift in Meaning

FOR THIS CHAPTER OF translation analysis, the relevant passages for consideration are deemed to be Mark 16:17, Acts chapters 2, 10, 19 and 1 Corinthians 12, 14, concluding with Revelation 5:9, 7:9, 10:11, 11:9, 13:7, 14:6, 17:15.

6.1 WYCLIF BIBLE TRANSLATION OF "LANGUAGES/ TONGUES" (1380 AD)

The Wyclif Bible, the first-ever complete English translation of Scripture, was a literal translation of the Latin Vulgate, instigated by Oxford professor and theologian John Wycliffe. The majority of instances of γλῶσσα/γλῶσσαι (*glóssa/glóssai*) are translated *langagis* (languages) and not *tungis* (tongues) in the relevant texts, and most noticeably in the focal 1 Corinthians chapter 12 (verses 10, 28, 30) and chapter 14 (verses 6, 10, 18, 22), which are the subject of debate, without ever prefacing any with the adjective "unknown." For example, in 1 Corinthians 12:10, Wyclif reads *"kyndis of langagis"* (Bagster, 1841:770). It is definitional to observe how Wyclif translates I Corinthians 14:18: "I thanke my god, for I speke in the *langage* of alle you . . . " (Bagster, 1841:776).

The term *langagis* (languages) appears to have been the appropriate word in that day, although Wyclif is not entirely averse to using *langagis* and *tungis* as synonyms. *The Latin Vulgate, which Wyclif and associates translated from, traces back to Jerome in 382 AD, so I have used a Latin-English Dictionary that has classical Latin definitions into the third century AD (Oxford Latin Dictionary, 1968:v–vi).

6.2 TYNDALE BIBLE TRANSLATION OF "LANGUAGES/ TONGUES" (1535 AD)

The 1525 AD Tyndale translation was the first English version to be made also using the original Hebrew and Greek (Weigle, 1962:vii). At 1 Corinthians 13: 8, the adjective "other" misleadingly prefaces "tonges" in the Tyndale Bible (Weigle, 1962:976). The Tyndale final revision published in 1535 AD, in the relevant passages of Mark 16:17, Acts 2, 10, 19 and 1 Corinthians 12, 14, as well as the pertinent, figurative seven references from Revelation 5:9, 7:9, 10:11, 11:9, 13:7,14:6, 17:15 (Weigle, 1962:656, 658, 774, 972, 974, 976, 978–984, 1414ff), used the term *tonges* (plural) to consistently translate the Latin word *lingua*, which in the figurative, non-anatomical sense of the word is the "particular mode of speech prevalent in a given country, region, period, etc., a language, dialect" (Oxford Latin Dictionary, 1968:1033, §4). In respect to the translated old Latin term *lingua*, under the six variations listed, there is not an option of non-earthly, ecstatic, heavenly/angelic language (Oxford Latin Dictionary, 1968:1032–1033, §1–6).

6.3 CRANMER BIBLE TRANSLATION OF "LANGUAGES/ TONGUES" (1540 AD)

An interesting insight to begin this section is the biographical note about King Edward VI (October 12, 1537 AD–July 6, 1553 AD) that he began his formal education, under tutors concentrating, as he himself recalled, on "learning of tongues, of the scripture, of philosophy, and all liberal sciences" (Loach, 1999:11–12; Jordan, 1968:42). We find out that these "tongues" he learned were French, Spanish and Italian (Jordan, 1968:40; MacCulloch, 2002:8). Clearly, he was not learning ecstatic, non-earthly *glossolalic* tongues, but rather "tongues," as it was defined in those days, of normal, earthly languages, which required study.

Cranmer's Great Bible used the term *tonges* (plural) to consistently translate the Latin word *lingua*, which is defined as the "particular mode of speech prevalent in a given country, region, period, etc., a language, dialect" (Oxford Latin Dictionary, 1968:1033, §4).

Cranmer's Great Bible of 1540 AD (Weigle, 1962: 658), in Acts 2:6, uses the phrase "speake with his awne langage" and then "his awne tong" (Acts 2:8) and "oure awne tonges" (Acts 2:11), so there is interchangeability within the close context, obviously meaning native, earthly languages.

At 1 Corinthians 13: 8, the adjective "other" misleadingly prefaces "tonges" in the Cranmer Great Bible (Weigle, 1962:976).

6.4 GENEVA BIBLE TRANSLATION OF "LANGUAGES/ TONGUES" (1562 AD)

By 1562 AD, the Geneva Bible illegitimately added the adjective "strange" before "tongue" in 1 Corinthians 14:2, 4, 5, 13, 14, 19, 22, 23, 27, with "divers" being the unwarranted insertion before "tongues" in 1 Corinthians 14:6. In all cases, these spurious and misleading insertions are bracketed in the 1962 Weigle edition of the New Testament *Octapla*.

The idiom "unknown tongues" and its variants took on seemingly authoritative status after 1562 AD, when they were introduced in the Geneva Bible as a targeted partisan shot against the Catholic Church's liturgical use of the Latin unknown to their parishioners, which by the Reformers was regarded as spiritually "unprofitable" (see excellent expose by Blosser & Sullivan, 2022:Kindle Location p. 282–294). Even then, the polemic descriptor "unknown" carried no suggestion in the sixteenth century such as later attached to it by *glossolalic* Pentecostals and Charismatics of the modern era (Blosser & Sullivan, 2022:Kindle Location p. 293). Nevertheless, in the early twentieth century AD, in a marriage of convenience between German liberal, historical-critical theologians and Pentecostals, *glossolalia* became the new reinterpretation of "speaking in tongues" (Boddy, 1914:88–89; Bartleman, 1980:77, 167; Boddy, 1908:4).

The Geneva Bible "(strange) tongue" and KJV "unknown tongues" idiom was not meant to alter the traditional Christian understanding of "tongues" away from earthly languages, but such was the distortion that occurred over time. The "strange tongues" or "unknowen tongues" held to the universal understanding of "tongues" in church writings from the first century AD up to the nineteenth century AD, which "was understood to mean nothing more than *actual human languages*" (Blosser & Sullivan, 2022:Kindle Location p. 287).

Indeed, we glean this helpful understanding of the Apostle Paul's intent directly from the Geneva Bible translators of 1 Corinthians 14:18, which reads: "I thanke my God, I speake *langages* more than ye all" (Bagster, 1841:777; Weigle, 1962: 981).

6.5 RHEIMS BIBLE TRANSLATION OF "LANGUAGES/TONGUES" (1582 AD)

The Rheims Bible uniformly uses the word "tonge/tongue" or "tonges/tongues" through all the previously noted relevant verses (Mark 16:17, Acts 2, 10, 19 and 1 Corinthians 12, 14; Revelation 5:9, 7:9, 10:11, 11:9, 13:7,14:6, 17:15). However, in 1 Corinthians 12:10 (Weigle, 1962:972) and 1 Corinthians 14:21–22 (Weigle, 1962:980), within the same verse(s), Rheims interestingly uses "languages" and "tonges" interchangeably. Even through the above-noted seven pertinent Revelation verses, wherein the references undisputably mean earthly language groups, the Rheims Bible consistently translates "tonge" or "tonges."

The Rheims Bible does not use the adjective "unknowen" or any such variation in the relevant verses (Weigle, 1962). This is understandable in that this New Testament English translation was done by Roman Catholic scholars, closely adhering to the Latin Vulgate, in 1582 AD, as part of the Counter-Reformation (Weigle, 1962:ix). Understandably, these Catholic scholars would not be conceding any insertion of "unknowen" which the Protestants aimed at the unprofitableness of the Latin liturgy not understood by the common people (Blosser & Sullivan, 2022:Kindle Location p. 293).

6.6 BISHOP'S BIBLE TRANSLATION OF "LANGUAGES/TONGUES" (1568/1602 AD)

The Bishop's Bible as the successor to the Geneva Bible and the predecessor to the King James Bible reflects the trend to inserting adjectives meant to bolster the Protestant attack on the "unknowen" tongues/languages of the Roman Catholic Church.

The Acts 2 uses in the Bishop's Bible exhibit the momentum in the trajectory to the interchangeability of the two terms "languages" and "tongues" from the Wyclif Bible (1380 AD), the earliest under consideration, where *langage* (singular) and *langagis* (plural) were used in the 4 occurrences of Acts 2:4, 6, 8, 11 (Bagster, 1841:524, 526).

In the Acts 2:4, 6, 8, 11 verses, the Geneva Bible (1562 AD) uses *langage* in 2 out of the 4, specifically Acts 2:6, 8 (Weigle, 1962:659), and in the evident trajectory, the Bishop's Bible (1602 AD) uses *language* in only 1 of those 4 verses, namely, in Acts 2:6 (Weigle, 1962:659).

In the Bishop's Bible (1602 AD), with no support in the Greek text of 1 Corinthians 12:10, we begin to see the addition of "divers" to "kindes of tongues," while the Greek text simply has γένη (*genē*), so should be one or the other ("divers" or "kindes") but not both. Doubling up like that gives it perverse connotations, not intended in the Greek text. It should be "kinds of languages" or "divers (different) languages," but in their zeal to win the debate against the Catholic Church, to get the Bible translated into understandable, vernacular languages, the Reformers piled it on and inadvertently introduced terms that were seized upon and perilously distorted in course of time. The Bishop's Bible doesn't italicize the unfounded "divers" (1Cor 12:10). The KJV does.

6.7 AUTHORISED (KJV) BIBLE TRANSLATION OF "LANGUAGES/TONGUES" (1611/1873 AD)

To define the term "tongues," in the King James era, one six-word phrase in the title page of the King James Bible (1611:3) tells us everything: "THE HOLY BIBLE, Conteyning [Containing] the Old Teſtament, AND THE NEW: Newly Tranſlated [Translated] out of the Originall tongues: & with the former Tranſlations [Translations] diligently compared and reuiſed [reused], by his Maieſties [Majesty's] ſpeciall [special] Comandement. Appointed to be read in Churches. Imprinted at London by Robert Barker, Printer to the Kings moſt Excellent Maieſtie. Anno Dom. 1611." The "tongues" herein are specified as "Originall," understood to be Hebrew and Greek, which emphatically tells us that they were normal, earthly, learned languages. That, of itself, tells us what the word "tongues" meant in that milieu and should determine how we decipher that word every time we read it thereafter in the biblical books of the King James Version.

In offering more proof, the subsequent 28 mentions of "tongue(s)" (KJV, 1611:4–18), which concludes the prefatory explanation of "The

The Earliest View of New Testament Tongues

Tranflators [Translators] To the Reader" make it abundantly clear, in every instance, that "tongue(s)" means "language(s)" in the normal, earthly sense because they are designated: English or Hebrewe or Latine or Greeke or Dalmatian or Gothicke or Ethiopian, or original or sacred or vulgar or barbarous or mother tongue. In a same sentence, the Translators referred to the original sacred tongues (Hebrew and Greek), foreign languages and the English tongue, when describing the nature of their task—"that out of the Originall facred tongues, together with comparing of the labours, both in our owne and other forreigne Languages, of many worthy men who went before vs, there fhould be one more exact Tranflation of the holy Scriptures into the Englifh tongue." So, there was some interchangeability between "language(s)" and "tongue(s)" but no hint of extraterrestrial languages. *The "Translators To the Reader" piece was written, on behalf of the translators, by Dr. Myles Smith of Oxford University (Weigle, 1962:ix).

Furthermore, in the contexts of the word "tongue(s)" in "The Epistle Dedicatorie" and "Tranflators To the Reader," there's not the slightest hint that the languages possessed by the modest, self-effacing KJV translators were obtained by a supernatural dump of languages into their heads (cf. KJV, 1611:13). The translators regarded themselves as "poore Inftruments [Instruments] to make Gods holy Trueth to be yet more and more knowen vnto [unto] the people" (KJV, 1611:6). Thus, in the KJV context, it would be absurd to draw any other conclusion than that "tongue(s)" means "language(s)" in the non-supernatural, learned earthly sense, if one consults the KJV (1611 AD) title page, "The Epistle Dedicatorie" and "Tranflators To the Reader," (KJV, 1611:8–18).

If one distils the lengthy preface of the KJV (1611 AD), one discerns the castigation of the Pope and Catholic Church and the passionate concern to get the "word of God" out of the exclusive Latin and translated into understandable, known "tongues [languages]," in this case the English of the common people, so they could read it for themselves and be nourished (KJV, 1611:10–11). The Translators said that the "Popifh [Popish] perfons [persons]" "defire [desire] ftill [still] to keepe [the people] in ignorance and darkneffe [darkness]" (KJV, 1611:6). On the other hand, the Translators fervently wanted "to deliuer [deliver] Gods booke vnto [unto] Gods people in a tongue which they vnderftand [understand]" (KJV, 1611:13).

It's crucially important to keep this to the fore, that the KJV and its predecessor translations were being shaped in the cauldron of the

Reformation (1517–1648 AD), where deep political and religious tremors were convulsing the western world. The KJV Translators said that "a voice [voice] forſooth [forsooth] was heard from heauen [heaven], ſaying [saying], Now is poiſon [poison] powred [poured] down into the [Romish] Church" (KJV, 1611:6), so there was perceived to be a lot at stake.

The KJV of 1611 AD used the term *tonges* (plural) to consistently translate the Latin word *lingua*, which is defined as the "particular mode of speech prevalent in a given country, region, period, etc., a language, dialect" (Oxford Latin Dictionary, 1968:1033, §4), with no lexical option of non-earthly, ecstatic or celestial language (Oxford Latin Dictionary, 1968:1032–1033, §1–6). Even with that clear definition, the word "tongues" has become a significant theological problem because there are more than one thousand English words in the KJV which are now used in a substantially different sense (Weigle, 1962:xiii).

The KJV translators of 1611 AD used the term "unknown," before "tongue(s)," as a vigorous argument against the Roman Catholic church conducting services in the Latin language not understood by the common people in much of Europe (Blosser & Sullivan, 2022:Kindle Location p. 283).

The KJV insertion of the adjective "unknown" was not originally intended to give the impression that the tongues were "non-earthly languages." Speaking in γλῶσσα/γλῶσσαι (*glṓssa, glṓssai*) in the original KJV was not meant to classify it as a non-earthly, extraterrestrial language. This is an erroneous understanding of a translator's polemic insertion, which is straightforwardly acknowledged not to be in the original Greek text by the type set of italicization. Unfortunately, some less informed lay people misread the KJV text at this point, and some preachers, using the KJV text, urge less informed people to believe that the "unknown" tongues of the KJV is proof of ecstatic utterances (Blosser & Sullivan, 2022:Kindle Location p. 293–295).

With the addition of "strange" before "tongue(s)" in I Corinthians 14, the Geneva Bible had set the course for the Bishop's Bible and the Kings James Bible. So, in 1 Corinthians 14:2, the King James translators of 1611 AD inserted and italicized the adjectival phrase "unknowen" before tongue (Bagster, 1841:775) and made five more like insertions thereafter. The 1873 AD King James Bible retains the same six insertions (1 Cor 14:2, 4, 13, 14, 19, 27) of the adjectival "unknown" before "tongue" (Weigle, 1962:978, 980, 982).

The irony here is that many of us would now contend that the implied earthly, foreign language(s) referred to in 1 Corinthians 14, although known by the speaker, is actually unknown to the listening congregation and thus Paul's insistence that it be translated. However, the onus is on the exegete to make his case based on Paul's helpful contextual clues and the more clear passages in Acts. It is without warrant to place this in translation whereby uninformed preachers and misguided lay persons, not knowing the reasons for its original insertion, will make of it something quite different from what the Reformation translators intended. It's most unfortunate that the King James Version particularly misleads English Bible readers by using that descriptor "unknown" before "tongue." If an English reader is paying close attention, he will notice that the term "*unknown*" is italicized in the King James Version, acknowledging that it has no support in the underlying Greek text.

The other irregularity we notice in the King James Version is the italicized "diuers/divers" adjective placed before "kindes/kinds of tongues" in 1 Coritnhians 12:10 (Bagster, 1841:771; Weigle, 1962:972). It is also without basis in the underlying Greek text and it too has become harmful to sound interpretation for those who only work off an English text.

6.8 LUTHER'S TRANSLATION OF "LANGUAGES/TONGUES" (1483–1546 AD)

Martin Luther doesn't follow the English translators by adding the corresponding adjective of "unknown" in the German language.

In 1 Corinthians 12:10, 28, 30 and 1 Corinthians 13:8 and Revelation 5:9; 7:9; 10:11; 11:9; 13:7; 14:6; 17:15 (Luther, 1545:453–455; 638ff), Luther translates γλῶσσα (*glōssa*) and its various forms as "languages" (German "*Sprachen*"). On the book of Corinthians, Meyer (1884:285) noted that "In chap. xiv., however, he has still 'tongues' [*Zungen*] in 1545." We don't know why Luther had "*Sprachen*/languages" in most places but not in 1 Corinthians 14. In any event, we know that "For Luther and his foes, 'speaking in tongues' had to do with the Roman Mass offered in Latin: Luther said the vernacular is needed" (Spittler, 1988:339).

Martin Luther (Bergendoff, 1958:142) alleged that the Apostle Paul was, in 1 Corinthians 14, primarily concerned with the role of preaching and the listening and learning of the congregation. The German Luther used 1 Corinthians 14 to elaborate his position on preaching in the vernacular:

> Who ever comes forward, and wants to read, teach, or preach, and yet speaks with tongues, that is, speaks Latin instead of German, or some unknown language, he is to be silent and preach to himself alone. For no one can hear it or understand it, and no one can get any benefit from it. Or if he should speak with tongues, he ought, in addition, to put what he says into German or interpret it in one way or another, so that the congregation may understand it (Bergendoff, 1958:142).

Luther insisted that the Scripture reading and teaching and preaching in the believer's assembly be the vernacular language, using 1 Corinthians 14 to support his position. For Scripture reading and teaching and preaching in the believer's assembly, not in the language of the recipients, Luther insisted on the need for those *Zungen*/tongues (earthly, foreign languages) to be translated into the congregation's German vernacular for their benefit. The cure for the Epiphanius diagnosis of the Corinthian malady is remedied by Luther's prescription on 1 Corinthians 14.

6.9 CALVIN'S TRANSLATION OF "LANGUAGES/TONGUES" (1509-1564 AD)

John Calvin worked from the Greek text, but with the Vulgate open as he wrote in Latin. To him γλῶσσαι (*glōssai*) always referred to known languages. Calvin (1573:374–375) knew of many languages; he applauds learning them; he castigates his opponents for preventing people from learning them; he believes that in the Apostle Paul's day some might have had a miraculous knowledge of languages not learned by normal processes; but he never allows that Paul would have condoned truly unknown, non-earthly languages.

Calvin (1573:374–375) writes: "For it is incredible (at least we do not read of any instance) that there were any people who spoke by the influence of the Spirit, in a language they did not themselves know. For the gift of tongues was not bestowed merely for the purpose of making a noise, but rather for the purpose of communication, of course." Calvin, contemporaneous with the KJV, was not at all influenced by the English practice of having two synonymous words ("languages" and "tongues") to render γλῶσσαι (*glōssai*), and in Calvin's French translation, he expounded it as "languages" in the most consistent and normal use of the Greek (Buchanan, 2012:13).

In respect to Acts 2, Calvin, saw the "cloven tongues" as a signification that the preaching of the gospel was to spread abroad through all languages (Calvin, 1959:I, 34). This gift instigated preaching in foreign languages to reach the Gentiles (Calvin, 1965:I, 51). In Calvin's Acts Commentary (Vol. 1), Calvin (1965:318) rather specifically refers to "a variety of *tongues* to praise God in many languages" and they were given "for the Gospel had to be preached to foreigners with a different language, but also for the adornment and honour of the Gospel itself." Calvin then immediately goes on in the next sentence to write that "ambition afterwards corrupted this second use, when many carried over to ostentation and display" and that as a result "Paul has sharp things to say against this fault in the case of the Corinthians."

Calvin (1573:366), in commenting on 1 Corinthians 14:2, writes of the "gift of tongues" which was pursued by the Corinthians because it "had more of show connected with it, for when persons hear a man *speaking in a foreign tongue* [italicized emphasis mine], their admiration is commonly excited" and then Calvin goes on, with comment on the same verse, to explicitly say that "The term denotes a foreign language."

On 1 Corinthians 14:3, in elucidating the Apostle Paul, Calvin (1573:367) emphasizes that "Prophecy is profitable to all," "while a foreign language is a treasure hid in the earth" reiterating for the third time in the span of two short verses that it is an earthly, foreign language.

In commenting on 1 Corinthians 14:5, Calvin (1573:367-368) elaborates on his understanding of the efficacy of "foreign tongues" by asserting that this "knowledge of languages is more than simply necessary" and "the use of a foreign tongue is seasonable" as long as we "have an eye to this as our end—that edification may redound to the Church." Calvin here has his eye on the Catholic Church ultimatum that the teaching and rituals of the Church should be conducted in Latin, to which he and other Reformers strongly objected, because they wanted church services understandable in the various vernacular languages of the laity.

TRANSLATION ANALYSIS OF ANY SHIFT IN MEANING

On 1 Corinthians 14:11, Calvin (1573:372) states that "Paul views it as the height of absurdity, that a man should be a barbarian to the hearers, by chattering in an unknown tongue, and at the same time he elegantly treats with derision the foolish ambition of the Corinthians, who were eager to obtain praise and fame by this means." Like Epiphanius, Calvin understands the Corinthian problem to have been an issue of pompous people, with inflated egos, ostentatiously using earthly, foreign languages, in elevated manner, to pridefully posture in the assembly.

On 1 Corinthians 14:13, Calvin (1573:373), in interpreting the Apostle Paul, writes: "If any one, therefore, is able to speak a foreign language, will the gift be useless? Why should that be kept back, which might be brought out to light, to the glory of God? He shows the remedy. Let him, says he, ask from God the gift of interpretation also. If he is without this, let him abstain in the meantime from ostentation."

In expounding on 1 Corinthians 14:14, Calvin (1573:374-375) bluntly writes:

> It is not credible (at least we nowhere read of it) that any spoke under the influence of the Spirit in a language that was to themselves unknown. For the gift of tongues was conferred—not for the mere purpose of uttering a sound, but, on the contrary, with the view of making a communication. For how ridiculous a thing it would be, that the tongue of a Roman should be framed by the Spirit of God to pronounce Greek words, which were altogether unknown to the speaker, as parrots, magpies, and crows, are taught to mimic human voices!

On 1 Corinthians 14:16, in expositing the Apostle Paul, Calvin (1573:377) states that it is a plain prohibition: "What can be plainer than this prohibition—let not prayers or thanksgivings be offered up in public, except in the vernacular tongue."

Calvin's biblical commentary clearly demonstrates that he viewed "tongues" as earthly, foreign languages. Calvin, in the 1 Corinthians 14 passages above, does not posit the "gift of tongues" (earthly, foreign languages) for evangelism but primarily for edification. This supports the Epiphanius view that the languages (γλῶσσαι/*glōssai*) were to be used in the normal course of teaching Corinthian congregants and bringing spiritual understanding to those new believers. That Calvin (1965:318) believed it was being used in the ancient Corinthian congregation for "ostentation and display" also parallels the Epiphanius understanding.

7.0 CONCLUSIONS

For the translations of the Geneva Bible, the Bishop's Bible and the King James Bible, the idiomatic expression of "unknown tongues" solely referred to the Catholic Church's use of liturgical Latin. The idiomatic expression was not meant as a reference to anything mystical, such as an esoteric, unintelligible, celestial *glossolalic* language for public or private use (Blosser & Sullivan, 2022:Kindle Location p. 293–295).

The translators of the KJV New Testament knew the comparable words "language" and "translate," but always translated γλῶσσα/*glōssa* as "tongue," and *hermēneuō* or *diermēneuō* as "interpret." They used "tongue" as their normal synonymous word for "language," whereas for moderns it has taken on an esoteric, mystical meaning. As The New Testament Octapla editor, Weigle (1962:xii) candidly assessed: "The greatest problem is presented by those English words which are still in constant use but now convey a different meaning from that which they had in 1611 and in the King James Version." The KJV translators significantly confused the picture with the italicized "unknown" prefixed to "tongues" as a polemic against the Roman Catholic unknown Latin mass, so they did not see in γλῶσσα/*glōssa*, a language unknown on earth, which is today termed "*glossolalia*."

So what is the best way of rendering *glōssai* and *diermēneuō* in English? The flawed tradition, beginning with the Geneva Bible, enshrined in the King James Version, and followed by most main English versions ever since, has been to, without qualification, embrace the terms "tongues" and "interpret." Admittedly, middle-age English did use "tongues" for "languages" in an interchangeable sense. As with other KJV words: "These words were once accurate translations of the Hebrew and Greek Scriptures; but now, having changed in meaning, they have become misleading. They no longer say what the King James translators meant them to say" (Weigle, 1962:xii –xiii). It is unfair to the KJV translators, and to the truth they expressed, to retain words which now convey meanings they did not intend (Weigle, 1962:xiii).

In 1 Corinthians 12–14 the former interchangeability has been forfeited in regard to "tongues" and "interpret," and these innocent English equivalents for the Greek, have acquired a special religious sense from the KJV use of "unknown" in 1 Corinthians 14. And "it is that use we must revisit" (Buchanan, 2012:3), as, with the passage of time, it appears to no longer be a valid use. Other less confusing English words exist, such as "language(s)" and "translate."

To reiterate, *glossolalia* is actually not a term used in the New Testament by the Apostle Paul nor any other writer in the entire Bible and was first invented in the English by the theological writer, Frederic William Farrar, in about 1879 AD (Oxford English Dictionary, 1933:232). It is therefore anachronistic and misleading to put that meaning into the mouth of earlier translators, especially when contrary to their clear meaning in numerous places.

This translation analysis has not in any way undermined the Epiphanius thesis and appears rather supportive in that the earliest English translations essentially understood the original and pivotal Greek terms, γλῶσσα/γλῶσσαι (*glōssa/glōssai*), as normal, earthly language(s), and even the addition of the adjectival and polemical "unknown" was acknowledged, by bracketing or italicization, to have no textual basis. However, that eventually became a significant interpretational problem for the non-Greek lay reader as the mists of time obscured the polemic intent aimed at the *unknown* Latin of the Catholic liturgy.

In this chapter, the Epiphanius thesis has been shown to be compatible with the intent of the earliest English translations.

7

Summary, Findings, Conclusions

WITH ENGLISH SPEAKERS, THE term "languages" eventually overtook the term "tongues" in normal, street-level parlance, but the mystically suggestive "tongues" remained in the King James Version, and so to a great extent shaped biblical exegesis in the last century (Buchanan, 2012:5). The illegitimate KJV addition of the adjective "unknown," confirmed it in the minds of those illiterate in Greek and so "interpretation" arose alongside it (Buchanan, 2012:5). It's worth reiterating that in the New Testament alone, apart from those places where the Greek word γλῶσσα (*glōssa*) obviously means the literal tongue, the organ of speech, and leaving aside the debated 1 Corinthians occurrences, all the figurative references clearly mean earthly, learned "language(s)" (cf. esp. the seven references in Revelation).

It is important to remember that the Greek terms, of Luke in Acts and of Paul in 1 Corinthians, are identical on this matter. When one adds the weight of Luke and Paul's close personal and ministry companionship over a number of years, it is inescapable that if they used the same Greek term, they would have used it in the same sense (Johnson, 1963:310). It is most logical that Luke who wrote Acts, after Paul's Corinthians Epistles, would not have deviated from the terminology of the Apostle Paul (Johnson, 1963:310). Luke was undoubtedly informed by Paul about the event of John's twelve disciples at Ephesus, which Luke dutifully recorded in Acts 19:1–7, and Luke likely knew of the Corinthian tensions directly from Paul (Johnson, 1963:311).

SUMMARY, FINDINGS, CONCLUSIONS

Luke accompanied Paul on his final journey from Caesarea to Rome when Paul was a prisoner while Luke was his attending physician. Paul and Luke were shipwrecked off the coast of Malta in approximately 60 AD. It was probably during Luke's stay with Paul under house arrest in Rome that Luke wrote the book of Acts. Acts had to have been written before Paul's possible second imprisonment and martyrdom and the fall of Jerusalem in 70 AD because these momentous events are not mentioned in the book of Acts (Marshall, 1980:48; LaSor, 1972:22; Ger, 2004:6; MacArthur, 1994:3–5). Luke and Paul had intensive time together (Acts 16:10–40; Acts 20:5–21:18; Acts 27:1–28:14; Col 4:14; Phlm 24; 2 Tim 4:11), so it is to be expected that they would be consistent in their definition of γλῶσσαι (*glōssai*). Consequently, the full description of the language speaking at Pentecost "must be allowed to explain the more limited descriptions that occur elsewhere" (Johnson, 1963:311). The onus would be on skeptics to negate the above Scripture passages indicating that Luke and Paul spent significant time together and to conclusively prove that the use of "we" in the Acts passages (Acts 16:10–40; Acts 20:5–21:18; Acts 27:1–28:14) was no more than a literary convention and doesn't mean what it actually says. The skeptic would then also have the burden of responsibility to persuasively articulate why two close companions would use distinctly different meanings for the same Greek word when having a document scribed.

The Apostle Paul regarded the speaking and translating of multiple, learned, earthly languages to be "manifestations of the Spirit" (1 Cor 12:7–10) and "appointments of God" (1 Cor 12:11, 28) for the "common profit" (1 Cor 12:7), for the "edification" of other believers (1 Cor 14:5, 12, 26). The Apostle Paul emphasized that instead of insisting on using one's own distinctive language, be that Hebrew or a minority dialect of Greek, which would polarize the church and undermine the prophetic word and not edify, the overriding concern should be to communicate to others.

This required translation into the majority language, and prophets yielding the floor to one another, was so that clear verbal communication could be obtained. The individual speaking in a language, not familiar to most of those present, should translate it (1 Cor 14:5, 13) or be sure that someone else could (1 Cor 14:28). This kind of communication would build others up. The Apostle Paul set the stellar example, and although able to speak a number of foreign, earthly languages in the Corinthian assembly, he was willing to forego that to the end of speaking less but comprehensibly to his audience.

If we translate γλῶσσα (*glōssa*) as "language" and understand it as a language known and natural to the speaker, but not the majority language of the assembly, it is another foreign, earthly language, not mysterious, unearthly tongues. For a person to speak, pray, or sing "with the spirit" (1 Cor 14:13–15) is to use his natural, mother tongue because the speaker's "spirit" would instinctively vocalize this, whereas to speak, pray, or sing "with the mind" is to more consciously and cerebrally translate that into the majority language of the congregation, and therefore it could be said that the mind of the speaker is fruitful in respect to the hearers (Buchanan, 2012:8).

In integrating these migrant believers into the life of the congregation, Paul gave them the liberty to speak in their first language, be that Hebrew or a migrant minority Greek dialect, but required them to translate it into the majority Greek dialect (1 Cor 14:5, 13), and if they did not have that language facility, to check that someone in the assembly could translate on that occasion (Buchanan, 2012:9). If neither scenario for translation was viable, then the prospective minority language speaker should not address the assembly but should commune with himself and God while seated right there in the gathered assembly (1 Cor 14:28). After all, in 1 Corinthians 14, Paul's instruction for believers was in regard to their conduct in their gatherings, not advice for their private devotional times in their respective homes.

The huge advantage that Bishop Epiphanius had in understanding the Corinthian congregation scenario, borne out of the Hebraistic synagogue, was that he was born of Jewish parents in Judea and spent much of his life there (Thomassen & van Oort, 2009:xiii, iv et al.), which would tend to his having a more Hebraistic and less Gentile mindset. That he knew Hebrew seems likely based on his periodic Hebrew quotations.

This Jewish Hebrew background of his is unique among the post-Apostolic Greek and Latin Fathers where we get the first mentions of γλῶσσαι (*glōssai*). A few of the post-Apostolic Fathers may have been closer in time to the first-century Corinthian church, but not knowing Hebrew or the Hebrew culture and tradition firsthand, as Epiphanius did, put them at a significant disadvantage in understanding the Corinthian squabble.

SUMMARY, FINDINGS, CONCLUSIONS

Epiphanius, Romaniote Jew, who eventually became Bishop of Salamis, an ancient Greek city-state on the east coast of Cyprus, thus also had one foot in the Greek world of his day, and therefore would have been aware of the historic struggles for Greek dialect dominance throughout that region.

The huge factor, as described in the foregoing chapter 5.1, is the need to understand "other tongues/languages" from a first-century AD Jewish perspective in place of our Gentile understanding. Using the proper holy language in the worship service would have been a significant issue in the first century AD because the early assemblies of Jesus' believers were initially Jewish converts. And we know that the first controversy among the early Jewish believers was related to language, with the neglect of Hellenistic Jewish widows by the native Hebrew Jews (Acts 6:1ff). The Hellenistic Jews would have primarily used Greek in their worship services, whereas the Hebraistic Jews would have used Aramaic and Hebrew in their worship services (Zerhusen, 2020a).

In due course, there was the development of a predominantly Gentile church (ἐκκλησίᾳ/ekklēsia) caused by: the outward spread from Jerusalem of the Jewish believers because of persecution; the success of the Apostle Paul's missionary endeavours outside of Israel; the demolition of the Temple and devastation of Jerusalem in 70 AD, destroying the centre of Jewish ritual; the rejection of Christ by the majority of Jews and Christ's reception by many Gentiles (Zerhusen, 2020a).

As a result, the almost exclusively Jewish church (ἐκκλησίᾳ/ekklēsia) became almost exclusively Gentile and lost the Hebraic understanding of the scandal involving the use of profane languages in the Temple courts on the occasion of the Acts 2 Pentecost. In the 100-year gap thereafter, there was no discussion of the "other tongues" (Acts 2:4) controversy.

It is crucial to recognize this very telling gap of about 100 years, from the writing of Corinthians/Acts to the first known mention (about 160 AD), by any church figure, of γλῶσσαι (glōssai/languages), subsequent to the Apostolic Age. There is no relevant mention of the issue by any of the Apostolic Fathers, those handful who are reckoned to have directly known some of the twelve Apostles or to have been considerably impacted by them.

It is also significant that these first recorded remarks, ambiguous and misconstrued, on the γλῶσσαι (glōssai/languages) issue, were by

The Earliest View of New Testament Tongues

a Gentile, the post-apostolic Irenaeus (c. 130–c. 202 AD), bishop of what is now Lyons, France, who was far removed geographically and culturally from the Judean setting at the time of Jesus the Messiah. Greek-minded and Greek-speaking Irenaeus would have been without an indigenous knowledge of how important the Hebrew language was to the Temple ritual and to the first believers in Jesus who were all Jewish, as noted in the first several sections of chapter 3 of this book.

By the middle of the second century AD, the number of Gentiles in the church swamped the number of Jews. The Gentile and Greek domination would have decimated the Hebrew language ethos held by the first-generation believers in Judea and to which the Diasporan pilgrims to the major Jewish festivals were also exposed prior to the 70 AD destruction of the Jerusalem Temple.

The Gentile Church Father, Irenaeus, does not appear to have recognized that, to the Judeans and Diasporan Jews, Hebrew was ingrained as the "holy language" for a number of centuries, prior to Jesus' ministry, and all other earthly languages were viewed as just that—"other tongues/languages" (cf. Acts 2:4).

Irenaeus did not discuss Jewish culture in his interpretation of the phrase "other tongues" nor apply such first-century Jewish differentiation but, with his ambiguous statement on "other tongues," inadvertently shaped the discussion for almost the next seventeen hundred years. This Gentile understanding gripped the church for many centuries followed by our last century's misplaced vigorous debate around "cessationism" and "continuationism." With a wrong starting point, we have got way off track.

So if one asks about the audacity of this book's thesis, and that of other proponents herein, challenging the *xenolalic* language-miracle view of the Church Fathers, dominant for over seventeen centuries, the rejoinder is that this reasonable claim, of known, learned, earthly languages, actually takes us back to the original Acts and Corinthian contexts in the first half of the first century AD, about a hundred years prior to the first comment by a post-apostolic Early Church Father (Irenaeus) on the γλῶσσαι (*glṓssai*) topic. The ambiguous comment of Irenaeus appears to have confused or misled centuries of scholars, so modern-day advocates of that position ought not to feel shame-faced or defensive or the need to dig in, but should instead, with humility, carefully mull over the information herein.

SUMMARY, FINDINGS, CONCLUSIONS

A Romaniote Jewish Bishop, Epiphanius, born of Jewish parents in Judea, having spent much of his life there (Thomassen & van Oort, 2009:xiii, iv et al.), contended that the γλῶσσαι (*glōssai*) conflict in Corinth was a problem of prideful people using Hebrew and certain Greek dialects to posture as superior to others in the assembly. This interpretation meant that 1 Corinthians chapter 14 was not referring to a non-earthly phenomena nor being spontaneously given a previously unknown, unlearned, earthly, foreign language.

The Older Testament Scripture, which was originally in Hebrew, the prideful and inconsiderate use of Greek dialects—these components seem to have created a significant issue around the lack of verbal interpretation/translation and a resulting edification void and teaching deficiency within the Corinthian assembly. These indicators combined seem to have indicated it to be an interpretive or didactic problem within the Corinthian assembly rather than non-earthly utterance or supernaturally bestowed earthly languages. By the different sections and chapters in this book, the Epiphanius interpretation has been shown to be linguistically sound, culturally relevant, historically viable, contextually consistent, compatible with the intent of the earliest English translations, and therefore exegetically preferable.

The Apostle Paul's first canonical letter to the Corinthians and Acts 2, 10 and 19, appear to be unreliable support for modern-day ecstatic or non-ecstatic non-earthly "tongues." When these γλῶσσα/γλῶσσαι (*glōssa/glōssai*) passages are recognized as uncertain for building their case, I have encountered some Charismatics who resort to extra-biblical rationale and subjectivism on the matter before us. Some Charismatics might be okay with that approach of "tongues" not needing support in Scripture. However, to admit a questionable scriptural basis, but still dogmatically insist that it's from God, would make my more biblically-based Charismatic/Pentecostalist friends uncomfortable. Like all evangelical Christians, they require the sanction of Scripture to justify those things they most hold dear.

Over the years, some open-minded Charismatics/Pentecostalists have questioned their presuppositions. On this note, Zerhusen, whom I have quoted on the *diglossia* perspective, personally learned "to speak in tongues" in his home church, an Assemblies of God congregation, but he came to realize his "tongues" were what linguists call "free vocalization" (Maclachlan, 2015:Kindle Location 1736).

The Earliest View of New Testament Tongues

To reiterate and conclude this chapter on a practical basis, for the maximum edification of the congregants, Paul's basic guidelines were:

1. Those whose first language is different from the majority language of the congregation, may, with competent translation by oneself or another, make valued speaking contributions in the assembly of believers (1 Cor 14:5).

2. Speaking in a foreign language, with translation, may be the offering of a song, a teaching, or a disclosure of truth (1 Cor 14:26).

3. Foreign language speaking should be restricted to two or three persons maximally (1 Cor 14:27).

4. If no translator is known to be available, in advance of speaking, then the person should quietly express himself to God in his thoughts, right there in the assembly (1 Cor 14:28).

8

Contribution and Recommendations

THIS BOOK'S THESIS AFFIRMS the intrinsic value of the various languages throughout the world in that the gospel can now be disseminated to all nations. In that sense, languages can be considered a remarkable endowment of the Holy Spirit. Since that paradigm-shifting Pentecost which birthed the universal church, the good news can be proclaimed in common languages to all people and not just in Hebrew, Aramaic or dominant Greek dialects to Hebraistic or Hellenistic Jews. God's outreach is well beyond his chosen people who were subject to the Old Covenant.

As in the foregoing, the Epiphanius thesis has been shown to be linguistically sound, culturally relevant, historically viable, contextually consistent, compatible with the intent of the earliest English translations, and therefore argued to be exegetically more likely. So, we can adduce with reasonable certitude that, among Messianic believers, in the first century AD, γλῶσσαι (*glōssai*) was regarded as earthly, human, learned languages.

Nevertheless, the Holy Spirit can do something different in our time that does not violate the character of God. In other words, one can't put God in a box. The Spirit moves wherever he wants and, at times, does some surprising things. The Holy Spirit like "the wind blows where it wishes and you hear the sound of it, but do not know where it comes from or where it is going" (John 3:8). God doesn't need my consent. The stories of both Testaments demonstrate that God is creative, to put it mildly. He is frequently doing a new thing. Despite being skeptical of the modern phenomena, because of its susceptibility to fakery, manipulation and self-inducement since Azuza, as detailed in the chapter 4 historical analysis, it's fair to say that the Holy Spirit could do something different with γλῶσσαι (*glōssai*) than he did in the first century AD.

Nevertheless, we should also be candid to acknowledge that what is occurring these days with *glossolalia* is different from the description of "languages/tongues" as laid out in the pages of Holy Writ. Faupel (1996:108), at the time of his writing, stated that his Wesleyan church denomination questions "whether it [*glossolalia*] reflects New Testament practice. The primary reason given is the conviction that biblical tongues were actual languages while the contemporary phenomenon is not." At the conclusion of his academic article on the subject, Weaver (1973:23) concludes that "The present day phenomenon of Christians claiming to speak in tongues has some other explanation than that it is a continuation of the New Testament practice of the gift."

In assessing the hermeneutics of Pentecostals, Cargal (1993:180) admits that their modern phenomena, although using labels from the New Testament, are not in fact the same as in the first-century church. Pentecostalist Fee confesses (1976:122) that "in general the Pentecostal's experience has preceded their hermeneutics. In a sense, the Pentecostal tends to exegete his or her experience." Firstly, in the matter of recommendations, this "cart-before-the-horse hermeneutic" must be thoroughly re-examined by my Pentecostal and Charismatic friends.

The inference of an extra-biblical consensus of the Early Church Fathers (Greek and Latin), when alluding to Acts chapter 2, that γλῶσσαι (*glōssai*/languages) meant a supernatural ability to instantaneously speak previously unlearned, earthly languages, is not definitive proof that it actually was. It is an unproven presumption cogently contested in the foregoing for its lack of linguistic, cultural and historical support.

Because the Church Fathers are extra-biblical sources, without fear of being labelled a liberal, it is fair to call for further examination of why there may have been embellishment by some of the Early Church Fathers, especially as the pages of canonical Scripture do not make any explicit claim to all the Apostles having received a supernatural dump of certain foreign languages (*xenolalia*) nor all languages (*pan-xenolalia*). Even the Acts 2:4ff passage doesn't indicate that the speaking with "other languages" was previously unlearned languages, and the Apostle Peter makes no mention of it in his preaching that followed.

CONTRIBUTION AND RECOMMENDATIONS

In 1 Corinthians 14:11, the use of "if... then" (ἐὰν οὖν/*ean oun*) indicates that the Apostle Paul was well aware that he could not speak and understand all languages (Collins, 1999:499) and he did have the traumatic language deficiency of Acts 14:11–18, which turned concussive (Acts 14:19). As well, the several languages, for which Paul is thankful to God that he could speak (1 Cor 14:18), were most likely his learned languages, with no statement to the contrary supporting *xenolalia*.

Not a single one of the Apostles made the claim that they were given the supernatural ability to speak foreign languages. It seems to be an allegation that arose after the New Testament period. To play loose with a Scripture author's original meaning or overlay a meaning over the original intention damages the authority of inspired Scripture. On the other hand, the Epiphanius comments on the 1 Corinthians 14 passage demonstrates a literal, historical approach without discounting genre, immediate and broader context, and authorial intent.

Secondly, therefore, in recommendations, because of the 100-year gap before an Early Church Father commented on γλῶσσαι/*glōssai* (languages), which statement has been misconstrued to mean supernatural ability to instantaneously speak previously unlearned, earthly languages, there needs to be more scholarly scrutiny of the hermeneutical methods that may have affected a Church Father's interpretation of Acts 2, and corollary passages, perpetuating somewhat of a hagiographical commentary on this issue.

Because the whole matter of supernatural languages was "obscure" as Chrysostom says (NPNF, Series 1, Chrysostom Volumes, Vol. 12, Homily XXIX, p. 168) and not occurring, it may be because it had never started up in the first place and from the first mention of γλῶσσαι/*glōssai* (languages), by Irenaeus, in about 160 AD, there was misunderstanding. It may be that at that first mention onward there was embellishment and aggrandizement to legendary proportions, eventually arriving at the hagiographic status of supernaturally "speaking all languages."

Speaking all languages would hardly be necessary when the Apostles could get by quite well with Greek and Aramaic and some dialectal variations of same to the extent they fanned out in the first century AD (Beare, 1963:237; Haenchen, 1971:169; Neusner, 1965:10; Bruce, 1988:55; Hengel, 1980:115). Most of the 12 Apostles, who spread out from Jerusalem, missionized in close Greek lands and the remainder in near-by Aramaic-speaking countries. Thomas went the farthest, to

The Earliest View of New Testament Tongues

southern India, where they still use the liturgical Syriac language—a dialect of the Aramaic spoken by Thomas. (Tongue-in-cheek, none of the Apostles got as far as the Inuit or the Saami of the Arctic north polar regions.) Thus, there needs to be serious research on this strange exponential development to supernaturally "speaking all languages," when only the Greek and Aramaic languages were needed by the 12 Apostles for the limits of their missionary travels, and they had already learned those languages.

Thirdly, in the matter of recommendations, on the important issue of Bible translations/versions, going forward, it would be quite preferable to consistently use the updated terms "language/languages" everywhere the Greek words γλῶσσα (*glōssa*) or γλῶσσαι (*glōssai*) are in the New Testament text.

As a cautionary, regressive tale on this point, according to their "Q&A: Translation Decisions For The Christian Standard Bible" (Christian Standard Bible, 2017), the 2017 CSB appears to have backpedalled on this *glōssa/glōssai* issue from their earlier commendable approach in the Holman Christian Standard Bible® (Copyright © 2009 by Holman Bible Publishers) which "rendered the *lalein + glossa construction as 'languages'* rather than the traditional 'tongues' because the translators saw 'tongues' as an archaic way of referring to verbal communication. (For instance, people today write and speak of 'the Spanish language' rather than 'the Spanish tongue.')." Now in the more recent 2017 CSB version, the translators, not wanting "to exclude charismatic views of ecstatic speech" have reverted to "tongues." Having felt the heat of "many readers" (i.e., Charismatic complainants), and complicit with the Holman Bible Publishers, the translators caved in and have done a disservice to objective Bible translation in the contemporary era. "Though well-publicized and well-received in many circles, the HCSB [Holman Christian Standard Bible of 2009] never achieved a significant market share of Bible sales" (Strauss, 2019:260). Strauss (2019:277) gauges that with the change of language with reference to "tongues," etc., "the CSB will likely gain wider acceptance in the Christian community." Indeed, publishers need to sell lots of Bibles into the large Charismatic market, so alas, archaic, misleading, mystical language is reinserted or retained.

If, for reasons of marketing to the large Charismatic constituency, translators and publishers feel that they must use "tongue/tongues," at minimum, they should have clear and obvious footnotes which explain that the underlying Greek term(s), up until the present era, have been understood to mean "language/languages" in the ordinary, earthly sense of those words.

The world has many languages, and many local churches are comprised of people having diverse languages. In 1 Corinthians 14, God has provided instructions for navigating the issue of multiple languages and their beneficial utilization in a local assembly.

In 1 Corinthians 14, the Apostle Paul is emphatic that he wants clear translation of the various languages to occur so that congregants can comprehend what is said and be edified! This is God's Magna Carta—his Great Charter—for dealing with what could be a challenging and problematic issue in multilingual churches. May God bless multilingual churches as they use the principles laid out in the foregoing chapters to bring honor and glory to him. Soli Deo Gloria!

Bibliography

Abbott-Smith, G. 1922. A manual Greek lexicon of the New Testament. New York: Charles Scribner's Sons.

Adiego, J. 2007. Greek and Lycian. (*In* Christidis, A.F., ed. A history of ancient Greek: from the beginnings to late antiquity. New York: Cambridge University Press. p. 763–767).

Akers, B. 1995. The Gift of Tongues in 1 Cor. 14:1–5. *Paraclete*, Winter 1995, 29: 13–21.

Aland, B. and K., Karavidopoulos, J., Martini, C. & Metzger, B., eds. 2012. Novum Testamentum Graece (Nestle-Aland). 28th rev. ed. Stuttgart: Deutsche Bibelgesellschaft.

Aland, B. and K., Karavidopoulos, J., Martini, C. & Metzger, B., eds. 2014. The Greek New Testament (UBS GNT). 5th rev. ed. Swindon, England: United Bible Societies.

Alford, H. The New Testament for English Readers, volume 2. London: Rivingtons.

Ambrosiaster. 2009. Commentaries on Romans and 1–2 Corinthians. Translated from the Latin and edited by Gerald Bray. Downers Grove, IL: IVP Academic.

Amidon, P. 1990. The Panarion of St. Epiphanius of Salamis, Selected Passages. New York: Oxford University Press.

Andersen, F. I. (trans.). 1983. 2nd Enoch (Slavonic Apocalypse of). (*In* Charlesworth, J.H., ed. Old Testament Pseudepigrapha, Vol. 1: Apocalyptic Literature and Testaments. Garden City, NY: Doubleday. p. 91–221).

Anderson, A. 2006. The Azusa street revival and the emergence of Pentecostal missions in the early twentieth century. *Transformation*, April 2006, 23(2):109.

Anderson, R. 1979. Vision of the disinherited: the making of American Pentecostalism. New York: Oxford University Press.

ANF The Ante-Nicene Fathers: Translations of the Writings of the Fathers Down to A.D. 325, edited by Alexander Roberts and James Donaldson. 10 vols. 1885–1887. Grand Rapids: Eerdmans.

Anon. 1832. Revelation–The "Tongue." *The Monthly Review*, Jan. to April 1832, 1(1):32–33.

Appletons. 1889. Appletons' Cyclopedia of American Biography, Vol. 6, Zinzendorf. Edited by James G. Wilson and John Fiske. New York: D. Appleton.

Aquinas, T. 1947. The Summa Theologica. 1st complete American ed. Translated from the Latin by Fathers of the English Dominican Province. New York: Benziger Bros. https://www.ccel.org/a/aquinas/summa/SS/SS176.html#SSQ176OUTP1 Date of access: 24 Jan. 2023.

———. Super I Epistolam B. Pauli ad Corinthios lectura; Commentary On the First Epistle to the Corinthians by Saint Thomas Aquinas. Translated by Fabian Larcher, O.P. (987–1046 by Daniel Keating) Html-edited by Joseph Kenny, O.P. https://isidore.co/aquinas/SS1Cor.htm#141 Date of access: 24 Jan. 2023.

Babcox, N. 1985. A search for charismatic reality. Portland: Multnomah Press.

Bachmann, H. & Slaby, W.A., eds. 1980. Computer Konkordanz Zum Novum Testamentum Graece. Berlin: Walter de Gruyter.

Bagster, S. 1841. The English Hexapla. London: Samuel Bagster & Sons.

Baltes, G. 2014. The use of Hebrew and Aramaic in epigraphic sources of the New Testament era. (*In* Buth, R. & Notley, S., eds. The language environment of first century Judaea. Leiden: Brill. p. 35–65).

Barclay, W. 1958. The mind of St Paul: a lucid exposition of many aspects of St. Paul's thought. London: William Collins.

———. 1975. The letters to the Corinthians. Daily Study Bible Series. Philadelphia: Westminster.

Barentsen, J. 2011. Stephanas as model leader: a social identity perspective on community and leadership (mis)formation in Corinth. *Journal of Biblical perspectives in leadership*, Summer 2011, 3(2): 3–14.

Barnes, A. 1949. Notes on the New Testament: 1 Corinthians. Grand Rapids: Baker.

Barnett, P. 2012. Luke's Acts as a historical source for Paul. https://paulbarnett.info/2012/12/lukes-acts-as-a-historical-source-for-paul/ Date of access: 02 May 2024.

Barrett, C.K. 1968. The first epistle to the Corinthians. Harper's New Testament Commentaries. New York: Harper & Row.

———. 1971. Paul's opponents in II Corinthians. NTS, 17:233–254.

———. 1976. Acts and the Pauline Corpus. *Expository Times*, 88(1):2–5.

———. 1982. Essays on Paul. Philadelphia: Westminster Press.

———. 2004. Acts 1—14. The International Critical Commentary on the Holy Scriptures of the Old and New Testaments. London & New York: T & T Clark.

———. 2004. Acts 15—28. The International Critical Commentary on the Holy Scriptures of the Old and New Testaments. London & New York: T & T Clark.

Bartoli, D. & Maffei, J. 1889. St. Francis Xavier, Apostle of the Indies and Japan. Tenth American from the last London edition. Translated from the Italian. New York: P. O'Shea.

Bartleman, F. 1980. Azusa Street (Reprint of the 1925 ed. titled "How Pentecost came to Los Angeles" with foreword by Vinson Synan). Plainfield, NJ: Logos International.

Bauer, W. 2021. A Greek-English lexicon of the New Testament and other early Christian literature, 4th ed. Translated and adapted from the German 6th revised and augmented edition by W.F. Arndt and F.W. Gingrich and F.W. Danker. Revised and edited by F.W. Danker from W. Bauer's 6th ed. Chicago: University of Chicago press.

Bauman, R. 1992. Women and politics in ancient Rome. New York: Routledge.

Baur, F.C. 1845. Paulus, der Apostel Jesu Christi, sein Leben und Wirken, seine Briefe und seine Lehre. Stuttgart : Berlag von Becher & Muller.

———. 1875. Paul the apostle of Jesus Christ, his life and work, his epistles and his doctrine. Second German Edition, edited after the death of the author by Eduard Zeller. Translated by A. Menzies. Edinburgh: Edinburgh University Press.

Baxter, R. 1981. Charismatic gift of tongues. Grand Rapids: Kregel.

Beale, G. 2005. The descent of the eschatological temple in the form of the Spirit at Pentecost. Part 2, Corroborating evidence. *Tyndale Bulletin*, 56(2): 63–90.

Beare, F. 1964. Speaking with tongues: a critical survey of the New Testament evidence. *Journal of Biblical Literature*, 83: 229–246.

———. 1986. Speaking with tongues: a critical survey of the New Testament evidence. (*In* Mills, W. ed. Speaking in tongues: a guide to research on glossolalia. Grand Rapids: Eerdmans. p. 107–126).

Beckwith, R. 2008. The Old Testament Canon of the New Testament Church. Eugene, Oregon: Wipf and Stock Publishers.

Bengel, J. 1873. Gnomon of the New Testament, Volume 2. Translated by Andrew Fausset. Edinburgh: T. & T. Clark.

Benson, J. 2019 (originally published 1811–1818). Joseph Benson's commentary of the Old and New Testaments [Kindle ed.]. Available http://patristic.altervista.org

Berding, K. 2000. Confusing word and concept in "spiritual gifts": have we forgotten James Barr's exhortations? *Journal of the Evangelical Theological Society*, March 2000, 43(1):37–54.

Bergendoff, C. 1958. Luther's works, volume 40: church and ministry II. Philadelphia: Fortress Press.

Berkhof, L. 1952. Principles of Biblical Interpretation. 2nd ed. Grand Rapids: Baker.

Bernadette, J. 1990. Paul and the Law: how complete was the departure? *The Princeton Seminary Bulletin*, 1:71–89.

Bickerman, E. 1985. The Jews in the Greek age. Cambridge, MA: Harvard University Press.

Bietak, M. 2003. Israelites found in Egypt. *Biblical Archaeology Review*, 29(5):1–13.

Bigg, C. 1902. Epistles of St. Peter and St. Jude. 2nd ed. Edinburgh: T. & T. Clark.

Billings, B. 2014. The apistoi and idiotes in 1 Corinthians 14:20–25: The Ancient Context and Missiological Meaning. *The Expository Times*, 126(3):277 –285.

Birnbaum, P. 1964. A book of Jewish concepts. New York: Hebrew Publishing Company.

Bittlinger, A. 1967. Gifts and graces: a commentary on 1 Corinthians 12–14. Translated by Herbert Klassen. London: Hodder & Stoughton.

Black, M. 1962. Pharisees. (*In* Buttrick, G., ed. The Interpreter's Dictionary of the Bible. Nashville: Abingdon Press. p. 774–781).

Blackwelder, B. 1971. Letters from Paul: an exegetical translation. Anderson, IN: Warner Press.

Blanc, M. 1994. Societal bilingualism. (*In* Asher, R., ed. Encyclopedia of Language and Linguistics, 1. Oxford: Pergamon Press. p. 355).

Bloch, R. 1978. Methodological note for the study of rabbinic literature. (*In* Green, W., ed. Approaches to ancient Judaism: Theory and Practice. Missoula, MT: Scholars. p. 51–75).

Blomberg, C.L. 1994. 1 Corinthians. The NIV Application Commentary [Kindle ed.]. Grand Rapids: Zondervan.

Blosser, P. & Sullivan, C. 2022. Speaking in tongues: a critical historical examination: volume 1: the modern redefinition of tongues. [Kindle ed.] Eugene, OR: Wipf and Stock. Available: https://www.amazon.ca

Blumhofer, E. 1993. Restoring the faith: the Assemblies of God, Pentecostalism, and American culture. Chicago: University of Illinois Press.

Bock, D. 2007. Acts (Baker Exegetical Commentary on the New Testament). Grand Rapids: Baker.

BIBLIOGRAPHY

Boddy, A. 1908. *Confidence*. May 1908, 1(2):4.

———. 1914. *Confidence*. May 1914, 7(5):88–89.

Bollandists. 1897. Analecta Bollandiana, volume XVI, edited by Carolus de Smedt et al. Brussels: Société des Bollandistes.

Boote, D. & Beile, P. 2005. Scholars before researchers: On the centrality of the thesis literature review in research preparation. *Educational Researcher*, 34(6):3–15.

Borgen, P. 1996. Early Christianity and Hellenistic Judaism. Edinburgh: T&T Clark.

Borst, A. 1957. Der Turmbau von Babel: Geschichte der Meinungen iiber Ursprung und Vielfalt der Sprachen und Volker (The tower of Babel: history of opinions on the origin and diversity of languages and peoples), Vol. 1. Stuttgart: Anton Hiersemann.

Bouhours, D. 1688. The Life of Francis Xavier. Translated by John Dryden. London: Printed for Jacob Tonson, at the Judges-Head in Chancery-lane.

Bradshaw, P. 2008. Daily prayer in the early church: A study of the origin and early development of the divine office. Eugene, OR: Wipf and Stock.

Branick, V. 1989. The house church in the writings of Paul. Wilmington, DE: Glazier.

Britannica, Encyclopedia. 2023. Edict of Villers-Cotterêts. https://www.britannica.com/topic/Edict-of-Villers-Cotterets Date of access: 26 Feb. 2023.

Britannica, Encyclopedia. 2023. Edward Irving. https://www.britannica.com/biography/Edward-Irving Date of access: 13 Feb. 2023.

Britannica, Encyclopedia. 2023. Francis Xavier. https://www.britannica.com/biography/Saint-Francis-Xavier Date of access: 28 Jan. 2023.

Britannica, Encyclopedia. 1911. Irving, Edward, Encyclopedia Britannica, Vol. 14. 11th ed. Cambridge, UK: Cambridge University Press.

Britannica, Encyclopedia. 2023. John Calvin. https://www.britannica.com/biography/John-Calvin Date of access: 03 Feb. 2023.

Britannica, Encyclopedia. 09 2023. Michael Psellus. https://www.britannica.com/biography/Michael-Constantine-Psellus Date of access: 20 Jan. 2023.

Britannica, Encyclopedia. 2023. Occitan Language. https://www.britannica.com/topic/Occitan-language Date of access: 20 Jan. 2023.

Britannica, Encyclopedia. 2023. St. Leo I. https://www.britannica.com/biography/Saint-Leo-I Date of access: 05 Feb. 2023.

Britannica, Encyclopedia. 2023. Zinzendorf. https://www.britannica.com/biography/Nikolaus-Ludwig-Graf-von-Zinzendorf Date of access: 10 Feb. 2023.

British Museum. 2023. François Maximilien Misson. https://www.britishmuseum.org/collection/term/AUTH224990 Date of access: 04 Feb. 2023.

Brixhe, C. 2007. Greek translation of Lycian. (*In* Christidis, A.F., ed. A history of ancient Greek: from the beginnings to late antiquity. New York: Cambridge University Press. p. 924–934).

Brock, S. 1972. The phenomenon of the Septuagint. *Oudtestamentische Studiën, Old Testament Studies* (OtSt), 17:11–36.

———. 1992. To revise or not to revise: attitudes to Jewish biblical translation. (*In* Brooke, G. & Lindars, B. eds. Septuagint, scrolls and cognate writings, Society of Biblical Literature Septuagint and Cognate Studies Series, Number 33. Atlanta: Scholars Press. p. 301–338).

Broneer, O. 1951. Corinth. *The Biblical Archaeologist*, 14(4):77–96.

Brown, R. & Meier, J. 1983. Antioch and Rome: New Testament cradles of Catholic Christianity. New York: Paulist Press.

Bruce, F. F. 1952. The Acts of the Apostles: the Greek text with introduction and commentary. 2nd ed. Grand Rapids: Eerdmans.
———. 1954. Commentary on the book of Acts, NICNT. Grand Rapids: Eerdmans.
———. 1977. Paul: Apostle of the heart set free. Grand Rapids: Eerdmans.
———. 1988. The book of the Acts. Grand Rapids: Eerdmans.
———. 1990. The Acts of the Apostles: the Greek text with introduction and commentary. 3rd ed. Grand Rapids: Eerdmans.
Bubenik, V. 2007. The decline of the ancient dialects. (*In* Christidis, A.F., ed. A history of ancient Greek: from the beginnings to late antiquity. New York: Cambridge University Press. p. 482–485).
Buchanan, C. 2012. 1 Corinthians and tongues revisited. [Kindle ed.]. (*In* Bridger, F., ed. Conversations at the edges of things: reflections for the church in honor of John Goldingay. Eugene, OR: Pickwick Publications. p. 1–13).
Buck, C.D. 1900. The source of the so-called Achaean-Doric Koine. *The American Journal of Philogy*, 21(2):193–196.
Budiselić, E. 2016. Glossolalia: why Christians can speak in tongues in a church service without interpretation. *Kairos—Evangelical Journal of Theology*, 10(2):177–201.
Burgess, S. 1976. Medieval examples of charismatic piety in the Roman Catholic Church. (*In* Spittler, R., ed. Perspectives on the new Pentecostalism. Grand Rapids: Baker. p. 14–26).
Burkert, W. 1995. Lydia between East and West or How to date the Trojan War: a study in Herodotus. (*In* Carter, J.B. & Morris, S.P. eds., The ages of Homer, a tribute to E.T. Vermeule. Austin: University of Texas Press. p. 139–148).
Burton, E. 1955. Syntax of the Moods and Tenses in New Testament Greek, 3rd ed. Edinburgh: T & T Clark.
Busenitz, N. 2006. The Gift of Tongues: Comparing the Church Fathers with contemporary Pentecostalism. *Master's Seminary Journal*, Spring 2006, 17(1):61–78.
Busenitz, N. 2014. Are tongues real foreign languages?: A response to four continuationist arguments. *Master's Seminary Journal*, Fall 2014, 25(2):63–84.
Butler, A. 1938. Butler's lives of the saints, 12 volumes, edited by H. Thurston. [Kindle ed.]. Available: https://www.amazon.ca
Butler, C. 1985. Test the spirits: the charismatic phenomenon. Great Britain: Evangelical Press.
Buttmann, A. 1891. A grammar of the New Testament Greek. Translated from the German by J. H. Thayer. Andover, MA: Warren F. Draper Publisher
Calvin, J. 1573. Commentaries on the epistles of Paul the Apostle to the Corinthians, volume 1. Translated from the original Latin, and collated with the author's French version by John Pringle. Grand Rapids: Christian Classics Ethereal Library. https://ccel.org/ccel/c/calvin/calcom39/cache/calcom39.pdf (Adobe Acrobat printing) Date of access: 31 Jan. 2023.
———. 1959. Commentaries: the gospel according to John, volume 1. Grand Rapids: Eerdmans.
———. 1965. Commentaries: the acts of the Apostles, volume 1. Translated from the Latin and compared with the French by W.J.G. McDonald and John W. Fraser. Grand Rapids: Eerdmans.

BIBLIOGRAPHY

Campbell, W. 2016. Paul, antisemitism, and early Christianity identity making. (*In* Boccaccini, G. & Segovia, C., eds. Paul the Jew: rereading the Apostle as a figure of second temple Judaism. Minneapolis: Fortress Press. p. 301–340).

Cantarella, E. 1987. Pandora's daughters: the role and status of women in Greek and Roman antiquity. Baltimore: Johns Hopkins University Press.

Cargal, T. 1993. Beyond the Fundamentalist-Modernist Controversy: Pentecostals and Hermeneutics in a Postmodern Age. *Pneuma* 15(2):163–187.

Carson, D.A. 1987. Showing the Spirit: a theological exposition of 1 Corinthians 12–14. Grand Rapids: Baker.

Carter, C.W. 1969. A Wesleyan view of the Spirit's gift of tongues in the book of Acts. *Wesleyan Theological Journal*, 4:39–68.

Chadwick H. & Edwards, M. 2012. Theodoret. (*In* Hornblower, S. & Spawforth, A. eds. Oxford Classical Dictionary, 4th ed. Oxford: Oxford University Press. p. 1457).

Chancey, M. 2005. Greco-Roman culture and the Galilee of Jesus. Cambridge, UK: Cambridge University Press.

Chapman, H. 1908. Clement I, Saint, Pope. (*In* Catholic Encyclopedia. 4:12–17).

Charlesworth, J.H., ed. 1983. The Old Testament pseudepigrapha, volume 1. Garden City, New York: Doubleday.

———. 1985. The Old Testament pseudepigrapha, volume 2. Garden City, New York: Doubleday.

Chow, J. 1992. Patronage and power: a study of social networks in Corinth. Sheffield: JSOT.

Christian Standard Bible. 2017 https://csbible.com/wp-content/uploads/2017/01/Translation-Decisions-QA.pdf. Date of access: 11 Dec. 2023.

Christidis, A.F., ed. 2007. A history of ancient Greek: From the beginnings to late antiquity. English translation from original Greek version of 2001. New York: Cambridge University Press.

Chrysostom, J. 1984. On the incomprehensible nature of God: the fathers of the church, Vol.72. Translated by Paul Harkins. Washington, D.C.: Catholic University of America Press.

———. 1998. John Chrysostom, against the Jews. Homily 1. Translator unknown. http://www.tertullian.org/fathers/chrysostom_adversus_judaeos_01_homily1.htm Date of access: 1 Nov. 2019.

Ciampa, R.E. & Rosner, B.S. 2006. The structure and argument of 1 Corinthians: A Biblical/Jewish approach. *New Testament Studies*, 52(2):205–218.

———. 2010. The first letter to the Corinthians. The Pillar New Testament Commentary. [Kindle ed.]. Grand Rapids: Eerdmans. Available: https://www.amazon.ca

Cite langue francaise. 2023. Ordinance of Villers Cotterets. https://www.cite-langue-francaise.fr/en/Discover/The-monument/the-Ordinance-of-Villers-Cotterets-the-founding-myth-of-the-French-language Date of access: 26 Feb. 2023.

Clark, G. 1975. 1 Corinthians: a contemporary commentary. Nutley, NJ: Presbyterian and Reformed Publishing Company.SSS

Clarke, Adam. 1967. Adam Clarke's commentary: one volume edition. Grand Rapids: Baker.

Clarke, A. 1993. Secular and Christian leadership in Corinth: a socio-historical and exegetical study of 1 Corinthians 1–6. Leiden: Brill.

Clemen, C. 1931. Religions of the world. Translated from the German by A. K. Dallas. London: George G. Harrap.

BIBLIOGRAPHY

Cohen, S.J.D. 1998. A portrait of Jesus' world—The Jewish Diaspora | From Jesus to Christ—The first Christians | FRONTLINE | PBS. Date of access: 30 June 2022.

———. 1999. The beginnings of Jewishness: boundaries, varieties, uncertainties, Hellenistic culture and society. Berkeley: University of California Press.

Collins, R. 1999. First Corinthians. Sacra Pagina. Collegeville, Minnesota: The Liturgical Press.

Conway, P. 1911. Saint Thomas Aquinas of the order of preachers. London: Longmans, Green.

Conybeare, W. & Howson, J. 1863. The life and epistles of St. Paul, two volumes in one. People's ed. London: Longman, Green, Longman, Roberts, & Green.

Conzelmann, H. 1975. 1 Corinthians: a commentary on the first epistle to the Corinthians. Hermeneia. Philadelphia: Fortress Press.

Cooper, D. 1947, 1949. Rules of interpretation: third rule, the golden rule of interpretation. *Biblical Research Monthly*. https://www.biblicalresearch.info/page47.html Date of access: 25 Aug. 2023.

Cooper, H. 2010. Research synthesis and meta-analysis: A step-by-step approach. 4th ed. Thousand Oaks, CA: Sage.

Copeland, L. 1991. Speaking in Tongues in the Restoration Churches. *Dialogue: A Journal of Mormon Thought*, 24(1):13-35.

Cremer, H. 1895. Biblico-Theological Lexicon of New Testament Greek. Edinburgh: T&T Clark.

Creswell, J.H. & Creswell, J.D. 2018. Research design qualitative, quantitative, and mixed methods approaches. 5th ed. Thousand Oaks, CA: Sage.

Crystal, D. 1989. The Cambridge encyclopedia of language. New York: Cambridge University Press.

Currie, S. 1965. "Speaking in Tongues": early evidence outside the New Testament bearing on "Glossais Lalein." *Interpretation: A Journal of Bible and Theology*, 19(3):274-94.

Cyril of Alexandria. 1872. Cyrilli: Archiepiscopi Alexandrini. In Epistolam I Ad Corinthios, 14:10. (*In* Pusey, P., ed. D. Joannis Evangelium. London: Oxford. p. 293-294).

Dalman, G. 1929. Jesus-Jeshua. New York: Macmillan.

Daniel-Rops, H. 1962. Daily life in the time of Jesus. New York: Hawthorn.

Daube, D. 1956. The New Testament and rabbinic Judaism. London: Athlone.

Davies, J.G. 1952. Pentecost and glossolalia. *Journal of Theological Studies*, 3(2):228-231.

Deissmann, A. 1927. Light from the ancient east. Translated from the German by L.R.M. Strachan. New York: George H. Doran.

De Waard, J. 1965. A comparative study of the Old Testament text in the Dead Sea Scrolls and in the New Testament. Leiden: Brill.

Dines, J. 2004. The Septuagint. New York: T&T Clark.

Dio Chrysostom. 1946. Dio Chrysostom, Vol. 4, Discourses 37-60, Loeb Classical Library 376. Translated by H. Lamar Crosby. Cambridge, MA: Harvard University Press.

Dix, G. 1953. The 'Hellenization' of the Gospel. Uppsala: Almqvist & Wiksells.

Dorson, R. 1973. Introduction: folklore and traditional history. (*In* Dorson, R., ed. Folklore and traditional history. Berlin: De Gruyter Mouton. p. 7-9).

BIBLIOGRAPHY

Dosuna, J. Mendez. 2007. The Doric dialects. (*In* Christidis, A.F., ed. A history of ancient Greek: from the beginnings to late antiquity. New York: Cambridge University Press. p. 444–459).

Drimbe, A. 2019. Paul's use of the Old Testament in the First Letter to the Corinthians (I): exegetical techniques and devices. *Jurnal teologic*, 18(2):37–82.

Dryer, M. 1989. Large linguistic areas and language sampling. *Studies in Language*, 13(2):257–292.

Dunn, J. 1975. Jesus and the Spirit. Philadelphia: Westminster.

———. 1985. Works of the Law and the curse of the Law. *New Testament Studies*, 31:423–434.

———. 1996. The Acts of the Apostles. Grand Rapids: Eerdmans.

———. 1999. Who did Paul think he was? A study of Jewish-Christian identity. *New Testament Studies*, 45:174–193.

———. 2006. The Partings of the ways between Christianity and Judaism and their significance for the character of Christianity. 2nd ed. London: SCM.

Du Toit, P. 2016. Was Paul fully Torah observant according to Acts? *HTS Theological Studies*, 72(3):1–9.

———. 2019. God's saved Israel. Eugene, OR: Pickwick Publications.

Eberhard, D., Simons, G., & Fennig, C., eds. 2023. Ethnologue: languages of the world. 26th edition. Dallas, TX: SIL International. Online version: http://www.ethnologue.com.

Eddy, P. & Boyd, G. 2007. The Jesus legend: a case for the historical reliability of the synoptic Jesus tradition. Grand Rapids: Baker.

Edersheim, A. 1876. Sketches of Jewish social life in the days of Christ. Grand Rapids: Eerdmans.

Edgar, T. 1996. Satisfied by the promise of the Spirit. Grand Rapids: Kregel.

Edmundson, G. 1913. The church in Rome in the first century. London: Nabu.

Edwards, T.C. 1886. A commentary on the first epistle to the Corinthians. 2nd ed. New York: A.C. Armstrong & Son.

Ekem, J.D. 2004. "Spiritual gifts" or "spiritual persons"? 1 Corinthians 12:1a revisited. Neot 38: 54–74.

Ellis, E. 1975. Paul and his opponents. (*In* Smith, M. & Nuesner, J., eds. Christianity, Judaism and other Greco-Roman cults. Leiden: Brill. p. 264–298).

———. 2003. Paul's use of the Old Testament. Eugene, OR: Wipf and Stock.

Engelbrecht, E. 1996. "To speak in a tongue": The Old Testament and early rabbinic background of a Pauline expression. *Concordia Journal*, July, 22(3):295–302.

Engels, D. 1990. Roman Corinth: an alternative model for the classical city. Chicago: University of Chicago Press.

Epiphanius. 2009. *The Panarion of Epiphanius of Salamis*. Book I (Sects 1–46), edited by E. Thomassen & J. van Oort. Second Edition, Revised and Expanded. Translated by Frank Williams. Leiden: Brill. (Nag Hammadi & Manichaean studies, Vol. 63).

Eerdman, C. 1966. The first epistle of Paul to the Corinthians. Philadelphia: Westminster.

Eisenbaum, P. 2009. Paul was not a Christian: The original message of a misunderstood apostle. New York: Harper Collins.

Eusebius, P. 1926. Eusebius: the ecclesiastical history, volume 1. With an English translation by Kirsopp Lake. London: William Heinemann.

Eusebius, P. s311–325 AD? Eusebius Caesariensis Historia ecclesiastica (Greek version) http://www.documentacatholicaomnia.eu/03d/0265-0339%2C_Eusebius_

Caesariensis%2C_Historia_Ecclesiastica%2C_GR.pdf. Date of access: 17 Dec. 2022.

Farrar, F. 1880. The life and work of St. Paul, volume 1. New York: E.P. Dutton.

Faupel, D.W. 1996. Glossolalia as Foreign Language: Investigation of the Early Twentieth-Century Pentecostal Claim. *Wesleyan Theological Journal*, Spring 1996, 31:95–109.

Fausset, A. 1873. A Commentary, critical and explanatory, on the Old and New Testaments by Jamieson, Fausset, Brown, Vol. 2, New Testament. New York: S. S. Scranton and Company.

Fee, G.D. 1976. Hermeneutics and historical precedent. (*In* Spittler, R., ed. Perspectives on the new Pentecostalism. Grand Rapids: Baker. p. 118–132).

———. 1987. The first epistle to the Corinthians. The New International Commentary on the New Testament. Grand Rapids: Eerdmans.

———. 1990. God's empowering presence: The Holy Spirit in the letters of Paul. Peabody, MA: Hendrickson.

———. 1993. Gifts of the Spirit. (*In* Hawthorne, G. & Martin, R. & Reid, D. eds. Dictionary of Paul and his letters. Downers Grove, IL: IVP. p. 339–347).

———. 2002. New Testament exegesis: A handbook for students and pastors. Philadelphia: Westminster.

———. 2014. The first epistle to the Corinthians, revised edition. The New International Commentary on the New Testament. Grand Rapids: Eerdmans.

Feldman, L. 1986. The omnipresence of the God-Fearers. *Biblical Archaeology Review*, 12(5):58–63.

Ferguson, C. 1959. Diglossia. *Word*, 15(2):325–340,

Ferguson, E. 2013. Church history, volume one: from Christ to the Pre-Reformation: the rise and growth of the church in its cultural, intellectual, and political context. Grand Rapids: Zondervan.

Filastrii Episcopi Brixiensis. 1898. Diversarum hereseon liber. Corpus Scriptorum Ecclesiasticorum Latinorum (38). Edited by Friderici Marx. Prague: F. Tempsky

Fitzmyer, J. 2008. First Corinthians. London: Yale University.

Flusser, D. 1989. Jewish Sources in Early Christianity. Tel Aviv, Israel: MOD.

Forbes, C. 1995. Prophecy and inspired speech in early Christianity and its Hellenistic environment. Tübingen, Germany: Mohr (Paul Siebeck).

Ford, J. 1966a. The first epistle to the Corinthians or the first epistle to the Hebrews? *The Catholic Biblical Quarterly*, 28(4): 402–416.

———. 1966b. Hast thou tithed thy meal? and Is thy child kosher? *Journal of Theological Studies*, 17(1):72–79.

———. 1986, Toward a theology of "speaking in tongues." (*In* Mills, W. ed. Speaking in tongues: a guide to research on glossolalia. Grand Rapids: Eerdmans. p. 263–294).

Fotopoulos, J. 2010. 1Corinthians. (*In* Aune, D., ed. The Blackwell companion to the New Testament. Chichester, West Sussex: Blackwell. p. 413–433).

Fox, George. 1659/1831. The works of George Fox, Vol. 3: The great mystery of the great whore unfolded; and Antichrist's kingdom. https://www.books.google.ca/books?id=OUBUXRr-4C&pg=PA13&redir_esc=y#v=onepage&q&f=false Date of access: 04 Mar. 2023.

———. 1909. George Fox: an autobiography. Edited with an introduction and notes by Rufus Jones. Philadelphia: Ferris & Leach.

―――. 1952. The Journal of George Fox, edited by John Nickalls. Cambridge, UK: Cambridge University Press.
Frankenberg, W. De Syrischen Clementinem mit Griechischem paralleltext. Leipzig: J.C. Hinrichs. 1937.
Frier, B. & McGinn, T. 2004. A casebook on Roman family law. Oxford: Oxford University Press.
Frodsham, S. 1941. With signs following: the story of the Pentecostal revival in the twentieth century. Springfield, MO: Gospel Publishing House.
Furnish, V. 1988. Corinth in Paul's time—what can archaeology tell us? *Biblical Archaeology Review*, 14(3):14–27.
Gamble, H. 1995. Books and readers in the early church. New Haven, CT: Yale University.
Gardner, P. 2018. 1 Corinthians: Zondervan Exegetical Commentary on the New Testament. Grand Rapids: Zondervan.
Garland, D. 2003. 1 Corinthians: Baker Exegetical Commentary on the New Testament. Grand Rapids: Baker.
Garland, D. 2003. 1 Corinthians: Baker Exegetical Commentary on the New Testament. [Kindle ed.] Grand Rapids: Baker. Available: https://www.amazon.ca
Garnsey, P. & Woolf, G. 1989. Patronage of the Rural Poor in the Roman world. (*In* Wallace-Hadrill, A. ed. Patronage in ancient society. London: Routledge. p. 153–70).
Garroway, J.D. 2011. Ioudaios. *JANT*, 2011:524–525.
Geisler, N. 2019. Signs and wonders: healings, miracles, and unusual events. Matthews, NC: Bastion.
Ger, S. 2004. Acts: witnesses to the world. Chattanooga, TN: AMG.
Geraty, L. 2013. From Sabbath to Sunday: why, how and when? (*In* Shanks, H. ed. Partings: how Judaism and Christianity became two. Washington, DC: Biblical Archaeology Society. p. 255–268).
Gerhardsson, B. 1986. The Gospel tradition. Lund, Sweden: Wallin & Dalhom.
―――. 1990. The Gospel tradition. (*In* Dungan, D. ed. The Interrelations of the Gospels. Leuven: Peeters.
Germano, M. 2002. The upper room: was it the site of the first Christin Pentecost? https://biblicaltongues.com/article-germano/ Date of access: 25 Nov. 2023.
Giles, J. 1839. A lexicon of the Greek language, for the use of colleges and schools. London: Paternoster-Row.
Gill, J. 1746–1748. Gill's exposition of the whole Bible. https://www.sacred-texts.com/bib/cmt/gill/co1014.htm Date of access: 22 Aug. 2023.
Godet, F. 1890. Commentary on St. Paul's First Epistle to the Corinthians, volume 2. Translated from the French by A. Cusin. Edinburgh: T. & T. Clark.
Goldsworthy, A. 2016. In the name of Rome: the men who won the Roman Empire. New Haven, CT: Yale University Press.
Goodman, M. 1996. Sacred space in Diaspora Judaism. (*In* Isaac, B. & Oppenheimer, A. eds. Studies on the Jewish Diaspora in the Hellenistic and Roman periods, Teʻuda volume 12. Tel Aviv: Ramot. p. 1–16).
Goodspeed, E.J. 1950. Gaius Titius Justus. *Journal of Biblical Literature*, 69(4):382–383.
Gorman, M.J. 2009. Elements of biblical exegesis: A basic guide for students and ministers. Peabody, MA: Hendrickson.

Goulder, M. 1995. St. Paul versus St. Peter: a tale of two missions. Louisville: Westminster.

———. 2001. Paul and the competing mission in Corinth. Peabody, MA: Hendrickson.

Graves, M. 1980. The public reading of Scripture in early Judaism. *Journal of the Evangelical Theological Society*, September 2007, 50(3):467–487.

Grintz, J. 1960. Hebrew as the spoken and written language in the last days of the Second Temple. *Journal of Biblical Literature*, 79(1):32–47.

Gromacki, R. 1967. The Modern Tongues Movement. Philadelphia: Presbyterian & Reformed.

Grosheide, F. 1953. The first epistle to the Corinthians. The New International Commentary on the New Testament. Grand Rapids: Eerdmans.

Groves, J. 1830. A Greek and English dictionary, comprising all the words in the writings of the most popular Greek authors. Boston: Hilliard, Gray, Little and Wilkins.

Grudem, W. 1999. Bible Doctrine. Grand Rapids: Zondervan.

Gundry, R. 1966. "'Ecstatic Utterance' (N.E.B.)?" *The Journal of Theological Studies*, 17(2), October:299–307.

———. 2010. Corinthians in the commentary on the New Testament. Grand Rapids: Baker.

———. 2011. Commentary on First Corinthians [Kindle ed.]. Grand Rapids: Baker. Available: https://www.amazon.ca

Hachlili, R. 2015. Synagogues: Before and After the Roman Destruction of the Temple. *Biblical Archaeology Review*, 41(3):30–38, 65.

Haenchen, E. 1971. The Acts of the Apostles. Philadelphia, PA: Westminster.

Haidir, H., Simanjuntak1i, F., Junaidi, Pujiono, M. 2019. Diglossia: phenomenon and language theory. *European Journal of Literature, Language and Linguistics Studies*, 3(2):58–65.

Hakola, R. 2017. The production and trade of fish as source of economic growth in the first century CE Galilee. *Novum Testamentum*, 59:111–130.

Hamilton, H. 1859. A lexicon of the Greek language: exhibiting in a concise form. London: John Edward Taylor.

Hamilton, J. 1900. The History of the Moravian Church. Bethlehem, PA: Times Publishing.

Hanegraaff, W. 2012. Esotericism and the academy: rejected knowledge in western culture. Cambridge, UK: Cambridge University Press.

Hannan, M. 2017. Profile: Reverend Edward Irving; prophet to some, heretic to others, Aug. 3, 2017 https://www.thenational.scot/news/15453072.profile-reverend-edward-irving-prophet-to-some-heretic-to-others/ Date of access: 13 Feb. 2023.

Hanson, Kenneth C. & Oakman, Douglas E. 2002. Palestine in the Time of Jesus: Social Structures and Social Conflicts. Minneapolis: Augsburg Fortress.

Harnack, A. 1908. The mission and expansion of Christianity, Vol. 1. Translated from the German and edited by James Moffatt. London: Williams and Norgate.

———. 1925. New Testament studies VI: the origin of the New Testament and the most important consequences of the new creation. Translated from the German by J. R. Wilkinson. London: Williams and Norgate. http://www.ccel.org/ccel/harnack/origin_nt.v.i.html Date of access: 7 Jan. 2023.

Harris, S. 1985. Understanding the Bible. Palo Alto, CA: Mayfield.

Harris, W. 1989. Ancient Literacy. Cambridge: Harvard University Press.
Hasel, G. 1991. Speaking in tongues: Biblical speaking in tongues and contemporary glossolalia. Berrien Springs, MI: Adventist Theological Society Publications.
Hatch, E. & Redpath, H.A., eds. 1983 printing. A concordance to the Septuagint. Grand Rapids: Baker.
Hawthornthwaite, S. 1857. Mr. Hawthornthwaite's adventure among the Mormons as an elder during eight years. Manchester.
Hays, R. 1989. Echoes of Scripture in the letters of Paul. New Haven, CT: Yale University Press.
Hengel, M. 1980. Jews, Greeks, and Barbarians. Translated by John Bowden. Philadelphia, PA: Fortress.
———. 1989. The "Hellenization" of Judea in the first century after Christ. Translated by John Bowden. London, UK: SCM.
———. 2010. Saint Peter—the underestimated Apostle. Grand Rapids: Eerdmans.
Hering, J. 1962. The First Epistle of Saint Paul to the Corinthians. Translated from the second French edition by A. W. Heathcote and P. J. Allcock. London: Epworth.
Hezser, C. 2001. Jewish Literacy in Roman Palestine. Tübingen, Germany: Mohr Siebeck.
Higley, S. 2007. Hildegard of Bingen's unknown language: an edition, translation, and discussion. New York: Palgrave Macmillan.
Hinson, E. 1967. A brief history of glossolalia. (In Stagg, F. & Hinson, E. & Oates, W. eds. Glossolalia: tongue speaking in biblical, historical, and psychological perspective. Nashville: Abingdon. p. 45–75).
———. 1986. The significance of glossolalia in the history of Christianity. (In Mills, W. ed. Speaking in tongues: a guide to research on glossolalia. Grand Rapids: Eerdmans. p. 181–203).
Hodge, C. 1860. An exposition of the first epistle to the Corinthians. New York: Robert Carter & Brothers.
Holl, K. 1910. Die handschriftliche Überlieferung des Epiphanios (Ancoratus und Panarion), Leipzig: J. C. Hinrichs.
———. 1915. Epiphanius: Ancoratus und Panarion (haer. 1–33). Leipzig: J. C. Hinrichs.
———. 1980. Epiphanius II: Panarion (haereses 34–46), GCS. Revised by Jürgen Dummer. Berlin: De Gruyter.
———. 1985. Epiphanius III: Panarion (haereses 65–80). De Fide, GCS. Revised by Jürgen Dummer. Berlin: De Gruyter.
———. 2006. Register zu den Bänden I-III (Ancoratus, Panarion 1–80, De Fide), GCS. Revised by Friedrich-Christian Collatz et al. Berlin: De Gruyter.
Holladay, C. 1990. 1 Corinthians 13: Paul as apostolic paradigm. (In Balch, D., Fereguson, E. & Meeks, W. eds. Greeks, Romans and Christians—in honor of A. J. Malherbe. Minneapolis: Fortress. p. 80–98).
Holmes, M. 2007. The Apostolic Fathers: Greek Texts and English Translations. 3rd ed. Grand Rapids: Baker.
House, H. Wayne. 1983. Tongues and the mystery religions of Corinth. *Bibliotheca Sacra*, April, 140 (558):134–148.
Hughes, P. 1974. The languages spoken by Jesus. (In Longenecker, R. & Tenney, M. eds. New dimensions in New Testament study. Grand Rapids: Zondervan. p. 127–143).
Hull, J. 1967. The Holy Spirit in the Acts of the Apostles. Cleveland: World Pub.
Hunter, C & F. 1976. Why should I speak in tongues??? Houston: Hunter Ministries.

Hunter, H. 1980. Tongues-Speech: a patristic analysis. *Journal of the Evangelical Theological Society*, June 1980, 23(2):125–137.
Hyatt, E. 2002. 2000 years of charismatic Christianity. Lake Mary, FL: Charisma House.
Idelsohn, A. 1932. Jewish liturgy and its development. New York: Dover Publications.
Irenaeus. 1885. Against heresies. Denver, Colorado: New Advent.
Irving, E. 1825. For missionaries after the apostolical school, a series of orations: in four parts (Part 1). London: Hamilton, Adams.
———. 1864. The Collected Writings of Edward Irving in Five Volumes, volume 5, edited by G. Carlyle. London: Alexander Strahan.
Isbell, C. 1975. Glossolalia and propheteialalia: a study of 1 Corinthians 14. *Wesleyan Theological Journal*, Spring 1975, 10:15–22.
Jeremias, J. 1988. Jerusalem in the time of Jesus. Philadelphia, PA: Fortress.
Jewish Encyclopedia. 2023. Epiphanius. https://www.jewishencyclopedia.com/articles/5819-epiphanius Date of access: 26 May 2023.
Johnson, L.T. 1992. Tongues, gift of. (*In* Anchor Bible Dictionary, 6:596–600).
Johnson, S.L. 1963. A symposium on the tongues movement. Part II: The gift of tongues and the book of Acts. *Bibliotheca Sacra*, October, 120 (480):309–311.
Johnston, D. 1999. Roman Law in Context. Cambridge, UK: Cambridge University Press.
Joosten, J. & Kister, M. 2010. The New Testament and rabbinic Hebrew. (*In* Bieringer, R. ed. The New Testament and rabbinic literature. Leiden: Brill. p. 333–350).
Joosten, J. 2017. How Hebrew became a holy language. *Biblical Archaeology Review*, 43(1):44–49, 62.
Jordan, W. 1968. Edward VI: the young king. The protectorship of the Duke of Somerset. London: George Allen & Unwin.
Josephus, F. 1852. The works of Josephus. Translated by William Whiston. Halifax, Eng.: Milner and Sowerby.
———. 1943. Jewish antiquities, Books 12–13. Translated by Ralph Marcus. Cambridge, MA: Harvard University Press.
———. 1963. Jewish antiquities, Books 14–15. Translated by Ralph Marcus. Cambridge, MA: Harvard University Press.
———. 1982. Josephus: the Jewish war, edited by Gaalya Cornfield. Grand Rapids: Zondervan.
Jubilees, Book of. 1917. Translations of early documents, Series 1, Palestinian Jewish texts (pre-Rabbinic). Translated from the Ethiopic by R.H. Charles. New York: Macmillan Co.
Kaplan, M. 1972. Judaism as a civilization. New York: Schocken.
Karali, Maria. 2007. The classification of the ancient Greek dialects. Translated from the Greek by Chris Markham. (*In* Christidis, A.F., ed. A history of ancient Greek: from the beginnings to late antiquity. New York: Cambridge University Press. p. 387–394).
Kazazis, John. 2007. Atticism. Translated from the Greek by Deborah Kazazis. (*In* Christidis, A.F., ed. A history of ancient Greek: from the beginnings to late antiquity. New York: Cambridge University Press. p. 1200–1212).
Keener, C. 2005. 1–2 Corinthians. New Cambridge Bible Commentary. New York: Cambridge University Press.
———. 2014. Acts: An exegetical commentary, volume 3. Grand Rapids: Baker.

BIBLIOGRAPHY

Kelsey, M. 1968. Tongue speaking: an experiment in spiritual experience. Garden City, NY: Doubleday.

Kennedy, A. & Reed, W. 1963. House. (*In* Grant, F. & Rowley, H. eds. Hastings Dictionary of the Bible, Revised Edition. New York: Charles Scribner's. p. 401–406).

Kent, J. 1966. Corinth: results of excavations conducted by the American School of Classical Studies at Athens, Vol. 3, part 3: the inscriptions. Princeton, NJ: American School of Classical Studies at Athens.

Kildahl, J. 1972. The Psychology of Speaking in Tongues. New York: Harper & Row.

———. 1974. Six behavioral observations about speaking in tongues. (*In* Agrimson, J. ed. Gifts of the Spirit and the body of Christ. Minneapolis: Augsburg. p. 71–70).

Kinzig, W. 2012. Ambrosiaster. (*In* Hornblower, S. & Spawforth, A. eds. Oxford Classical Dictionary, 4th ed. Oxford: Oxford University Press. p. 69–70).

Kistemaker, S. 1990. Acts New Testament Commentary. Grand Rapids: Baker.

Kittel, G. 1964. Theological Dictionary of the New Testament, Vol. 1–10. Translated and edited by Geoffrey W. Bromiley. Grand Rapids: Eerdmans.

Kittel, R. et al, eds. 1967/77. Biblia Hebraica Stuttgartensia. 4th ed. Stuttgart: Deutsche Bibelgesellschaft.

KJV. 1611. The holy Bible, conteyning the Old Testament and the New. London: Robert Barker Printer.

Knox, W. 1948. The Acts of the Apostles. Cambridge, UK: Cambridge University Press

Koch, K. 1980. Occult ABC. Grand Rapids: Kregel.

Koenig, J. 1978. Charismata: God's gifts for God's people. Philadelphia: Westminster.

Koester, H. 1990. Ancient Christian Gospels: Their history and development. Harrisburg, PA: Trinity Press International.

Koet, B. 1996. As close to the synagogue as can be: Paul in Corinth [Acts 18:1–18]. (*In* Bieringer, R., ed. The Corinthia Correspondence. Leuven: Leuven University Press. p. 409ff).

Korner, R. 2015. Ekklēsia as a Jewish synagogue term: Some implications for Paul's socio-religious location. *Journal of The Jesus Movement in Its Jewish Setting (From the First to the Seventh Century)*, 2:53–78.

Kraeger, S. 2010. Toward a mediating understanding of tongues: a historical and exegetical examination of early literature. *Eleutheria*, 1(1): 43–58.

Kydd, R. 1984. Charismatic gifts in the early church. Peabody, MA: Hendrickson.

Kreiser, B. 1978. Miracles, convulsions, and ecclesiastical politics in early eighteenth-century Paris. Princeton, NJ: Princeton University Press.

Lake, K. (trans.). 1912. The apostolic fathers, 2 vols. Cambridge: Harvard University Press.

———. 1914. The earlier epistles of St. Paul: their motive and origin. 2nd ed. London: Rivingtons.

Lamm, M. 1991. The mikveh's significance in traditional conversion. https://www.myjewishlearning.com/article/why-immerse-in-the-mikveh/ Date of access: 1 Nov. 2022.

Lampe, G., ed. 1961. A patristic Greek lexicon. London: Oxford University Press.

Larsson, E. 1985. Paul: Law and salvation. *New Testament Studies*, 31:426–436.

LaSor, W. 1972. Church alive. Glendale, CA: Regal.

Leithart, P. 2002. Synagogue or temple? Models for the Christian worship. *Westminster Theological Journal*, 64(1):122.

Lenski, R. 1946. The interpretation of St. Paul's First and Second Epistle to the Corinthians. Columbus, OH: Wartburg.
Levine, L. 2005. The ancient synagogue: The first thousand years. New Haven, CT: Yale University Press.
Levine, A. 2006. The misunderstood Jew: the church and the scandal of the Jewish Jesus. San Francisco: Harper.
Lias, J. 1905. First Epistle to the Corinthians. Cambridge Greek Testament for Schools and Colleges. Cambridge, UK: Cambridge University Press
Liddell, H.G. & Scott, R., eds. 1968. A Greek-English lexicon of the New Testament, revised and augmented by Henry Stuart Jones with the assistance of Roderick McKenzie. Oxford: Clarendon.
Liddell, H.G. & Scott, R., eds. 1892. A lexicon: abridged from Greek-English lexicon of the New Testament. London: Oxford at the Clarendon.
Lightfoot, J. 1859. Horae Hebraicae et Talmudicae: Hebrew and Talmudical exercitations upon the Gospels, the Acts, some chapters of St. Paul's epistle to the Romans, and the First Epistle to the Corinthians, in 4 volumes. Translated by Robert Gandell. Oxford: Oxford University Press.
Loach, J. 1999. Edward VI, edited by G. Bernard & P. Williams. New Haven, CT: Yale University Press.
Lockwood, G. 2000. 1 Corinthians. St. Louis, MO: Concordia Publishing House.
Loisy, A. 1920. Les actes des apôtres. Paris: Émile Nourry.
Longenecker, R. 2007. Acts (The Expositor's Bible Commentary). Grand Rapids: Zondervan.
Louw, J.P. & Nida, E.A., eds. 1988. Greek-English lexicon of the New Testament based on semantic domains. New York: United Bible Societies.
———. 1992. Lexical semantics of the Greek New Testament. Atlanta: Scholars.
Lust, J., Eynikel, E. & Hauspie, K., eds. 2003. A Greek-English Lexicon of the Septuagint, Revised Edition. Stuttgart: Deutsche Bibelgesellschaft.
Luther, M. 1545. Das Neue Testament unsers herrn und heilandes Jesu Christi nach der deutschen ubersetzung D. Martin Luthers. Stuttgart: Wurttemberg Bible Institute.
Lyons, J. 1981. Language and linguistics: an introduction. Cambridge, UK: Cambridge University Press.
MacArthur, J. 1984. 1 Corinthians, The MacArthur New Testament Commentary. Chicago: Moody.
———. 1992. Charismatic Chaos. Grand Rapids: Zondervan.
———. 1994. Acts 1–12. Chicago: Moody.
———. 1996. Acts 13–28. Chicago: Moody.
MacCulloch, D. 2002. The boy king: Edward VI and the Protestant Reformation. Berkeley, CA: University of California Press.
———. 2010. Christianity: the first three thousand years. 1st American edition. New York: Viking Penguin.
MacDonald, W. 1986. Glossolalia in the New Testament. (*In* Mills, W. ed. Speaking in tongues: a guide to research on glossolalia. Grand Rapids: Eerdmans. p. 127–140).
MacGregor, K. 2018. 1 Corinthians 14:33b-38. *Priscilla Papers*, Winter 2018, 32(1):22–28.
MacKenzie, R. & Pettem, M. 1990. Review of [Johannes P. LOUW et Eugene A. NIDA (eds.) (1988): Greek-English Lexicon of the New Testament Based on Semantic

Domains, New York, United Bible Societies, Vol. 1: 843 p., Vol. 2: 375 p.] Meta, 35(2), June:439–441.

Maclachlan, R. 2015. Tongues revisited: a third way. [Kindle Edition.] Porirua, New Zealand: Clearsight. Available: https://www.amazon.ca

MacLennan, R. & Kraabel, A. 1986. The God-Fearers: a literary and theological invention. *Biblical Archaeology Review*, 12(5):46–53.

McClung, G. 2006. Azusa Street and beyond. New Kensington, PA: Bridge Logos.

McGuckin, J. 2001. Saint Gregory of Nazianzus: an intellectual biography. Crestwood, NY: St Vladimir's Seminary Press.

McNamara, M. 1983. Palestinian Judaism and the New Testament. Wilmington, DE: Michael Glazier.

Machiela, D. 2013. Hebrew, Aramaic, and the Differing Phenomena of Targum and Translation in the Second Temple Period and Post-Second Temple Period. (In Buth, R. & Notley, R. eds., The Language Environment of First Century Judaea. Leiden: Brill. p. 209–246).

Malina, B. & Neyrey, J. 1991. First-century personality: dyadic, not individualistic. (*In* Neyrey, J., ed. The social world of Luke-Acts: models for interpretation. Peabody, MA: Hendrickson. p. 67–96).

Malina, B. & Pilch, J. Social-Science Commentary on the Letters of Paul. 1517 Media, 2006. https://doi.org/10.2307/j.ctv19cwbcq Date of access: 9 July 2022.

Manson, W. 1962. Studies in the Gospels and Epistles. Manchester: Manchester University Press.

Marcos, N. 2000. The Septuagint in context: Introduction to the Greek version of the Bible. Translated by Wilfred G.E. Watson. Leiden: Brill.

Mare, W. 1976. 1 Corinthians: The Expositors Bible Commentary, Vol. 10. Grand Rapids: Zondervan.

Marshall, C. & Rossman, G. B. 2016. Designing qualitative research. 6th ed. Thousand Oaks, CA: Sage.

Marshall, I. H. 1977. The significance of Pentecost. *Scottish Journal of Theology*, 30:347–369.

———. 1980. The Acts of the Apostles, Tyndale New Testament Commentaries. Grand Rapids: Eerdmans.

———. 1999. A Critical and Exegetical Commentary on the Pastoral Epistles, International Critical Commentary. Edinburgh: T & T Clark.

Martin, D. 1995. The Corinthian body. New Haven: Yale University Press.

Martin, R. 1987. The opponents of Paul in 2 Corinthians: an old issue revisited. (*In* Hawthorne, G. & Betz, O., eds. Tradition and Interpretation in the New Testament. Grand Rapids: Eerdmans. p. 279–289).

Marulli, L. 2011–2012. Paul and his Jewish identity: an overview. *Spes Christiana*, 22–23:85–104.

Marzano, A. 2013. Harvesting the sea: the exploitation of marine resources in the Roman Mediterranean. Oxford: Oxford University Press.

Mason, S. 2009. Josephus, Judea and Christian origins: Method and categories. Peabody, MA: Hendrikson.

Masters, P. & Whitcomb, J. 1982. The charismatic phenomenon. London:Wakeman Trust.

Mathieu, P. 1864. History of the miraculous and convulsionaries of Saint-Médard; preceded by the life of the deacon Pâris, a notice on Carré de Montgeron and a glance at Jansenism from its origin to the present day (French Version). Paris: Didier.

May, L. 1956. A survey of glossolalia and related phenomena in non-Christian religions. *American Anthropologist*, February 1956, 58(1):75–96.

Meeks, W.A. 1975. Am I a Jew? Johannine Christianity and Judaism. (*In* Neusner, J., ed. Christianity, Judaism, and other Greco-Roman cults: studies for Morton Smith at sixty. Part One: New Testament. Leiden: Brill. p. 163–186).

———. 1983. The first urban Christians: The social world of the Apostle Paul. New Haven: Yale University Press.

Meggitt, J. 1998. Paul, poverty, and survival. Edinburgh: T&T Clark.

Meier, J. 1991. A marginal Jew, vol. 1. New York : Doubleday.

Mendels, D. 2011. Why Paul went west. *Biblical Archaeology Review*, 37(1):49–54, 68.

Merriam-Webster Dictionary. s.a. www.merriam-webster.com/dictionary/Camisard Date of access: 03 Feb. 2023.

Metzger, B. 1968. "Methodology in the Study of the Mystery Religions and Early Christianity," Historical and Literary Studies, Pagan, Jewish, and Christian. Grand Rapids: Eerdmans.

———. 1975. A textual commentary on the Greek New Testament. London: United Bible Societies.

———. 1994. A textual commentary on the Greek New Testament. 2nd ed. Stuttgart: German Bible Society.

Meyer, H. 1884. Critical and exegetical hand-book to the epistles to the Corinthians. Translated from the German by Douglas Bannerman. New York: Funk & Wagnalls.

Meyers, E. 2013. Living side by side in Galilee. (*In* Shanks, H. ed. Partings: how Judaism and Christianity became two. Washington, DC: Biblical Archaeology Society. p. 133–150).

Michael, B. & Lancaster, T. "One Law" and the Messianic Gentile. *Messiah Journal*, Summer 2009:46–70.

Migne, J. 1859. Patrologia Graeca—Greek and Latin, Vol. 74, Explanatio in Epistolam I ad Corinthos. Paris: Imprimerie Catholique.

Migne, J. 1863. Patrologia Graeca—Greek and Latin, Vol. 74, Fragmenta in Acta Apostolorum (Ex Catena Crameri, Oxonii 1838). Paris: Imprimerie Catholique.

Migne, J. 1863. Patrologia Graeca—Greek and Latin, Vol. 76, S. Cyrilli Alexandrini, Contra Julianum. Paris: Imprimerie Catholique.

Milik, Jozef T. 1959. Ten years of discovery in the wilderness of Judaea. 1st English ed. Chatham, UK: SCM.

Miller, David M. 2014. Ethnicity, religion and the meaning of Ἰουδαῖος in ancient 'Judaism'. Currents in Biblical Research, 12(2):216–265.

Miller, E. 1878. Irvingism, Vol. 1 & 2, The history and doctrines of Irvingism. London: C. Kegan Paul.

Miller, J. 1980. Listening for the African Past. (*In* Miller, J., ed. The African past speaks: essays on oral tradition and history. Folkestone: England. p. 51–52).

Milligan, G. 1908. St. Paul's epistles to the Thessalonians. London: Macmillan and Company.

Millis, B. 2010. The social and ethnic origins of the colonists in early Roman Corinth. (*In* Friesen, S., Schowalter, D. & Walters, J. eds. Corinth in context: comparative studies on religion and society. Leiden: Brill. p. 13–36).

———. 2013. The local magistrates and elite of Roman Corinth. (*In* Friesen, S., James, S. & Schowalter, D. eds. In Corinth in contrast: studies in inequality. Leiden: Brill. p. 38–53).

Misson, F. 1847. Les Prophètes Protestants, edited by A. Bost. Paris: s.n.

Moravian Church. 2020. The Moravian catechism. Bethlehem, PA: IBOC, Moravian Church in America.

Morris, L. 1958. The first epistle of Paul to the Corinthians. Tyndale New Testament Commentaries. Grand Rapids: Eerdmans.

Moule, C. 1959. An idiom book of New Testament Greek. Cambridge, UK: Cambridge University Press.

Moulton, J. 1908. A grammar of New Testament Greek, vol. 1, 3rd ed. Edinburgh: T & T Clark.

Moulton, J.H. & Milligan, G., eds. 1930. The vocabulary of the Greek Testament. Grand Rapids: Eerdmans.

Muller, M. 1996. Die Abraham-Gestalt im Jubilaenbuch: Versuch einer Interpretation (The figure of Abraham in the Jubilee book: an attempt at an interpretation). *SJOT*, 10:238–57.

Murphy-O'Connor, J. 1996. Paul: A critical life. Oxford: Clarendon.

———. 2002. St. Paul's Corinth. Collegeville, MN: Liturgical.

———. 2009. Keys to first Corinthians: Revisiting the major issues. Oxford: Oxford University Press.

Murray, O. 1987. Herodotus and oral history. (*In* Sancisi-Weerdenburg, H. & Kuhrt, A, eds., Achaemenid history II: the Greek sources. Leiden: Nederlands Instituut voor het Nabije Oosten. p. 93–115).

Musée protestant. 2023. The Bible in times of persecution for the French Protestants. https://museeprotestant.org/en/notice/thebibleintimesofpersecutionforthefrenchprotestanta1685–1760/ Date of access: 26 Feb. 2023.

———. 2023. Prophetic Movement. https://museeprotestant.org/en/notice/prophetic-movement/ Date of access: 26 Feb. 2023.

———. 2023: 16th century translations of the Bible into Latin and French. https://museeprotestant.org/en/notice/xvith-century-translations-of-the-bible-into-latin-and-french/ Date of access: 26 Feb. 2023.

Nash, R. 1984. Christianity and the Hellenistic World. Grand Rapids: Zondervan.

Neander, A. 1900. Planting and training of the Christian Church by the Apostles, Vol. 1. 3rd ed. Translated from the 1841 German 3rd edition by J.E. Ryland. London: George Bell.

Neusner, J. 1965. A history of the Jews in Babylonia, l. The Parthian Period. Studia Post Biblica. Leiden, Netherlands: Brill.

Newton, B.E., Ruijgh, C.J., Lejeune, M. and Malikouti-Drachman, A. "Greek language." Encyclopedia Britannica, 13 Apr. 2018, https://www.britannica.com/topic/Greek-language Date of access: 8 July 2022.

NPNF *A Select Library of the Nicene and Post-Nicene Fathers of the Christian* Church, edited by Philip Schaff and Henry Wace. 28 vols. in 2 series. 1886–1889. Reprint, Peabody, MA: Hendrickson, 1995.

Oliphant, M. 1862. The Life of Edward Irving, Minister of the National Church, Vol. 2. London: Hurst and Blackett.

BIBLIOGRAPHY

Oliver, I. 2021. The parting of the ways: When and how did the ekklesia split from the synagogue https://www.academia.edu/43765735/ThePartingoftheWaysWhen andHowDidtheEkklēsiaSplitfromtheSynagoguepostprintdraft Date of access: 2 July 2022. (now in McDermott, G., ed. Understanding the Jewish roots of Christianity: Biblical, theological, and historical essays on the relationship between Christianity and Judaism.) Bellingham, WA: Lexham, chapter 6.

Ong, H. 2014. Is "spiritual gift(s)" a linguistically fallacious term? A lexical study of Χάρισμα, Πνευματικός, and Πνεῦμα. *The Expository Times*, 125(12):583 –592.

———. 2016. The language of the New Testament from a sociolinguistic perspective. *Journal of Greco-Roman Christianity and Judaism*, 12:163–190.

Origen, A. 2001. Commentary on the Epistle to the Romans: the fathers of the church, book 1. Translated by Thomas Scheck. Washington, D.C.: Catholic University of America Press.

Orlinsky, H. 1974. Essays in biblical culture and Bible translation. New York: KTAV Publishing House.

Oropeza, B.J. 2009. Jews, Gentiles, and the Opponents of Paul: A Synopsis of Apostasy in the Pauline and Deutero-Pauline Letters (This is a seminar paper presented at the University of Tubingen, which was an early synopsis of a pre-published version of B.J. Oropeza's 2012 book titled Jews, Gentiles, and the Opponents of Paul: Apostasy in the New Testament Communities, Vol. 2. Eugene, OR: Cascade.)

———. 2017. 1 Corinthians, New Covenant Commentary Series. Eugene, OR: Cascade/Wipf & Stock.

Osborne, G. 2004. Romans. Downers Grove, IL: IVP.

Oster, R. 1995. 1 Corinthians, The College Press NIV Commentary. Joplin, MO: College Press

Ott, M. 1910. Blessed Jacopo de Voragine. The Catholic Encyclopedia, Vol. 8. New York: Robert Appleton. https://www.newadvent.org/cathen/08262b.htm Date of access: 28 Jan. 2023.

———. 1912. Unigenitus. The Catholic Encyclopedia, Vol. 15. New York: Robert Appleton. https://www.newadvent.org/cathen/15128a.htm Date of access: 07 Feb. 2023.

Oxford Dictionary of the Christian Church. 1958. 1st ed. London: Oxford University Press.

Oxford Dictionary of the Christian Church. 1997. 3rd ed. New York: Oxford University Press.

Oxford English Dictionary. 1933. Volume 4. Oxford: Clarendon.

Oxford Latin Dictionary. 1968. London: Oxford University Press.

Pachomius *et al.* 1932. Sancti Pachomii vitae Graecae. (*In* Halkin, F., ed. Subsidia Hagiographica 19. Brussels, Belgium: Société des Bollandistes. p. 154–155).

———. 1981. Pachomian Koinonia: Pachomian chronicles and rules. Cistercian Studies Series: Number 46. Volume 2. Translated by Armand Veilleux. Kalamazoo, MI: Cistercian Publications. p. 51–52).

Packer, J. 1985. Keep in step with the Spirit. Downers Grove, IL: IVP

Paget, J. 2014. The origins of the Septuagint, chapter 7, from Part III—Greek Bible and language. (*In* Aitken, J. & Paget, J. eds. The Jewish-Greek Tradition in Antiquity and the Byzantine Empire. Cambridge, UK: Cambridge University Press. p. 105–119).

BIBLIOGRAPHY

Panayotou, Anna. 2007. Ionic and Attic. (*In* Christidis, A.F., ed. A history of ancient Greek: from the beginnings to late antiquity. New York: Cambridge University Press. p. 405–416).

Parham, S. 1930. The life of Charles F. Parham: founder of the Apostolic Faith Movement. Joplin, MO: Hunter Print.

Parkhurst, J. 1817. A Greek and English lexicon to the New Testament. London: Thomas Davison, Whitefriars.

Pawlak, M. 2013. Corinth after 44 BC: ethnical and cultural changes. *Electrum*, 20:143–162.

Pender-Cudlip, P. 1972. Oral traditions and anthropological analysis: some contemporary myths. *Azania: Archaeological Research in Africa*, 7(1):3–24.

Perkins, P. 2012. First Corinthians. Paideia Commentaries on the New Testament. Grand Rapids: Baker.

Perrot, C. 1988. The reading of the Bible in the ancient synagogue. (*In* Mulder, M. ed. The literature of the Jewish people in the period of the second temple and the Talmud, volume 1 Mikra. Leiden: Brill. p. 137–159).

Pervo, R. 2009. Acts, Volume 58 of Hermeneia. Minneapolis, MN: Fortress.

Petersen, W. 2006. Patristic Biblical Quotations and Method: Four Changes to Lightfoot's Edition of "Second Clement. *Vigiliae Christianae*, Brill, 60(4):389–419.

Peterson, D. 2009. The Acts of the Apostles (The Pillar New Testament Commentary). Grand Rapids: Eerdmans.

Pickering, J. 1855. A comprehensive lexicon of the Greek language: adapted to the use of colleges and schools. Boston: Rice and Kendall.

Pietersma, A. 2002. A new paradigm for addressing old questions: The relevance of the interlinear model for the study of the Septuagint. (*In* Cook, J. ed. Bible and Computer: The Stellenbosch AIBI-6 Conference. Proceedings of the Association Internationale Bible et Informatique "From Alpha to Byte." University of Stellenbosch, 17–21 July 2000. Leiden: Brill. p. 337–64).

Pilkington, G. 1832. The Unknown Tongues discovered to be English, Spanish, and Latin... *The Monthly Review*, January to April, 1832, 1(1):21–40.

Plumptre, E. 1863. Tongues, gift of. (*In* Smith, W. ed Dictionary of the Bible, volume 3. Boston: Little, Brown. p. 1555–1562).

Pohl, A. 1982. 17 reasons why I left the tongues movement. London: Bethel Baptist Print Ministry.

Pond, E. 1839. Memoir of Count Zinzendorf. Boston: Masachusetts Sabbath School Society.

Powell, B. 1903. Greek inscriptions from Corinth. *American Journal of Archaeology*, Second Series, Volume 7, No. 1:26–71.

Poirier, J. 2010. The tongues of angels: the concept of angelic languages in classical Jewish and Christian texts. Scientific Studies on the New Testament 2nd Series (Wissenschaftliche Untersuchungen zum Neuen Testament II, 287). Tübingen: Mohr Seibeck.

Poythress, V. 1977. The nature of Corinthian *glossolalia*: possible options. *Westminster Theological Journal*, Fall 1977, 40(1):130–135.

———. 2001. Greek lexicography and translation: Comparing Bauer's and Louw-Nida's lexicons. *Journal of the Evangelical Theological Society*, June 2001, 44(2):285–296.

Prior, D. 1985. The Message of 1 Corinthians. Downers Grove, IL: InterVarsity.

BIBLIOGRAPHY

Psellos, M. 1989. To the disciples, about the Apostles speaking various languages [English translated from Latin section 74 title]. (*In* Gautier, P. ed. Michaelis Pselli Theologica. volume 1. Leipzig: BSB B.G. Teubner Verlagsgesellschaft. p. 292-297).

Rabin, C. 1976. Hebrew and Aramaic in the first century. (*In* Safrai, S. & Stern, M. eds. The Jewish People in the First Century, Compendia Rerum Iudaicarum ad Novum Testamentum. Volume 2. Philadelphia: Fortress. p. 1007-1039.

Rackham, R. 1901. The acts of the apostles. London: Methuen & Co.

Rahlfs, A. & Hanhart, R., eds. 2006. Septuaginta. 2nd rev. ed. Stuttgart: Deutsche Bibelgesellschaft.

Randall, C. 2009. From a far country: Camisards and Huguenots in the Atlantic World. Athens, GA: University of Georgia Press.

Ramsey, A. 1908. Speaking with tongues: an exegetical study. *The Christian and Missionary Alliance*, April 4, 1908, 30(1):7-9, 17.

Reitzenstein, R. 1978. Hellenistic mystery religions: their basic ideas and significance. Translated from the German by John E. Steely. Pittsburgh: Pickwick.

Richards, E.R. 2004. Paul and First Century Letter Writing: Secretaries, Composition and Collection. Downers Grove, IL: InterVarsity Press.

Rienecker, F. & Rogers, C. 1982. Linguistic key to the Greek New Testament. One-volume edition, Grand Rapids: Zondervan.

Roberts, A., Donaldson, J. & Coxe, A., eds. 1885. Ante—Nicene Fathers. Translations of the writings of the Fathers down to A.D. 325, Volume I: The Apostolic Fathers — Justin Martyr, Irenaeus. Reprint, Grand Rapids: Eerdmans, 2001.

———. 1885. Ante—Nicene Fathers. Translations of the writings of the Fathers down to A.D. 325, Volume II: Fathers of the Second Century. New York: Christian Literature.

———. 1885. Ante—Nicene Fathers. Translations of the writings of the Fathers down to A.D. 325, Volume III: Latin Christianity: Its Founder, Tertullian. Grand Rapids: Eerdmans.

———. 1885. Ante—Nicene Fathers. Translations of the writings of the Fathers down to A.D. 325, Volume IV: The Fathers of the Third Century. Grand Rapids: Eerdmans.

Robertson, A.T. 1931. Robertson's New Testament word studies, Vol. 4, Epistles of Paul. Grand Rapids: Baker.

———. 1934. A grammar of the Greek New Testament in the light of historical research. Nashville: Broadman.

Robertson, A. & Plummer, A. 1914. First epistle of St. Paul to the Corinthians, ICC. 2nd ed. Edinburgh: T & T Clark.

Rogers, C. 1965. The gift of tongues in the post-apostolic church. Bibliotheca Sacra, April-June, 122 (486):134-145.

Rose, S. 1979. Orthodoxy and the Religion of the Future. Platina, CA: St Herman.

Runesson, A. 2001. Origins of the Synagogue: A Socio-Historical Study. Stockholm: Almqvist & Wiksell.

———. 2014. The historical Jesus, the Gospels and first-century Jewish society; the importance of the synagogue for understanding the New Testament. (*In* Warner, D. & Binder, D., eds. A city set on a hill: essays in honor of James F. Strange. Mountain Home, AR: BorderStone. p. 265-297).

Runesson, A. & Binder, D. & Olsson, B. 2008. The ancient synagogue from its origins to 200 AD: a source book. Leiden: Brill.

Ryrie, C. 1960. Especially the parchments. *Bibliotheca Sacra*, July, 117(467):242-248.

Safrai, S. 1976. The Jewish People in the First Century—Historical Geography, Political History, Social, Cultural and Religious Life and Institutions. Amsterdam: Van Gorcum.

Safrai, S. 1976. The Temple. (*In* Safrai, S. & Stern, M. eds. The Jewish People in the First Century. Stichting Compendia Rerum Iudiacarum ad Novum Testamentum, Vol. 2. Assen, Netherlands: Van Gorcum. p. 865-907).

Safrai, S. 1975. The temple and the divine service. (*In* Avi-yonah, M. ed. The World History of the Jewish People: The Herodian Period. Jerusalem: Masada. p. 326ff).

Samarin, W. 1972. Tongues of men and angels: The religious language of Pentecostalism. New York: Macmillan.

Sanders, E. 1992. Judaism: practice and belief. London: SCM.

———. 1999. Common Judaism and the synagogue in the first century. (*In* Fine, S. ed. Jews, Christians, and polytheists in the ancient synagogue: cultural interaction during the Greco-Roman period. London: Routledge. p. 1-15)..

Sandmel, S. 1978. Judaism and Christian beginnings. New York: Oxford University Press.

Sawyer, J. 2002. Sacred languages and sacred texts [Kindle ed.]. London: Taylor & Francis e-library. (Religion in the first Christian centuries). Available: https://www.amazon.ca

Schiffman, L. 2015. A short history of the Dead Sea Scrolls and what they tell us. *Biblical Archaeology Review*, 41(3):45-53.

Schaff, P. 1910a. History of the Christian Church, Volume I: Apostolic Christianity (A.D. 1-100). Grand Rapids: Eerdmans.

———. 1910b. History of the Christian church, Volume II: Ant-Nicene Christianity (A.D. 100-325). Grand Rapids: Eerdmans.

———. 1910c. History of the Christian church, Volume III: Nicene and Post-Nicene Christianity (From Constantine the Great to Gregory the Great, A.D. 311-600). Grand Rapids: Eerdmans.

Schattschneider, D. 1998. Zinzendorf, Nikolaus Ludvig von. (*In* Anderson, G., ed. Biographical Dictionary of Christian Missions. New York: Simon & Schuster Macmillan, p. 762).

Schnabel, E. Acts (Zondervan Exegetical Commentary on the New Testament). Grand Rapids: Zondervan.

Schreiner, T. 2018. First Corinthians. Downers Grove, IL: InterVarsity.

Schurhammer, G. 1977. Francis Xavier: his life, his times—Vol. 2, India. Rome: The Jesuit Historical Institute.

Schwartz, D. 2007. "Judean" or "Jew'? How should we translate ᵒΙουδαῖος' in Josephus? (*In* Frey, J., Schwartz, D.R. & Gripentrog, S. eds. Jewish identity in the Greco-Roman world. Leiden: Brill. p. 3-27).

Schweitzer, A. 1950. Paul and His Interpreters. Translated from the German by G. W. Montgomery. New York: Macmillan.

Segal, M.H. 1927. A grammar of Mishnaic Hebrew. Oxford, UK: Oxford University Press.

Seltman, M. 2015. The changing faces of antisemitism. Leicestershire, UK: Troubador.

Selwyn, E. 1947. The first epistle of St. Peter. 2nd ed. London: Macmillan and Company.

Sevenster, J. 1968. Do you know Greek? Leiden, Netherlands: E. J. Brill.

Severian of Gabala. 2006. 1—2 Corinthians, ACCS, NT volume 7. 2nd ed. Edited by Gerald Bray. Downers Grove, IL: IVP Academic.

BIBLIOGRAPHY

Silva, M. 1993. Old Testament in Paul. (*In* Hawthorne, G., Martin, R. & Reid, D. eds. Dictionary of Paul and his letters: a compendium of contemporary biblical scholarship. Downers Grove, IL: InterVarsity. p. 631).

Simpson, A.B. 1892. The Gift of Tongues. *The Christian Alliance and Missionary Weekly*, February 12, 1892, 8(7):98.

———. 1898. The Worship and Fellowship of the Church. *The Christian and Missionary Alliance*, February 9, 1898, 20(6):126.

Smith, J. 1902. History of Joseph Smith, the prophet, Vol. 1. Salt Lake City, UT: Deseret News

Smith, M.J. 2013. Paul in the twenty-first century. (*In* Harding, M. & Nobbs, A. eds. All things to all cultures: Paul among Jews, Greeks and Romans. Grand Rapids: Eerdmans. p. 1–33).

Snyder, G. 2003. Ante Pacem: archaeological evidence of church life before Constantine. Macon, GA: Mercer University Press.

Souris, Georgios. & Nigdelis, Pantelis. 2007. The parallel use of Greek and Latin in the Greco-Roman world. (In Christidis, A.F., ed. A history of ancient Greek: from the beginnings to late antiquity. New York: Cambridge University Press. p. 897–902).

Southey, R. 1846. The life of John Wesley, and rise and progress of Methodism, Vol. 1. 3rd ed. London: Spottiswoode.

Spinckes, N. 1710. The new pretenders to prophecy re-examined. London: printed for Richard Sare.

Spittler, R. 1988. Glossolalia. (*In* Burgess, S., ed. Dictionary of Pentecostal and Charismatic Movements. Grand Rapids: Zondervan Publishing House. p.335–341).

Spolsky, Bernard. 1997. Multilingualism in Israel. *Annual Review of Applied Linguistics*, 17. Cambridge, UK: Cambridge University Press.

Storms, S. 2019. The language of heaven: crucial questions about speaking in tongues. [Kindle ed.]. Lake Mary, FL: Charisma House. Available: https://www.amazon.ca

Stott, J. 1976. Baptism and fullness: the work of the Holy Spirit today. Downers Grove, IL: InterVarsity.

Strauss, M. 2019. A review of the Christian Standard Bible. *Themelios*, August, 44(2):258–277.

Strayer, B. 2008. Suffering Saints: Jansenists and Convulsionnaires in France, 1640–1799. Brighton, UK: Sussex Academic.

Sullivan, C. 2013. Gift of tongues project: notes about the Epiphanius text on the problem tongues of Corinth. https://charlesasullivan.com/4555/notes-about-the-epiphanius-text-on-the-problem-tongues-of-corinth/#easy-footnote-1-4555/ Date of access: 02 May 2024.

———. 2014. Gift of tongues project: the language of instruction in the Corinthian Church. https://charlesasullivan.com/4683/the-language-of-instruction-in-the-corinthian-church/ Date of access: 22 Sept. 2023.

———. 2020. Gift of tongues project: notes on the Cyrillian catena on I Corinthians 14:10. https://charlesasullivan.com/3179/notes-on-the-cyrillian-catena-on-i-corinthians-1410/ Date of access: 16 Jan. 2023.

Sullivan, F. 1977. "Speaking in Tongues" in the New Testament and in the modern charismatic renewal. (*In* Malatesta, E., ed. The Spirit of God in Christian Life. New York: Paulist. p. 23–74).

BIBLIOGRAPHY

Sweet, J.P. 1986. A sign for unbelievers: Paul's attitude to glossolalia. (*In* Mills, W. ed. Speaking in tongues: a guide to research on glossolalia. Grand Rapids: Eerdmans. p. 141–164).

Sweet, J. 1991. A house not made with hands. (*In* Horbury, W., ed. Templum Amicitiae. Sheffield: JSOT. p. 368–390).

Talbert, C. 2002. Reading Corinthians—a literary and theological commentary, revised edition. Macon, Georgia: Smyth & Helwys.

Taylor, M. 2014. 1 Corinthians. New American Commentary, Vol. 28. Nashville, TN: B&H Publishing Group.

Tertullian. 1972. Adversus Marcionem. Translated and edited by Ernest Evans. Glasgow: The Oxford University Press.

Thayer, J. 1889. A Greek-English lexicon of the New Testament. New York: American Book Company.

Theissen, G. 1982. The social setting of Pauline Christianity: essays on Corinth. Translated and edited from the German and with an introduction by John H. Schutz. Philadelphia: Fortress.

Theodoret of Cyrus. 2006. 1—2 Corinthians, ACCS, NT volume 7. 2nd ed. Edited by Gerald Bray. Downers Grove, IL: IVP Academic.

Thiselton, A.C. 1979. The "interpretation" of tongues: a new suggestion in the light of Greek usage in Phil and Josephus. *Journal of Theological Studies*, 30:15–36.

———. 2000. The first epistle to the Corinthians. The New International Greek Testament Commentary. Grand Rapids: Eerdmans.

Thomas, D. 2011. Acts, Reformed Expository Commentary. Phillipsburg, NJ: P&R Publishing.

Thomas, R. 1978. Understanding spiritual gifts: the Christian's special gifts in the light of 1 Corinthians 12–14. Chicago: Moody.

Thrall, M. 1980. Super-Apostles, servants of Christ, and Servants of Satan. *JSNT*, 6:42–57.

Tomson, P.J. 1990. Paul and the Jewish law: halakha in the letters of the Apostle to the Gentiles. Minneapolis: Augsburg Fosrtress.

Topf, D. 2020. Fundamentalism, marginalization, and eschatology: historical, socio-economic, and theological factors influencing early Pentecostal theological education. *Spiritus*, 5(1):99–119.

Toussaint, S. 2015. Rethinking tongues. *Bibliotheca Sacra*, April-June, 172(686):177–191.

Tov, E. 2008. Hebrew Bible, Greek Bible and Qumran: collected essays. Tubingen, Germany: Mohr Siebeck.

Trench, R. 1865. Synonyms of the New Testament. London: MacMillan.

Tucker, B. 2011. "Remain in your calling": Paul and the continuation of social identities in 1 Corinthians. Eugene OR: Pickwick Publications.

Turner, M. 1985. Spiritual gifts then and now. *Vox Evangelica*, 15:7–63.

United Bible Societies. 2014. The Greek New Testament. 5th rev. ed.

Van Kley, D. 2006. The rejuvenation and rejection of Jansenism in history and historiography: recent literature on eighteenth-century Jansenism in French. *French Historical Studies*, Fall 2006, 29 (4):649–684.

Vansina, J. 1985. Oral tradition as history. Madison, WI: University of Wisconsin Press.

Venn, H. 1862. Francis Xavier and the Jesuit Missions in the Far East. an anniversary exhibition of early printed works. Cambridge, UK: Cambridge University Press.

Verbrugge, V. & Harris, M. 2008. 1 Corinthians. The Expositor's Bible Commentary [Kindle ed.] Grand Rapids: Zondervan. Available: https://www.amazon.ca

Voragine, J. 1914. The Golden Legend. Translated from the Latin by William Caxton. London: Cambridge University Press.

Wacker, G. 2001. Heaven below: early Pentecostals and American culture. Cambridge, MA: Cambridge University Press.

Wagner, W. 1994. After the Apostles: Christianity in the second century. Minneapolis: Augsburg Fortress.

Walker, W. 1970. A history of the Christian Church. New York: Charles Scribner's Sons.

Warfield, B. 1953. Miracles: yesterday and today—true and false. Grand Rapids: Eerdmans.

Watson, F. 2004. Paul and the hermeneutics of faith. London: T&T Clark.

Weaver. G. 1973. Tongues shall cease. *Grace Journal*, Winter 1973, 14(1):12–24.

Weigle, L. 1962. The New Testament Octapla. New York: Thomas Nelson & Sons.

Weitzman, S. 1999. Why did the Qumran community write in Hebrew? *JAOS*, 119:35–45.

Williams, C.G. 1981. Tongues of the Spirit: study of Pentecostal *glossolalia* and related phenomena. Cardiff: University of Wales Press.

Williams, C.K., II. 1993. Roman Corinth as a commercial center. (*In* Gregory, T.E., ed. The Corinthia in the Roman period (JRASup 8). Ann Arbor, Michigan: JRA. p. 31–46).

Williams, G. 1962. The radical reformation. Philadelphia: Westminster.

Williams, G. & Waldvogel, E. 1975. A history of speaking in tongues and related gifts. (*In* Hamilton, M. ed. The charismatic movement. Grand Rapids: Eerdmans. p. 61–113).

Wilson, A. Fishy business: Roman exploitation of marine resources. *JRA*, 19: 525–537.

Winer, G. B. 1882. A Treatise on the grammar of Greek New Testament, 9th English ed. Translated from the German by W.F. Moulton. Edinburgh: T & T Clark.

Winter, B. 1999. Gallio's ruling on the legal status of early Christianity (Acts 18:14–15). *Tyndale Bulletin*, 50(2):213–224.

———. 2001. After Paul left Corinth: the influence of secular ethics and social change. Grand Rapids: Eerdmans.

Witetschek, S. 2018. Peter in Corinth? A review of the evidence from 1 Corinthians. *The Journal of Theological Studies*, 69(1):66–82.

Witherington, B. 1995. Conflict and community in Corinth: a socio-rhetorical commentary on 1 and 2 Corinthians. Grand Rapids: Eerdmans.

———. 1998. The Acts of the Apostles: a socio-rhetorical commentary. Grand Rapids: Eerdmans.

———. 2015. Biblical views: speaking in the tongues of men or angels? *Biblical Archaeology Review*, 41(4):30, 66.

Woodard, R. 2004. The Cambridge encyclopedia of the world's ancient languages. Edited by Roger Woodard. Cambridge, UK: Cambridge University Press. https://commons.wikimedia.org/wiki/File:AncientGreekDialects_(Woodard)_en.svg Date of Access: 02 Mar. 2023

Wright, A. 1898. Some New Testament problems. London: Methuen & Co.

Wright, B. 2008. Praise Israel for wisdom and instruction: Essays on Ben Sira and wisdom, the letter of Aristeas and the Septuagint. Leiden: Brill.

BIBLIOGRAPHY

Wright, N.T. 1992. The New Testament and the People of God. Minneapolis: Augsburg Fortress.

Yule, G. 2020. The study of language. Cambridge, UK: Cambridge University Press.

Zerhusen, B. 1995. An Overlooked Judaean Diglossia in Acts 2? *Biblical Theology Bulletin*, 25(3):118–130.

———. 1997. The problem tongues in 1 Corinthians 14: a re-examination. *Biblical Theology Bulletin*, 27(4):139–152.

———. 2020a. Answer. biblicaltongues.com/article-zerhusen-answer/ Date of access: 24 Oct. 2023.

———. 2020b. Critique of review by Chris Good. www.biblicaltongues.com/review-chris-good/ Date of access: 24 Oct. 2023.

Zerwick, M. 1963. Biblical Greek. Rome: Scripta Pontificii Instituti Biblici.

Zerwick, M. & Grosvenor, M. 1996, 5th ed. A grammatical analysis of the Greek New Testament. Rome: Gregorian & Biblical.

Zsengellér, J. 2016. The Samaritan diaspora in antiquity. *Acta Ant. Hung*, 56:157–175.

www.ingramcontent.com/pod-product-compliance
Lightning Source LLC
Chambersburg PA
CBHW050613300426
44112CB00012B/1487